Cracking the
AP*

U.S. GOVERNMENT
& POLITICS Exam
2008 Edition

Tom Meltzer and Paul Levy

PrincetonReview.com

Random House, Inc. New York

The Princeton Review, Inc
2315 Broadway
New York, NY   10024
E-mail: editorialsupport@review.com

ISBN: 978-0-375-42850-0
ISSN: 1097-2757

AP and Advanced Placement Program are registered trademarks of the College Entrance Examination Board.

Editor: Rebecca Lessem
Production Editor: M. Tighe Wall
Production Coordinator: Suzanne Barker

Printed in the United States of America.

10   9   8   7   6   5   4   3   2   1

2008 Edition

ACKNOWLEDGMENTS

The Princeton Review would like to thank John Hoj of Nordhoff High School in Ojai, CA for reviewing the book in preparation for our last two revisions, including this one, and Matthew Polazzo of Stuyvesant High School in New York, NY for his conscientious work as author of the 2008 edition. Thanks also to the members of the Princeton Review staff who worked on this title: Rebecca Lessem, Mary Kinzel, M. Tighe Wall, and Suzanne Barker as well as freelancer Matthew Sheehy.

Thanks to Linda, Naomi, and all my students and alumni at Stuy.

—Matt Polazzo

I want to thank all the great Princeton Review teachers I've worked with over the years. They are quite simply the brightest, most creative, and most energetic group of people I've ever come across and are undoubtedly The Princeton Review's greatest asset.

Thanks also to John Katzman for entrusting me with this book; to my editor on the 2006-2007 edition, Christiane Angeli, who demonstrated the patience of Job on this project; and to the production editorial staff of the 2006-2007 edition, Trish Dublin and Katie O'Neill.

Special thanks also go to Richard Strean, Matthew Polazzo, and John Hoj for their expertise. Thanks finally to my family, the guys in my band—5 Chinese Brothers—and most especially to Lisa.

—Tom Meltzer

CONTENTS

INTRODUCTION

WHAT IS THE PRINCETON REVIEW?

The Princeton Review is an international test preparation company with branches in all major U.S. cities and several abroad. In 1981, John Katzman started teaching an SAT prep course in his parents' living room. Within five years, The Princeton Review had become the largest SAT prep program in the country.

Our phenomenal success in improving students' scores on standardized tests is due to a simple, innovative, and radically effective philosophy: Study the test, not just what the test claims to test. This approach has led to the development of techniques for taking standardized tests based on the principles the test writers themselves use to write the tests.

The Princeton Review has found that its methods work not just for cracking the SAT, but for any standardized test. We've already successfully applied our system to the GMAT, LSAT, MCAT, and GRE, to name just a few. Obviously you need to be well versed in government and politics to do well on the AP U.S. Government & Politics Exam, but you should remember that any standardized test is partly a measure of your ability to think like the people who write standardized tests. This book will help you brush up on your political knowledge and prepare for the exam using our time-tested principle: Crack the system based on how the test is created.

We also offer books and online services that cover an enormous variety of education and career-related topics. If you're interested, check out our website at **PrincetonReview.com**.

PART I

The Test and How to Crack It

1

ABOUT THE ADVANCED PLACEMENT PROGRAM

WHAT IS THE ADVANCED PLACEMENT PROGRAM?

The fact that you're reading this book means that you probably already know something about the Advanced Placement (AP) program: After all, how many people pick up a test-preparation guide for a little light reading? So, you probably already know that the AP courses at your high school are supposed to be the toughest available and that, at the end of the school year, you can take an AP exam that may allow you to earn college credit for your work in the course. However, there are a few things you probably don't know: Who decides what constitutes an AP course? Are AP courses the same at every high school? Who writes and grades the AP exam? This section of the book answers these and other related questions.

The Advanced Placement program is coordinated by an organization called the College Board. The College Board oversees college-admissions examinations; it also publishes test and course materials from previous years, holds seminars on college admissions, and sponsors educational research. Its membership is made up of college administrators and educators; college admissions officers; and high school administrators, college counselors, and teachers.

The College Board appoints a development committee for each of the 32 subjects in which AP exams are available. Each committee meets to decide what should be covered in an AP course and what should be on the AP exam. The Government and Politics Examination Committee, which writes both the U.S. Government and the Comparative Government Exams, is made up of six people—two high school government teachers and four college professors (two experts in U.S. government, two experts in comparative government). Its decisions are included in a publication called *Advanced Placement Course Description: Government and Politics*, which is available from the College Board. Don't bother buying it—this book includes all the pertinent information from that booklet. If you want to take a look at it, ask your teacher if he or she has a copy; most social studies departments have copies of all the important College Board AP publications. Since they are all available for sale to the general public, there's no reason your teacher should refuse to let you see them. They're also available on the College Board's website: **www.collegeboard.com.**

The development committee has two important jobs: to update the course description to reflect recent events and trends in political science and to write the AP U.S. Government and Politics examinations. The committee is therefore responsible for making changes to both the course syllabus and to the test content and format. When the committee finishes writing an exam, it hands it over to the Educational Testing Service (ETS), which prints and administers the exam. ETS also "normalizes" the multiple-choice section; that is, ETS makes sure that it is no harder or easier than the previous year's multiple-choice section. Yes, ETS is the same group that administers the SAT and many other annoying admissions exams; fortunately, its role in creating AP exams is more limited than it is on the SAT.

No one forces teachers to teach AP Government in a particular way; the committee's requirements are actually more like suggestions. If you discuss your AP Government course with a friend taking the same course at a different school, you will likely find that his or her course is noticeably different from yours (especially if you are using different textbooks). Don't worry about these differences: There is no one *right way* to teach AP Government. All teachers will interpret the meaning and importance of events in their own manner. In that way, your AP Government course is similar to a college course. In most other ways, it will probably be easier than a typical college course, although much harder than a typical high school course.

Should You Take AP Classes? Should You Take AP Exams?

There's an obvious downside to taking AP classes: They are more difficult than regular classes. AP classes mean more detailed lectures, more homework, more research papers, more tests, and possibly a lower grade. So why take an AP course?

First, if you're thinking about going to college, you want as many AP courses on your transcript as you can comfortably handle. These classes indicate to your prospective schools that you are serious about studying. Many admissions offices will give your AP grade a one-level "bump"; that is, they will treat your C as a B. (By the way, that's how some high school students end up with GPAs above 4.0; they get almost all A's, including their AP courses.) College admissions officers are more favorably disposed to students who take AP courses.

Second, AP courses help you develop skills you will need in college. A good AP teacher will assign research papers and administer essay tests; require you to study primary source material, maps, census data, and many other resources beyond your textbook; encourage discussion of course material;

and lecture in a way that prompts you to take good notes in order to pass the course. All these aspects of AP courses will help prepare you for your college courses.

Third, AP courses are supposed to prepare you for AP exams, which can be quite helpful in getting your college degree. Many schools award college credit for good grades on AP tests. Because college credits cost money, success on AP exams could save you and/or your parents a lot of money. In some cases, a school will allow you to skip an introductory class if you have a good AP score. In a best case scenario, taking AP tests can help you skip a year of college (and save a year's tuition). It's important to note that you do not have to take an AP course to take an AP exam. If you feel you're up to speed in a subject, you should take the AP exam regardless of the course you took. Remember also that it is the individual college, and not the College Board, that decides whether to grant advanced placement for AP scores; the schools themselves also determine what is considered a satisfactory grade. Before committing to an AP exam, contact your prospective schools and find out their AP policies. You can also check the school's course catalogue: Almost all schools print their AP policies in their catalogues, which are often available at the better local libraries. Ask the reference librarian for assistance.

Taking AP tests can help your college application in other ways as well. The College Board confers a number of awards to students who excel on three or more AP exams. The **AP Scholar Awards** are given to students who exceed an average grade of 3 on three or more AP exams; more prestigious awards are given to students who take more tests and receive higher grades. These awards are noted on the score reports that are sent to your prospective colleges.

How Do You Sign Up for the Exam? What Will Happen on Test Day?

If you want to take one or more AP exams, the first thing you should do is visit your college counselor. He or she will direct you to the AP coordinator for your school. The AP coordinator is usually a teacher or counselor who is in charge of collecting exam fees and telling you when and where the exam will be held. If for some reason you can't take the test through your school—for example, if you're the only student who wants to take an AP exam or your school has not designated a coordinator—you can still take the test through another school. To find out which schools in your area offer the test, call the College Board's AP Services office at 609-771-7300, or look on their website at **www. collegeboard.com.**

It costs $83 to take exams for full-year AP courses. This fee is expensive, but still much cheaper than the cost of the college course that you may place out of. Your school keeps $7 for administrative fees, and the College Board suggests that the school refund that money to you if you and your family have financial difficulties. You may also apply to the College Board for a $22 fee reduction based on financial need. If, for some reason, you need to take the test at a time other than when it is being offered, you may be charged an additional fee.

THE COLLEGE BOARD'S SUGGESTED TIMETABLE FOR STUDENTS PREPARING TO TAKE AN AP TEST

- **January**—discuss with your government teacher and your college counselor whether you should take the exam. If you decide to take the test, meet with the AP coordinator and hand over your fees. If you need to make special arrangements because of a disability, do so at this time. If your school does not offer AP exams, contact the College Board to find the location of the nearest school offering the tests.

- **Mid-February**—if you need to take the exam at another school and you still haven't made plans to do so, DO IT NOW!

- **May**—AP exams are administered.

- **Early and mid-June**—AP exams are graded. If you want your score report sent to schools other than those you indicated on your test registration, or if you want to cancel your test scores, you have until **June 15** to contact the College Board with your request (learn more about canceling your test scores on the next page, under the heading **Special Circumstances**).

- **Early July**—your prospective colleges start to receive your grades.

- **Early to mid-July**—you receive your grades.

The AP U.S. Government and Politics Exam is usually offered at 8:00 A.M. The test may start a little earlier or later at your school, but not by much: College Board rules prohibit starting before 6:00 A.M. or after 10:00 A.M. On test day, you will need to bring

- two number-two pencils (for the multiple-choice section). Make sure you have an eraser.

- a dark-blue or black pen (with which to write your essays).

- a watch (in case there's no clock in your testing room). Do not bring a watch that beeps or has an alarm or a calculator; it will be confiscated by the proctor.

THINGS YOU MAY NOT BRING TO THE EXAM

- Cell phones, PDA's, MP3 players, pagers, or any other electronic or communication device

- Books, compasses, correction fluid, dictionaries, highlighters, notes, or colored pencils

- Scratch paper (notes can be made on portions of the exam booklets)

- Watches that beep or have an alarm

- Portable listening or recording devices (even with headphones) or photographic equipment

- Computers

- Clothing with subject-related information

Some exceptions to these rules are made by the College Board for students with disabilities.

SPECIAL CIRCUMSTANCES

SPECIAL CONDITIONS FOR STUDENTS WITH DISABILITIES

Students who seek special testing conditions to accommodate disabilities should have either a current Individualized Education Program (IEP) on file at their school *or* a signed letter from a doctor describing the disability. The following options are available to qualified students: large-type tests and Braille tests for those with poor or no vision (poor-sighted students may also have an aide read to them and take dictation for the essays); the right to take the exam at a different, more accommodating location; and the right to take the exam untimed. Take note: You must present documentation of your disability for your score report to indicate "Certified Disability." Make sure your documentation is in order long before test day.

PROBLEMS ON TEST DAY

On rare occasions, the College Board writes a lousy question. Sometimes ETS misprints a question, misprints a page of the exam (or leaves it blank), or makes some other error. If, during the test, you believe that one or more of the questions on the test doesn't work, you should contact the College Board as soon as possible after the test. Provide the test title, the question number, and a description of what you think was wrong with the question. But honestly, this is extremely unlikely to happen in a government exam—such errors almost invariably occur on math or science tests. If you do see a misprint, you should report it immediately to the proctor, and after the exam, to the College Board at the phone number, address, and e-mail address provided at the end of this chapter.

More common are problems in test administration. Maybe your proctor gave the directions incorrectly. For you, that should be no big deal, as you'll know all the directions well before test day because you read this book. The big problem is a proctor who times the exam incorrectly, particularly if he or she gives you too little time (you *could* report an error if your proctor gave you too *much* time, but why would you want to?). In the case of a timing error, notify the school's AP coordinator immediately. If the coordinator doesn't help (maybe he or she is the proctor who screwed up the timing), go see the principal. If you wait too long, you may get stuck with the score you got on the mistimed exam.

That covers what happens when the College Board, ETS, or your proctor messes up. What about when you screw up? If you think (or know) that you blew the exam, you have until **June 15** to contact the College Board and cancel your score. **June 15** is also the date by which you have to contact the College Board if you want to withhold your grades from certain colleges, or add schools to the list of those receiving your grades. Unless you're reasonably certain you got a 1 on an AP exam, you probably shouldn't cancel your grade.

Finally, here's a list of things that will get you thrown out of the test, lead to your scores being canceled, and raise serious suspicions that you are a cheater.

- leafing through the exam booklet before the exam begins

- trying to give answers to or receive answers from someone else during the exam

- working on the wrong section of the exam

- continuing to work on the exam after you have been instructed to stop

- tearing a page out of your test booklet or trying to sneak the entire exam out of the test site

- looking in a textbook, notebook, or encyclopedia during the exam

- behaving disruptively

WHAT IS THE AP U.S. GOVERNMENT AND POLITICS EXAM LIKE? HOW IS IT GRADED?

The AP U.S. Government and Politics Exam is a two-part test. The chart below illustrates the test's structure.

Section	Question Type	Number of Questions	Time Allowed	Percent of Final Grade
I	Multiple-Choice	60	45 minutes	50
II	Essay	4	100 minutes	50

The test is designed to test an overview of U.S. government. It doesn't give all subjects equal weight, however. Here's how the test questions break down.

Subject	Percent of Questions
Constitutional underpinnings	5 to 15
Political beliefs and behavior	10 to 20
Political parties, interest groups, and mass media	10 to 20
Institutions of government: congress, president, judiciary, and bureaucracy	35 to 45
Public policy	5 to 15
Civil rights and liberties	5 to 15

While most of the questions deal with the institutions of government, the questions are nearly evenly divided among the four institutions. There are no definition questions, although you need to know the definitions of words to understand the questions. The questions tend to deal with the dynamics of how government operates within a political environment. For example, you may be asked how interest groups attempt to influence policy making in Congress and the bureaucracy or how the president attempts to influence Congress through public opinion. The test writers want to know whether you understand the general principles that guide U.S. government and the making of public policy.

In addition to the multiple-choice questions, there are four mandatory essay questions. You'll have a total of 100 minutes to answer all of them. You should spend approximately 25 minutes per question, but be aware that you must manage your own time. Additional time spent on one question will reduce the time that you have left to answer another. Writing more than is necessary to answer the question will not earn you extra points.

The graders assign each of your essays a numerical score. Weighing the average on the essays and the score on the multiple-choice questions each as 50 percent, they create a final score from a low of 1 to a high of 5. The chart below tells you what that final score means.

Score (Meaning)	Percentage of test takers receiving this score	Equivalent grade in a first-year college course	Credit granted for this score?
5 (extremely qualified)	9	A	Yes
4 (well qualified)	20	B+	Almost always (contact admissions department to ask)
3 (qualified)	26	C+	Some do, but some don't (contact admissions department to ask)
2 (possibly qualified)	35	C-	Very few do (contact admissions department to ask)
1 (no recommendation)	10	D	No

After you've read this book, take our practice tests. To score your multiple-choice questions, award yourself one point for every correct answer, subtract $\frac{1}{4}$ point for every incorrect answer, and credit 0 points to your score for questions you left blank. This will give you your raw score.

Here's what that score would translate into on the AP U.S. Government and Politics Exam, assuming you performed as well on the essay questions.

Multiple-Choice Raw Score	AP Score
0 to 18	1
19 to 27	2
28 to 39	3
40 to 48	4
49 to 60	5

Of course, if you follow our advice for how to write a good essay, you could score higher on the essays than on the multiple-choice section and potentially increase your final grade by one point.

FINALLY...

A lot of the information in this chapter also appears in a free College Board publication called *Advanced Placement: Bulletin for Students and Parents*. It includes sample test questions and updated information about the exam. It also contains some test-taking suggestions. We at The Princeton Review think our suggestions are much better.

You should be able to get a copy from your counselor. If not, go to **www.collegeboard.com** to request one. The phone number is 609-771-7300, and the e-mail address is apexams@info.collegeboard.org.

2

BEING A GOOD TEST-TAKER

Very few students stop to think about how to improve their test-taking skills. Most assume that if they study hard, they will test well; if they don't study, they will do poorly. Most students continue to believe this even after experience teaches them otherwise. Have you ever studied really hard for an exam, then blown it on test day? Have you ever aced an exam you thought you weren't well prepared for? Most students have experienced one, if not both, of these scenarios. The lesson should be clear: Factors other than how many hours you spend studying influence your final score on any test.

This section will provide you with insights that will help you perform better on the AP U.S. Government and Politics Exam—and on other exams as well.

Test Anxiety

Everybody experiences some anxiety before and during an exam. To a certain extent, test anxiety can be helpful: Some people find that they perform faster and more efficiently under stress. If you've ever pulled an all-nighter to write a paper and ended up doing good work, you know the feeling.

However, too much stress is definitely a bad thing. Hyperventilating during the test, for example, almost always leads to a lower score. If you find that you stress out during exams, here are a few preemptive actions you can take.

- **Eliminate as many surprises as you can before taking the test.** Make sure you know where the test is being held, when it starts, what type of questions are going to be asked, and how long the test will take. Have all your test-taking supplies, such as pencils, pens, a watch, and ID, laid out the night before your exam. You don't want to be worrying about any of these things on test day or, even worse, after the test has already begun.

- **Take a reality check.** Evaluate your situation realistically before the test begins. If you've studied well, remind yourself that you are prepared for the test. Remember that many others taking the test are not as well prepared, and (in your classes, at least) you are being graded against them, so you have an advantage. If you didn't study enough, accept the fact that you will probably not ace the test. Don't stress out or fixate on how much you don't know. Make sure you get to every question you know something about. Your job is to score as high as you can by maximizing the benefits of what you do know. In either case, it is best to think of a test as if it were a game: How can you get the most points in the time allotted to you? Always pick questions you can answer easily and quickly before you answer questions that will take more time.

- **Try to relax.** Slow, deep breathing works for almost everybody. Take a few seconds, close your eyes, take a few slow, deep breaths, and concentrate on nothing but your inhalation and exhalation for a few seconds. This is a basic form of meditation, and it should help you clear your mind of stress and, as a result, better concentration on the test. If you've ever taken yoga classes, you probably know some other good relaxation techniques. Use them when you can (obviously, anything that requires leaving your seat and, say, assuming a handstand position won't be allowed by any but the most free-spirited proctors).

The best way to avoid stress is to study both the test material and the test itself. By reading this book, you are taking a major step toward a stress-free AP U.S. Government and Politics Exam. Congratulations!

Pacing

A big part of scoring well on an exam is working at a consistent pace. The worst mistake test-takers make is that they come to a question that stumps them and, rather than just skip it, they panic and stall. Time doesn't stand still when you're working on a question you can't answer, and it's not unusual for students to waste five minutes on a single question because they are too stubborn to cut their losses.

Don't make that mistake. Tests are like marathons—you do best when you work through them at a steady pace. You can always come back to a question you don't know. When you do, very often you will find that your previous mental block is gone, and as you gleefully move on to the next question, you'll wonder why the question perplexed you the first time around. Even if you're still stumped, you won't have wasted valuable time you could have spent on questions you do know.

The benefit of keeping a steady pace is particularly obvious on multiple-choice tests such as the SAT or Part I of the AP U.S. Government and Politics Exam. On these tests, every question is worth the same amount toward your final score. When all the questions on a test are equally valued, no individual question is that important. You should always skip questions that give you trouble until you've answered every question that you know the answer to.

Finally, you should set a realistic goal for your final score. If you simply try to get the best score you possibly can, you will probably overextend yourself. In trying to do too much, you will hurt your score with careless mistakes. Check with the schools you are applying to. Do you need a 3 to earn credit for the test? If you get a raw score of 35 (out of 60) on the multiple-choice section *and* do as well on the essays, you'll get a 3. The raw score is determined by adding up the number of questions you answer correctly and subtracting $\frac{1}{4}$ of the number of questions you answer incorrectly. In other words, you could answer 45 questions, get 37 right, get 8 wrong, and leave 15 blank and still earn a score of 3. Only students who are shooting for a 5 should try to answer every question on the multiple-choice section; everyone else should go slower and spend more time on each question to avoid careless mistakes.

The following is an approximation of how to pace yourself on the AP test:

If you want to get a	answer this many	and leave this many blank
2	30 to 38	22 to 30
3	45	15
4	52	8
5	as many as you can	as few as possible

We'll talk more about pacing on the multiple-choice section in the next chapter.

IN THE WEEKS BEFORE THE EXAM

There are a few things you should start doing any time after January 1 (but certainly before **May 1**). One of them is to read this book. Here are some others.

- **Ask your teacher for copies of old AP U.S. Government and Politics Exams.** The College Board releases an AP exam every five years. The first was released in 1989, the second in 1994, and the last in 1999. Your teacher may have worked with you on these released exams. If not, see if your teacher has copies of them. They are all available through the College Board.

  You should also visit the College Board's website and download the free sample essay questions from past years. These can be found at **www.collegeboard.com/ student/testing/ap/prep_free.html.**

Make sure you get the most out of the released exams by understanding why you got some wrong. Go over your incorrect answers, and even your correct ones, with your teacher after school or in a free period. Note that the subject matter of many of the questions is similar from year to year. Doing well on a practice test, and understanding why you did well, is the best confidence-builder for the real thing.

- **Commit a little time every night to test preparation**. A little studying every night is much better than a lot of cramming during the week before the exam. In early to mid-April, try to set aside 20 to 30 minutes three or four times a week to review this book, the textbook you used in class, your notes on your teacher's lectures, and any other class materials. You can also surf the Web for government-related sites. There are thousands of them.

- When reviewing the material in this book don't forget to use the index. It's useful in the course of your studying when you want information and can't remember where you read it—but there's more to it than that. When you've just about finished with the book, take a look at the entries that have several page references; these are some of the most important subjects, and you would do well to review them again. Also read through the glossary. Finally, you'll find that the explanations to both tests do double duty as supplementary review as well.

In the Final Week Before the Exam

In a best case scenario, you should not cram for the test. However, cramming is better than not studying at all. If it's one week before the test and you haven't started studying yet, you should devote as many hours as possible to studying.

If, however, you have been preparing, you should do the following:

- **Maintain your usual routine.** Try not to go to bed much later or earlier than usual. Don't start a new diet or exercise program. In other words, stay the course.

- **Do a general subject review**. Stop concentrating on memorizing details. Focus instead on "big picture" issues, such as political, social, and economic trends. Stop asking yourself questions like, "What are the responsibilities of the House Judiciary Committee?" and start asking yourself questions like, "How many examples of the system of checks and balances can I come up with?"

- **Read and become familiar with all the directions for the exam**. They're all in this book. Don't waste valuable time during the exam trying to understand instructions. Know what you're supposed to do on each section of the test long before test day.

ON TEST DAY

- **Start the day with a reasonable, but not huge, breakfast.** You'll need energy for the exam. Have a nice breakfast, but nothing so filling that it will put you to sleep. Beware of coffee, tea, or anything else that will make you have to use the restroom during the test.

- **Bring everything you need.** You'll need two number-two pencils (for the multiple-choice section), an eraser, a dark-blue or black pen (for the essay sections), and a watch. Do not bring a watch with an alarm or one that beeps; it will be taken away from you.

- **Wear comfortable clothing.**

- **Bring a snack.** A piece of fruit or a candy bar during the break can give you a much-needed energy boost. Some proctors don't allow any food or drinks in the testing room, but many will let you eat during your break.

FINALLY...

Learn everything you can about the exam. The more you know, the less you will be surprised during the test, and the more easily and quickly the exam will go. The following chapters will tell you all about the multiple-choice and essay sections of the exam.

SUMMARY

- Start studying for the test a month or more in advance. Just 30 to 45 minutes of studying a few nights per week will make a huge difference.

- Ask your teacher for copies of old AP U.S. Government and Politics exams. Write some practice essays and review them with your teacher.

- Don't change your regular routine in the week leading up to the test, but refocus your studies from details to "big picture" questions. Get a good night's sleep before the test day.

- On test day, wear something comfortable. Have a nice and sensible breakfast. Bring pencils, an eraser, a pen, and a watch to the test. Also, bring a snack.

- Beat test anxiety. Prepare for the test so there will be few surprises on test day. Take deep, slow breaths to relax during the test.

- Maintain a steady pace throughout the exam. Don't get hung up on any individual question. Set a target score and pace yourself to achieve your goal.

3

Cracking the Multiple-Choice Section

THE BASICS

The directions for the multiple-choice section of the AP U.S. Government and Politics Exam are pretty simple. They read

Directions: Each of the questions or incomplete statements below is followed by five suggested answers or completions. Select the one that is best in each case and then fill in the corresponding oval on the answer sheet.

In short, you're being asked to do what you've done on many other multiple-choice exams: Pick the right answer, then bubble in your answer on a separate sheet of paper. You will *not* be given credit for answers you record in your test booklet (e.g., by circling them) but not on your answer sheet. The section consists of 60 questions, and you will be given 45 minutes to complete it.

The College Board also provides a breakdown of the general subject matter covered on the exam. This breakdown will not appear in your test booklet; it comes from the preparatory material the College Board publishes. Here again is the chart we showed you in Chapter 1.

Subject	Percent of questions
Constitutional underpinnings	5 to 15
Political beliefs and behavior	10 to 20
Political parties, interest groups, and mass media	10 to 20
Institutions of government: Congress, president, judiciary, and bureaucracy	35 to 45
Public policy	5 to 15
Civil rights and liberties	5 to 15

Constitutional underpinnings	• the political and economic circumstances at the time of the framing of the Constitution • the motivation of the framers • the weaknesses of the Articles of Confederation • the strengths of the Constitution • separation of powers • the nature and political impact of federalism • principles of democratic government • system of checks and balances
Political beliefs and behavior	• the ideological beliefs people maintain regarding their government • political socialization • public opinion and its impact on policy • how and why citizens vote as they do • the methods of political participation • the reasons citizens disagree over political beliefs and behavior

Political parties, interest groups, and mass media	• what parties do • how they operate • how they are organized • how they link citizens to government • how they help make and use the rules of elections • how electoral laws affect the outcome of elections • what interest groups do and what makes them effective • the role of PACs and their impact on the political process • the types of mass media • the purpose of the media • the impact of the media on the political agenda
The institutions of government: Congress, president, judiciary, and bureaucracy	• the structure and function of the legislature, executive branch, judiciary, and bureaucracy • the structural and political interrelationships of the institutions of government • the connections between the national government, citizens, political parties, interest groups, and the states
Public policy	• the process of making public policy • citizen participation in policy making • the interactions between Congress, the courts, and the bureaucracy on policy making • the impact of elections in policy making • the participants in domestic and economic policy making • the limitations of domestic and economic policy making
Civil rights and liberties	• substantive and procedural rights and liberties • the impact of the Fourteenth Amendment on rights and liberties • the consequences of judicial interpretation on rights and liberties

As you can see, the primary focus of the test is the nuts and bolts of the federal government. The test also emphasizes political activity—the factors that influence individual political beliefs, the conditions that determine how and why people vote, and the process by which groups form and attempt to influence the government. All these subjects, you should note, are important. As much as 30 percent (or as little as 10 percent) of your exam may focus on constitutional issues and civil rights.

TYPES OF QUESTIONS

The majority of questions on the multiple-choice section of the test are pretty direct. Here's an example.

1. A "pocket veto" can occur only when

   (A) Congress amends a bill
   (B) the president is out of the country
   (C) a bill passes Congress with a greater than
       two-thirds majority in each house
   (D) the Supreme Court has ruled that the
       proposed legislation is unconstitutional
   (E) a bill reaches the president's desk within 10
       days of the end of a congressional session

Sometimes, the College Board makes the questions a little trickier. One way it does this is by phrasing a question in such a way that four answers are correct and one is incorrect. We call these questions "NOT/EXCEPT" questions because they usually contain one of those words (in capital letters, so they're difficult to miss). Here's an example.

2. In the twentieth-century, the Democratic Party
   traditionally received majority support from all of
   the following groups EXCEPT

   (A) the wealthy
   (B) African Americans
   (C) Jews
   (D) union members
   (E) teachers

Another way is the Roman-numeral format question. This type of question can have more than one correct answer. Here's an example.

3. The increased use of the presidential primary since
   the 1960s has had the following effect(s)

   I. Weakened the power of the political parties
   II. Increased the power of political activists in the parties
   III. Increased the cost of running for political office
   IV. Increased the drama of the party convention
   V. Decreased the number of persons challenging incumbents

   (A) I only
   (B) I, II, and III only
   (C) II and III only
   (D) II and IV only
   (E) III, IV, and V only

Once or twice during the multiple-choice section, you will be asked to interpret an illustration, often a map or a political cartoon. These are usually rather easy. The key is *not* to try to read too much between the lines. Here's an example.

"Sorry, but all my power's been turned back to the states."

Lee Lorenz ©1981 from *The New Yorker Collection*. All Rights Reserved.

4. The principle of government most relevant to the cartoon is

   (A) judicial restraint
   (B) checks and balances
   (C) federalism
   (D) executive privilege
   (E) representative democracy

Finally, there will be one or two questions on the test asking you to interpret a graph or chart. Again, these are usually very direct, and the most important thing for you to do is *not* to overinterpret the data. The correct answer will be indisputably supported by the information in the chart. Here's an example.

Average, highest, and lowest approval ratings, by percentage of all eligible voters, for U.S. presidents, 1953 to 1974			
	Average	Highest	Lowest
Eisenhower	65	79	48
Kennedy	70	83	56
Johnson	55	79	35
Nixon	49	67	24

Source: Gallup poll

5. Which of the following conclusions can be drawn from the information presented in the chart above?

(A) Eisenhower was the most consistently popular president in the nation's history.
(B) Kennedy received greater congressional support for his programs than did any other president during the period in question.
(C) Nixon's lowest approval rating was the result of the Watergate scandal.
(D) The difference between Johnson's highest and lowest approval ratings was the greatest for any president during the period in question.
(E) Eisenhower and Johnson were equally well liked by all Americans.

Answers to these and other drill questions appear at the end of this chapter.

HOW TO CRACK THE AP U.S. GOVERNMENT AND POLITICS MULTIPLE-CHOICE SECTION

The AP U.S. Government and Politics Exam is, by ETS standards, a straightforward test. Unlike the SAT, for example, on the AP U.S. Government and Politics Exam neither the questions nor the answers are designed to trick you. The subject matter can be found easily in this textbook, often in the chapter summaries. You should, however, not be lulled into believing the test is easy because it covers material that can be readily obtained from reading the newspaper and watching television. This so-called "street knowledge" is not enough to ensure a passing grade on the exam. The AP U.S. Government and Politics Exam is an academic test that requires knowledge from the textbook. Information acquired from contemporary sources such as newspapers and television will probably not be needed in the multiple-choice sections of the test. It will, however, be needed for the Essay sections of the test, particularly if you are asked for examples.

If you've paid attention in class, you should do well on this test. If you haven't paid close attention, you may still be able to master the material if you review intensively. Use the subject review that appears later in this book as your guide. Either way, you will do better if you know what to expect of the test. On the next few pages, we'll discuss some things that all AP U.S. Government and Politics multiple-choice sections have in common.

THE QUESTIONS ARE OF MIXED DIFFICULTY

The examination is made up of questions of varying difficulty. It is not unusual to have many questions on the examination that fewer than 50 percent of the students answer correctly. Some are so difficult that fewer than 25 percent of students answer them correctly. There are even some very easy questions, which the vast majority of students answer correctly. But watch out for the really difficult questions that may involve very technical issues, such as committee seniority or campaign finance reform. These may be good questions to skip if you're not sure of your answer.

QUESTIONS APPEAR IN A GENERAL ORDER OF DIFFICULTY

As you take the test, remember this general order of difficulty. You will probably sense that the questions are getting more difficult as you progress through the section. Knowing that the questions are indeed supposed to become increasingly difficult is one more way to be prepared for the test.

Although there are some easy questions and some difficult questions sprinkled throughout the exam—for example, on a recent exam one of the most difficult questions appeared in the first quarter of the test—questions toward the end of the section are, on the whole, more difficult than questions at the beginning of the section. Make this system work for you. You will be able to warm up on a few relatively easy questions before you see anything too scary. That said, everyone perceives questions differently, so don't panic if you think the first few are difficult; you might have more luck with questions in the middle.

THERE ARE NO TRIVIAL PURSUIT QUESTIONS ON THIS EXAM

Here's some more good news. The AP U.S. Government and Politics Exam doesn't ask about trivial matters. You will never see a question on the exam such as this one.

6. The American equivalent of the British Exchequer is the

    (A) House Finance Committee
    (B) Internal Revenue Service
    (C) United States Mint
    (D) Office of Budget and Management
    (E) Federal Reserve Board

To answer this question correctly, you would have to be fairly familiar with the British government. The AP U.S. Government and Politics Exam does not require such knowledge. This question is atypical in another way as well: It does not reward partial knowledge. Even if you had known that the British Exchequer has something to do with money and government, you could not have eliminated any of the incorrect answers on this question. On an actual AP test, at least a couple of these answers would have been completely unrelated to finance, and you could have eliminated them and guessed from among the remaining answers.

THE GUESSING PENALTY AND PROCESS OF ELIMINATION

Were you surprised by the suggestion (made on the preceding page) that you should guess? Many students think that they should never guess on an exam. But even the College Board will tell you that's not true. This passage appears on the first page of the AP U.S. Government and Politics Exam.

> Many candidates wonder whether or not to guess the answers to questions about which they are not certain. In this section of the examination, as a correction for haphazard guessing, one-fourth of the number of questions you answer incorrectly will be subtracted from the number of questions you answer correctly. It is improbable, therefore, that mere guessing will improve your score significantly; it may even lower your score, and it does take time. If, however, you are not sure of the best answer but have some knowledge of the questions and are able to eliminate one or more answer choices as wrong, your chance of getting the right answer is improved, and it may be to your advantage to answer such a question.

The only thing wrong with this advice is that it understates the value of guessing once you have eliminated one or more answer choices. Statistically speaking, guessing after you have eliminated one or more incorrect answer choices *will* improve your final score on the multiple-choice section.

Here's why. Suppose you guess randomly on five questions. Probability tells you that you should get one correct and four incorrect. Your raw score for those five questions would be +1 for the correct answer and $-4\left(\frac{1}{4}\right) = -1$ for your four incorrect answers. Your guesses would net exactly 0 points. That's the exact same score you would have received if you had skipped all five questions. There is, then, no guessing penalty. Random guesses cancel one another out, unless you are either very lucky or very unlucky.

However, you will rarely find a question for which you can't eliminate at least one of the answer choices. In many cases, you will be able to eliminate two or even three incorrect answers. Whenever you get this far but can get no further, you *must* take a guess from among the remaining answer choices.

Consider this scenario: Billy and Cal are both taking the AP U.S. Government and Politics Exam. Each one knows the answers to 36 of the 60 multiple-choice questions. Each of them has time to look at most of the other questions—let's say 18 of the remaining 24—and in each case, each could eliminate two incorrect answers but could go no further. Billy doesn't guess on those 18 questions, and he ends up with a raw score of 36. He's right on pace for a final score of 3. Cal, however, guesses on all 18. Because he is guessing from among three answer choices, he will likely get one out of every three correct. He ends up with +6 for his correct answers and $-12\left(\frac{1}{4}\right) = -3$ for his incorrect answers. Cal's raw score of 39 gives him a boost toward the final score of 4 that he is shooting for.

Had Billy and Cal been able to eliminate three answer choices on each of the 18 questions, the results would have been even more dramatic. Billy, who didn't guess, would have gotten that same raw score, 36. Cal, however, would have gotten 9 of the 18 correct for a +9, while losing only $-9 \left(\frac{1}{4}\right) = -2\frac{1}{4}$ for his incorrect answers. His final raw score of 42.75 would have sent him well on his way to a score of 4.

Does that mean you should take a guess on every question on the test? No. Because you have only a limited amount of time to spend on the multiple-choice section, you have to maximize that time. The first thing you want to do is make sure you've answered every question to which you know the answer. Only then do you want to guess on questions to which you don't know the answer. However, once you have worked on a question, eliminated some answers, and convinced yourself that you cannot eliminate any other incorrect answers, you should guess and move on to the next question.

If it seems that we are focusing more on eliminating incorrect answers than on finding the correct answers, it is because that is the most efficient way to take a multiple-choice exam. Use Process of Elimination (POE) to whittle down the answer choices to one because incorrect answers are much easier to identify than the correct one is. When people look for the correct answer among the answer choices, they have a tendency to try to justify how each answer may be correct. They'll adopt a forgiving attitude, but this is a situation in which savage brutality is rewarded. Don't fall into this trap. Eliminate incorrect answers. Terminate them with extreme prejudice. If you've done your job well, only the correct answer will be left standing at the end.

All this probably sounds pretty aggressive to you. It is. Good test takers take multiple-choice tests aggressively. They sift through the answer choices, discard incorrect answers without remorse, guess with impunity, and prowl the test searching for questions they can answer, all with the tenacity and ruthlessness of a shark. Alright, maybe that overstates the case a little, but you get the point. So, eliminate as many answers as you can. Any time you don't know the answer but are able to eliminate at least one answer choice, guess.

COMMON SENSE CAN HELP

Sometimes answers on the multiple-choice section contradict common sense. Eliminate those answers because common sense works on the AP U.S. Government and Politics Exam.

Which of the answer choices to the question below go against common sense?

7. Which of the following best explains the way in which federal legislation is implemented?

(A) Most laws outline general goals and restrictions, which the federal bureaucracy interprets and translates into specific guidelines.

(B) The manner of implementing federal legislation is negotiated between a joint congressional committee and a presidential advisory committee.

(C) All of the regulations pertaining to a piece of legislation are contained within the legislation itself.

(D) After a bill is signed, all disputes pertaining to its implementation are decided by the congressional committee responsible for the bill.

(E) The details of implementing congressional legislation are worked out in the courts on a case-by-case basis.

Here's How to Crack It

You should have been able to apply common sense to eliminate answers (D) and (E) pretty quickly. Congressional committees (D) work on bills *before* they reach the floor for a vote, and this work takes up all their time. They would hardly have time to hear all disputes concerning bills that have already passed. Furthermore, such a system would violate the system of checks and balances, because the responsibility for interpreting laws belongs to the judiciary. All the same, the details of congressional legislation could never be worked out in the courts (E). There would simply be too many cases for the courts to be able to process them all. Similarly, answer (B) contradicts the principle of separation of powers. It is the executive branch's responsibility to enforce the law; it is not required to confer with Congress on the manner in which it performs this task. Answer (C) is impractical. You have no doubt seen "photo ops" of politicians standing before the mountains of federal regulations on the books. Those regulations are created by the federal bureaucracy as guidelines for implementing legislation. They are not contained within the legislation itself. The correct answer, by Process of Elimination, is (A).

SUMMARY

- Familiarize yourself with the different types of questions that will appear in the multiple-choice section.

- Tailor your studying to suit the test's most common topics. Don't spend a lot of time studying civil rights and civil liberties until you have completely reviewed the workings of the federal government and the basics of political behavior.

- Rest assured that the AP U.S. Government and Politics Exam tests a relatively small amount of information. Be confident: You can review this material fairly quickly and get a good grade on this exam.

- Remember also that most of the questions on this exam are of medium difficulty. The test does not bother with trivial matters or minute exceptions to general trends. The test writers want to know that you understand the general principles underlying U.S. government.

- Use Process of Elimination on all but the easiest questions. Once you have worked on a question, eliminated some answers, and convinced yourself that you cannot eliminate any other incorrect answers, you should guess and move on to the next question.

- Use common sense.

ANSWER KEY FOR SAMPLE QUESTIONS IN THIS CHAPTER

1. E
2. A
3. B
4. C
5. D
6. B
7. A

4

CRACKING THE ESSAY SECTION

Most students hear the word *essay* and cringe. An essay, after all, is long and complicated. It has to be thorough. It has to begin with a thesis statement, proceed to a discussion of one idea in each of several paragraphs, and finish with a finely drawn conclusion. It has to include clear transitions to lead the reader along a single train of thought.

Good news! You have only 100 minutes to answer four questions, but the graders know you cannot possibly write four eloquent essays, each in 25 minutes. So you don't have to produce brilliant, detailed, original examinations of broad issues. Focus: Depth—not breadth—scores points.

WHAT ARE THE AP U.S. GOVERNMENT AND POLITICS EXAM ESSAY QUESTIONS LIKE?

The AP U.S. Government and Politics Essay section has four essay questions. Each counts equally. The entire essay section counts as 50 percent of your examination grade. Even though the essays are all mandatory, you may have some choices within an essay. For example, a question may look like this:

> How have procedural due-process rights been expanded by the Supreme Court in the twentieth-century? You must refer in your answer to one of the following cases: *Miranda v. Arizona*, *Mapp v. Ohio*, *Gideon v. Wainwright*.

Choices within questions will give you the opportunity to write as much as you know in the limited time available. They allow you to highlight what you know best instead of having to write about many subjects, some of which you might not remember as well. Again, depth not breadth. Note that you will get no more points for writing more than what the question requires. You cannot make up points lost in a previous essay question, so be sure to focus on only one topic if one is what the question asks for. If there is a choice within a question, make certain you choose the subject you know the most about. Be explicit. Also remember that if the question deals with a Supreme Court case, you shouldn't worry about the background of the case. It is the ruling and the consequences that are important.

If you are confronted by an essay that you feel unprepared to answer, don't panic. Skip it and come back to it later. Writing another essay may prompt you to recall your knowledge of the first subject. Remember to keep track of your time.

Unlike the multiple-choice section of the test, you cannot be penalized for attempting to write an answer. Therefore, never leave an essay blank. Write something about the subject, even if it is knowledge you picked up from a magazine or newspaper.

The essays are graded using an answer standard, to which only the graders have access. A certain number of points is given for each piece of information supplied correctly. The numerical grade of the essay is determined by adding the points earned for each part of the essay.

Each essay uses a different scoring standard. One essay could be graded using a total of five points, another a total of seven points, and another a total of ten points. While the total score for each question may differ, the value of each question is equal in determining the final score on the essay section. Each of the four essay questions is worth one-eighth of the total exam, or 12.5 percent.

A simple way for you to get an idea of the kinds of essay questions that might be asked and the structure of an answer standard is to visit the College Board website at **www.collegeboard.com.** In the section devoted to Advanced Placement, you will find a file that contains the AP U.S. Government and Politics essay examination questions for the last five years, with the grading standard for each question.

Another way to understand the types of questions that may be asked is to look in the table of contents of a textbook. Test writers essentially take the concepts found in individual chapters and combine them into a question. For example, they may ask about the ways in which interest groups attempt to influence policy. Political action committees operating as political arms of interest groups try to influence both the nominating process for public office and the outcome of general elections. Interest groups also try to influence policy making both at the legislative and enforcement levels. Information about such a question will be found in the chapters on interest group politics, elections, and the branches of government. The test writers are trying to force you to combine many separate pieces of information into a coherent point of view. They are trying to get you to analyze, assess, and evaluate. Therefore the question may be written as shown:

1. Interest groups can have both a positive and negative impact on American politics. Assess the impact that one of the following interest groups has had on American politics. Your answer must include one positive and one negative effect.

   - NRA
   - AARP
   - AMA
   - NOW

Or

1. What impact have the following PACs had on those running for office and policy making?

Or

1. What resources must a PAC employ to successfully influence policy making? Make certain to include in your answer three resources used by PACs.

All essay questions will ask you to display knowledge you have acquired. Some questions will ask you to assume a position and prove that position. You should **never give your personal opinion in an essay**. The graders refer to this as editorializing, and it is the "kiss of death." When the question asks you to choose a position, it is asking for an academic reason as to why a certain position is correct. There is often no single correct answer. But sometimes it is easier to prove one side than the other. In the examples above, it may be easier to argue the negative impact of PACs rather than the positive. But remember, you can make an argument for both sides, and sometimes the question may ask you to do that.

You should be very careful when you answer the four questions in the essay section. It is quite possible that you will not be required to write a complete essay with a thesis statement, evidence, and conclusion. In fact, if you were to write such an answer, and it was inappropriate, your score would probably suffer. **Do exactly the tasks that the question asks for.** If the question asks you to analyze data by explaining trends shown in a graph, do so. Make sure your analysis can be backed up by the data in the graph. If the graph question contains a part B (it often does), it will probably ask for an explanation of the data in the graph. This part of the answer will come from your knowledge of the subject. Because time is a factor and you will be awarded no more points for extras, do nothing more than what the question asks. Remember: You could be asked to write an essay explaining a graph, chart, data, historical quotation, or political cartoon; assuming or analyzing a position; or completing some other task.

An example of a stimulus-type essay question may look as follows:

Percentage of U.S. Population Affiliated with a Political Party

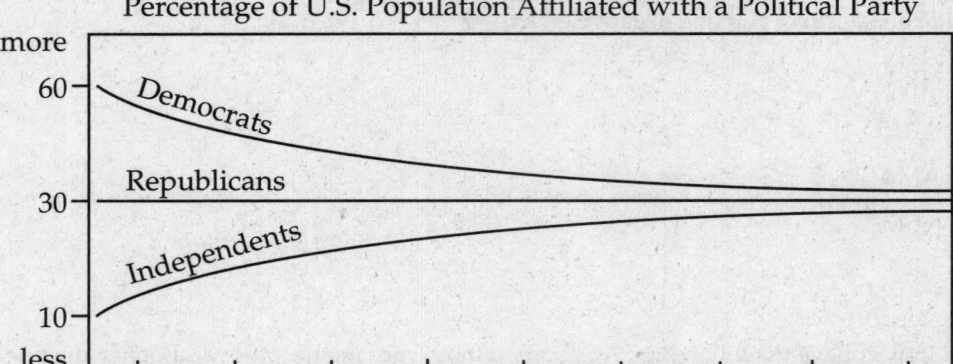

2. Using the information in the figure above and your knowledge of United States politics, complete the following tasks.

   (a) From the data in the chart above, what trends have occurred in the membership of the political parties in the past 40 years?

   (b) Based on your knowledge of American politics, explain what impact the trends have had on those running for political office.

Part (a): Answer (Keep in mind that this is just an outline; you will have to write in complete sentences and paragraphs.)

- The data shows that the number of Republicans has remained constant.

- The data shows that the number of Democrats has declined.

- The data shows that the number of Independents has increased.

- The data shows that the two political parties are approximately equal in number.

- The data shows that the Independents have come from the Democratic Party.

- The data shows that there are now almost as many Independents as members of the two major parties.

Part (b): Answer

- Independents are people who belong to no party. They vote for the candidate they
  ~~~~~~~~~~~~~~~ of the party with whom the candidate is affiliated. Independents
  ~~~~~~~~~~ e of the parties because of the positions they have taken
  ~~~~~~~~~~ pendents tend to be centrists. Therefore candidates will try
  ~~~~~~~~~~ s by taking centrist positions because they will probably
  ~~~~~~~~~~ election. This often makes it difficult to differentiate the
  ~~~~~~~~~~ dates. Perhaps this is one reason voters say it doesn't mat-
  ~~~~~~~~~~ ich in turn can cause depressed voter turnout.

Note that the question in part (a) does not ask for a thesis statement. It simply asks you to analyze the data. Part (b) also does not require a thesis statement. It contains an explanation of the data and the impact of decreasing party affiliations on elections. In answering these kinds of questions, it is always advisable to write complete sentences.

BE OPTIMISTIC

Both the exam writers and the graders realize that 25 minutes is not very much time to respond to a question. They understand that it will take about five minutes for you to understand the question and begin to organize your answer. Obviously, there is not enough time to give a very in-depth answer. Because of the time constraint, you will have to choose only those parts of your answer that give the strongest response to the question. The graders are not looking for the final word on the subject. Instead, they are checking to see whether you can

- address the question

- clearly explain the issues involved

- if required, assume a position and back it up with evidence and examples

- if required, acknowledge several points of view

These should be your four goals in writing your AP U.S. Government and Politics essays. Let's look at another essay question and go over each of the points.

ADDRESS THE QUESTION

3. It has been said that U.S. presidential election processes are inherently undemocratic and unrepresentative. Using your knowledge of election practices since 1992, to what degree is the above statement accurate?

Read the question very carefully. Make sure that you understand exactly what the question is asking. Students often start writing about something not asked in the question because they did not think and organize first. Don't panic. Read the entire question and make sure you address every part of it. Have you ever said to a teacher, "I knew that, but I forgot to write it down," or "I knew that but didn't see it in the question"? Essays that address the question fully earn more points; those that ignore parts of the question are doomed to low scores.

After reading the question above, you can determine that

- the claim you should discuss is that the election process is undemocratic

- there is a time limitation of 1992 to the present

- the question deals only with presidential elections

- you have to think about what practices may be unfair and undemocratic; there are potentially many, so decide which are the most important

- the reverse may be true, that elections are fair and democratic

- you should choose one position and give some evidence to support it

This question has what we call "limiters" to the response. "Since 1992" is one of the limiters; the phrase "presidential elections" is the other. There are many reasons to use limiters. One is to make things easier on the graders. If no date were given, you could write about any election in U.S. history and it would, therefore, be impossible to grade the exam. The limiter may also be a significant hint to answering the question. 1992 is the year that Ross Perot ran for president as an Independent against Bill Clinton and George H. W. Bush. This is a significant factor in this answer.

Some students find it helpful to underline significant parts of a question. If you were to do this, your question would probably look as follows:

3. It has been said that U.S. <u>presidential elections processes are inherently undemocratic</u> and unrepresentative. Using your knowledge of <u>election practices since 1992, to what degree is the above statement accurate</u>?

Unlike the previous sample question on political parties, this question will require a **thesis statement**. This should be an easy thesis statement to write, because the question requires you to assume a position and prove it. Assuming that you agree with the statement, your thesis statement may simply be: *U.S. presidential elections are inherently undemocratic and unrepresentative.*

You have assumed a position and now have to find the best pieces of evidence to support the claim. Note that the question does *not* tell you how many pieces of evidence to use. If it doesn't tell you how many, use three, but watch your time carefully, and be sure to relate each of the three points back to the thesis. Your three pieces of evidence, which you could introduce in the first paragraph, could be the following: low voter turnout caused by cumbersome registration laws; the state-by-state, winner-take-all system of determining electoral votes in the electoral college; and the large number of votes that are cast but not counted because of voting-machine malfunction or voter error.

THE EVIDENCE

Let's walk through how an essay should be structured using the question above as an example.

Be sure to clearly explain the issues involved and carefully pick the best pieces of evidence to prove your point. As you write, **assume that your reader knows very little about the topic. Define your terms, explain concepts,** and **provide historical background** whenever appropriate. Don't be afraid that you will bore the grader or that your essay will appear overly simple. On the contrary, defining terms, explaining concepts, and giving historical background in your first paragraph are all ways of indicating to the grader that you have a firm grasp of the subject.

The second paragraph of your essay should deal with the first piece of evidence to support the thesis—in this case, the issue of voter registration. You should discuss how each state has its own set of laws dealing with voter registration. There is no uniformity throughout the country. Some states make registration easy by allowing registration on election day. Others make registration cumbersome by requiring it to be completed weeks prior to election day. Or they require re-registration in the event of an address change or a failure to vote in the last election. These obstacles tend to depress voter turnout. You would want to note that U.S. voter turnout is only slightly higher than 50 percent, which is one of the lowest rates of any industrialized nation. All of these points are pieces of evidence to support the thesis statement.

The third paragraph should discuss the electoral college and the winner take all method of distributing electoral votes. Give a short explanation of the purpose of the electors, and describe how the number of electors is determined for each state. Explain what "winner-takes-all" means and why you believe that this is an inherently unfair method of counting votes. A good example would be Ross Perot receiving 19 percent of the popular vote but no votes in the electoral count. Another example would be George W. Bush losing the popular vote to Al Gore in 2000 but winning the election through the electoral vote. You may want to add that, in some states, the electors aren't required to vote as the popular vote indicates.

You should note that the difficulty of this question lies in picking only those pieces of information that simply and explicitly respond to the question. You could write a book on the electoral college and another on its history; the only thing that is important to answer in the essay is its misrepresentation of the popular vote, resulting in an undemocratic outcome.

The fourth paragraph should deal with the lack of a uniform voting method in all states or within a single state. This lack of uniformity can result in ballots that count in some states not counting in others, or counting in some counties, but not in others within a state. The Florida debacle in the 2000 election would be a great example. You could even throw in the Supreme Court case *Bush v. Gore*, which deals with multiple criteria for determining how to count ballots.

The conclusion in the last paragraph needs to link all the pieces of information to the thesis statement in the first paragraph. It should summarize how the electoral college, cumbersome registration laws, and differing state laws regulating the casting and counting of various types of ballots cause undemocratic results in presidential elections.

Note that this essay example has five paragraphs. The only reason is that five fits the format. If the question asked for one example, there would only be three paragraphs. There is no hard rule as to how many paragraphs should be written to answer a question. Remember, some questions may not even require multiple paragraphs.

ACKNOWLEDGE OTHER POINTS OF VIEW

The College Board scoring guide for the AP U.S. Government and Politics essay states the following:

> ....students should not simply summarize the arguments for or against a position but should evaluate the arguments. Specific examples should be incorporated to support their evaluation. Students should also develop the ability to acknowledge the opposite viewpoint without reducing the strength of their argument.

Whenever appropriate, include or acknowledge at least one viewpoint other than the one you have chosen in your essay. Briefly explain that viewpoint, and say why it is not the viewpoint you have chosen to argue. Again, look at our sample question. You could acknowledge the fact that registration is intended to reduce voter fraud, therefore promoting democracy. You could acknowledge that the electoral college was intended to keep small state populations from being swamped by the large states, thus ensuring a more democratic outcome. Finally, you could acknowledge that states have a right to determine election criteria for their own citizens, which is also democratic. **Exercise extreme caution when you discuss the opposing view.** Do not make it appear that you are arguing against your thesis. All you are doing here is stating that there can be another side to the argument.

A final caution. *Watch your time.* If you are running out, don't acknowledge the opposing view. Just write a simple conclusion.

PLANNING AND WRITING YOUR ESSAY

There are two essential components to writing a successful timed essay. The first is to plan what you are going to write before you start writing. The second is to use a number of tried-and-true writing techniques that will make your essay better organized, better thought out, and better written.

BEFORE YOU START WRITING

Read the question carefully. Figure out what you are being asked. Then brainstorm for a minute or two. In your test booklet, write down everything that comes to mind about the subject; there is room on the back pages of the booklet and on the blank space at the bottom of pages. Look at your notes and consider the results of your brainstorming session as you decide what points you will argue in your essay. Make the core of your argument into your thesis. Tailor your argument to the information, but don't make an argument that you know is wrong or with which you disagree. If you do either of these things, your essay will probably be awful. Finally, go through the results of your brainstorming. Some of what you wrote down will be "big picture" conclusions; some will be facts that can be used as evidence to support your conclusions; and some will be interesting material that, nonetheless, will not fit into a well-organized essay and should be discarded.

Next, make an outline. The outline should be brief—just a few words for each paragraph. You should plan to write as many paragraphs as are appropriate for answering the question. For example, some essays will require two paragraphs on relevant issues; others will need five. Or as the first essay example indicates, if the question does not require a full essay, you should not write one.

AS YOU ARE WRITING

Observe the following guidelines:

- **Keep sentences as simple as possible.** Long sentences get convoluted very quickly and will give your graders a headache.

- **Use appropriate political science terminology.** Don't overdo it, however, because it will look as if you're trying to show off. Remember that good writing doesn't have to be complicated; most great ideas can be stated simply. *Never* use a word if you are unsure of its meaning or proper usage. A malapropism may give your graders a good laugh, but it won't earn you any points and will probably cost you.

- **Write clearly and neatly.** Here's an easy way to put graders in a good mood. Graders look at a lot of chicken scratch; it strains their eyes and makes them grumpy. Also keep in mind that they have as little as two minutes to read each essay. Neatly written essays make them happy. When you cross out, do it neatly. Write in black ink. If you're making any major changes—if you want to insert a paragraph in the middle of your essay—make sure you indicate them clearly.

- **Define your terms.** Most questions require you to use terms that mean different things to different people. One person's "liberal" is another person's "conservative" and yet another person's "radical." The folks who grade the test want to know what *you* think these terms mean. When you use them, define them. Take particular care to define any such terms that appear in the question. Almost all official College Board materials stress this point, so don't forget: Define any term that you suspect can be defined in more than one way.

- **Use transition words to show where you are going.** When continuing an idea, use words such as "furthermore," "also," and "in addition." When changing the flow of thought, use words such as "however" and "yet." Transition words make your essay easier to understand by clarifying your intentions. Better yet, they indicate to the graders that you know how to make a coherent, persuasive argument.

- **Use structural indicators to organize your paragraphs.** Another way to clarify your intentions is to organize your essay around structural indicators. For example, if you are making a number of related points, number them ("First…Second…Finally…"). If you are attempting to compare and contrast two viewpoints, use the indicators "on the one hand" and "on the other hand" or "whereas."

- **Stick to your outline.** Unless you get an absolutely brilliant idea while you're writing, don't deviate from your outline. If you do, you'll risk winding up with an incoherent essay.

- **Try to prove one "big picture" idea per paragraph.** Keep it simple. Each paragraph should make one point; substantiate that point with evidence.

- **Back up your ideas with examples.** Yes, we've said it already, but it bears repeating. Don't just throw ideas out there and hope that you're right. You will score big points if you substantiate your claims with facts.

- **Try not to write just one or two paragraphs.** A short essay will hurt you more than will one that is too long.

- **Make sure your first and last paragraphs address the question directly.** Nothing will cost you points faster than if the graders decide you didn't answer the question. It's always a safe move to start your final paragraph by answering the question directly; if you've written a good essay, that answer will serve as a legitimate conclusion.

How to Crack the Essay Questions

Answering the essay questions on the AP U.S. Government and Politics Exam is not very different from answering the essay questions you have been answering all your life. The keys to success are:

- **Read the question carefully.** Tailor your answer to the question. When you have written all your notes and outline and you are prepared to begin writing your response, reread the question to ensure your answer is right on target.

- **Answer each part of the question directly.** If one part of the question asks how Jefferson's concern about term limitations is relevant today, you should probably have a sentence in your essay—and in a fairly prominent place such as the first paragraph or the first line in a subsequent paragraph—that reads "Jefferson's concern is very relevant (or irrelevant) today." Don't be coy.

- **Don't panic.** As you scan the four questions, you may well come to rest on the one that deals with a subject your teacher didn't cover or you didn't get around to studying. Don't worry: Everyone finds some questions harder than others. To build your confidence, answer the question you find easiest before turning to the intimidating one.

- **Watch your time.** You need to average no more than 25 minutes per question. The biggest mistake you can make, with the exception of failing to respond to the question, is failing to leave yourself enough time to answer all four questions. It's okay to spend as much as 30 minutes on a given question but you'd better make it worth it, and you probably don't want to do it on the first essay or you'll feel rushed while writing the remaining three.

- **If you draw a total blank on a question, take a deep breath, and ask yourself what you do know about the topic.** You may realize that you know more that you think. Try to figure out what the question is trying to get at or how you can approach it.

- **If you are running out of time on your fourth essay, abbreviate and write partial sentences.** The graders know that you may have to rush to finish the last essay. Although, under ideal circumstances, you would write in complete, well-considered sentences, you may not have time to do so. Don't panic; do the best you can, knowing that the graders will give you some leeway at the end of your essay, especially if you are clear and coherent at the beginning and in the middle. It is better to get all of your points down on paper with bullets than to have three beautiful introductory sentences that don't answer the question.

SUMMARY

- The essay questions are similar to the essays you have been assigned in your class. They require you to break down the information contained in the question and state a clearly reasoned point of view.

- Read questions carefully. Look for the multiple parts of the question. Make sure you respond to every part of the question—the graders will be looking for your response to each part.

- Mark up the question. You may bracket the core of the question, underline the operative words such as *evaluate, discuss, describe, analyze, agree with*, and *disagree with*, or circle limiters like, "since 1992," "give one example," and "list three."

- Look out for questions that require a definition of a term. If they ask for a definition, write one.

- Although you are not writing a history essay, making chronological points can strengthen your writing in certain areas (for example, the development of civil rights law). Do not write a mere list of historical data points in chronological order. Political science relies on analytical writing to substantiate viewpoints, so back up your position with proofs.

- Don't start writing until you have brainstormed, chosen a thesis if required, and written a brief outline.

- Make sure your conclusion does not contradict your hypothesis and your data does not contradict your thesis. Also make sure one sentence does not contradict another. Be consistent in your thinking.

- Follow your outline. Stick to one main idea per paragraph. Support your ideas with facts.

- Write clearly and neatly. Don't use sentences that are too long. Toss in a couple of political science terms that you know you won't misuse. When in doubt, stick to simple syntax and vocabulary.

- Use transition words to indicate continuity of thought or changes in the direction of your argument.

- Bring a watch to the exam and spend 25 minutes on each essay. Write explicitly and without equivocation.

- Every piece of data that supports your argument should be linked to it. Do not just list information without relating it to the point you are trying to make.

- Do not use slang, do not editorialize (do not give your personal opinion), do not inject your own politics, do not write jokes or make comments, do not make vague references to authors, do not preach, and do not moralize.

- Do not highlight or underline parts of your essay—the reader will figure it out. Highlighting looks amateurish and will distract the reader.

PART ◆ II

AP U.S. Government and Politics Review

5

THE CONSTITUTIONAL UNDERPINNINGS

THE CONCEPTS

- Why did the Articles of Confederation fail?
- What was the immediate impact of Shays's Rebellion?
- What motivated the Framers of the Constitution? Were they elitists or pragmatists?
- Why did the Framers create a republican form of government?
- Why did the Framers create a federal system of government?
- What is the purpose of checks and balances and the separation of powers?
- Why are plurality systems democratic but unstable?

THE TERMS

- Articles of Confederation
- Shays's Rebellion
- New Jersey Plan
- Virginia Plan
- Great Compromise
- Three-Fifths Compromise
- federalism
- dual federalism
- Federalists
- Antifederalists
- *Federalist Papers*
- Bill of Rights
- judicial review
- representative democracy
- delegated powers
- reserved powers
- concurrent powers
- full faith and credit clause
- privileges and immunities clause
- extradition
- supremacy clause
- categorical grants
- block grants
- separation of powers
- checks and balances
- veto
- override
- amendment
- ratify
- establishment clause
- selective incorporation
- cabinet
- governor
- line-item veto
- pardons and reprieves
- bicameral legislature
- revenue sharing

ENLIGHTENMENT PHILOSOPHIES

The Framers of the Constitution lived in a unique time when new ideas on how government should be organized and run challenged conventional wisdom regarding the roles of people and their government. The Enlightenment was an eighteenth-century philosophical movement that began in western Europe with roots in the Scientific Revolution. The focus was on the use of reason rather than tradition to solve social dilemmas. The following Enlightenment philosophers contributed directly to the formation of thought that led to the creation of the American Constitution and government.

- Thomas Hobbes: Hobbes's famous work *Leviathan* argued that if humans were left to their own devices, chaos and violence would ensue. In a state of nature, life would be "solitary, poor, nasty, brutish, and short." He argued that the best way to protect life was to give total power to an absolute monarch.

- John Locke: While Hobbes was concerned primarily with the protection of life, Locke went further and argued in his *Second Treatise on Civil Government* that liberty and property also needed to be respected. According to Locke, life, liberty and property were natural rights granted by God; it was the duty of all governments to respect and protect these rights.

- Charles de Montesquieu: Montesquieu was a French philosopher who greatly influenced the founders. His *De l'Esprit des Lois* (The Spirit of the Laws) advocated for the separation of power into three branches of government.

- Jean Jacques Rousseau: Rousseau argued that the only good government was one that was freely formed with the consent of the people. This consent was shown in a powerful "social contract," which was an agreement among people.

- Voltaire: This was the pen name of François-Marie Arouet. In works like *Candide*, Voltaire acts as a strong proponent of individual freedom, and a staunch defender of free speech.

THE WEAKNESS OF THE ARTICLES OF CONFEDERATION

The first government of the newly born United States of America was formed under the **Articles of Confederation**, the predecessor to the Constitution. These Articles were informally followed from 1774 to 1781 when they were ratified and so named. The government under the Articles achieved some notable accomplishments.

- They established the methods by which new states would enter the Union.

- They negotiated the treaty that ended the Revolutionary War.

- They set the precedent of **federalism**, whereby the states and central government shared governing responsibilities.

However, the Articles of Confederation had insurmountable weaknesses that placed the newly independent states at risk. By 1787, trade between the states was in decline, the value of money was dropping, potential threats from foreign enemies were growing, and there was the real threat of social disorder from groups within the country. The inability of the state of Massachusetts to effectively deal with **Shays's Rebellion**, in which more than 1,000 armed farmers attacked a federal arsenal to protest the foreclosure of farms in the western part of the state, was a major concern at the Constitutional Convention.

The federal government under the Articles:

- could not raise an army

- was completely dependent on the state legislatures for revenue—the federal government was not permitted to tax citizens

- could not pay off the Revolutionary War debt

- could not control interstate trade

- had no Supreme Court to interpret law

- had no executive branch to enforce national law

- had no national currency

- had no control over import and export taxes imposed between states

These deficiencies of the Articles of Confederation were the direct causes for calling a convention. But amending the articles became so difficult that James Madison did not have difficulty persuading the other delegates that a complete rewrite was necessary. The result was the **Constitution,** and the convention came to be known as the **Constitutional Convention**.

THE CONSTITUTIONAL CONVENTION

When the Framers of the Constitution met in Philadelphia in 1787, they were divided over their views of the appropriate power and responsibilities of government. Some saw the current government, formed under the Articles of Confederation, as weak and ineffective, while others believed that changes to the Articles would be infringements on the responsibilities of state governments and intrusions into the lives of citizens. Some historians (such as Charles Beard) see the convention as an elitist conspiracy to protect the wealth of the rich, while others (such as John Roche) see the convention as a meeting of political pragmatists who knew that by protecting everyone's property and rights, they could best protect their own. Today, the generally accepted view is that the Framers were pragmatists.

The delegates agreed that a stronger central government was necessary but were fearful of the corrupting influences of power. How to control the federal legislature was a central theme at the convention. The large states seized the agenda at the beginning of the convention and proposed the **Virginia Plan**, a recipe for a strong government with each state represented proportionately to its population. The small states worried that a government dominated by the large states would be overly strong, so they proposed the **New Jersey Plan**, under which each state would be represented equally. The **Great** (or **"Connecticut"**) **Compromise** created the solution: a **bicameral** (two-house) **legislature** with a House of Representatives, based on population, and a Senate, with equal representation for all states.

Another major conflict arose over the representation of slaves. (Remember that slaves obviously could not vote then.) Northerners felt that slaves should not be counted when determining each state's number of electoral votes, while Southerners obviously disagreed. The "solution" was the infamous **Three-Fifths Compromise**, in which the decision was made that slaves would count as three-fifths of a person when apportioning votes.

Under the Articles of Confederation there was no executive authority to enforce laws. The Framers of the Constitution corrected the problem with the chief executive, or president. Under the Constitution, the executive is the enforcer of law and a second check on the power of the legislature. Before bills become law, they require presidential approval, and the president has the power to veto acts of the legislature. However, presidential power is not absolute. Congress can override a presidential veto if two-thirds of both houses of the legislature vote to do so.

In order to arbitrate disputes between the Congress and the president, between states, and between the states and the central government, the Framers created the Supreme Court.

Despite all the compromises agreed to at the convention, acceptance of the Constitution was by no means assured. It had to be submitted to the states for ratification. Supporters and opponents of the Constitution broke into two camps, **Federalists** and **Antifederalists**. Alexander Hamilton, James Madison, and John Jay wrote a series of newspaper articles supporting the Constitution, collectively known as the *Federalist Papers*. These essays are the primary source for understanding the original intent of the Framers. They were designed to persuade the states of the wisdom of a strong central government coupled with autonomous political power retained by the states.

The opposition to the Constitution centered around the lack of a **Bill of Rights** that would protect the rights of individuals from government usurpation. Once the Federalists guaranteed that a Bill of Rights would be added to the Constitution immediately after ratification, opposition diminished and the Constitution became the foundation of American government.

THE CONSTITUTION AS AN INSTRUMENT OF GOVERNMENT

THE "LIVING CONSTITUTION"

The Constitution is vague and skeletal in form, containing only about 5,000 words. It was intended to be a blueprint for the structure of government and a guide for guaranteeing the rights of citizens. It was written to allow change, anticipating unknown needs of future generations. The branches of government have all grown and evolved since the ratification of the Constitution.

- The **necessary and proper clause** of the Constitution (Article I, Section 8) allows Congress to "make all laws" that appear "necessary and proper" to implement its delegated powers. This is also called the **elastic clause.** For example, there is nothing in the Constitution that creates the Federal Reserve System, which is the central bank for the United States. Neither is there any mention of a Cabinet in the executive branch. The Federal District Courts and the Courts of Appeals were both created by congressional elaboration.

- Executive power has expanded through the use of **presidential practice.** Executive orders, which have the same effect as law, bypass Congress in policy making and are not mentioned in the Constitution. Presidents use them as part of the enforcement duties of the executive branch. Executive agreements between heads of countries have many of the same elements as treaties. These agreements bypass the ratification power of the Senate but are not mentioned in the Constitution. Use of the Oval Office and the media as a communication link directly to the electorate were never anticipated by the Framers.

- When the Supreme Court decided the case of *Marbury v. Madison* in 1803, it drastically increased its own power by granting itself the power to overturn laws passed by the legislature, also known as **judicial review.**

- Finally, custom and usage have changed the system to meet differing needs. The political-party system, with its organization, technology, and fund-raising capabilities, was created from custom and usage. The rules used in Congress were also created from custom and usage.

FEDERALISM

Central to the Constitution is the idea that the United States government is a federal government. The term **federalism** describes a system of government under which the national government and local governments (state governments, in the case of the United States) share powers. Other federal governments include Germany, Switzerland, and Australia.

Under federalism, some government powers belong exclusively to the national government, some exclusively to the states, and some are shared by the two. Those **powers that belong to the national government** only are called **delegated powers** or **enumerated powers**. Among them are

- printing money
- regulating interstate and international trade
- making treaties and conducting foreign policy
- declaring war

Powers that belong exclusively to the states are called **reserved powers.** According to the Tenth Amendment, these powers include any that the Constitution does not either specifically grant to the national government nor deny to the state governments. These powers are not listed in the Constitution; in fact, they are made up of all powers *not* mentioned in the Constitution. They include

- the power to issue licenses
- the regulation of intrastate (within the states) businesses
- the responsibility to run and pay for federal elections

Some powers are shared by the federal and state governments. These are called **concurrent powers.** Among them are the powers to

- collect taxes
- build roads
- operate courts of law
- borrow money

The Constitution specifies which powers are denied to the national government and which powers are denied to the states. Those powers are listed in the chart on the next page.

The Constitution also obliges the federal government to guarantee the states a republican form of government and protection against foreign invasion and domestic rebellion. The federal government must also prevent the states from subdividing or combining to form new states without Congressional consent. The states, in turn, are required by the Constitution to accept the court judgments, licenses, contracts, and other civil acts of all the other states; this obligation is contained in the **full faith and credit clause.** The states may not refuse police protection or access to their courts to a U.S. citizen just because he lives in a different state; this provision appears in the **privileges and immunities clause.** Finally, the states usually must return fugitives to the states from which they have fled; this process is called **extradition.**

The **supremacy clause** of the Constitution requires conflicts between federal law and state law to be resolved in favor of federal law. State laws that violate the Constitution, federal laws, or international treaties can be invalidated through the supremacy clause.

The nature of federalism has changed over time. For the first part of the nation's history, the federal and state governments remained separate and independent. The relationship between the national and state governments during this period is called **dual federalism**. What little contact most Americans had with government occurred on the state level, as the national government concerned itself primarily with international trade, the construction of roads, harbors, and railways, and the distribution of public land in the West.

The Federal Government Does Not Have the Power to:

Suspend the *writ of habeas corpus*, (which protects against illegal imprisonment), except in times of national crisis

Pass *ex post facto* (retroactive) laws or issuance of bills of attainder (which declare an individual guilty of a capital offense without a trial)

Impose export taxes

Use money from the treasury without the passage and approval of an appropriations bill

Grant titles of nobility

The State Governments Do Not Have the Power to:

Enter into treaties with foreign countries

Declare war

Maintain a standing army

Print money

Pass *ex post facto* (retroactive) laws or issuance of bills of attainder (which declare an individual guilty of a capital offense without a trial)

Grant titles of nobility

Impose of import or export duties

As with all parts of the Constitution, the definition of federalism is in the eye of the beholder. Ideological **States' Rightists** define federalism as a relationship in which the states retain most of the political power. **Nationalists** often see the federal government as being supreme in all matters and ultimately in control.

Most federal government programs, such as those to aid the poor, clean the environment, improve education, and protect the handicapped, are administered through the states. The federal government pays for these programs through grants-in-aid, outright gifts of money to the states. Nationalists prefer to tie strings to the grants, ensuring that the federal government maintains control over the money. States' Rightists want no strings attached, leaving decisions about how the grant money is to be used to state and local governments, who they believe know best how to use it.

Nationalists like **categorical grants**, the type of aid that has federal strings attached. States' Rightists like **block grants**, which give the states broad powers to experiment and use the money as they see fit. In the final analysis, however, the federal government can use a number of techniques, including direct orders and preemption, to force the states to abide by federal law. The federal government can also use a crossover sanction, which requires a state to do something before a grant will be awarded. An example would be to raise the drinking age to 21 before federal highway money to build state roads is released.

Federalism allows states to experiment with solutions to solve their own state problems. Funds that a poor state could never raise can come from the federal government. This allows for diversity and greater equality between the states.

SEPARATION OF POWERS

The Framers of the Constitution decided that no one faction of the government should be able to acquire too much power. To prevent this, they borrowed the concept of the **separation of powers** from the French political philosopher **Charles de Montesquieu**. The Framers delegated different but equally important tasks to the three branches of government. The **legislative branch** (Congress) makes the laws; the **executive branch**, led by the president, enforces the laws; and the **judicial branch** interprets the laws.

Separation of powers also prevents a person from serving in more than one branch of the government at the same time. A congressperson (legislative branch), for example, may not also be a judge (judicial branch), nor a cabinet member (executive branch). If a congressperson were appointed to one of these positions, he or she would first have to resign his or her seat in Congress.

THE SYSTEM OF CHECKS AND BALANCES

The system of **checks and balances** is another constitutional safeguard designed to prevent any one branch of government from becoming dominant. The system of checks and balances requires the different branches of government to share power and cooperate with one another to accomplish anything of importance. See the following page for some examples of the system of checks and balances.

- **Nomination of federal judges, cabinet officials, and ambassadors.** The president chooses nominees for these positions. However, the president's nominees must be approved by the Senate.

- **Negotiation of treaties.** The president is empowered to negotiate treaties. No treaty can go into effect, however, until it is approved by two-thirds of the Senate.

- **Enactment of legislation.** Only Congress may pass laws. However, the president has the power to **veto**, or reject, legislation. The president's veto power forces the legislature to consider the president's position on a law, and to negotiate with the president to prevent a veto. Congress can also check the president's veto by **overriding** the veto, but to do so it must pass the same law with a two-thirds majority in both houses (a congressional override is difficult, but not impossible). If Congress succeeds in overriding the president's veto, the legislation becomes law regardless of the president's position. Finally, the courts may determine the constitutionality of the law. Thus, the courts have the power to overturn laws passed by Congress and approved by the president (only on constitutional grounds, however; judges may not overturn laws simply because they don't like them).

AMENDMENT PROCESS

One reason that the Constitution has lasted more than 200 years is that it is flexible. Many of its provisions require interpretation, allowing the document to become more conservative or progressive as the times warrant. Furthermore, the Constitution can be changed through **amendments** (the addition of provisions to the document).

To amend the Constitution, a **proposed amendment must be introduced to both houses of Congress and approved by a two-thirds majority in each.** The amendment is then passed on to each of the 50 state legislatures. **Three-fourths of the state legislatures must ratify** the amendment for it to become part of the Constitution. The states themselves are allowed to determine how many votes are required to ratify an amendment. Most states require a simple majority of their legislatures, but seven states require either three-fifths or two-thirds majorities. Also, rather than use the state legislatures, Congress can mandate that each state use a **ratifying convention**, with delegates expressly elected to vote on the proposed amendment. This method was once used to ratify the Twenty-first Amendment, which ended Prohibition.

The Constitution allows for a second means of amendment. Two-thirds of the state legislatures could petition Congress to call a constitutional convention. Because no constitutional convention has ever taken place, nobody knows for certain how extensively conventioneers would be allowed to alter the Constitution. Could they rewrite it entirely, or would they be restricted to amendments mentioned specifically in their petitions for a convention? Fear that a constitutional convention could attempt drastic alterations has persuaded many state legislators to oppose any call for a convention. A recent movement for a convention to add a balanced budget amendment to the Constitution was narrowly defeated.

Proposal Methods	Ratification Methods
• Proposed amendment wins 2/3 majority in the House and Senate • Used for all 27 amendments	• 3/4 of all state legislatures approve of the amendment • Used 26 times (not for 21st Amendment)
• A constitutional convention is called by 2/3 of state legislatures. Any amendment can now be proposed at the convention • This method has never been used	• 3/4 of special state ratifying conventions approve the amendment • Used only once, for the 21st Amendment

AMENDMENTS

THE BILL OF RIGHTS (DECEMBER 15, 1791)

The first ten amendments were added to the Constitution within three years of its ratification. These amendments are known collectively as the Bill of Rights. Originally written by James Madison, many provisions of the Bill of Rights have been expanded and clarified over the years.

The First Amendment

Supreme Court Justice Benjamin Cardozo said that the First Amendment of the Bill of Rights contains "the fundamental principles of liberty and justice which lie at the base of all of our civil and political institutions."

- **Freedom of religion.** The government may not interfere with an individual's right to practice his or her faith as described in the **free exercise clause**. Furthermore, as stated in the **establishment clause**, Congress may not establish an official church of the United States nor give a particular faith or sect preferential treatment over others. This constitutional provision is usually referred to as the separation of church and state.

- **Freedom of speech and freedom of the press**. Congress may not pass a law that prevents citizens from expressing their opinions, either in speech or in writing. Nevertheless, the Supreme Court has placed some limits on these freedoms. Speech or writing intended to incite violence or used to intentionally slander or libel are not protected. Justice Oliver Wendell Holmes articulated the "clear and present danger" test, in which the government has the right to interfere in free speech if it poses a threat to others, in the case of *Schenck v. United States* (1917). Nevertheless, criticism of the government and its politics is protected. When it comes to censoring the press, the government can almost never use *prior restraint*—crossing out sections of an article before publication. These strong protections for the press were established in the case of *New York Times v. U.S.* (1971).

- **Freedom of assembly and freedom to petition the government**. The Constitution protects the people's rights to assemble peacefully, to hold demonstrations, and to ask the government for changes in policy. Rallies and demonstrations that encourage or incite violence and those that do not seek official sanction to trespass on public property are not protected.

The Second Amendment
The Second Amendment to the Constitution, which protects the citizen's right to bear arms, has led to a debate over whether the Constitution protects citizens' right to bear arms under all circumstances, or only when those citizens serve in "well-regulated militias."

The Third Amendment
The most antiquated of all the amendments, though not at the time of its creation, the Third Amendment forbids the quartering of soldiers and the direct public support of armed forces. It was a direct reaction to the British practice of using civilian support to conduct military operations. Still, it later had importance as it became part of the foundation of the **Right to Privacy** as established in the case of *Griswold v. Connecticut* (1965).

The Fourth Amendment
The Fourth Amendment places restrictions on government agencies regarding criminal or civil procedural investigations and does much to protect an individual's "person, house, papers, and effects against unreasonable searches and seizures." This amendment was most dramatically reviewed in the twentieth-century, as evidenced in *Mapp v. Ohio* (1961). Questions regarding the use of probable cause, traffic stop searches, and the use of search warrants have led to challenges regarding the interpretation of the **exclusionary rule** regarding evidence seized without proper procedures. In its original form, the exclusionary rule holds that all evidence unlawfully gathered must be excluded from judicial proceedings.

The Fifth Amendment
The Fifth Amendment does the most to protect an individual from the broad powers of the Federal government. It provides a guarantee of a **grand jury** when a suspect is held for a capital or other

"infamous" crime. It eliminates the possibility of a person being maliciously prosecuted for the same crime again and again by prohibiting **double jeopardy**. It establishes the right of the government to seize property for public use under the auspices of **eminent domain** but only if such seizure can be "justly compensated." Nor may defendants be forced to testify against themselves if on trial, thus prohibiting **self-incrimination**. The most significant attribute of the Fifth Amendment is its mandate that the federal government not deprive an individual of "life, liberty, or property by any level unless **due process of law** is applied."

The Sixth Amendment
This amendment allows persons accused of a crime to be prosecuted by an impartial jury in a "speedy" public trial. Individuals have the right to be informed of their charges (**habeas corpus**), to confront witnesses, to subpoena witnesses for their defense, and to have a lawyer for their defense.

The Seventh Amendment
Although statutory law has come to replace or supersede common law, the Seventh Amendment allows for trial by jury in common-law cases.

The Eighth Amendment
The Eighth Amendment prohibits excessive bail in federal cases. Yet its most significant challenges have arisen from the clause which prohibits "cruel and unusual punishment." **Capital punishment**, the twentieth-century. Does it constitute "cruel and unusual punishment?" Various Supreme Courts have taken different positions on this issue.

The Ninth Amendment
The Ninth Amendment reaffirms the principles of a limited federal government. "The powers not delegated to the United States by the Constitution, nor prohibited by it to the States, are reserved to the States respectively, or to the people" means that rights not specifically mentioned in the Constitution are still protected—everyone has the right to brush their hair, for example—even though that right is mentioned nowhere in the Bill of Rights. Although somewhat vague in its premise, the Ninth Amendment has led to the implied right to privacy and other questions regarding individual rights not identified or even understood at the time of the creation of the Constitution.

The Tenth Amendment
The Tenth Amendment defines the relationship between the states and the national government under the concept of federalism. It states that when powers are not defined or delegated by the Constitution, the states have **reserved power** to make their own individual judgments—so long as they do not infringe with the explicit rules of the Constitution and the federal government. State issues such as death penalty, speed limit, and drinking age are within the jurisdiction of the states to decide so long as they do not contradict the Constitution.

EARLY AMENDMENTS (1795–1804)

The Eleventh Amendment (1795)
This amendment was passed as a response to the Supreme Court ruling of *Chisholm v. Georgia* (1793), which held that states did not enjoy sovereign immunity from lawsuits brought by residents of other states. In order to overrule *Chisholm*, the Eleventh Amendment provides that states may not be sued in federal court by citizens of another state or country without the consent of the states being sued.

The Twelfth Amendment (1804)
Originally, under Article II of the Constitution, those selected as electors for choosing the president got to cast *two* votes. The candidate who got the highest number of votes won the presidency, while the runner-up got the vice presidency as a consolation prize. The Twelfth Amendment was created

following the debacle of the election of 1800—a tie between Thomas Jefferson and Aaron Burr, who split the Republican vote. This amendment ensured that electors would now have to cast separate votes for the president and the vice president.

THE CIVIL WAR AMENDMENTS (1865–1870)

The Thirteenth Amendment (1865)
This amendment prohibited the institution of slavery except as punishment for a convicted crime, and was a direct result of the Union victory in the Civil War.

The Fourteenth Amendment (1868)
Remember, the Bill of Rights did not originally apply to state law. After the Civil War, Northerners pushed for a constitutional amendment that would prevent the South from denying equal rights to the newly freed slaves. The Fourteenth Amendment was designed to accomplish this purpose, stating that

> No state shall make or enforce any law which shall abridge the privileges or immunities of citizens of the United States; nor shall any state deprive any person of life, liberty, or property, without due process of law; nor deny to any person within its jurisdiction the equal protection of the laws.

The Fourteenth Amendment expanded the right to due process to all Americans; however, it did not immediately apply the protections of the Bill of Rights to all state laws. Instead, the Supreme Court has used the "due process" and "equal protection" clauses to extend most of the Bill of Rights protections but has done so on a case-by-case basis. This process of incorporating some of the Bill of Rights protections to state law is called **selective incorporation**.

The Fifteenth Amendment (1870)
The Fifteenth Amendment granted voting rights to males of all races, and was originally designed to extend voting rights to newly freed male slaves. Ultimately, the Supreme Court and southern states later narrowed, and in some cases eliminated, the provisions of this amendment during the late nineteenth and early twentieth-century. Voter rights were only later made secure by the passage of the **Twenty-fourth Amendment** and the **Voting Rights Act of 1965**.

PROGRESSIVE ERA AMENDMENTS (1913–1920)

The Sixteenth Amendment (1913)
Before the passage of this amendment, most revenue was gathered through tariffs that placed a large burden on the poor. The Sixteenth Amendment gave Congress the power to collect taxes on income, which allowed for the creation of a progressive income tax that fell more on the rich.

The Seventeenth Amendment (1913)
This amendment provided for the direct election of United States senators. Previously, senators had been selected by the state legislatures. The Seventeenth Amendment shifted the responsibility for choosing senators from the legislatures to the general voting public.

The Eighteenth Amendment (1920)
Known as the Prohibition amendment, this amendment prohibited the manufacture, sale, and transportation of alcohol in or out of the United States.

The Nineteenth Amendment (1920)
This amendment granted voting rights to all American women.

LATER AMENDMENTS (1933–1992)

The Twentieth Amendment (1933)
Before the passage of the Twentieth Amendment, there was a long gap in between the time that the outgoing president left and the time that he was succeeded by his replacement. This gap proved especially damaging to the nation as it was in the grip of the Great Depression and anxiously waiting for FDR to take the reigns. As a result, this amendment clearly defined the procedures regarding the specifics of presidential and legislative terms, and shortened the amount of time between presidential election and inauguration.

The Twenty-first Amendment (1933)
Prohibition had largely led to the rise of organized crime and widespread lawbreaking. The Twenty-First Amendment recognized the failure of this government experiment and repealed prohibition, allowing for the legalization of the sale of alcohol.

The Twenty-second Amendment (1951)
In response to Franklin Delano Roosevelt's unprecedented four presidential election victories, this amendment limited the president to two terms.

The Twenty-third Amendment (1961)
This amendment allowed the residents of Washington, DC to vote in presidential elections, bringing the total national electoral count to 538.

The Twenty-fourth Amendment (1964)
The Twenty-Fourth Amendment eliminated the racially discriminatory practice of forcing African Americans to pay poll taxes when attempting to vote in southern state elections.

The Twenty-fifth Amendment (1967)
Following the assassination of John Kennedy and given the age of his successor, Lyndon Johnson, this amendment provided clarity regarding the selection of a new vice president should the position become vacant. The Twenty-fifth Amendment also formally permitted the vice president to assume the presidency temporarily in the event of a presidential disability.

The Twenty-sixth Amendment (1971)
In response to the number of young people fighting in the Vietnam War, the Twenty-sixth Amendment lowered the voting age from 21 to 18.

The Twenty-seventh Amendment (1992)
This is a sleeper amendment that was passed over 203 years after it was first proposed. If Congress votes itself a pay increase, that increase cannot take effect until after the next election.

THE "UNWRITTEN CONSTITUTION"
Certain deeply ingrained aspects of our government are not specified in the Constitution. These traditions are called the unwritten Constitution. **Judicial review**—the power of the Supreme Court to declare laws and executive actions unconstitutional—for example, is not mentioned in the Constitution. The principle was established by Chief Justice **John Marshall** in 1803 and has been observed ever since, so it has become as real and integral a part of U.S. government as are those principles described in the Constitution.

Other prominent examples of the unwritten Constitution are as follows:

- **Political parties and political conventions.** The Framers of the Constitution disliked political parties and had hoped they would not develop in the United States. Parties did arise, however, and soon became a fixture of the U.S. political landscape. Political conventions, at which delegates choose their party's presidential candidate and draw up the party's **platform** (a list of its political objectives), have played an important role in U.S. politics since the early 1800s.

- **The Cabinet.** The president's Cabinet is a group of advisors made up of the heads of various executive departments of the government. The Constitution mentions the executive departments but does not require the president to meet with them as a group to seek their advice. George Washington established the tradition and every president since has followed it.

Until the Twenty-second Amendment was ratified, the two-term limit on the presidency was also a part of the unwritten Constitution. **Franklin D. Roosevelt** broke that tradition (because the country was about to enter World War II) and, soon after his death, the Twenty-second Amendment was proposed to ensure that no other president could do so.

STATE AND LOCAL GOVERNMENTS

The Constitution does not stipulate the form state governments must take. The states are instead free to form whatever governments they choose, provided that the government is defined by a state constitution and that the constitution is approved by Congress. However, most state governments are structured after the federal government.

All states have an executive branch led by a **governor**, whose duties to the state are similar to the president's duties to the nation. Governors direct state executive agencies, which oversee areas such as education, roads, and policing. They command the state National Guard and may grant **pardons** and **reprieves.** Most have the power to appoint state judges, with the "advice and consent" of one of the state's legislative bodies. Governors have veto power over acts of the state legislature.

All states but one have bicameral legislatures modeled after the House of Representatives and the Senate (Nebraska has a unicameral legislature.). In the same way that Congress enacts federal law, the state legislatures enact state law. The legislatures have the power to **override** the **gubernatorial veto** (the word *gubernatorial* means *relating to the governor*). Governors have many of the same executive powers as presidents. However, many governors may use a **line-item veto** to reject only parts of bills. Presidents were denied this power by the Supreme Court under the ruling that a federal line-item veto would take too much power away from the legislative branch (see page 84).

All states also have state judiciaries to interpret state law. These judicial systems consist of trial courts and appeals courts, as does the federal judiciary. They hear both criminal cases (in which an individual is accused of a crime) and civil cases (in which disputing parties can sue to receive compensation).

Local governments—that is, governments on the city, town, and county levels—are somewhat more varied than are state governments. There are more than 86,000 local governments in the United States. Most have executive, legislative, and judicial branches whose actions must comply with state and (when applicable) federal law.

State and local governments raise revenues through taxes. Both may impose income taxes, although not all do. **Property taxes** generate a large portion of state revenues, as do taxes on local businesses; states must be careful about tax rates, however, because businesses may relocate when tax rates increase. Many states sponsor lotteries to increase revenues. States also receive federal funds through block grants and **revenue sharing** (federal money granted to the states for general purposes).

SUMMARY

- Remember that the Articles of Confederation were ultimately too weak to serve as a viable government for the new nation.

- Know the important philosophers that influenced the Framers: Hobbes, Locke, Montesquieu, and Rousseau.

- The Constitutional Convention in Philadelphia resulted in a new governing document that sought to balance the autonomy of the states with a stronger federal government.

- The vagueness of some sections of the Constitution along with elements like the elastic clause make the document adaptable to changing times, earning it the title of the "living Constitution."

- The United States, through the Constitution, was the first nation to practice federalism: a balance of power between the states and the federal government.

- In keeping with the principles of Montesquieu, the Founders created a government split into three branches and gave each branch the power to check the other two.

- To keep the Constitution adaptable to changing times, the Framers added an amendment process that made it hard, but not impossible, to change the document.

- Try to remember all 27 Amendments: the Bill of Rights, the early amendments, the Civil War Amendment, the Progressive Era Amendments, and the later amendments.

- Many powers that are not formally declared in the Constitution have been taken on by the president and Congress—you should be aware of this "unwritten Constitution."

- Know a bit about how state and local governments function with their own executive, legislative, and judicial branches.

PRACTICE QUESTIONS

1. Shays's Rebellion is significant because it

    (A) led to the overthrow of British rule
    (B) scared American elites, leading to the adoption of the Constitution
    (C) caused the American colonies to join together in the face of a threat from the French
    (D) led to the enactment of slavery in the South
    (E) narrowly avoided overthrowing the government of Vermont

2. Which of the following was NOT a problem with the Articles of Confederation?

    (A) There was no strong federal army to prevent revolutions.
    (B) The Articles were almost impossible to amend.
    (C) Each state was taxing trade with other states.
    (D) States were establishing ties with foreign powers.
    (E) The articles did not adequately protect the freedom of the states.

3. The issue of the representation of slaves was decided by the

    (A) Three-Fifths Compromise
    (B) Connecticut Compromise
    (C) Commerce and Slave-Trade Compromise
    (D) Bill of Rights
    (E) Articles of Confederation

4. The principle of American government that establishes concurrent state and national governments is known as

    (A) separation of powers
    (B) limited government
    (C) federalism
    (D) checks and balances
    (E) judicial review

5. The Virginia Plan would have created a

    (A) legislature dominated by the small states
    (B) legislature dominated by the big states
    (C) legislature controlled by the slave states
    (D) legislature that balanced control between the large and small states
    (E) constitutional monarchy

6

PUBLIC OPINION AND THE MEDIA

THE CONCEPTS

- What is public opinion?
- What is the public agenda, and how is the agenda shaped?
- How is public opinion measured?
- What role does the media play in shaping public opinion?
- What effect does the media have on individual political beliefs and voting behavior?

THE TERMS

- saliency
- intensity
- stability
- public opinion
- random sampling
- exit polls
- Gallup poll
- political socialization
- liberal ideology
- conservative ideology
- news media
- public agenda

Public opinion, simply put, is how people feel about things. Pollsters measure the public's opinion of everything from television programs to commercial products to political issues. Networks, companies, and politicians commission these polls because they seek the approval of the public.

Obviously, public opinion is not uniform: Even the most popular television shows attract a minority of all Americans. Furthermore, many programs are designed to receive favorable ratings from a specific subgroup of society rather than from the public at large. Networks, for example, seek high ratings from young, middle-class audiences, as these are the audiences most sought after by advertisers. Because advertisers are less interested in senior citizens, networks seek their approval less aggressively.

The same holds true for political issues. Most Americans—the **general public**—care more about the political issues that affect their day-to-day lives directly. A political issue does not have to interest the majority of Americans, then, to be considered important by politicians. If an issue is of enough importance to a smaller group—the **issue public**—to cause those voters to become more politically active, that issue may well become an important political issue. Furthermore, very few politicians seek the approval of the general public as a whole. With the exception of the president, all politicians have much smaller constituencies, and they measure the public opinion of these constituencies in order to appeal to them. Members of the House of Representatives, for example, are interested primarily in the concerns of their home districts, which are often quite different from the concerns of the general public.

CHARACTERISTICS OF PUBLIC OPINION

Those who measure public opinion are not just interested in the direction of public opinion—that is, how the public is feeling at a given moment. They also want to know how strongly the public feels and how likely people are to change their minds. That is why they try to gauge the following characteristics of public opinion:

- **Saliency.** The saliency of an issue is the degree to which it is important to a particular individual or group. For example, Social Security is an issue with high salience for senior citizens. Among young voters, Social Security has a much lower salience.

- **Intensity.** How strongly do people feel about a particular issue? When the intensity of a group's opinion is high, that group can wield political influence far beyond their numbers. For example, the majority of Americans have favored some form of gun control for decades. However, the intensity of that opinion is not high, and most Americans consider other issues when they vote. The National Rifle Association (NRA) represents a minority position. However, the intensity of their opposition to gun control is high. As a result, its members are likely to decide how they will vote based primarily on a candidate's position on gun control. This, in turn, has made the NRA one of the nation's most powerful lobbying organizations.

- **Stability.** Public opinion on issues changes over time. Some dimensions of public opinion, such as support for democracy and a controlled free-market economy, remain relatively stable. Others can change quickly, as was the case during the last two years of George Bush Sr.'s administration. During the Gulf War (January 1991), President Bush recorded the highest approval ratings of any president since 1945. Less than two years later, the majority of Americans showed their disapproval of his performance as president by voting against him.

In the United States, public opinion is measured regularly through elections. Elections measure public opinion indirectly, however, because votes for—or against—candidates can rarely be translated into clear and specific opinions. Referenda measure the public's opinion on specific issues but do so infrequently (a referendum submits to popular vote a measure passed by a legislative body). Public opinion is measured most frequently and directly by **public opinion polls.**

POLLS MEASURE PUBLIC OPINION

Public opinion polls are designed to determine public opinion by asking questions of a much smaller group. Pollsters achieve this through **random sampling**, a method that allows them to poll a representative cross-section of the public. When polling by phone, pollsters use a machine that dials numbers randomly. When conducting **exit polls** at polling places on election day, they target voting districts that collectively represent the voting public and randomly poll voters who are leaving the voting place. This method prevents bias, which may occur if pollsters were to approach only those voters who seemed most friendly or anxious to participate. When performed correctly, polls can measure the opinions of 300 million Americans by polling a mere 1,500 of them.

For a poll to accurately reflect public opinion, its questions must be carefully worded. A poll that asks, "Do you approve or disapprove of the death penalty?" would likely yield a very different response from one that asks, "Would you want the death penalty imposed on someone who killed your parents?" Most pollsters try to phrase questions objectively. Polls generally ask multiple-choice questions, which are closed-ended, as opposed to open-ended questions (such as, "Explain why you approve or disapprove of the death penalty"). Closed-ended questions yield results that are more easily quantifiable, providing a more accurate read of the direction and intensity of public opinion.

Even with those controls, polls cannot be 100 percent accurate. Polling organizations know how accurate their polls are and include this information with the poll results. The accuracy is measured as a sampling error and appears as a percentage with a plus and minus sign to the left (example: ±4 percent). The **sampling error** tells how far off the poll results may be. Suppose a poll indicated that 60 percent of Americans favored the death penalty. If that poll had a sampling error of ±4 percent, the actual percentage of Americans favoring the death penalty could be anywhere between 56 and 64 percent. Generally, the more respondents a poll surveys, the lower the sampling error.

Another cause of inaccurate poll results is dishonesty among poll respondents. Although few people purposely attempt to subvert polls, some respondents answer polls as they feel they should answer as opposed to how they really feel. Some white voters will profess support for black candidates, for example, because they do not want the pollster to think of them as racist; when it comes time to vote, however, these voters choose white candidates.

The best-known polls are the Harris poll and the Gallup poll. Many major newspapers and television networks conduct public opinion polls, as do academic and public interest institutions.

WHERE DOES PUBLIC OPINION COME FROM?

Public opinion is made up of the views of individuals. Individuals develop their political attitudes through a process called **political socialization.** Why, and when, do they change? What factors influence a person's political beliefs?

The first factor that influences individual political beliefs is **family.** Most people eventually affiliate with the same political party as their parents. Children's political beliefs are also greatly affected by the moral and ethical values they learn from their parents. Political values learned in childhood stay with many Americans throughout their entire lives. Also important is their **location**—people born in rural states may develop political views that are more socially conservative than those of city dwellers.

As children grow, other factors influence their political socialization. In **school** they learn about history and government and are exposed to the political perspectives of teachers and peers. **Religious institutions** have a similar influence on many Americans. **Mass media** such as television, radio, and magazines further influence political attitudes. In general, however, youth is a time when many Americans pay relatively little attention to and have little interest in political issues. This is because most political issues have little direct impact on their day-to-day lives.

Those who progress to **higher education** often find themselves questioning their social and political assumptions for the first time. As a result, college can be a time of radical change in an individual's political beliefs. This is particularly true of students at campuses that are heavily politicized and that lean strongly in one political direction, either conservative (such as Texas Christian University) or liberal (such as Reed College). Studies have shown that students retain throughout their lives many of the political attitudes they acquire in college.

As individuals reach adulthood, **real-life experiences** become the primary influence on their political beliefs. Family responsibilities and property ownership tend to make people more conservative. Conversely, individuals who experience bias based on their earning power, race, or gender may grow more liberal or more cynical about government. Adults continue to be influenced by participation in religious organizations, by the attitudes of their peers, and by what they learn through the news media.

POLITICAL IDEOLOGIES

The terms *liberal* and *conservative* in the previous paragraph refer to the predominant **ideologies** in the United States. An ideology is a coherent set of thoughts and beliefs about politics and government. The three most common political ideologies in the United States are the following:

- **Conservative.** Conservatives stress that individuals should be responsible for their own well-being and should not rely on government assistance. As a result, they tend to oppose government interference in the private sector. They also oppose most federal regulations, preferring that the market determine costs and acceptable business practices. Social conservatives, who make up a powerful wing of the conservative movement, do support government action on social issues.

- **Liberal.** Liberals believe that the government should be used to remedy the social and economic injustices of the marketplace. They tend to support government regulation of the economy. They also support government efforts to redress past social injustices through programs such as affirmative action. Most liberals believe the government should strictly enforce the separation of church and state, and therefore oppose school-sponsored prayer and proposed bans on abortions, which they perceive as motivated by religious beliefs.

- **Moderate.** Moderates make up the largest portion of the American public. In a 1993 poll, nearly half of all Americans identified themselves as politically moderate. The beliefs of moderates do not constitute a coherent ideology. Instead, moderates view themselves as pragmatists who apply common sense rather than philosophical principles to political problems.

Compared with citizens of other Western democracies, Americans have fewer main ideological groups. The many extreme political parties that exist in Europe, ranging from right-wing nationalists to left-leaning communists, are practically nonexistent in the United States. Furthermore, perhaps because of the paucity of viable groups, Americans readily vote outside of their self-professed political beliefs. In 1996, for example, 30 percent of self-identified conservative voters chose the more liberal Bill Clinton over conservative Republican candidate Bob Dole.

Americans who are strongly ideological tend to be the most politically active citizens. They are more likely than other Americans to join political organizations and participate in political activities, such as rallies and boycotts. They are more likely to take an active role in the leadership of their political parties. One result of this phenomenon is that candidates in the presidential primaries must perform a balancing act. To win the primaries, they must first appeal to the more ideological party faithful. Then in the general elections, they must move back to the political center or risk alienating the general voting public.

Determining Factors in Ideological and Political Behavior

Although there is no one-to-one correlation between people's backgrounds and their political beliefs, people who share certain traits tend to share political beliefs. Here are some of the factors that influence people's ideological and political attitudes.

- **Race/ethnicity.** Racial and ethnic groups who disproportionately populate the lower income levels tend to be more liberal than other Americans. Blacks and Hispanics are more likely than other Americans to support liberal social programs, for example. There are exceptions to these rules, however: Cuban Americans, for one, tend to be very conservative. Among Americans of European descent, southern and eastern Europeans are generally more liberal on economic issues than are those of British and French descent. On social issues, however, southern and eastern Europeans tend to be more conservative, in accordance with their religious beliefs.

- **Religion.** Among the various religious groups in the United States, Jews and African American Protestants are generally the most liberal. Catholics also lean toward the political left, although many are conservative on social issues. Devout white Protestants tend to be more conservative. This is particularly true in the south, where white Protestants who attend church regularly are among the nation's strongest supporters of the Republican Party.

- **Gender.** Women tend to be more liberal than men. They are more likely to vote Democratic, more likely to support government social welfare programs, and less likely to support increases in military spending.

- **Income level.** Americans in higher income brackets tend to be more supportive of liberal goals such as racial and sexual equality. They also support greater international cooperation. However, they tend to be less sympathetic to government social welfare goals, and are fiscally conservative. Poorer Americans, conversely, are generally more conservative on all issues except those concerning social welfare.

- **Region.** Regional differences arise from different economic and social interests. In the heavily unionized midwest, for example, Democratic candidates and goals are generally successful. In the more religious South, conservatism is predominant. The ethnic and racial mix of the east coast has made it the most liberal region of the country. The west coast, toward which many Americans continue to migrate, is the most polarized, with strong liberal and conservative contingencies scattered up and down the coast. Liberals tend to congregate in the cities; elsewhere, westerners are generally conservative.

PUBLIC OPINION AND THE MASS MEDIA

The **news media** play an important role in the development of public opinion. News media include all of the following:

- news broadcasts on television and radio
- newspapers
- news magazines, such as *Time* and *Newsweek*
- magazine broadcast programs, such as *60 Minutes* and *20/20*
- newsmaker interview programs, such as *Meet the Press* and *Larry King Live*
- political talk radio
- websites, blogs (weblogs), and online forums

These media provide most Americans with their most extensive exposure to politicians and the government. In many ways, they act as an intermediary between the people and the government, constantly questioning the motives and purposes of government actions and then reporting their findings to the public.

Throughout American history, public exposure to news media has consistently increased, both through higher literacy rates and through the expansion of news sources available in print and broadcast. As a result, the media have played an increasingly significant role over the years in shaping public opinion.

The most important role the media play is in setting the **public agenda.** By deciding which news stories to cover and which to ignore, by returning to some stories night after night while allowing others to die after a few reports, the news media play an important part in determining the relative importance of political issues. This power of the media is limited by the public's inherent interest in a story, however. Prior to American involvement in Bosnia, constant coverage of the crisis there did little to raise public awareness of or interest in the story, because many Americans perceived the crisis as too remote to be of interest. In general, the process of setting the national agenda is a dynamic one. The media generally try to report stories they believe will interest the public. As interest grows, coverage increases and the story becomes more important.

Less clear is whether the media have the power to alter public opinion. It is generally believed that the media affect public opinion only when news coverage is extensive and is either predominantly negative or positive. Positive news coverage of the Gulf War is believed to have increased American support for President Bush's actions. A constant barrage of negative images broadcast from Vietnam in the 1960s, conversely, is credited with having turned many Americans against the war. The news media can also alter public opinion when it is volatile: Studies have demonstrated, for example, that public approval of the president is quite volatile and changes depending on whether news coverage of the president is positive or negative. In most other instances, however, the media do not greatly impact public opinion. This is in part because the news media cover many stories simultaneously, thus diluting their ability to influence public opinion on any single issue. It is also due in part to the fact that most Americans choose those news media that reinforce their political beliefs. For example, conservative magazines such as the *National Review* are read almost exclusively by conservatives; liberal magazines, such as *The Nation*, are read primarily by liberals and progressives.

ARE THE NEWS MEDIA BIASED?

Critics from both ends of the political spectrum claim that the news media interject their political beliefs in their reports. Conservatives cite polls that have consistently shown that news reporters are more likely to hold liberal views and vote Democratic than are average Americans. Liberals point out that the major news media are owned by large, conservative companies, such as General Electric (NBC) and Disney (ABC). They argue that these companies exert pressure on the networks to downplay or ignore stories that reflect badly on the companies or the economic and political forces that support them.

To date, no study has conclusively demonstrated consistent ideological bias in news reporting, either in the stories news organizations choose to report or in the way they report them. Over the course of American history, the news media have in fact grown markedly less biased. Most newspapers in the eighteenth and nineteenth centuries were openly partisan; today, news organizations attempt to maintain journalistic integrity by remaining as objective as possible.

Commercial concerns reinforce this trend toward objectivity. Biased reporting may appeal strongly to one segment of the population, but it would just as surely alienate another segment. Seeking to offend the fewest possible audience members, most news organizations attempt to weed out bias from their reports.

This does not mean, however, that the news media achieve complete objectivity. News organizations must make hundreds of decisions each day about what to report and how prominently to report it. Many local newspapers, for example, ignore all but the most major international stories, not because they are not newsworthy but rather because their readers are generally uninterested in such stories. Network news broadcasts shy away from more complex stories, both because of time constraints and out of fear that they may bore viewers and listeners. A primary source of media bias, then, is the media's need for an immediate audience appeal.

Time and space constraints also result in bias in news reporting. Editors must decide which facts can be omitted from stories and which stories are not newsworthy enough to include. Time and space concerns affect all news organizations, but they are most acutely felt by television news programs, which report up to 20 stories during their 18 minutes of broadcast time (some half-hour programs feature as many as 12 minutes of advertising!).

Finally, news reports can be biased by the sources that reporters use for their information. Reporters in Washington, DC, must rely heavily on politicians and government sources for information, for example. The effect of this reliance is complicated. On one hand, reporters try to not offend their government sources with uncomplimentary reports, because they will need to return to those sources for future stories. Furthermore, there is the danger that reporters in Washington will become too close to the people and events they cover, resulting in bias. On the other hand, reporters must maintain their credibility and so must demonstrate their independence. They cannot consistently file favorable reports on the subjects they cover and expect to remain credible. Furthermore, surveys have demonstrated that reporters are more skeptical about the motives of politicians than average Americans are. This skepticism is reflected in their reporting. This may in part explain why public confidence in the government has decreased as the news media have grown more prominent.

Most modern politicians understand the power of the media and, accordingly, attempt to influence coverage. They stage events that yield appealing photographs (photo ops) and provide voluminous documented information in support of their positions (press releases). Attempts to manipulate media reports have grown more frequent and more sophisticated in recent years. Many politicians have studied the masterful way in which Ronald Reagan handled press coverage and have attempted to copy his successes.

SUMMARY

- Public opinion is measured by looking at saliency, intensity, and stability.

- Data about what people think come from polls, and many politicians base their decisions on polling data.

- Political socialization is the term used to describe how people learn about politics as they grow and mature.

- There are three basic political ideologies in America: conservative, liberal, and moderate.

- Know which factors tend to lead to which ideologies. A black woman in Chicago is more likely to be liberal than a white man from the rural South.

- The media plays a major role by placing certain policies and news events in the spotlight. This is also known as creating a public agenda.

PRACTICE QUESTIONS

1. The strength of the public's feelings about an issue is known as

   (A) intensity
   (B) saliency
   (C) stability
   (D) intransigence
   (E) zealotry

2. Which of the following is generally NOT a source of political socialization?

   (A) Family
   (B) School
   (C) Life experiences
   (D) Indoctrination by the two major political parties
   (E) Religion

3. A liberal would probably support

   (A) lower taxes
   (B) deregulation of industry
   (C) larger welfare payments to the poor
   (D) restrictions on the right to abortions
   (E) a ban on gay marriage

4. A conservative would probably support

   (A) higher taxes
   (B) scaling back laws that regulate industry
   (C) affirmative action
   (D) increasing access to abortions
   (E) increasing the power of bureaucracies like the Environmental Protection Agency

5. Which of the following is generally NOT a factor in determining ideological behavior?

   (A) Race/Ethnicity
   (B) Religion
   (C) Gender
   (D) Region
   (E) Birth order

7

POLITICAL PARTIES, INTEREST GROUPS, AND PACs

THE CONCEPTS

- What coalitions make up the two main political parties in the United States?
- Why do third parties so often fail in U.S. politics?
- What effect has dealignment had on political parties?
- Are there serious policy differences between Democrats and Republicans?
- Who supports the two parties and why?
- How does the Constitution control special interests?

- How have interest groups helped to democratize the U.S. political system?

- Why are interest groups a threat to democracy?

- What role do interest groups play in setting the political agenda?

- What techniques do PACs use to get their messages across?

- How do interest groups achieve and exert their influence?

THE TERMS

- political parties
- two-party system
- primary elections
- bolter parties
- doctrinal parties
- single-issue parties
- Independent candidates
- platform
- national convention
- soft money
- split-ticket voting
- party dealignment
- party realignment
- divided government
- critical election
- coalition
- *amicus curiae* briefs
- class action suits
- influence peddling
- Federal Election Campaign Act
- political action committees (PACs)

In the previous chapter we reviewed how individuals develop their political beliefs. Few political acts, however, are the work of a single person. Rather, most politically active people work within groups to achieve common political goals. The AP U.S. Government and Politics Exam expects you to know about three types of political groups. They are **political parties, interest groups,** and **political action committees (PACs).** This chapter reviews everything you need to know about the organization and activities of these groups.

POLITICAL PARTIES

As we've mentioned, few successful political accomplishments are the work of one person. More often, such a person joins with other like-minded individuals to form organizations that try to influence the outcomes of elections and legislative struggles. **Political parties** are unique among these groups in that they play a formal role in both of these processes. Although they are not mentioned in the Constitution—in fact, the Framers of the Constitution disliked political parties and hoped to prevent them—political parties became a mainstay of U.S. elections by the year 1800. Parties arose in the United States as a means of uniting those who shared political ideals, enabling them to elect like-minded representatives and pursue similar legislative goals. To those ends, parties endorse candidates for office and assist in their election efforts. In return for this support, parties expect candidates to remain loyal to goals defined by the party leadership.

The United States has two major political parties: Democrats and Republicans. This **two-party system** is reinforced by the nation's electoral system. U.S. election rules, which have agreed upon by members of the two parties, also make it difficult for all but the two major parties to win a place on the ballot, further strengthening the two-party system.

Party Characteristics

Don't forget these facts about political parties.

- Parties serve as intermediaries between people and the government.

- Parties are made up of grassroots members, activist members, and leadership.

- Parties are organized to raise money, present positions on policy, and get their candidates elected to office.

- Parties were created outside of the Constitution—they are not even mentioned in the document.

The major purpose of political parties is to get candidates elected to office. In the past, candidates were chosen by the party hierarchy, with little or no public input. However, since 1960, more states have passed laws requiring parties to select candidates through state-run **primary elections**. These primaries have reduced the power of political parties. Candidates must raise their own money for primaries, campaigning for their party's nomination with little to no support from the party itself. If the parties don't control the money, they can't control the candidates. This levels the playing field, but multiple candidates for the nomination can splinter the party membership.

Third Parties

New parties are occasionally formed in the United States. Unless and until these parties reach the level of a major party, they are called third parties. Third parties form to represent constituencies that feel disenfranchised from both of the major parties. These **bolter parties** usually unite around a feeling that the major parties are not responding to the demands of some segment of the electorate. The Reform Party, under whose banner Ross Perot ran for president in 1996, was an example of a bolter party whose constituency was fed up with politics as usual.

Sometimes third parties form to represent an ideology considered too radical by the mainstream parties. These **doctrinal parties** reject the prevailing attitudes and policies of the political system. The Socialist Party and the Libertarian Party are examples. **Single-issue parties** are formed to promote one principle. The American Independent Party, which sponsored the segregationist candidacy of George C. Wallace in 1968, is an example. Third parties can have a major impact on elections. The Green Party, which favors strict environmental policies, more government social programs, and controls over big business, ran Ralph Nader for president in 2000. Nader's candidacy took votes from Al Gore, thus tipping the scales in favor of George W. Bush.

Third-party candidates should not be confused with **Independent candidates.** Independent candidates run without party affiliation. It is very difficult for Independent candidates to overcome the money and organization of the two major parties. Eugene McCarthy, an anti-Vietnam War candidate in 1968, and John Anderson, a fiscal conservative and social liberal in 1980, are two examples.

WHY THIRD PARTIES FAIL

The failure of third parties to elect presidential and other candidates to office is a direct result of an American political system designed to support only two major parties. National campaigns in countries using equal, single-member, plurality voting-district systems (like the United States) require huge sums of money and vast organizations. Also, in American presidential elections, almost all states have a winner-take-all system for electoral votes; the candidate who receives the most votes, even if it is only by one, wins all of the electors in the state. In effect, each state has its own presidential campaign and the candidates have to treat each state as though it were a separate election. Because the losers get no electoral votes, the electoral count usually does not accurately reflect the popular vote. In 1968, **George Wallace** won 14 percent of the vote and received 46 electoral votes. In 1992, however, Ross Perot won 19 percent of the vote and yet received 0 electoral votes. Neither result was a proportionate reflection of the popular vote.

FUNCTIONS OF MODERN POLITICAL PARTIES

Political scientists identify three major subdivisions of political parties.

- **The party among the electorate.** Voters enroll in and identify with political parties. They generally vote for candidates who represent their party.

- **The party in government.** Government officials belong to political parties. They act together to pursue common goals, although regional and ideological differences sometimes subvert their efforts.

- **The party organization.** A group of people who are neither elected officials nor average voters, the party organization is made up of political professionals who recruit candidates and voters, organize campaign events, and raise money to promote the party.

Political parties perform all of the following functions:

- **Recruit and nominate candidates.** The parties are the major players in electoral politics. They seek out candidates to run in their primary elections. They also create the rules by which candidates seek their nominations. In nearly all elections, nomination by one of the major parties is a prerequisite to victory.

- **Educate and mobilize voters.** Political parties fund propaganda campaigns to persuade voters to choose their candidates. They send mailings, hold rallies, and run advertisements. They target regions in which their support is strong and campaign to persuade voters in those regions to vote on election day.

- **Provide campaign funds and support.** The national parties have committees dedicated to raising funds for House and Senate campaigns. State parties also raise funds for candidates for both state and national office. Although most candidates rely primarily on their own personal campaign support staff, they also need the help of the state or national party organizations.

- **Organize government activity.** Parties act as an organizing force in government. The House and Senate organize their leadership and committee systems strictly along party lines, as do state legislatures.

- **Provide balance through opposition of two parties.** Each party serves as a check on the other by constantly watching for and exposing weakness and hypocrisy. The minority party (provided a single party controls both the White House and the Congress) performs the role of the *loyal opposition*, constantly critiquing the performance of the party in power.

- **Reduce conflict and tension in society.** The two-party system promotes compromise and negotiation in two ways: by encouraging parties to accommodate voters, and encouraging voters to accept compromises in policy. The Republican Party, for example, includes both religious social-conservatives and libertarians. To assemble winning coalitions, the party must somehow appease both groups. The groups, in turn, must be willing to compromise if they wish to prevent the Democrats from prevailing.

U.S. political parties are not hierarchical. The national party organization and each of the state and local organizations are largely autonomous and serve different functions; one does not take orders from the other.

Party committees are organized by geographic subdivisions. Locally, committees at the precinct, town, ward, and electoral district levels coordinate get-out-the-vote drives, door-to-door canvassing, and leaflet distribution. These party committees are staffed mostly by volunteers, and their work is largely concentrated around election time. The next largest geographic grouping is the county. County committees coordinate efforts in local elections and organize the efforts of committees on the precinct level. They also send representatives to each polling place to monitor voting procedures. State committees raise money and provide volunteers to staff campaign events. They provide support to candidates for both state and national offices. National legislative elections, however, are also the responsibility of the powerful congressional district and senatorial committees. These committees, chaired by incumbents and staffed by professionals, are part of the national party organization. They are most likely to become involved in these legislative elections when the possibility exists of gaining or losing a seat. Because incumbents usually run for reelection and are often reelected easily, the congressional and senatorial committees are active in a minority of election efforts during each electoral cycle.

The national party plans the **national conventions** held every four years to nominate a presidential candidate. It sponsors polls to keep party members informed of public opinion and manages issue-oriented advertising and propaganda.

Are Parties in Decline?

Some political scientists believe that the parties are no longer as powerful or as significant as they once were. Prior to 1968, one party typically controlled both the executive and legislative branches of government. Since that year, however, there have been only eight years of one-party control of these branches (1977 to 1980, 1992 to 1994, and 2002 to 2005). Americans are voting a **split ticket** (see page 78) more frequently than ever before. They are more likely to consider the merits and positions of a particular candidate than to merely consider his or her party affiliation. As a result, no one party dominates government, and officials with different political agendas are elected to work together. Split-ticket voting leads to divided government, when one party controls Congress and the other controls the White House. This can create policy gridlock because these two branches are often at odds with each other. Conversely, it can cause them to work together in the creation of moderate public policy. Lastly, it encourages party dealignment because voters do not align with their parties as uniformly as they once did.

Increasingly, modern candidates have taken control of their own election campaigns, relying less on party support than did past candidates. They are now able to appeal directly to the public through television. This has left the parties—which once wielded great power over the electoral process—with less power. In their place, media consultants have become the chief movers and shakers in political campaigns.

PARTY COALITIONS

Political parties consist of combinations of groups, which consist of combinations of individuals. The larger the coalition the more likely the candidate will win. Party candidates and party positions on policy are designed to attract more groups of voters, putting together a winning **coalition.**

In the presidential elections of 2004 and 2008, the Republican coalition included the following:

- disaffected conservative Democrats called "blue-dogs"
- veterans' groups
- the religious right
- pro-lifers
- opponents of gay rights
- missile-defense supporters
- opponents of affirmative action
- Cuban Americans
- supporters of the development of natural resources on public lands
- religious conservatives

In the same elections, the Democratic coalition included the following:

- pro-choicers
- African Americans
- labor unions
- intellectuals
- people with lower incomes
- city dwellers
- non-Cuban Latinos
- feminists
- Jewish people
- environmentalists

While there are always exceptions to the rule, the two parties rely on these groups as a base of support. Regionally, it appears that the east and west coasts and the upper midwest are more Democratic, while the south and lower midwest are more Republican.

IDEOLOGICAL DIFFERENCES BETWEEN THE PARTIES

While there are general ideological differences between the two parties, there are also a number of similarities. Neither party, for example, questions the validity of the nation's capitalist economic system.

Although both parties tend to be centrist, there are nevertheless differences in the ways the two parties view the role of government. The greatest ideological differences are between the liberals in the Democratic Party and the conservatives in the Republican Party, the so-called **party bases.** While appealing to the independent centrist voter during election campaigns, each party counts on its base to get out and vote. Party leaders must use great care in choosing policy positions so they do not lose their party base. They must also avoid alienating the moderates of the party by taking extreme left or right positions.

Democrats tend to be

- less disposed to spend on defense.
- less disposed to use vouchers, or other public funds, to let students attend private schools.
- more disposed to spend money to advance social-welfare programs.
- more disposed to use government money for public education.
- more disposed to spend money on government-run health programs.
- more disposed to grant tax relief to targeted groups such as the lower and middle classes.
- against private ownership of assault weapons and for broader regulations on the ownership of firearms.

Republicans tend to be

- more disposed to spend on defense.

- more disposed to use vouchers for private schools and to give government aid to parochial schools.

- more disposed to grant tax relief to everyone, including the wealthy and corporations.

- less disposed to spend money on social-welfare programs.

- less disposed to spend money on government-run health programs.

- less disposed to regulate firearms.

PARTY REALIGNMENT

Party realignment occurs when the coalitions making up the two parties fall apart, such as when many of the groups that make up the majority party defect to the minority party. Realignments are very rare and usually occur as a result of some major traumatic event, such as an economic depression or a war. They are signaled by what is called a **critical election,** when a new party comes to dominate politics. The last realignment took place in 1932, as a result of the Great Depression, when the Republican Party became the minority party and the Democratic party became the majority party, with overwhelming numbers of Democrats being elected to every branch of government at every level. Realignments occur over a period of time and show permanence. The New Deal coalition of the 1930s lasted for decades. There have been no realignments since the 1930s.

The trend today seems to be toward dealignment. Dealignment is usually a result of party members becoming disaffected as a result of some policy position taken by the party. These disaffected party members join no political party, and vote for the candidate rather than the party he or she belongs to. Since the 1960s, membership in the Democratic party has declined while the number of independents has increased. During the same time period, the number of Republicans has remained constant. The two major parties are now nearly equal in party membership. This is a classic example of dealignment.

INTEREST GROUPS AND LOBBYISTS

Interest groups are organizations dedicated to a particular political goal or to a set of unified goals. Group members often share a common bond, either religious (**Christian Coalition**), racial (**National Association for the Advancement of Colored People**), or professional (**American Medical Association**). In other cases, they simply share a common interest, such as the environment (**Sierra Club**) or political reform (**Common Cause**). In either case, they are similar to political parties in that they try to influence the outcome of elections and legislation. Unlike political parties, however, they do not nominate candidates, nor do they normally try to address a wide range of issues.

When interest groups try to influence legislators, we say they are **lobbying** for a bill or issue. The term originated with the historical practice of early lobbyists; they waited in the lobby of the capitol so they could catch legislators coming in and out of session. Today, most lobbyists are highly paid professionals. A number are former legislators, whose experience and friendships in the capitol make them particularly effective.

There are literally thousands of interest groups in the United States. Most groups fall under one of the following categories:

- **Economic groups.** Economic groups are formed to promote and protect members' economic interests. They include peak business groups such as the U.S. Chamber of Commerce, which represents the interests of all businesspeople. Other groups represent specific trades and industries; among these are the American Farm Bureau Federation and the American Nuclear Energy Council. Labor groups such as the AFL-CIO and the United Auto Workers represent union members. Professional groups include the American Medical Association and the American Bar Association. Most economic groups have existed a long time and have developed strong ties with legislators and bureaucrats. They are also extremely well funded, and either represent or employ large constituencies. As a result, they are usually the most powerful interest groups in Washington, DC.

- **Public interest groups.** Public interest groups are nonprofit organizations that are generally organized around a well-defined set of public policy issues. Consumer groups usually work to promote safer products and more informative labeling; the most prominent of these groups is Public Citizen, led by **Ralph Nader**. Environmental groups, such as the Sierra Club, advocate preservation of wildlife and wilderness areas. Religious groups such as the Christian Coalition attempt to influence public policy in such a way as to promote or protect their beliefs. Other groups promote causes such as women's rights, minority rights, and political reform. Single-issue groups like the **National Rifle Association** and the **National Right to Life Committee** are often among the most powerful public interest groups because of the intensity of their supporters. Single-issue constituents are more likely than other voters to use a single issue as a litmus test for candidates. Thus, a candidate who advocates gun control runs the risk of losing the votes of all 3 million NRA members.

- **Government interest groups.** Most states and many cities and other localities maintain lobbying organizations in the nation's capital. A separate group represents the nation's governors, and yet another represents mayors. Most foreign governments and businesses lobby the government as well.

HOW INTEREST GROUPS INFLUENCE GOVERNMENT

Interest groups use a number of tactics to persuade Congress, the president, the judiciary, and federal bureaucrats. They include the following:

- **Direct lobbying.** Representatives of the interest group meet privately with government officials to suggest legislation and to present arguments supporting their positions.

- **Testifying before Congress.** Interest groups provide expert witnesses at committee hearings.

- **Socializing.** Social events in Washington, DC, are often political events as well. Interest groups hold social functions and members attend other functions to meet and forge relationships with government officials.

- **Political donations.** Interest groups provide financial support to candidates and parties that champion their causes. Those that are forbidden to do so by law—corporations, trade groups, and unions—may do so by forming political action committees (PACs) for that purpose.

- **Endorsements.** Many groups announce their support for specific candidates. Some groups rate legislators on the basis of their voting records; a high rating constitutes an implicit endorsement of that candidate.

- **Court action.** Interest groups file lawsuits or **class action suits** to protect and advance their interests. They will also submit *amicus curiae* (friend of the court) **briefs** in lawsuits to which they are not a party so that judges may consider their advice in respect to matters of law that directly affect the case in question.

- **Rallying their membership.** Public interest groups sometimes contact members and ask them to write, phone, or e-mail their legislators in support of a particular program or piece of legislation.

- **Propaganda.** Interest groups send out press releases and run advertisements promoting their views.

LIMITS ON LOBBYING

Several laws limit the scope of lobbyists' activities. Most are ineffective, but stronger efforts to regulate lobbying run the risk of violating the First Amendment right to free speech. The 1946 Federal Regulation of Lobbying Act was intended to allow the government to monitor lobbying activities by requiring lobbyists to register with the government and publicly disclose their salaries, expenses, and the nature of their activities in Washington, DC. The Supreme Court has interpreted this law so narrowly, however, that it currently applies to only a small percentage of active lobbyists.

Other laws prohibit, for limited amounts of time, certain lobbying activities by former government officials. These laws are meant to counteract the appearance of **influence peddling**, the practice of using personal friendships and inside information to get political advantage. Former legislators must wait one year before lobbying Congress directly, for example. However, they may lobby the executive branch immediately after leaving office. They may also work as consultants to interest groups. In short, they may do everything *except* call congresspersons to plead directly for a bill. A similar limit applies to former executive officials. It prevents them from lobbying for five years after they leave the agency that employed them. These limits were determined in *Buckley v. Valeo* (1976), the case that equated donations with free speech.

Finally, federal laws prohibiting campaign contributions from corporations, unions, and trade associations can be sidestepped through the formation of a political action committee or PAC.

POLITICAL ACTION COMMITTEES (PACs)

The 1974 **Federal Election Campaign Act** allows corporations, unions, and trade associations to form **political action committees** as a means of raising campaign funds. Certain restrictions apply to PACs: They must raise money from at least 50 contributors; they must donate to at least five different candidates; they may not donate more than $5,000 per year to any single candidate nor more than $15,000 to a national party per year. Corporate, union, and trade PACs must raise money from employees and members and may not simply draw it from their treasuries.

Corporations, unions, and trade associations are not the only groups that form PACs. Many other interest groups form PACs to collect and distribute contributions, as do legislators (these PACs are called leadership PACs). Federal law limits the amount donors may contribute to candidates ($2,300), national parties ($28,500), and individual PACs ($5,000). Furthermore, the sum of all such contributions may not exceed $108,200 over two years. These numbers are accurate for the 2008 election cycle, but are scheduled to increase slightly for each future cycle.

Currently there are more than 4,000 PACs registered with the federal government. Nearly half represent corporations; more than 1,000 are issue oriented. PACs contribute most heavily to House campaigns, although they also contribute heavily to senatorial campaigns. They contribute predominantly to incumbents who are likely to win reelection, hoping thereby to purchase access to legislators in the next Congress.

SUMMARY

- Though they are not mentioned in the Constitution, political parties have become an integral part of American government. They may embrace a wide variety of ideologies, but ultimately both parties share the same goal: to be elected by any means necessary.

- American history has been marked by numerous third parties that have challenged the prevailing duopoly. All have died, but if it is popular enough, a third party may influence the two major parties to adopt its ideas.

- Parties serve many functions in American democracy: they recruit and fund candidates, educate voters, provide a loyal opposition, and run the government—all while mitigating societal tension.

- When we look at parties, they often turn out to be broad coalitions of disparate ideologies and groups. The Republican Party, for example, blends libertarians who are hostile to government regulation with religious evangelists who want government to play a greater role in stamping out immorality.

- Generally speaking, Democrats tend to be in favor of government regulation of industry, redistribution of government money to the poor, and social freedom. Republicans tend to want to empower business to free itself from government rules, encourage people to earn money with assistance from the state, and want more social and moral controls on society.

- Interest groups are large organizations with strong policy goals, but are different from political parties in that they do not change their ideologies. These groups try to control the political process by hiring lobbyists to influence legislators and by giving them money as well.

- When labor unions or corporation want to fund candidates, they do so by forming Political Action Committees, or PACs. PACs provide a means to funnel money to a candidate of choice and are regulated by the Federal Election Commission (FEC).

PRACTICE QUESTIONS

1. Which of the following could be defined as a "bolter" party?

   (A) The Libertarian Party
   (B) The Socialist Labor Party
   (C) The Communist Party
   (D) The Reform Party
   (E) The Green Party

2. Which of the following is NOT a function of American political parties?

   (A) Serving as the loyal opposition
   (B) Fomenting armed rebellion
   (C) Selecting and funding candidates
   (D) Educating the public on issues
   (E) Governing the nation

3. Who of the following people would be most likely to be a Democrat?

   (A) A Cuban American
   (B) A religious evangelical
   (C) A White southerner
   (D) A Mexican American
   (E) A pro-lifer

4. Which of the following is NOT generally a method that interest groups use to influence the government?

   (A) Bribery
   (B) Direct lobbying
   (C) Testifying before Congress
   (D) Political donations
   (E) Endorsements

5. Political Action Committees (PACs) were formed to allow unions and corporations to

   (A) run their own members for political office
   (B) funnel limited amounts of money to candidates of their choice
   (C) funnel unlimited amounts of money to candidates of their choice
   (D) have a voice in government policy meetings
   (E) sit down together to work out their differences

8

ELECTIONS

THE CONCEPTS

- Does the media place too much emphasis on irrelevant issues in presidential campaigns?
- Why do incumbents win at such high rates?
- Why is voter turnout so low in the United States?
- What is the impact of primary elections, and who votes in them?
- Why do political parties have such a difficult time holding their coalitions together?
- Why are soft money contributions considered a threat to the election process?
- Why did the Supreme Court have a problem with the imposition of spending limits on PACs?
- Has the Federal Election Campaign Reform Act succeeded in fulfilling the intent of the legislation?
- What accounts for the so-called gender gap?

THE TERMS

- nominations
- general elections
- closed primary
- open primary
- blanket primary
- plurality
- runoff primary
- super-delegates
- federal matching funds
- Super Tuesday
- front-loading
- Federal Election Commission
- brokered conventions
- electoral college
- winner-take-all system
- mandate

The federal government holds elections every two years. Each election gives voters the chance to select a new representative in the House of Representatives. Every other election allows them to vote for president. Each of a state's two seats in the Senate is contested every six years; as a result, state voters select a senator in two out of every three federal elections.

To cut expenses and to encourage voter turnout, states hold their elections at the same time as federal elections. Thus, voters choose not only federal officials at election time, but also state legislators, judges, the governor, and local officials. They may also be asked to vote on referenda and state bond issues.

Thus, many officeholders are chosen and many issues decided during each election. When the AP U.S. Government and Politics Exam asks about elections, however, it nearly always focuses on the presidential election. This chapter will do the same.

There is one exception to this rule. The AP U.S. Government and Politics Exam always asks at least one question about the advantage **incumbent** congresspersons enjoy in their reelection campaigns. Be sure you know the following two facts, as they will almost certainly be tested on the AP exam: 1) representatives who run for reelection win approximately 90 percent of the time; and 2) while incumbent senators also have a tremendous electoral advantage, their advantage is less than that of House incumbents. Senators must run statewide, and incumbents almost always face a serious challenger. House members run in their home districts, where constituents are often overwhelmingly of one party due to **gerrymandering**, partisan redrawing of congressional district borders. In such races, victory in the primary election virtually guarantees victory in the general election. In fact, each year a number of House incumbents run for reelection unopposed.

THE ELECTION CYCLE

Elections consist of two phases: **nominations**, during which the parties choose their candidates for the general elections, and **general elections**, during which voters decide who will hold elective office.

The majority of states (39) use primary elections to select presidential nominees. All states use some form of primary election to select legislative and state nominees. These elections are usually held between early February and late spring of an election year. Each state sets its own rules for these elections, and there is considerable variation in primary procedures from state to state. There are several types of primaries.

- **Closed primary.** This is the most common type. In a closed primary, voting is restricted to registered members of a political party. Voters may vote only for candidates running for the nomination of their declared party. In a closed presidential primary, Democrats choose among the candidates for the Democratic nomination, while Republicans choose among Republican hopefuls.

- **Open primary.** In open primaries, voters may vote only in one party's primary, but they may vote in whichever party primary they choose. Voters select the party primary in which they wish to participate in the privacy of the voting booth. Critics argue that open primaries allow voters to sabotage their opponents' primaries by crossing party lines to vote for the candidate *least* likely to win the general election. This is likely to happen only when there are no close contests in one party, however.

- **Blanket primary.** Blanket primaries use the same procedure as the general elections. In blanket primaries, voters may vote for candidates of either party. They may vote for only one candidate per office. Only Alaska and Washington state use this primary system.

In primary voting for legislators and state officials, the candidate who receives a **plurality** (greatest number) of the votes cast in each primary is declared the winner. Some states require the winner to receive a minimum percentage of the vote, however. If no candidate receives the required share of votes, a **runoff primary** is held between the two top vote-getters. Runoffs occur most often when many challengers vie for an open office, especially when none of the candidates is well known.

In primary elections for the presidency, voters also choose delegates pledged to a particular presidential candidate. Winning delegates attend their party's national convention. Some states select presidential convention delegates at **state caucuses** and **conventions.** This process begins with local meetings of party members, who select representatives to send to statewide party meetings. Compared with primaries, the state caucus and convention process usually attracts fewer participants. Those who participate tend to be more politically active and better informed than typical voters; they are also less likely to be political moderates.

The Democratic Party uses a third method to choose some delegates to its national convention. It grants automatic delegate status to many elected party leaders, including congresspersons and important state leaders. These **super-delegates** generally support the front-runner. Critics complain that the super-delegates dilute the importance of the primary elections by making it easier for the party elite to control the nominating process. The Republican Party does not have super-delegates.

General elections for federal office are held on the first Tuesday of November. Elections in which the president is being chosen are called **presidential elections.** Those that occur between presidential elections are called **midterm elections.**

FIRST STEPS TOWARD NOMINATION

Nearly all elected officials first receive the endorsement, or nomination, of one of the two major parties. Nominees usually have extensive backgrounds in government. Some presidential candidates are current or former members of the Senate. Many have served as governors. Gubernatorial experience allows candidates to claim executive abilities, because governors serve many of the same government functions in their states as the president does in the federal government. Governors also have the advantage of being able to run as Washington outsiders, as opposed to Senators, who usually have extensive federal experience. At a time when public distrust of Washington is high, outsider status can be a significant benefit. **Bill Clinton**, **Ronald Reagan**, **Jimmy Carter,** and **George W. Bush** are four recent presidents who successfully exploited this factor.

On occasion, the major parties will pursue a candidate with little or no government experience. Such candidates are invariably popular and well-respected figures, often from the military. **Dwight Eisenhower** was such a candidate.

A presidential run is an all-consuming endeavor that must begin up to two years before the first primary. As a result, most candidates devote themselves to the effort full-time. Jimmy Carter and Ronald Reagan both left their governorships before running for the presidency; Bob Dole retired from the Senate in 1996 to commit himself more fully to his campaign. Others have remained in office and run successful campaigns. Bill Clinton and George W. Bush are two candidates who remained governors while successfully seeking their party's nomination. Presidents running for reelection and vice presidents seeking the presidency benefit from the prestige of their offices.

Those considering a run for the presidency must first seek support among the party organizations. They must especially seek the aid of influential donors to the party because elections are extremely expensive. Candidates spend much of the early stages of the nomination process meeting with potential donors, establishing PACs to raise funds (more about fund-raising below), and campaigning for the endorsements of important political groups and leaders. This entire process is often referred to as testing the waters. Many campaigns fail at this stage, long before the public is ever aware of them, due to lack of interest among the political elite.

In the year before the first primaries, potential candidates attempt to increase their public profile. They schedule public appearances and attempt to attract media coverage by taking stands on current issues and discussing the goals of their projected presidencies. Candidates are particularly vulnerable to the media during this period. Since the public knows little about most potential candidates, negative reports can quickly scuttle a campaign. As primary season begins, candidates try to raise as much money as possible, and to garner as many votes in the primaries as possible, in an effort to win the nomination. Candidates who can't raise their own money and don't get enough votes are quickly forced out of the race. The candidates also begin to assemble campaign personnel—advisors, political consultants, public relations experts, speechwriters, fund-raisers, lawyers, and office administrators—who will help manage the campaign.

Recently, very wealthy candidates have attempted to run for the presidency without needing, or using, federal matching funds. Ross Perot in 1992 and Steve Forbes in 1996 used their own money to campaign, but both campaigns failed. Ross Perot's 1992 campaign spent more money than the Democrat and Republican candidates combined.

FINANCING CAMPAIGNS

A successful presidential campaign requires much more than an appealing candidate. It needs a huge supporting staff, jets and buses, and the resources to hire consultants, pollsters, and advertising agencies. It should come as no surprise, then, that one of the most important skills a candidate can possess is the ability to raise money.

Presidential candidates who meet certain prerequisites may receive federal funding. Primary candidates who receive more than 10 percent of the vote in an election may apply for **federal matching funds.** These funds essentially double all campaign contributions of $250 and under by matching them. To receive matching funds, candidates must agree to obey federal spending limits: In 1996, the limit was $37 million for the primary elections. Furthermore, any candidate who receives less than 10 percent of the vote in two consecutive primaries loses his eligibility for matching funds until he wins more than 10 percent of the vote in another primary.

The federal government funds the general election campaigns of the two major presidential candidates, provided those candidates agree not to accept and spend other donations (an exception is made for up to $50,000 of the candidate's own money). In 1996, Bill Clinton and Bob Dole each received $62 million to finance their campaigns. Independents do not receive federal funding for their campaigns. Ross Perot financed his presidential runs with private donations and his personal wealth.

Despite attempts at campaign finance reform, the trend toward high levels of election spending has continued through the 1990s and into the first decade of the twenty-first-century. In the 2004 election, George W. Bush raised a whopping $272.5 million and John Kerry raised $250.3 million, making it the most expensive presidential race in history. Both candidates refused matching funds to avoid all spending limits.

There is currently no public financing of congressional campaigns, and there are no spending limits for congressional candidates. There are, however, limits on the amounts that individuals and political committees may donate to candidates. These limits, established by the **Bipartisan Campaign Reform Act (BCRA)** and enforced by the **Federal Election Commission,** are as follows:

	To a Candidate	To a National Party	To a Political Committee	Total per 2 Calendar Years
Individual may give	$2,300	$28,500	$5,000	$108,200
PAC may give	$5,000	$15,000	$5,000	no limit
Non-PAC committee may give[1]	$2,300	$28,500	$5,000	$108,200

Many Americans believe that the current campaign finance system has a corrupting effect on government. Efforts to change the system, however, run into several obstacles. The Supreme Court ruled in *Buckley v. Valeo* (1976) that mandatory spending limits on campaigns violate candidates' First Amendment rights to free expression. Furthermore, the system currently benefits incumbents. Accordingly, legislators are reluctant to make changes because changes would make their reelection more difficult. The permissible donations listed in the above table all will change if campaign finance reform is enacted.

---

[1] Political committees that do not meet legal requirements of a PAC (e.g., donations from at least 50 contributors).

PRIMARY SEASON

By January 1 of election year, candidates are campaigning widely among the public. From this point on, candidates participate in debates, campaign from state to state delivering their "stump speeches" (so called because campaigning is often referred to as "stumping"), and choreograph media events—in an effort to draw positive media coverage of their campaigns.

The earliest primaries (New Hampshire's is a prime example) provide a great boost to the campaigns of whoever wins, increasing the candidate's media exposure and making all-important fund-raising chores easier. Major financial contributors usually desert the campaigns of the losers in early primaries. Furthermore, candidates who receive less than 10 percent of the vote in two successive primaries lose their eligibility for crucial federal matching funds. As a result, those who fare poorly in early primaries usually have to drop out of the race long before the majority of delegates have been selected.

Because early primaries have grown increasingly important in recent years, many states have pushed forward the date of their primary elections. Many southern states even hold their primaries all on the same day in early March (called **Super Tuesday**). Large states such as New York and California have moved forward their primaries in hopes of having a greater influence on which candidates win the nominations. Political analysts refer to this strategy as **front-loading**, and the result has been to place increased pressure on candidates to succeed early. Critics argue that it unnecessarily forces voters to choose early in the election process, before they have gotten a chance to know the candidates well.

Primary elections and state caucuses continue into late spring. In most recent elections, however, the party nominee has been decided long before the last elections.

NATIONAL CONVENTIONS

After the primary season has ended, both parties hold national conventions to confirm their nominee. When no candidate has received the pledge of a majority of convention delegates, conventions decide who the nominee will be; such conventions are called **brokered conventions**. The parties have designed their primary systems to prevent brokered conventions, which can divide the party and cost it the election.

One of the main purposes of a national convention, in fact, is to **unify the party.** Primary elections can damage each party, as candidates attack each other and thereby expose rifts within the party membership. Another main purpose of conventions is to make a show of party unity for political gain. Both parties' conventions are nationally televised and are widely covered by the news media. Not surprisingly, most of what occurs on the convention stage is choreographed to appeal to the party faithful and undecided voters watching at home.

That does not mean that conventions are placid affairs, however. Conventions are the site of many political negotiations, as different factions of the party attempt to win concessions in return for their full support during the general election. There are often intense battles over the party platform, a statement of purpose and party goals, which, ironically, has little concrete significance. The conventions also offer some political drama, as nominees sometimes wait until the convention to announce their choice of running mates.

The greatest impact conventions can have on general election results is negative. In 1968, for example, rioting outside the Democratic convention created a bad impression among voters, especially when contrasted with the unified display at the Republican convention weeks later. In 1992, ultraconservatives were able to control key elements of the Republican convention. The image the convention created was one of an angry and activist party, which frightened voters and hurt President

Bush's reelection campaign. Under normal circumstances, however, conventions usually help their candidates considerably. Polls taken immediately after conventions show the candidates' approval ratings up significantly. This rise in public approval is called a **post-convention bump**.

Nonetheless, it is important to note that national conventions have been altered dramatically in the last century. Until about mid-century, conventions and convention delegates actually selected and nominated the candidate. With the adoption of primary elections, conventions have been transformed into mere coronations with the nominees generally being determined before the convention begins.

THE GENERAL ELECTION AND THE ELECTORAL COLLEGE

The remaining candidates continue to campaign for the general election in much the same way as they campaigned during the primaries: holding rallies, participating in debates, creating and running campaign advertisements, and pursuing positive media coverage. There are several key differences between the primaries and the general election. First, during the primaries, candidates run against members of their own party. Because primary candidates are often in general agreement about such big-picture issues as the proper role of government, their campaigns focus instead on the subtler differences between them. During the general elections, candidates often emphasize the general policy and philosophical differences between the two parties. Put simply, a candidate courts his or her political base during the primary season and then moves toward the center in the general election to win undecided votes in hopes of securing the majority.

Second, candidates planning their campaign strategies must consider the nature of the **electoral college.** This institution was created by the Framers of the Constitution as a means of insulating the government from the whims of a less educated public. Critics feel the electoral college system is antiquated, but no one has yet successfully proposed an amendment to change it. Presidential elections therefore continue to be determined not by the final popular vote but rather by this institution. Each state is given a number of electors equal to the sum of its federal legislators (senators plus representatives). The winner of the presidential election in each state wins all of that state's electors[2] (which is why it is often referred to as a **winner-take-all system**).

The electoral college system places greater emphasis on election results in large states. Victory by a single vote in California wins a candidate all of that state's 54 electoral votes; a similar margin of victory in Vermont yields only three electoral votes. Despite the number of votes at stake in the large states, candidates will often devote the bulk of their time to "swing" states—areas in which polling indicates a close race. This is the reason that during the 2000 presidential election, states like Pennsylvania and New Mexico were inundated with political ads while large states whose voters generally go with one party, such as New York, California, and Texas, were relatively quiet. Finally, candidates consider each other's electoral strategies in planning their campaigns. In 1968, the Democratic Party relied on the support of its southern base. Republican Richard Nixon realized that this support was weakening and campaigned aggressively in the region. Nixon's "southern strategy" worked in enough southern states to swing the election to the Republicans.

---

[2] The two exceptions are Maine and Nebraska, which give two electoral votes to the candidate who wins a plurality of the statewide vote, and one vote to the winner of each of the state's congressional districts. In 1996, Maine had four electoral votes, Nebraska had five.

MEDIA INFLUENCE ON ELECTIONS

With nearly 100 million voters participating in the general election, it is clear that candidates cannot come into direct contact with even a small portion of the electorate. Instead, they must rely on the media to get their political message across.

- **News media** provide many voters with daily campaign information. While most news programs occasionally report on the candidates' positions on the issues, they concentrate on the candidates' standing in the polls, or the horse race aspect of the election. This is because news directors prefer information that can be communicated quickly and that changes regularly, such as public opinion poll results. In contrast, candidates' positions on issues are often complex. Furthermore, they rarely change. Therefore, news programs may report such information once during an election, but they do not report it repeatedly as they do poll results. As a result, the attention of the network news audience is focused on the campaign game rather than on the candidates' political agendas.

- **Campaign advertisements** provide another, more controlled look at the candidates. Through advertising, candidates attempt to build a positive image with the public. In many cases, they also try to belittle their opponents through negative advertising. Negative advertising works best when the public knows little about a candidate. In 1988, for example, Democratic candidate Michael Dukakis was the subject of several effective negative advertisements. Although he led in the polls prior to the ads, Dukakis's support was weak, as most voters knew little about him. The negative advertisements were effective in destroying Dukakis's lead by portraying him as weak, incompetent, and soft on crime.

ELECTION DAY

There are nearly 200 million Americans of voting age. Of them, nearly 150 million are registered to vote. On a presidential election day, however, fewer than 100 million participate. **Voter turnout** is even lower for midterm elections: Typically less than 40 percent of all eligible voters participate in them. American voter turnout rates are among the lowest of all Western democracies.

Certain patterns are detectable in American voters' behavior. The likelihood that an individual will vote corresponds closely to his or her level of education: The more educated a person is, the more likely he or she is to vote. Age is also a factor: Turnout rates are highest among Americans over the age of 40, and lowest among those under the age of 20.

Voter turnout is also influenced in part by how close a race is. Voters are less likely to vote when they believe they know who will win the election. Such was the case in 1996, when many Americans were certain that Bill Clinton would be reelected. Remember, however, that many federal and state offices are up for grabs on election day. A closely contested race in any of those elections can be enough to motivate voters to participate.

On election day, the media report not only election results but also the results of exit polls that break down the vote by age, gender, race, income level, region, and nearly every other demographic imaginable. They do so in an effort to determine the meaning of the results. Why did voters choose one candidate over another? Were their votes an endorsement of the candidate's ideas, or did they instead vote against the winner's opponent? How satisfied were voters with the choices presented them? Were the voters sending a clear message—a **mandate**—or not? Winners search the results for evidence of a mandate. In 1992, Bill Clinton interpreted his victory as a mandate for a more active and progressive federal government. Several failures—on efforts to integrate homosexuals in the military and to establish nationalized health care—demonstrated that voter mandates are not always so clear. The voters' message has become more difficult to discern as **split-ticket voting**—voting for a presidential candidate of one party and legislators of the other—has grown more common.

SUMMARY

- Elections consist of two phases: nominations and the general election. Most nominations are made through party primaries. These can be open, closed, or "blanket."

- Candidates need the backing of the major parties along with a compelling back story before they can hope to make a strong campaign for national office.

- Campaign finance is restricted by a complicated web of regulations defined by the election laws of the 1970s along with the 2002 Bipartisan Campaign Reform Act. Candidates can get federal matching funds, but only if they agree to predetermined spending limits.

- Before the general elections, the candidates need to win their party primaries, which often involves energizing the base. Later, candidates may have to repudiate some of the more radical statements they made to court primary voters.

- Nominating Conventions used to be where the party nominees were selected, but now they are symbolic coronations of the candidate who has already been selected though the primary process. Still, delegates assemble, cheer, and argue over the drafting of the party platform.

- Presidential candidates must win each state's electors, which is done by getting a plurality of all the voters in that state. This method causes candidates to spend most all their time in "swing" or "battleground" states and can also result in the winner of the popular vote losing the election (as was the case with Al Gore in the election of 2000).

- After all the voting is done, pollsters, the parties, and the media try their best to determine why the people voted the way they did. Exit polls and surveys are the tools used to decipher these factors.

PRACTICE QUESTIONS

1. In an *open* Republican primary

   (A) only Republicans can vote
   (B) only Democrats can vote
   (C) only Republicans and Democrats can vote
   (D) only Independents can vote
   (E) every registered voter can vote.

2. In a given election cycle, a political action committee (PAC) may contribute to a candidate no more than

   (A) $2,000
   (B) $3,000
   (C) $4,000
   (D) $5,000
   (E) $6,000

3. At a nominating convention, the position that the political party will take is decided by the

   (A) Platform Committee
   (B) Committee on Permanent Organization
   (C) Credentials Committee
   (D) Rules Committee
   (E) Ideology Committee

4. In order to win the election for the presidency, a candidate must

   (A) receive a majority of the votes in the electoral college
   (B) receive a majority of the popular vote
   (C) receive a plurality of votes in the electoral college
   (D) receive a plurality of the popular vote
   (E) receive a unanimous vote from the electoral college

5. Which of the following people is *most* likely to vote in a general election?

   (A) a 25-year-old high school dropout
   (B) a 65-year-old professor
   (C) a 19-year-old college student
   (D) a 16-year-old high school student
   (E) a 30-year-old college graduate

INSTITUTIONS OF GOVERNMENT

CONGRESS

CONCEPTS

- Why do congressional incumbents have an advantage over challengers?
- Why did the Supreme Court strike down majority-minority voting districts?
- Why does Congress continue to maintain the seniority system?
- What is it about the way Congress operates that promotes factionalism?
- Why has it been argued that Congress contributes to the fragmentation of policy making?
- Why do we hate Congress but love our congressperson?

- Why would members of Congress vote against campaign finance reform?

- Why would members of the Senate engage in a filibuster?

- Why is the House Rules Committee so important?

- How does politics enter into the nomination process for independent agencies and the judiciary?

- What impact has the high cost of campaigning had on the legislative process?

TERMS

- census
- reapportionment
- gerrymander
- congressional district
- oversight
- House Rules Committee
- filibuster
- cloture
- pork barrel
- conference committee
- standing committee
- joint committee
- select committee
- pocket veto
- line item veto
- pigeonhole
- discharge petition
- Speaker of the House
- president *pro tempore*
- majority leader
- minority leader
- bills of attainder
- *ex post facto* laws

CONGRESSIONAL STRUCTURE

Congress is the bicameral (two-house) legislature responsible for writing the laws of the nation. Congress also serves other functions, such as overseeing the bureaucracy, consensus building, clarifying policy, legitimizing, and expressing diversity. It is made up of a House of Representatives of 435 members and a Senate of 100 members. The Constitution requires that all members of the House represent their constituents in equal single-member voting districts, with equal populations.

Every 10 years a **census** is taken by the federal government to count the population to determine the number of each state's congressional districts. Each state must then redraw its congressional boundaries to ensure that each district is equal in population. **Congressional reapportionment** is done by each state legislature. Therefore, the political party in control of the state legislature controls how the districts are drawn. As much as is legally possible, the legislature will **gerrymander** the district boundaries to give the majority party an advantage in future elections. This is true in every state with the exception of Iowa, which uses an independent commission to form districts. In some states, such as Alaska and Wyoming, the populations are so small that the entire state becomes a congressional district; all states are guaranteed at least one seat in the House.

CONGRESSIONAL ELECTIONS

Elections for all the **435 seats** of the **House of Representatives** occur **every two years.** House members must reside in the district they represent, be a citizen of the state, and be at least 25 years old. Election to the House takes place within each congressional district. The constituencies of representatives are relatively small compared with those of senators, and the House incumbent election rates are very high, averaging more than 90 percent. Many House members have safe seats and are not seriously challenged for reelection.

Elections for **one-third of the Senate** occur **every two years,** with a senator's term lasting six years. Every state is guaranteed two senators, elected on a staggered basis in statewide elections. Senate elections are generally more competitive, expensive, high profile, and generally draw candidates from other elected offices.

Important Voting Rights Court Cases

Smith v. Allwright (1944). The denying of African Americans the right to vote in a primary election was found to be a violation of the Fifteenth Amendment.

Baker v. Carr (1962). Authorized federal courts to be the final authority on the creation of House districts.

Wesberry v. Sanders (1963). Ordered House districts to be near as equal as possible— enshrined the principle of "one man, one vote."

Buckley v. Valeo (1976). The court ruled that giving money to a political campaign was a form of free speech and threw out some stringent federal regulations on fund-raising and election spending. This decision also allowed wealthy people to spend as much of their own money as they wanted if they chose to run for federal office.

Shaw v. Reno (1993) and *Miller v. Johnson* (1995). Race cannot be the sole or predominant factor in redrawing legislative district boundaries.

U.S. Term Limits v. Thornton (1995). States cannot set term limits on members of Congress.

Bush v. Gore (2000). Florida recount in the election of 2000 was ruled to be a violation of the Fourteenth Amendment's equal protection clause.

CONGRESSIONAL DISTRICTS AND REPRESENTATION

Descriptive representation means that the elected legislature should reflect the demographic characteristics of the constituency. Minorities and women have always been underrepresented in Congress and state legislatures, which is the reason that the **Voting Rights Act of 1965** encouraged states to take measures to increase minority representation in Congress. Into the early 1980s little progress had been made. Women, Latinos, and African Americans continued to be underrepresented. In 1982 Congress amended the Voting Rights Act to encourage states to create majority-minority districts, concentrating African American and Hispanic populations into distinct congressional districts. These districts were created to make it more feasible for minority candidates to get elected.

Following the 1990 census, many states redrew their congressional districts, which resulted in increasing African American representation by 50 percent and Hispanic membership by 70 percent. Various districts were drawn to conform to the Voting Rights Act. However, the shape of these districts was sometimes quite bizarre. North Carolina District 12, for example, stretched in a narrow band 160 miles down Interstate Highway 85. A Duke University professor joined with four other white plaintiffs to challenge the constitutionality of District 12. In *Shaw v. Reno* (1993), the Supreme Court surprised many with a split decision. The Court invalidated the district in question because its boundaries were neither contiguous nor compact and were drawn with the intent to discriminate through the use of racial gerrymandering. The Court ruled that any racial gerrymandering by the state required a compelling state interest, and it did not see such a compelling interest in this district. The Court went on to state that there was no constitutional guarantee of ethnic and racial representation in Congress, and that a person of different ethnic or racial background from the majority of the constituents could still effectively represent the constituents' needs. If the representative did not, there was always the solution of the ballot box.

North Carolina, Georgia, and Texas legislators have been accused by critics of playing dirty politics. African American and (to a lesser degree) Hispanic voters are overwhelmingly Democrat. (Cuban Americans in Florida tend to vote Republican.) Critics claim that Republican-controlled state legislatures were not motivated by any sense of duty. Instead, they stand accused of trying to remove racial-minority Democrats from other districts to ensure that more Republicans get elected. The political trade-off was to create a guaranteed Democratic district but at the same time gain more Republican seats from the surrounding districts. To isolate minorities in the district is known as "packing." To divide them across many districts is "cracking."

To add to the representation controversy, population shifts in the last 20 years have given additional seats in the House to southern states while reducing the number from other regions. In addition, suburban representation has increased, at the expense of both rural and urban areas.

Finally, Congress draws its members primarily from the legal and business worlds. Almost half of the House and more than half of the Senate have a legal background. The reason seems to be that lawyers have many of the prerequisites needed for a successful run for Congress: interest and experience in the law, prominence within the community, and the personal wealth to at least partially fund an election campaign.

Though they hold more seats than ever before, women still make up a small number of both houses: 16 seats in the Senate and 74 seats in the House. Currently, there are only three Hispanic senators, Ken Salazar (D-Colorado), Sam Zamarripa (D-Georgia), and Mel Martinez (R-Florida). Barack Obama (D-Illinois) is currently the only African American senator.

CONGRESSIONAL POWERS

The framers had a fear of the power inherent in legislatures. Because of that fear, the Constitution spells out the responsibilities of the legislature in more detail than those of the executive and judicial branches. To further guard against legislative usurpation (control of one house over the other), both houses have unique but complementary powers. The delegated powers, which require both houses to work in concert with each other, include taxing, borrowing money, regulating commerce, raising an army, creating and making rules for the federal courts, establishing naturalization laws, establishing post offices, providing for a militia, and making any law that is deemed necessary and proper for carrying out these powers.

Each house also has unique powers. Only the House of Representatives may initiate tax laws and spending bills. It is the **House Ways and Means Committee** that oversees taxing and spending legislation. The Senate has only amending powers on revenue bills.

The Senate's unique powers include confirmation of presidential nominations to the federal courts and ambassadorships to foreign countries. The Senate must also ratify all treaties signed by the president.

There are restrictions on congressional actions. Congress may not pass **bills of attainder** (laws that find people guilty of a crime and sentence them to prison) or **ex post facto laws** (that punish people for actions that occurred before the behavior was made criminal) and may not levy export taxes or grant titles of nobility. These same prohibitions apply to states.

THE NON-LEGISLATIVE TASKS OF CONGRESS

Congress's primary responsibility is to fulfill the legal needs of the nation by writing laws. However, Congress also performs other equally important functions. These include the following:

- **Oversight.** Through its committees and subcommittees, Congress reviews the work of the federal agencies. This helps check the executive branch. It investigates charges of corruption and waste, and it holds hearings where experts and citizens discuss the government's problems and suggest solutions. It is also the role of the Senate to confirm the members of the president's cabinet as well as to approve nominees for all positions in the federal court system.

- **Public education.** Committee hearings and floor debates increase public awareness of government and societal problems. Floor debates over gun control, tax cuts, Social Security reform, health care reform, and sending armed troops abroad all help to focus national attention on important issues.

- **Representing constituents within the government**. As representatives of their electorates, members of Congress not only vote on laws but also help constituents in their dealings with the government. They receive and can act on complaints about federal services, sponsor voters who seek scholarships or federal contracts, and solicit constituents' suggestions about how to improve the government. In performing this last task, some members of Congress consider themselves delegates whose job it is to mirror the views of their home districts. Others see themselves as trustees who should consider their constituents' views but should ultimately use their best judgment as experts when deciding how to vote.

THE LEGISLATIVE PROCESS

The legislative process is, by design, slow and complicated. This is to prevent Congress from acting hastily. The Framers intended for the process to foster compromise. The result has been that the final versions of bills are often radically different from initial versions. Without compromise there would be no legislative process.

As many as 10,000 bills are introduced on the floor of Congress each year. Some are written by members of Congress and their staffs; others are drafted by the executive branch and are introduced by a sympathetic member of Congress. Many are suggested or written by interest groups and their lawyers. Regardless of who authors a bill, a bill can only be proposed by a member of Congress. Whoever introduces a bill is called the **sponsor of the bill.**

The legislative process requires the two houses to work cooperatively with each other. **All bills must pass both houses in exactly the same form.** While the bills must be the same, the debate and voting processes in the two houses differ. Because there are 435 members of the House of Representatives, the process by which bills are debated is limited. The Senate, which is smaller, has fewer rules governing the legislative process.

Unlike the Senate, the House has a **Rules Committee,** which is responsible for determining how long a bill will be debated and, whether to allow an open or closed rule for amending the bill. Open rules allow amendments, closed rules prohibit amendments. When Republicans gained control of the House of Representatives in 1994, they promised most bills would be debated under open rules. Allowing 435 members an opportunity to add amendments to bills became so cumbersome, however, that the House leadership returned to the closed rule process. Because the Rules Committee controls crucial aspects of the legislative process, it is considered the most powerful committee in the House. The Rules Committee can kill a bill by delaying a vote or by making it easy for opponents to add **killer amendments**. The Rules Committee can also bring bills up for an immediate floor vote.

While the House strictly controls debate, the Senate does not. There are no time restraints placed on senators. **Filibusters** occur when senators speak with no intention of stopping. It is their intent to delay a vote on a bill and to tie up the work of the Senate. The only way to end a filibuster is to vote for **cloture**, but this requires the votes of 60 members, which is difficult to get when the two parties are evenly represented.

The Senate has no closed rules for amending legislation. Amendments, called riders, do not have to be germane to a bill. This allows individual senators an opportunity to add amendments, such as "pet" issues or projects for their home state, or to prohibit the actions of executive agencies. "Pet project" riders designed to bring federal money to a home state are called **pork barrel.** "Bringing home the bacon" is one of the reasons incumbent reelection rates are so high. The members of both houses love pork-barrel legislation.

After debates, bills usually end up passing the House and Senate in different forms, so both versions are sent to a **conference committee**. The members of these conference committees come from the respective committees of the two houses that wrote the bill. The conference committee tries to **negotiate a compromise bill,** acceptable to both houses of Congress. Once a compromise version has been written, the bill is returned to the two houses for a vote. Failure to pass a bill from a conference committee will kill a bill. If the bill is passed in both houses it is sent to the White House for the president's signature.

The president has options. If he does nothing for 10 days, the bill becomes law without his signature. If a congressional session ends during those 10 days, the president must sign every bill into law. If he doesn't, the bill will be **pocket vetoed**, requiring the bill go through the entire legislative process again. If there are more than 10 days left in a congressional session, and a president wants to prevent a bill from becoming law, he may veto the entire bill. The president must then give his reasons in writing and return the bill to the house of origination.

At that point, Congress has choices. The two houses may make the required changes, or they may attempt to override the president's veto by a two-thirds vote. If the bill passes both houses by the required two-thirds vote, the bill becomes law without the president's signature. If the house of origination (where the bill was originally introduced) does nothing with the presidential veto, the bill is dead.

In 1996, Congress gave the president the **line-item veto,** empowering the president to veto individual parts of a bill. The constitutionality of the line-item veto was immediately challenged in the Supreme Court *(Clinton v. New York City)*. The Court struck down the line-item veto as an unconstitutional delegation of legislative authority to the president.

Congress has also attempted to give itself veto power over the actions of the president. In specific instances, Congress would write legislation giving the president broad powers to act but reserve to itself the right to void presidential actions by a vote of one or both houses. This legislative veto was declared unconstitutional by the Supreme Court in *INS v. Chadha* (1983). The only form of veto mentioned in the Constitution is that used by the president.

LEGISLATION BY COMMITTEE

Most of the legislative business of Congress occurs in committees. Who serves on which committee and what position they hold is determined by a number of factors. **The majority party of each house holds all the committee chairs.** The majority party will also hold a **majority of the seats** on each committee, **effectively controlling all the business of the committee.** On the important committees, the majority usually holds two-thirds of the committee seats.

The committee member of the majority party with the most seniority becomes the chair and the senior member from the minority party becomes the ranking member. The ranking member becomes chair if the minority party becomes the majority party. This happened in 2001 when a member of the Republican-controlled Senate left the Republican Party to become an Independent. All Democrat ranking members of Senate committees became the chairs, while the Republican chairs became the ranking members. The same principle applies in the House of Representatives.

Committee assignments in the House and Senate are determined by the House and Senate leadership and a caucus of the two political parties. Members of Congress attempt to get on the committees that will allow them to do the most constituent service and help them get reelected. For example, representatives and senators from farm states try to get assigned to agriculture committees.

Committees serve as mini-legislatures, performing the tasks of investigating and debating bills that, due to time constraints, could never otherwise receive the consideration of Congress. Often, the congressional committee assigns the bill to an even smaller group, called a **subcommittee,** for initial consideration. Recently, there has been a proliferation of subcommittees. Subcommittees often determine how money is spent and have therefore become very powerful. In response to increased workloads, all committees and subcommittees have increased the size of their staffs.

The fate of a new bill depends on much more than its content. The membership of the committee and subcommittee that first considers the bill is crucial. Bill sponsors attempt to draft bills in such a way as to steer them toward sympathetic committees. Supporters of a bill must also decide which house of Congress should consider their bill first, because with the exception of revenue bills, federal bills may originate in either house. Supporters attempt to have the bill introduced in the house more sympathetic to their cause to build political momentum.

The House has more committees than the Senate. House members, however, due to their numbers tend to become more specialized because they serve on fewer committees. As a result, they are considered to have more expertise than senators. There are four types of committees in Congress.

- **Standing committees** are permanent, specialized committees. Examples include the House Ways and Means Committee, the Senate Judiciary Committee, and the Senate Armed Services Committee. There are 20 standing committees in the House and 17 in the Senate.

- **Joint committees** are made up of members of both the House and the Senate. These committees are normally used for communicating to the public or for investigations but generally do not send bills to the floor for votes.

- **Select committees** are temporary committees organized in each house for some special purpose. These committees usually carry out investigations for the purpose of writing special legislation. The House Watergate Committee and the Senate Select Committee on Unfair Campaign Practices are examples from the Nixon era. The work of these committees eventually led to campaign reform.

- **Conference committees** are temporary and include members from the committees of the two houses who were responsible for writing a bill. These committees try to negotiate compromise bills, which are then submitted to the two houses for an up or down vote without amendments. Once a compromise bill has been negotiated, the conference committee disbands.

Most bills die almost immediately in a subcommittee due to lack of interest from committee members; unless a committee member takes a special interest in a bill, the bill will either be quickly rejected or ignored until it dies a natural death at the end of the congressional session.

Committees and subcommittees function by calling interested parties and expert witnesses who have some information to give. Lobbyists often testify as expert witnesses. Congress can subpoena reluctant witnesses, forcing them to appear in hearings and can grant immunity to compel them to testify. Once their investigations have concluded, committees begin amending and rewriting sections of bills in meetings called markup sessions.

Committees will sometimes refuse to vote a bill out, hoping to keep it from being considered by the house. A bill stuck in a House or Senate committee is said to be **pigeonholed.** The parliamentary mechanism to force a bill out of committee for a floor vote is called a **discharge petition.**

Committees have responsibilities in addition to writing laws. For example, they are responsible for the oversight of many bureaucratic agencies and departments. Heads of regulatory agencies, which are responsible for enforcing the laws, often appear to give testimony before congressional committees with oversight jurisdiction. If the agency has not followed the intent of the law, the agency head will be in for a rough time.

Committees also hear testimony from agency heads pleading for money and personnel. Congressional budget cutting and agency reorganization can have a profound impact on an agency's ability to carry out its responsibilities. This is one way that Congress can use the budget to shape policy.

CONGRESSIONAL LEADERSHIP

The House

The leader of the House of Representatives is the **Speaker,** who is chosen by the majority party in a special election. The Speaker is powerful because he or she can direct floor debate and has influence over committee assignments and over the Rules Committee. The Speaker can also control which bills go to which committees. The **majority leader** of the House keeps party members in line and helps determine party policy and the party's legislative agenda. The **minority leader** keeps the minority party members in line and helps determine the minority party's legislative agenda. The House majority and minority whips also help their respective party leaders keep the members loyal to the party's legislative agenda.

The Senate

The vice president is the president of the Senate, and this is his only constitutionally delegated responsibility. However, the vice president is rarely on the floor of the Senate and only votes to break a tie. When the vice president is absent during Senate sessions, the **president** pro tempore is the presiding officer. The president *pro tempore* is largely an honorary position and is usually given to the most senior member of the majority party of the Senate. The majority leader has the real power in the Senate because he or she controls the legislative agenda and acts as a power broker and policy initiator. The minority leader can act as a power broker but usually cannot initiate policy and control the agenda.

WHY DO THEY VOTE THAT WAY?

Congresspersons are always cross-pressured to influence their vote. These pressures come from their own party and from the opposition. It also comes from the president through jawboning (trying to influence) and from their colleagues by logrolling ("you help me on this bill, and I'll help you on yours"). PACs try to influence votes through contributions, as do constituents and interest groups. Personal ideology and religious beliefs can also impact their judgment. The most important factor in determining the vote of a congressperson is party affiliation. Members of Congress usually—but not always—vote with their parties.

NOTABLE LEGISLATION

National Growth, Expansion and Institution Building

- **Northwest Ordinance (1789).** This law is one of the few successes of the Articles of Confederation; it provided clear guidelines for the settlement of new territories and provided a path to statehood.

- **Judiciary Act (1789).** This act of Congress was declared unconstitutional in the case *Marbury v. Madison* because it pre-dated the supremacy of court rules of the Constitution.

- **Missouri Compromise (1820).** An unsuccessful attempt to establish a line between the admission of free and slave states in the western territories. This law ultimately broke down in the run-up to the Civil War and was ruled unconstitutional in the *Dred Scott* decision.

Regulation of Government and Industry

- **Pendleton Act (1883).** Eliminated the spoils system of patronage in selection for government jobs and set up an exam-based merit system for qualified candidates.

- **Sherman Anti-Trust Act (1896).** This law provided Congress with authority to regulate and break up monopolies—known as "trusts"—in the United States.

- **Meat Inspection Act and Pure Food and Drug Act (1906).** In response to muckraking journalism and Upton Sinclair's novel *The Jungle*, Congress established federal guardianship over food and drug production.

- **National Labor Relations Act (1935).** Known as the Wagner Act, this law gave workers the right to join unions without fear of losing their jobs. It also created the National Labor Relations Board to facilitate collective bargaining.

- **Hatch Act (1939).** Permitted government employees to vote in government elections but forbade them from participating in partisan politics.

- **Taft-Hartley Act (1947).** Also known as the **Labor-Management Relations Act**, this law greatly reduced the power of unions by providing for a "cooling off" period and prohibited a list of "unfair labor practices." Seen as a curtailment of the Wagner Act.

- **Air Quality Act (1967).** The beginning of a series of acts to regulate impacts on the environment.

- **Federal Election Campaign Acts (1971–1974).** These laws created the Federal Election Commission and required disclosures of contributions and expenditures and limitations on contributions and presidential election expenditures.

- **War Powers Act (1973).** Limited President's power to use troops overseas in hostilities, put a time limit on use and gave Congress final power to withdraw troops.

- **Budget and Impoundment Control Act (1974).** Established Congressional budget committees and the Congressional Budget Office, and gave Congress the power to prevent the president from refusing to fund Congressional initiatives (known as "impoundment").

- **Freedom of Information Act (1974).** Declassified government documents for public use.

- **Gramm-Rudman-Hollings Bill (1985).** Set budget reduction targets to balance budget. Failed to eliminate loopholes.

Rights and Freedoms

- **Espionage Act (1917), Sedition Act (1918).** Severely curtailed the civil liberties of Americans during wartime and greatly increased the power of the federal government in controlling public activity.

- **Immigration Act (1924).** This law stringently limited the number of immigrants admitted into the United States and set strict quotas for entry.

- **Civil Rights Act (1964).** Title II banned discrimination in public places on the basis of race, color, national origin, or religion. Title VII prohibited employment discrimination based on gender.

- **Voting Rights Act (1965).** Suspended literacy tests, empowered federal officials to register voters, prohibited states from changing voting procedures without federal permission.

- **Age Discrimination in Employment Act (1967).** Banned age discrimination in jobs unless age is related to job performance.

- **Civil Rights Act (1968).** Banned housing discrimination based on race.

- **Title IX Education Act (1972).** Prohibited gender discrimination in federally funded education programs.

- **Americans With Disabilities Act (1990).** Protected civil liberties of disabled Americans and mandated "reasonable accommodations" to public facility use.

- **National Voter Registration Bill, (1993).** Also known as **The Motor Voter Act**, this law allowed people to register to vote when applying for driver's licenses.

- **The Patriot Act (2001).** In response to the terrorist attacks of September 11, 2001, Congress granted broad police authority to the federal, state, and local government to interdict, prosecute, and convict suspected terrorists. This law is formally known as the USA-PATRIOT Law, an acronym for "Uniting and Strengthening America by Providing Appropriate Tools Required to Intercept and Obstruct Terrorism"

Government Aid to the People

- **New Deal Legislation (1933–1939).** Legislation that expanded the role of government in the economy and society. Created entities like Social Security, the Securities and Exchange Commission, and the Tennessee Valley Authority. These laws also dramatically expanded the role and size of the federal government.

- **The G.I. Bill (1944).** Technically known as **The Serviceman Adjustment Act**, this law paid for college and living expenses for World War II veterans and provided low-interest home loans.

- **National Defense Education Act (1958).** This law provided for the use of federal funding to stimulate nationwide educational performance in science and mathematics in response to the launch of the Soviet satellite *Sputnik*.

- **Personal Responsibility and Work Opportunity Reconciliation Act (1996).** The Welfare Reform Act signaled a change in the role of the federal government in the relationship with the states. This law sought to increase the role of personal responsibility in welfare recipients and shifted many responsibilities for welfare provision to state governments.

- **Bipartisan Campaign Reform Act (2002).** Often known as the **McCain-Feingold Bill**, this law banned soft money contributions to national political parties and raised hard money limits to $2,000.

THE PRESIDENT

CONCEPTS

- How do presidents use their informal powers to get their legislative agenda passed?
- How can Congress curb the foreign policy making powers of the president?
- How does the president use the appointment power to ensure that policies are carried out?
- What techniques can presidents use to promote their legislative agenda in the face of divided government?
- What impact does the White House staff have on policy making?
- Why would Congress give the president a line-item veto?
- Do executive agreements go against the intent of the Framers of the Constitution?

TERMS

- executive agreements
- commander in chief
- Gulf of Tonkin Resolution
- War Powers Act
- chief of staff
- Office of Management and Budget
- cabinet
- impeachment
- secretaries

THE FORMAL POWERS OF THE PRESIDENCY

The original intent of the framers was to create an executive with limited formal powers. These powers are delegated in the Constitution in Article II, section 2, but they are less specific than the formal powers of Congress. The broadly defined powers were intended to give flexibility but have instead resulted in greatly expanded power.

The president is responsible for enforcing the laws, handling foreign policy, and serving as the ceremonial head of state. He is also the administrative head of the government. He can force Congress into session, must brief Congress on the "state of the nation," and can veto legislation and grant reprieves and pardons. But regardless of these expansive powers, he must cooperate with Congress because the powers of the presidency are intermingled with the powers of the legislature. The president's appointments of federal judges, Supreme Court justices, ambassadors, and department secretaries all require Senate approval. The president negotiates treaties, but they must be ratified by two-thirds of the Senate. Because Senate ratification is sometimes difficult to achieve, the broad powers of the president to initiate foreign policy now include **executive agreements** (which do not require Senate approval). These are agreements between heads of countries; under international and U.S. law they are as binding as a treaty. However, they usually deal with more routine, administrative matters.

THE PRESIDENT AS COMMANDER IN CHIEF

The president also serves as commander in chief of the armed forces. But the framers created a complex institutional situation regarding armed conflict. Only Congress has the power to declare war, but only the president can make war. In the nuclear age, the power of Congress to declare war could very well be obsolete. Because missiles can destroy cities within minutes of launch, congressional debate of the pros and cons of declaring war seems impractical, if not silly. While the United States has been in numerous wars since 1945, no declarations of war have been made.

While the president is the chief strategist and director of the military forces of the United States, he is at the mercy of Congress for the money to wage war. However, once the president has committed troops in conflict, it is inconceivable that Congress would refuse to fund the weapons needed for the military. For members of Congress such an action would mean political suicide and probably lead to a constitutional crisis within the U.S. government.

In a national crisis, the other branches of government and the American people look to the president for leadership. Initially, presidents will have strong support for their policies. This helps explain why Congress, in 1964, passed the **Gulf of Tonkin Resolution,** giving the president the broad powers to commit unlimited numbers of troops for an unlimited length of time in the Vietnam conflict. President Johnson was unable to bring that war to a conclusion. Strong criticism of his handling of the war led to a general lack of support for his policies, undermining his ability to govern. The same thing happened to President Carter when he was unable to successfully end the Iranian hostage crisis. George Bush Sr. was president during the Gulf War. His ability to quickly bring the war to a conclusion while suffering relatively few casualties resulted in the second-highest approval rating of any president, at 89 percent.

In the post–Vietnam War era, Congress has attempted to place controls on the war-making powers of the president. Congress passed the **War Powers Act** in 1973 in an attempt to force the president to seek congressional approval before making war. The act specifically limits the president to 10,000 troops for 60 days, with 30 additional days to withdraw the troops, unless Congress grants an extension or declares war. The Supreme Court has never ruled on the War Powers Act, and Congress has never invoked it, although whenever the president commits troops overseas, members of Congress have threatened the president with imposition of the War Powers Act.

THE INFORMAL POWERS

The presidential powers that are not enumerated in the Constitution are referred to as the informal powers, and they are sometimes more important than the formal ones. How well presidents use the informal powers can determine the success of their presidencies.

Presidents are supposed to be morale builders. President Carter's failure to improve the morale of the country contributed to his reelection defeat. President Reagan was a master at morale building, and this characteristic helps explain why he remained popular with the American people.

Presidents serve as legislative leaders and coalition builders. Failure to set and lead the legislative agenda and build coalitions in Congress can doom presidents, particularly when there is divided government (when one or both houses of the legislature are controlled by the opposition party). George Bush Sr. became the "foreign policy president" when he was unable to get his domestic policy agenda passed in a Democrat-controlled Congress. Ronald Reagan and his advisers were experts in building coalitions with Republicans and Southern conservative Democrats. This coalition of Republicans and southern Democrats gave Reagan his legislative agenda.

Perhaps the president's most important informal powers are as a policy persuader and communicator to Congress and the American people. Clinton and Reagan were superior communicators.

The ability of a president to communicate well with the American people is a very powerful tool for pressuring Congress. Communicating with Congress is also important. Having the congressional leadership down to the White House for lunch and a photo opportunity is another way that presidents try to persuade members of Congress to pass their legislative agenda.

EXECUTIVE OFFICE OF THE PRESIDENT

The Executive Office of the President helps carry out the president's administrative responsibilities. It is made up of more than half a dozen agencies involved in the day-to-day operations of the White House and is basically divided into three areas: domestic, foreign, and military affairs. It is staffed by hundreds of personnel located in the White House and the Executive Office Building. All are directly responsible to the president or his designees.

- **The Chief of Staff** is the top aide to the president. He or she is a person in whom the president has complete trust and is probably a longtime associate and friend. Considered one of the most powerful persons in Washington, the Chief of Staff is responsible for managing the Executive Office and can control access to the president, thus potentially controlling the information that the president receives. Some presidents, such as Bill Clinton, permitted easy access; others, such as **Richard Nixon**, tended to insulate themselves. Whoever the president chooses as Chief of Staff can have a tremendous impact on presidential effectiveness. Clinton's first Chief of Staff, **Thomas McClarty**, a Washington outsider and Clinton friend, ran an undisciplined White House, prone to many errors. He was replaced by a Washington insider, former Congressman **Leon Panetta**, who established order and discipline, emerging as a key policy player in the Clinton administration.

- **The National Security Council** is headed by the **National Security Advisor**, who has direct access to the president in matters relating to military and foreign policy. The NSC has been involved since the late 1940s in the decision-making process during national emergencies. President Kennedy used the NSC during the Cuban missile crisis, President Reagan during the Iran-Contra affair, and President Bush Sr. during the Gulf War. Unlike the State Department, the NSC is largely free from congressional oversight. For this reason, it has become one of the most favored institutions for many presidents.

- **The Domestic Policy Council** assists the president in formulating policies relating to energy, education, agriculture, natural resources, economic affairs, health and human resources, welfare reform, drug abuse, and crime.

- **The Office of Management and Budget** is responsible for preparing the budget of the United States and can be used to control and manage the executive agencies for the president. The OMB has enormous power because of its ability to allocate money to the cabinet departments through the budget process of the executive branch. Increasing or decreasing a department's budget affects how it carries out its responsibilities.

- **The Council of Economic Advisors** is responsible for helping the president make national economic policy. The Council is usually made up of the economists and advises the president on policies that are designed to increase prosperity.

- **The U.S. Trade Representative** is responsible for negotiating complex trade and tariff agreements for the president. Trade agreements such as GATT and NAFTA are negotiated by the Trade Representative on behalf of the president, with the guidance of the White House.

THE CABINET

The cabinet is not mentioned in the Constitution but was created through custom and usage. Each cabinet department was instituted by an act of Congress to help administrate the responsibilities of the executive branch.

Each cabinet secretary is appointed by the president and confirmed by the Senate. **Secretaries** can be dismissed at the president's will. Cabinet secretaries are supposed to run their departments and carry out the president's policies. Those who disagree with presidential policy are expected to resign. Secretaries tend to be lightning rods to be used for deflecting criticism and are responsible for explaining and promoting presidential policies. Over time, secretaries tend to represent their own departments more than the president's policies. They are expected to fight for their department's budget, jurisdiction, and personnel. This creates competition and friction between departments and accounts for why presidents usually do not hold full cabinet meetings. Presidents just don't have the time or inclination to listen to the bickering and arguing between department heads.

Still, despite these institutional shortcomings, cabinet secretaries do rule over vast departmental bureaucracies—each containing numerous powerful government agencies. With the recent addition of the **Department of Homeland Security,** there are now 15 cabinet departments. After the September 11th attacks, it was felt that a cabinet-level department was necessary to counter possible threats to the United States, and no fewer than 22 agencies were consolidated into the new department, making it the third-largest executive branch department. Agencies as disparate as the Immigration and Naturalization Service (INS), the Coast Guard, and the Secret Service were consolidated to shape a coherent agenda to protect the United States against potential attacks. The Department of Homeland Security has four functions: to protect the borders; to support local agencies like police and fire departments; to detect chemical, biological, and nuclear weapons; and to analyze intelligence. Homeland Security is the first top-level government position created since the Energy Department was formed in 1977 and the first large-scale government reorganization since Harry Truman created the Department of Defense in 1947. Other departments include Health and Human Services, Transportation, and Education.

IMPEACHMENT

The Constitution gives Congress the power to remove the president from office for "treason, bribery, or other high crimes and misdemeanors." The Constitution does not define high crimes and misdemeanors, leaving those definitions to politicians. The only direction in the Constitution is that the House of Representatives impeaches the president (or brings the charges) by a simple majority vote, and if the impeachment passes, the Senate holds a trial with the Chief Justice of the Supreme Court presiding. Removal of the president requires a two-thirds vote of the Senate. The entire process in Congress has been developed as a result of guesswork, custom, and usage.

Because the definition of an impeachable offense is left to the House, impeachment is a highly charged political process. Most constitutional scholars place the standard for impeachment as an act against the government or the Constitution, but there seems to be political disagreement over what standard should be used. Conservatives seem to have one standard, while liberals seem to have another. Every impeachment, or near-impeachment, has divided the Congress along party lines, and some scholars have accused members of Congress of using the process to undo the result of an election.

No president of the United States has been removed from office. The Senate failed to remove Andrew Johnson for his violation of the Tenure in Office Act by one vote. This act was later invalidated by the Supreme Court. Richard Nixon resigned as a result of the Watergate scandal. He knew that the Senate would convict if given the opportunity to vote. The impeachment of President Clinton for lying under oath was very political. All parties knew before the trial began that there was little chance of a Senate conviction. The general consensus was that, while Clinton's behavior had been improper and had brought dishonor to the Office of the President, his conduct had not risen to the level of an impeachable offense.

Federal judges are appointed for life and can be removed only by the impeachment process. Only seven federal judges have ever been removed by the Senate. One of them is **Alcee Hastings**, who was impeached for bribery and perjury, and is now a member of the same House of Representatives who voted for his impeachment.

THE JUDICIARY

CONCEPTS

- What circumstances are required for a case to be brought before the Supreme Court?
- How do politics enter into Supreme Court decisions?
- Why can it be said that all judicial decisions are activist?
- Why can it be said that a president's strongest legacy is found in the judiciary?
- What control does Congress have over the judiciary?

TERMS

- original jurisdiction
- appellate jurisdiction
- senatorial courtesy
- judicial restraint
- judicial activism
- judicial review
- *Marbury v. Madison*
- writ of *certiorari*
- justiciable
- standing

STRUCTURE AND JURISDICTION

The federal courts are responsible for interpreting and settling disputes arising out of federal law. State courts are responsible for interpreting and settling disputes arising out of state law. It is possible for a citizen to commit a single act that violates both state and federal law; trading in drugs and tax evasion are two examples.

There are three levels of federal courts: the Federal District Courts, which have **original jurisdiction,** the Federal Circuit Courts of Appeals, which hear cases on appeal from the District Courts, and the Supreme Court, which hears appeals of cases dealing with constitutional questions from the Circuit Courts and, in rare instances, original suits between states. The Supreme Court also has original jurisdiction in cases involving foreign ministers, which is intended to prevent states from deciding such cases.

The Supreme Court does not have a jury. It is considered a collegial court because its decisions are made by the nine justices. When the Court acts in **appellate jurisdiction,** it can only decide issues of law, never the facts of a case.

There are 91 **Federal District Courts**, created by Congress to fulfill its delegated responsibility of creating courts inferior to the Supreme Court. Federal District Courts decide both civil and criminal cases in original jurisdiction. The trial court that determines guilt or innocence is the court of original jurisdiction. These courts hear evidence and can use juries to decide the verdict. District Courts can also decide liability in civil cases where monetary losses have occurred. Civil cases can also have juries. It is always possible for a defendant to ask a judge to decide a case, but a judge can refuse the request and force the defendant to have a jury trial. (The Constitution guarantees a jury trial but not a trial decided by a judge.)

There are 13 **Circuit Courts of Appeals**, which hear cases on appeal from the Federal District Courts or from a State Supreme Court. In these cases someone has to claim that a federal constitutional right has been violated. The Circuit Courts decide issues of law, never issues of fact. Circuit courts have no juries. The decisions of these courts are made by panels of appointed judges. In almost every case, the Circuit Court of Appeals is the court of last resort because the Supreme Court rarely agrees to hear cases appealed from the Circuit Courts. Additionally, most Supreme Court judges rise form the Circuit Courts.

THE POLITICS OF THE JUDICIARY

All judges in the federal judiciary (only those on the Supreme Court are called justices) are appointed by the president for life terms. Appointees must go through a confirmation process in the Senate. To maintain judicial neutrality and integrity, impeachment is the only method of removal.

The appointment process has become very political. Some presidents have required potential appointees to fill out a judicial questionnaire to determine their political and judicial ideology. Nominees are almost always of the same party as the president. In nomination hearings before the Senate Judiciary Committee, members of both parties try to determine how potential judges would rule in cases dealing with issues such as abortion rights, affirmative action, or school prayer. The American Bar Association is asked to evaluate a nominee's qualifications and interest groups often present their opinions. Senators in a state where an appointee will sit have traditionally exercised **senatorial courtesy**—they submit a list of acceptable names of nominees to the president. Presidents usually choose a nominee from the list submitted.

Liberals and conservatives often argue over a nominee's judicial philosophy or level of judicial activism. The central point of the argument is whether the nominee is more or less inclined to second-guess a legislative enactment. As the conservatives see it, the courts are the least democratic branch of government (because judges are appointed, not elected), and when they overturn an act of a legislature they are overruling the will of the people, as expressed in the most democratic branch of government (the legislature). Judges who are reluctant to overturn the acts of a legislature are said to practice **judicial restraint.** Liberals often see judges as constitutional interpreters who should reflect current values. A judge who has no qualms about overturning a legislative action is considered a **judicial activist.** Compromise over these two positions is sometimes very difficult to achieve. The nomination of **Robert Bork** to be a Justice of the Supreme Court was defeated by liberals because of his judicial philosophy. **Clarence Thomas** was confirmed by the closest Senate vote in U.S. history, over concerns related to his conservative judicial philosophy, lack of experience, and the allegation that he sexually harassed an aide. Recently the arguments over activism and restraint have grown more complicated. Conservative judges are increasingly seen as activists in their rulings and liberal judges as more restrained.

PROCESS BY WHICH CASES REACH THE SUPREME COURT

The process that the Supreme Court uses to hear cases is not part of the Constitution. The process is a result of custom and usage, time and tradition.

The Supreme Court will not grant an appeal until all opportunities have been exhausted in the lower appellate courts. In the vast majority of cases, the Court refuses to hear the appeal because it agrees with the lower court decision. However, the Court may choose to review the decisions of lower courts. If four justices agree to this review, the court issues a **writ of *certiorari,*** a legal document used to request the lower court transcripts of a case.

The Supreme Court will rule only in cases that are real and adverse, which means that the case must involve an actual legal dispute. Such cases are said to be **justiciable.** Disputes over political issues cannot be decided by courts—political disputes are not justiciable. The Supreme Court cannot give advisory opinions. It can only rule in an actual legal case involving litigants. In other words, the Court will not rule on hypothetical cases.

The Court also places limits on who may bring cases before it. Simply disliking or disagreeing with a law is not sufficient to bring a case. The petitioner (the person who brings the case) must have some vested interest in the outcome of the case. Such petitioners are said to have **standing.**

JUDICIAL REVIEW

The Constitution does not specifically grant the Supreme Court the right to judge the constitutionality of laws. That power was established by the case of *Marbury v. Madison* **(1803)**. This extremely important power is called **judicial review** and was established by John Marshall, the fourth Chief Justice of the Supreme Court (he served from 1800 to 1835). Marshall was a Federalist who worked to increase the powers of the federal government over the states.

Under Marshall, the Court made several other rulings concerning the role of the Court and the relationship of the federal government to the states. They include the following:

- *Fletcher v. Peck* **(1810).** The first case in which the Court overturned a state law on constitutional grounds. *Fletcher* established the Court's right to apply judicial review to state laws. Previously, judicial review had only been applied to federal law.

- *McCulloch v. Maryland* **(1819).** The Court ruled that the states did not have the power to tax the national bank (and, by extension, the federal government). This decision reinforced the supremacy clause of the Constitution, which states that the Constitution "and the laws of the United States which shall be made in pursuance thereof...shall be the supreme law of the land; and the judges in every state shall be bound thereby, anything in the Constitution or laws of any State to the contrary notwithstanding."

- *Gibbons v. Ogden* (1824). The Court ruled that the state of New York could not grant a steamship company a monopoly to operate on an interstate waterway, even though that waterway ran through New York. The ruling increased federal power over interstate commerce by implying that anything concerning interstate trade could potentially be regulated by the federal government.

THE BUREAUCRACY

CONCEPTS

- To what degree is the bureaucracy able to maintain political neutrality?
- How do iron triangles and issue networks foster democratic principles?
- How does Congress control the bureaucracy?
- How does the bureaucracy act to implement the intent of Congress?
- How do regulatory agencies work to protect society?
- How do presidents control their policy preferences through the bureaucracy?

TERMS

- regulatory agency
- bureaucrat
- Federal Reserve Board
- iron triangle
- alliance (issue) network
- civil service system

The bureaucracy is responsible for ensuring that the policies and programs enacted by Congress and the executive departments are carried out. Because the bureaucracy is responsible for executing the laws, providing for defense, and administering social programs, it is considered part of the executive branch of government. To ensure impartiality, bureaucratic agencies are supposed to function above partisan politics and also ensure that the laws are administered without prejudice.

There are approximately four million bureaucrats who are salaried employees of the federal government, about 2.7 million civilians, and 1.4 million in the military. About 30 percent of the civilian employees work for the Defense Department, while about 15 percent work for various social agencies, including social security and welfare. No bureaucrat is elected. The 15 cabinet secretaries and the heads of independent agencies are appointed by the president with the consent of the Senate. Most of the hundreds of thousands of civilian employees who work for the government work for one of the 15 executive departments or one of the other "cabinet level" agencies considered by the White House to be part of the cabinet (such as the Director of Management and Budget or the Director of the Drug Control Office). These other cabinet level offices are not actual cabinet departments.

The largest department, the Department of Defense, is administered by the **Secretary of Defense**, who must be a civilian and reports directly to the president. Each of the five military services is headed by a uniformed chief of staff, and the five chiefs work together as the **Joint Chiefs of Staff**, headed by a chairman. The Joint Chiefs and their chairman are responsible for carrying out defense policy and report directly to both the Secretary of Defense and the president. The military is therefore subject to civilian control.

Reacting to complaints, the Clinton-Gore administration conducted a major review of the structure and performance of many executive branch agencies. The review resulted in more privatization of government responsibilities and more reliance on free market competition to ensure the government is paying the least and getting the best for the goods and services that it buys. There has also been a devolution of some responsibilities from the federal bureaucracy to the state bureaucracies. The shift has reduced the size of the federal government but has increased the size of state and local governments.

BUREAUCRATIC STRUCTURE

The bureaucracy is organized as a hierarchy of 15 pyramids, representing the 15 executive branch departments:

- Department of State
- Department of the Treasury
- Department of Defense
- Department of Justice
- Department of the Interior
- Department of Agriculture
- Department of Commerce
- Department of Labor
- Department of Health and Human Services
- Department of Housing and Urban Development
- Department of Transportation
- Department of Energy
- Department of Education
- Department of Veterans' Affairs
- Department of Homeland Security

At the top of each pyramid is the secretary of the department, who is appointed by the president and confirmed by the Senate. Directly subordinate to the secretary is the undersecretary, who is appointed by the president without Senate confirmation. Because secretaries and undersecretaries are presidential appointments, they are replaced at the end of a president's term. The position of undersecretary attracts young professionals. Because the pay is low compared with private industry, and the position is temporary, undersecretaries often use the appointment to step up to better positions in the private sector.

Below the secretaries are the personnel of the **Senior Executive Service**, including both appointees and non-appointees. Senior Executive Service appointees do not need Senate confirmation. These career officials are supposed to be responsive to the policy goals of the White House and help bureaucrats implement the policy preferences of the chief executive.

Each of the 15 departments is broken down into smaller units. These smaller units are called bureaus, offices, or services and are responsible for dealing with either a particular clientele or a specific subject. Examples are:

- The Bureau of Land Management (Department of the Interior)

- The Federal Bureau of Investigation (Department of Justice)

- The Internal Revenue Service (Department of the Treasury)

- The Immigration and Naturalization Service (Department of Homeland Security)

- The Federal Aviation Administration (Department of Transportation)

Government Corporations

Government corporations are hybrid organizations. They are a cross between a private business corporation and a government agency. Corporations are supposed to have freedom of action and flexibility and produce at least enough revenue to support themselves. Amtrak, the government corporation created to provide railroad passenger service, is an example. Unfortunately, Amtrak has never made a profit and must ask Congress for subsidies to keep itself from declaring bankruptcy and ending passenger rail service in the United States.

Originally created as a cabinet position, the United States Postal Service has become a government corporation. The intent of Congress was to create a mail delivery system that pays its own way without government assistance. Because of electronic messaging systems and competition from package delivery companies, the post office has had to increase its fees to stay solvent.

More successful, but at times controversial, is the Corporation for Public Broadcasting, which produces and airs both television and radio programs. Funding for the Public Broadcasting System (PBS) comes from both private and government subsidies. Most of its programming is related to public affairs, news, and cultural themes. The controversy often occurs when groups object to the content of programs. Still others object to the government being involved in any service that could be provided by private sector corporations.

REGULATORY AGENCIES AND COMMISSIONS

Government entities that are not within the 15 cabinet departments fall into two categories: the independent agencies and the **regulatory agencies,** sometimes called **independent regulatory commissions.** While independent agencies are generally run-of-the-mill bureaucracies with broad presidential oversight, regulatory commissions are given an extraordinary degree of independence to act as watchdogs over the federal government. Congress and the president are not supposed to become enmeshed in the workings of regulatory commissions. The safety regulations for nuclear power plants or securities exchange should not be regulated by politics.

In contemporary societies, the difficulties and complexities of writing legislation are often beyond the abilities and expertise of lawmakers. The result is that legislation is often written in general terms with many gaps that need to be filled in by the agency with jurisdiction. Independent agencies who have the responsibility for filling in these gaps and writing rules are referred to as **quasi-legislative agencies.** Those responsible for rule enforcement and punishing violators are **quasi-judicial agencies.**

Members of Congress do not have the education to deal with the scientific details that are often required to implement legislation. For example, House and Senate members who sit on committees that deal with environmental issues do not generally have advanced degrees in chemistry. It is the experts who work in the enforcing agencies who have that knowledge. Compounding the problems for Congress are the many competing interests that surround every major issue. Environmentalists have their agenda, while the petroleum industry, electric utilities, and lumber interests have theirs. Even the regulating agency with jurisdiction has its own agenda. These competing interests often delay or prevent legislation. This is the clash of the special interests.

In an age of science and technology, it is the faceless bureaucrat the public knows nothing about who often has the answers for Congress. These bureaucrats, on the one hand, are asked for advice and expertise, and, on the other hand, are often ignored because of the pressures from interest groups. Working within the regulatory commissions, they are the people responsible for writing and enforcing rules that regulate the environment, the economy, or industry. If they fail to implement the intent of Congress they are criticized by Congress and the parties regulated, usually for being too restrictive with their rules and too strict in their enforcement policies.

Examples of regulatory agencies include the following:

- **The Federal Trade Commission** is responsible for preventing fraud in the market-place by preventing price fixing and deceptive advertising.

- **The Securities and Exchange Commission** protects investors by regulating stock markets and policing corporations to prevent false and misleading claims of profits in an effort to increase stock prices.

- **The Nuclear Regulatory Commission** controls how electric power companies design, build, and operate nuclear reactors.

- **The Federal Communications Commission** is responsible for assigning broadcast frequencies, for licensing radio and television stations, and for regulating the use of wireless communication devices.

- **The Food and Drug Administration** is responsible for ensuring the health of the American people by inspecting the food supply for contaminants and spoilage. The agency is also responsible for regulating the sale of over-the-counter drugs and patent medicines.

- **The Federal Energy Regulatory Commission** is responsible for preventing price fixing and price manipulation in electric utilities, interstate oil and gas pipelines, and natural gas suppliers.

- **The Occupational Safety and Health Administration** is responsible for ensuring workers are employed in a safe work environment. For example, OSHA can regulate the type of ventilation in a factory, as well as the type of clothing worn and tools used.

Case Studies

Considered to be one of the most controversial government bureaucracies, the **Environmental Protection Agency (EPA)** was created in 1970 as an independent body. Its mission is the enforcement of the environmental laws passed by Congress. One of the agency's first responsibilities was to enforce the **1970 Clean Air Act.** The intent of the law was to reduce automobile pollution and increase automobile gasoline mileage. The automobile industry lobbied hard to defeat the bill and claimed they could not meet the requirements of the law by the time specified. They were granted extensions and eventually complied, although trucks and SUVs are still exempt from the law.

The Clean Air Act was amended in 1990 as a result of scientific evidence indicating that the refrigerants used in air conditioners were instrumental in depleting the ozone layer. The EPA successfully pressured chemical companies and air-conditioning manufacturers to find alternatives to the ozone-destroying chemicals. The EPA has also been successful in reducing the pollutants that cause acid rain.

Clean air is not the EPA's only problem. It is responsible for enforcement of the **Endangered Species Act.** This highly controversial law is intended to protect endangered wildlife habitats from human encroachment. To implement this goal, environmental impact statements are required whenever construction projects are planned. If there is any possibility that an endangered species could be adversely affected, the EPA has the power to prohibit construction. The EPA's ban on lumbering in areas of the Pacific Northwest, the habitat for the spotted owl, and its decision to block the construction of a dam in Tennessee because of the endangered snail darter fish are two examples. In the Tennessee dam case, Congress overruled the decision of the EPA, even though the Supreme Court had sided with the EPA to stop construction. In addition, Congress further weakened the EPA's enforcement powers by amending the Endangered Species Act to permit exemptions in the future. The EPA can sometimes become a foe of Congress, which originally gave the EPA its mandate to act.

Another agency that provokes political contention is the **Equal Employment Opportunities Commission (EEOC).** Created by the 1964 Civil Rights Act, the EEOC is responsible for enforcing the antidiscrimination laws of the United States. This commission has been susceptible to political pressure from both Congress and the White House. It is the EEOC's responsibility to implement affirmative action programs for minorities, to bring suits in cases of racial or sexual discrimination, and to enforce the **Americans with Disabilities Act.** The head of the EEOC is a presidential appointment and is supposed to carry out the policies of the president. If the law conflicts with presidential policy, the EEOC has a problem. How aggressively EEOC investigates charges of discrimination can cause conflict with Congress or the president.

The critics of affirmative action claim the policy is a form of reverse discrimination. Feeling pressure from voters, Congress, and the president, the EEOC first promoted affirmative action, then discouraged the policy. The attempts by this agency to implement the will of Congress have been complicated because both Congress and the White House seem to change their mind at will.

The Americans with Disabilities Act requires the EEOC to enforce laws against employers who discriminate against disabled employees or job seekers. In addition, part of the Disabilities Act requires that public buildings and large businesses be accessible to the disabled. Critics claim that this attempt at helping the disabled live normal lives has cost taxpayers hundreds of millions of dollars and the cost is too high in relation to the number of persons benefited. How aggressively EEOC investigates discrimination complaints may determine the future success of the act.

Who Runs Regulatory Agencies?

Independent regulatory agencies are run by panels of administrators called Boards of Commissioners. These commissioners are appointed by the president with the consent of the Senate. The terms of these commissioners usually overlap the term of the appointing president. The staggered term is intended to minimize political pressure from the White House. Depending on the commission, terms can range from 3 to 14 years.

Perhaps the best known regulatory board is the **Federal Reserve Board** (the Fed) because its policies directly affect the buying power of the public. The Fed accomplishes this by regulating banks, the value and supply of money, and interest rates. Its members serve 14-year terms. Its chairman serves a four-year term. The previous head, Alan Greenspan, has served both Democrat and Republican presidents. Today, the Fed is run by Ben Bernanke—a Bush appointee.

Because the Fed is an independent agency, its policies can sometimes conflict with the policies of the president. In 1993, in the first weeks of the Clinton administration, Fed Chairman Alan Greenspan told the president that the condition of the economy was worse than the Bush Sr. administration had told the American people. In addition, the national debt, as bad as it was perceived to be, was actually even greater than anyone realized. Clinton wanted an economic stimulus tax cut to get the economy out of recession. Greenspan told the president a tax cut should not be pursued, and if the White House went forward with the plan, the Fed would raise interest rates. Clinton was forced to break his campaign pledge to lower taxes. Even though the chairman and the president disagreed over economic policy, the president was powerless to do anything about it. In time, the Greenspan policy helped to get the economy out of the recession and into the longest economic boom in American history. Things went so well that Clinton reappointed Greenspan as chairman.

WHO CONTROLS THE BUREAUCRACY?

Because most boards of commissions and regulatory agencies are appointed by the president with Senate consent, political considerations always play a part in the appointment process. However, presidents come and go with great regularity, as do the appointed governing boards and commissions. It is the rank and file bureaucrats who are permanent, and they do not like political meddling.

While in office, presidents do have the power to promote their supporters and to use the budget to increase or decrease the influence of an agency. Reducing an agency's budget reduces its staff, which reduces its effectiveness. Increasing the agency's budget can have the opposite effect. Presidents can also reorganize an agency.

Congressional power over the bureaucracy is greater than that of the president. The Senate can affirm or reject presidential appointments. Congress can also abolish an agency or change its jurisdiction if it is unhappy with policy implementation. Finally, it is the Congress, through the appropriations process, that has the final say over how much money agencies will receive.

RULE SETTING, ALLIANCE BUILDING, AND IRON TRIANGLES

The regulatory agencies carry out their responsibilities by setting rules and regulations that industry must follow. Setting regulations is a participatory process in which industry becomes actively involved in determining the rules. Agencies welcome public participation by holding public hearings for testimony and advice. In most instances, the law requires agencies to consult with industry before rules and regulations can go into effect.

The rule-making process has fostered the creation of **iron triangles.** Typically iron triangles are informal alliances made up of three groups: 1) a particular industry and its lobbyists (for example, weapons manufacturers), 2) the congressional committee dealing with that industry (the Armed Services Committees of the Senate and House), and 3) the agency that actually is affected (in this case, the Pentagon). The groups that make up an iron triangle work together to formulate and implement policy in their area of interest. Lobbyists representing industry promote their special-interest agenda by claiming it is in the best interest of the American people. For example, drug companies may lobby the Food and Drug Administration to speed up the certification process for a medication because it will benefit the sick faster. Patients and drug companies will pressure Congress, which then pressures the FDA. These are powerful arguments, but speeding up the process can cause the FDA to overlook something dangerous about the medication.

Special interests also contribute money to congressional campaigns, and large contributors are never shy about asking for help from congressional representatives, who are asked to help put pressure on regulators, or at a minimum, to listen to the arguments that the special interests put forward for their cause.

Political scientists have recently seen a more complex political process at work. When issues affect many groups, pro and con coalitions of interest groups, members of Congress, and bureaucrats form a close working relationship. This political process is called either an **alliance network** or an **issue network** and is far more complicated than a simple three-part iron triangle.

For example, if a large factory was a polluter but had marginal profits, it would probably fight expensive environmental regulations. Compliance might drive the company into bankruptcy. But more is at stake than just the company. There are jobs involved and secondary industries that supply the raw materials for production at the company. A local government, which relies on the tax revenues from the company, also has something at stake. Environmental groups are going to be involved. This complicated situation would certainly result in the creation of issue networks for the purpose of influencing the regulatory agency's decisions.

After all the opportunities for input and debate have been exhausted, the regulatory agency writes and publishes the rules (this is its **quasi-legislative function**). If the industry still objects to the regulation, it can seek remedies in the courts by suing the regulatory agency. In the above example, if the company is forced to comply with the environmental laws, it could appeal the decision to the courts.

Because regulatory agencies invite so much controversy, there has been a recent trend toward deregulating the marketplace (removing government restrictions and regulations). Those in favor of **deregulation** claim that the competition of the marketplace is all the regulation that is needed. The deregulators say that regulation is too expensive and time-consuming and involves too much unnecessary red tape. They note that over the past 25 years, the **Civil Aeronautics Board**, which was responsible for regulating the airline industry, and the **Interstate Commerce Commission**, which regulated railroads and the trucking industry, were successfully phased out with little negative impact on consumers.

THE CIVIL SERVICE AND MAINTAINING NEUTRALITY

Today, the majority of government jobs are filled through the competitive **civil service** system. This system was established in 1883 with the passage of the *Pendleton Act*, a law that ended the "spoils system," or the practice of handing out government jobs in exchange for political support. The Office of Personnel Management acts as the bureaucracy's employment agency. OPM administers the civil service examination, publishes lists of job openings, and hires on the basis of merit. The intent is to create a competent, professional bureaucracy instead of one based on the "spoils system." A Merit Systems Protection Board investigates charges of agency corruption and incompetence and is supposed to protect "whistle blowers."

To ensure bureaucratic neutrality, Congress passed the **Hatch Act in 1939**. This law permitted bureaucrats the right to vote but not the right to actively campaign for political candidates, work for parties, or run for office. The act's revision of 1993 is less restrictive, allowing bureaucrats to join political parties, make campaign contributions, and display political advertising in the form of buttons and bumper stickers. Bureaucrats still cannot run for public office at any level, solicit campaign funds from subordinates, or make political speeches.

SUMMARY

- Remember that Congress is a bicameral (two-house) legislature, split into the Senate (in which all states receive equal representation) and the House of Representatives (in which representation is proportionate to population).

- The number of House seats a state gets is based on its population as determined by a census. Once the number of seats is determined, the state legislature draws the districts—often using partisan gerrymandering to ensure a majority for one party or the other.

- Congress has numerous powers that range from creation of all law, to funding all executive agencies, to declaring war. It is the first institution defined in the Constitution, and most scholars think that the Founders intended it to be the most powerful of the branches.

- How does a bill become a law? It is introduced to the House or Senate, referred to a committee, amended and debated, reintroduced to the general House and Senate, debated and amended once more, harmonized with its counterpart that has traveled through the other legislative body, voted on again and signed by the president.

- Given the large size of both houses of Congress, committees do most of the work of legislating. Committees can be standing, select, or joint, and are often further divided into subcommittees.

- The House is led by the speaker, while the Senate has two ceremonial leaders (the vice president and the president *pro tempore*) and one actual power broker—the majority leader.

- This chapter has a ton of laws. Try to remember them by using the four categories: (1) National Growth, Expansion, and Institution Building, (2) Regulation of Government and Industry, (3) Rights and Freedoms, and (4) Government Aid to the People.

- The president is the chief executive of the nation and is responsible for enforcing all laws. Over the years, the power of the presidency has grown dramatically—often at the expense of Congress.

- Even though the Constitution gives Congress the power to declare war, the nature of modern warfare has given the president control of this area. Though Congress does have tools to stop a wartime president, using them would generally be tantamount to political suicide.

- Being a good president often means going beyond the powers explicitly listed in the Constitution. Mastery of these "informal powers"—like consensus building or boosting the morale of the nation—often determines presidential greatness.

- The president relies a great deal on the Executive Office of the President (EOP)—his personal staff, which is ensconced within the west wing of the White House. The EOP is also home to a number of agencies that serve the president and are largely free from Congressional oversight.

- America has 15 cabinet departments, and each contains a huge array of agencies and bureaucracies designed to help enforce the law of the land. The cabinet secretaries are supposed to advise the president, but due to conflicting loyalties most presidents have kept them out of the loop and relied on the EOP and other informal advisors when making policy decisions.

- If a president has committed "treason, bribery, or other high crimes and misdemeanors," he can be impeached by a majority vote in the House and then removed from office with a two-thirds vote in the Senate.

- Remember that America has two legal systems: state and federal, and all people are under the jurisdiction of both. The federal system was created by the Constitution—all federal judges are appointed by the president and approved by the Senate, and the nation is divided into 91 federal districts.

- The Supreme Court rules on some very divisive social issues, and the battle to appoint new members has gotten more intense. Increasingly, presidents are looking to appoint younger and more ideological candidates who share their political philosophies.

- The Supreme Court is America's court of last resort and gets most all of its cases through appeals from lower courts or by granting writs of *certiorari* which cause cases to jump straight to their chambers.

- Though it is not mentioned in the Constitution, the Court's most important power is judicial review: the ability to strike down any state or federal law that is unconstitutional. This power was established in the case of *Marbury v. Madison* in 1803.

- Often called "the fourth branch of government," bureaucrats staff the gigantic executive agencies that run the federal government. To get these jobs, applicants must take competitive exams. Bureaucrats play a huge role in creating public policy by making rules that flesh out vague laws passed by Congress.

- We see four different types of bureaucracy in Washington: cabinet departments, independent agencies, regulatory commissions, and government corporations. Regulatory commissions are largely free of political control and have broad oversight responsibilities, while government corporations like the Postal Service are expected to turn a profit in the free market.

- Because the issues dealt with by bureaucrats are so technical and often pertain to a small interest group, we see the formation of iron triangles—cooperation between a bureaucracy (like the Department of Defense), a congressional committee (like the Senate Armed Services Committee) and an interest group (like weapons and aircraft manufacturers).

- Bureaucrats are supposed to be politically neutral and stable while their political overlords shift due to election results. Still, many suspect that they may take sides, and laws like the Hatch Act were designed to prevent this from happening.

PRACTICE QUESTIONS

1. The head of the Senate is the

   (A) President of the United States
   (B) Vice president of the United States
   (C) President *pro tempore*
   (D) Majority leader
   (E) Chief whip

2. One of the most important <u>legislative</u> powers of Congress is

   (A) the power to choose a president
   (B) the ability to propose amendments to the Constitution
   (C) the power to ratify treaties (in the Senate)
   (D) the power to confirm presidential appointments (in the Senate)
   (E) the ability to tax and spend

3. Congressional districts for the House are determined in the majority of states by

   (A) a vote held in the Senate by the majority party
   (B) an executive order of the president
   (C) the Supreme Court
   (D) a census and the various state legislatures
   (E) a nonpartisan commission

4. How are Cabinet members chosen?

   (A) By the president and are confirmed by the Senate
   (B) By the president and confirmed by both houses of Congress
   (C) By the House and confirmed by the Senate
   (D) By the Supreme Court
   (E) By the president alone—they need no confirmation

5. The Executive Office of the President (EOP) is

   (A) often a favored tool of the president due to the lack of Congressional oversight
   (B) relatively powerless since it is mentioned nowhere in the Constitution
   (C) located within the Department of Defense
   (D) a dumping ground for ex-cabinet secretaries who have done a poor job
   (E) always run by the vice president

6. What is the National Security Council (NSC) in charge of?

   (A) Matters relating to immigration
   (B) All matters relating to space exploration
   (C) Advising the president and helping to coordinate American foreign policy
   (D) The construction of nuclear weapons
   (E) Protecting the environment

7. "Senatorial courtesy" is

   (A) the process of getting judicial appointments approved by the House
   (B) when the Senate approves of the president's choice of Supreme Court Justice
   (C) when a Senator appoints a judge
   (D) when the president gets the approval of the two Senators from a state where he is about to name a federal judge
   (E) the law that makes Senators immune to prosecution

8. In the case of *United States v. Nixon*, the court ruled that

   (A) the legislative veto was unconstitutional
   (B) impoundment was illegal
   (C) the president has the power of executive privilege, but not in this case
   (D) President Nixon had the right to use executive privilege to withhold his tapes from investigators
   (E) President Nixon was guilty of high crimes and should be removed from office

9. The Pendleton Act

   (A) made it illegal for government employees to give money to political campaigns
   (B) was passed in the 1950's
   (C) was ruled unconstitutional
   (D) gave the Supreme Court the power to overturn Executive Privilege
   (E) ended the Spoils System and created a system of civil service exams

10. An iron triangle is

   (A) a name for an agreement between the secretaries of state, defense and treasury
   (B) the union of the army, navy and air force
   (C) a phenomenon that never occurs in American government
   (D) another name for the three branches of government
   (E) a policy-making group made of a committee of Congress, an interest group and a bureaucratic agency

10

PUBLIC POLICY

CONCEPTS

- Why do the poorest people in the United States have the least political power?
- What role does federalism play in the implementation of social welfare policy?
- Why is it so difficult to pass social welfare policy?
- Why are entitlement programs always a threat to the budget-making process?
- Why can it be said that the president is a secondary player when it comes to the economy?
- Why is it so difficult to write a budget for the United States?
- How can the president use the budget-making process to control his policy initiatives?

TERMS

- social welfare policy
- incrementalism
- policy fragmentation
- policy implementation
- agenda setting
- issue-attention cycle
- gross domestic product (GDP)
- laissez-faire economics
- Keynesian economics
- fiscal policy
- monetary policy
- trade deficit
- deficit spending
- Federal Reserve System
- supply-side economics
- Office of Management and Budget
- Congressional Budget Office
- mandatory spending
- discretionary spending
- social welfare
- entitlement programs
- Medicare
- Social Security
- COLAs
- food stamps
- supplemental public assistance programs
- Welfare Reform Act

The process of public policy making consists of first deciding what the problem is and then deciding how to solve it. Policy making can have three purposes.

- **Solving a social problem,** such as high crime rates, high unemployment, poverty among the aged, or teenage drinking

- **Countering threats,** such as terrorism or war

- **Pursuing an objective,** such as building a highway or finding a cure for cancer or AIDS

Policy can be achieved by prohibiting certain kinds of behavior, such as polygamy, murder, rape, and robbery. It can also be achieved by protecting certain activities. Granting patents and copyrights to individuals for their intellectual property, protecting the environment, and setting rules for workplace safety are all examples. Policy can promote some social activity; giving tax deductions for donations to charities is an example. Policy can be achieved by providing direct benefits to citizens. These benefits may include building roads, libraries, or hospitals. Benefits can also take the form of individual government subsidies, student loans, and pensions for the elderly.

Policy making can be frustrating because it often depends on public opinion, which can be fickle and unpredictable. The **issue-attention cycle** requires policy makers to act quickly, before the public becomes bored and loses interest. Public complaints over high energy prices can cause a flurry of policy making. But when prices go down, the public forgets about it until the next time.

Policy making often involves trade-offs between competing goods. To find additional energy resources may require access to pristine wildlife reserves. The risks to wildlife and the environment may be too high a price to pay for the additional energy. Conservation, smaller cars, and alternative energy sources may be better solutions, but each will have its supporters and opponents.

Because policy making can have unforeseen results and can touch off bitter disputes, legislators often use **incrementalism**—the slow, step-by-step approach to making policy. Or legislators may decide to use the policy of inaction because taking no action is one way of making policy. Conflicts over health care reform and social security entitlements can result in simply maintaining the status quo, not changing anything that is a policy.

MAKING POLICY

Policy making has a number of steps, and each is influenced by politics.

- The first involves **defining the role of government** in solving social and economic problems. The political left sees a greater responsibility for government than the right, with the result that governments on the left are larger, more active, and more expensive than on the right.

- **Agenda setting** identifies the social and economic problems, redefines them into political issues, and ranks them in order of importance. A citizen's socioeconomic status can determine which problems seem important and which don't. Poor people may rank job training high on the agenda, while the rich may rank tax cuts higher. When large numbers of people are affected, the concern will be ranked high. However, there are times when it is those with the most money who will have their issues placed high on the agenda. Large energy-producing corporations have a great deal of access to policymakers.

Policy can try to address the concerns of opposing sides. Strict environmental standards for oil exploration and refining try to address the concerns of two constituencies: the environmentalists and the petroleum producers.

A momentous event, such as a war, an oil embargo, or a collapsing stock market, may set the agenda. Old issues such as the quest for universal health care, the war on drugs, or environmental concerns can resurface. Scholars can force issues into the agenda through research studies. The discovery of the gap in the ozone layer is an example.

- **Policy formulation and adoption** can be accomplished in a number of ways. Sometimes the most difficult method is the legislative process in Congress, while the easiest may be through the executive branch by the use of executive orders from the president. Rules enacted by regulatory agencies or precedent-setting decisions by the Supreme Court are also sources of policy formulation and adoption. *Brown v. Board of Education* was certainly a policy-making decision.

- **Policy implementation** puts the policy into effect by enforcement through the appropriate government agency. Timetables and rules for carrying out policies as well as anticipating problems are all part of policy implementation. One of the major concerns of policy making is the unforeseen consequences. The three-strike rule, intended to get career criminals off the streets, has ended most plea-bargaining arrangements, causing overloaded courts, judges, and jails. The three-strike rule has turned out to be a much more expensive public policy than anticipated.

- **Policy evaluation** is the final step. Does a policy work? Have unforeseen consequences caused other policy problems? Evaluation provides feedback to the policy makers, so that modifications can be made to better solve the problems. Evaluation may determine that the problem has been solved and that the policy can be terminated.

OBSTACLES TO POLICY MAKING

The United States is a pluralist democracy, with multiple centers of power for making policy. Those interested in affecting policy-making concentrate their efforts at these many centers. Because the United States has a federal system of government, policy can be made at the local, state, and national levels. Separation of powers creates three policy-making centers: the executive, the legislative, and the judiciary. There is also the general bureaucracy, with its multiple policy-making centers. Trying to influence legislation, thousands of interest-group lobbyists descend upon these policy-making centers at all levels of government.

In their efforts to prevent tyranny and corruption, the framers created a policy-making nightmare by dispersing the power centers. Getting things done is cumbersome and frustrating. Multiple access points cause **policy fragmentation,** where many pieces of legislation deal with parts of policy problems but never deal with the entire problem. The war on drugs has at least 75 congressional committees with some type of jurisdiction or oversight; local and state law enforcement agencies are involved, as well as the Army, Navy, Air Force, Coast Guard, Border Patrol, Immigration and Naturalization Service, customs service, DEA, and the FBI.

Because so many agencies of government are involved, the drug war requires policy coordination. Interagency task forces try to iron out policy problems and conflicts between competing agencies, and Congress uses its oversight powers to change agency jurisdiction and give coherence to policy.

ECONOMIC POLICY

In 1992, Bill Clinton's informal campaign slogan was "It's the economy, stupid!" Of all the issues that face politicians, the economy is the most important. Success or failure usually rests with the person the public perceives as responsible for the condition of the economy; and whether it is true, the electorate usually holds the president responsible. Because of this phenomenon of responsibility, it can be said that Clinton was a very lucky candidate. In 1992 the economy was in recession and George Bush Sr. was blamed. In 1996 the economy was booming, and Clinton was given credit and reelected.

Because of the importance of the economy in the eyes of the voters, it is in a politician's self-interest to make policies that will increase people's standard of living. The electorate looks to Washington to achieve this objective. For the policy maker, the vexing question is how to achieve it.

Sound economic policy that achieves prosperity is probably the most elusive of all policies. There are many elements to the problem: inflation, deflation, interest rates, the supply of money in circulation, the profitability of corporations, foreign competition, international agreements, and consumer confidence, just to name a few. Complicating the problem are the various economic theories that drive policy decisions, and the various government agencies and institutions that make decisions affecting economic conditions.

ECONOMIC THEORY

Capitalist free-market systems in which both government and private industry play a role are called **mixed economies.** Mixed free-market systems are characterized by both private and public (government) ownership of the means of production and distribution of goods and services. The price of goods and services is determined by the free-market interplay of supply and demand. The profits after taxes are kept by the owners.

Free-market economic systems are plagued by periods of prosperity followed by periods of economic contraction (decreased activity, economic downturn). Because the United States has a mixed free-market system, the major problem for policy makers is how to maintain prosperity and economic growth while reducing the impact of the inevitable economic contraction. In capitalist systems, the basic question is to what extent the government should intervene.

Laissez-faire economists believe that the government should never become involved in economic issues. They believe that the narrow pursuit of individual profit serves the broader interest of society. Central to laissez-faire economics is the belief that free markets are governed by the laws of nature and government should not interfere with those laws. In vogue with rugged individualists in the nineteenth-century, laissez-faire economics disappeared as a viable government policy option during the Great Depression of the 1930s.

Perhaps the most influential economist of the twentieth-century was John Maynard Keynes, an interventionist. **Keynesian** economists believe the government can smooth out business cycles by influencing the amount of income individuals and businesses can spend on goods and services. This can be accomplished in two ways: fiscal policy and monetary policy.

Fiscal Policy

Fiscal policy refers to the government action of either lowering or raising taxes, which results in more or less consumer spending or enacting of government spending programs, such as building highways or hospitals. Keynesians believe that during economic downturns the government should spend money on projects to inject money into the economy. They are less worried about government deficit spending than about keeping the economy prosperous. A prosperous economy means a larger tax base, which will eventually correct deficit spending. In effect, the Keynesian school believes that when the economy is good, surplus taxes (money left over from tax revenues) should be saved to pay for the government spending that must take place during an economic downturn. Using this school of thought, the policy alternatives are obvious, but questions still remain. Should there be tax cuts? If so, how much, and who should get them? How much spending should the government engage in? How much **deficit spending** (funds raised by borrowing rather than taxation) should be allowed? The answers to these questions are extremely difficult, with major political consequences.

In the 1980s, the Reagan-Bush administration became the champion of the **supply-side** school of economic thought. The supply-siders take issue with supporters of Keynesian economics. Inflation is caused by too many dollars chasing too few goods. If the supply of goods is raised, the cost of the goods will decline. According to this theory, supply-siders argue that the government should cut taxes and spending on domestic programs to stimulate greater production.

Going along with supply-side theory, Congress in the 1980s enacted extensive tax cuts and reductions to social welfare programs, a policy later dubbed Reaganomics. Inflation was brought under control but huge yearly budget deficits, caused in part by a defense buildup, created a four-trillion-dollar debt. In the 1990s, budget surpluses began to shrink the deficit but these gains were reversed as a result of policies enacted during the Bush administration. Tax cuts followed by rising costs associated with the War on Terrorism and the invasion and occupation of Afghanistan and Iraq have resulted in record budget deficits. The Congressional Budget Office (CBO) estimated that the projected deficit total will grow from 7 trillion in 2005 to 12 trillion by 2015 if left unchecked.

Monetary Policy

Monetary policy refers to the process by which the government controls the supply of money in circulation and the supply of credit through the actions of the Federal Reserve Board (the Fed). The Fed can increase the amount of money in circulation by lowering interest rates. Rate reductions make borrowing money less expensive because interest on the money is low. This action usually inflates (expands) the economy, resulting in higher prices and wages. If the Fed raises interest rates, the impact on the economy will be deflationary, resulting in either more stable or lower prices or wages.

Monetary policy can be implemented by the Federal Reserve Board in three ways.

- By manipulating the **reserve requirement,** which raises or lowers the amount of money banks are required to keep on hand. Raising the reserve shrinks the amount of money available for borrowing, which raises interest rates. Lowering the reserve will have the opposite effect, lowering interest rates.

- By manipulating the **discount rate,** which raises or lowers the interest banks pay to the Federal Reserve Banks for borrowing money. Lowering the discount rate will lower the interest rates for consumer loans. Raising the discount rate will raise the interest rates for consumer loans. The higher the rate, the less consumers purchase.

- By manipulating **open market operations,** as the Federal Reserve buys and sells United States government bonds. People buy bonds because they have a better interest rate than savings accounts. When the Fed sells bonds, people withdraw money from banks to take advantage of the bond's higher interest rate. Because the bank has less to loan, consumer interest rates go up, which slows consumer spending and economic growth. When the Fed buys bonds, money flows back into the banks, which increases the money available for loans. With more money in the bank for consumers to borrow, interest rates are driven down. Lower interest rates means more consumer spending, which increases economic growth.

Some economists believe that government should intervene only to manipulate the money supply, an idea championed by Milton Friedman. These monetarists believe that the money supply should be increased at a constant rate to accommodate economic growth. Monetarists do not believe that interest rate changes and manipulation of tax rates have much of an impact on economic conditions.

In the 1990s, the U.S. economy expanded, creating record employment levels with little inflation. This expansion occurred without tax cuts. Many gave the credit to the monetary policy of Alan Greenspan and the Federal Reserve.

THE TOOLS OF ECONOMIC POLICY MAKING

The president receives advice on the state of the economy from the following departments and agencies:

- The Council of Economic Advisors
- The National Economic Council
- The Office of Management and Budget
- The Secretary of the Treasury

The president can influence the fiscal and monetary policies of these departments and agencies through his appointment power and policy initiatives. Remember that fiscal policy involves the budget, and monetary policy involves the money supply.

Fiscal Policy Making

The Director of the **Office of Management and Budget (OMB)** is responsible for initiating the budget process. The director meets with the president to discuss his policy initiatives. The state of the economy is discussed, centering on government revenue projections, which is the predicted income from taxes. Based on the president's priorities, some executive departments will receive more money than others. The OMB then writes the president's budget and submits it to Congress. Upon its arrival the budget is sent to three committees. The **House Ways and Means Committee** deals with the taxing aspects of the budget. **Authorization committees** in both houses decide what programs Congress wants to fund. **Appropriations committees** in both houses then decide how much money to spend for those programs that have been authorized.

The budget process is complicated, politically divisive, and in recent years nearly impossible to conclude. The president's projected revenues and expenditures often conflict with those of Congress. Congress often simply does not trust the president's numbers, and conversely, the president does not trust Congress's. These yearly budget problems forced passage of the **Budget Reform Act of 1974**, which created the Office of Management and Budget, as well as the **Congressional Budget Office**, with budget committees in both the House and Senate. The congressional committees set their own revenue and spending levels. Negotiations then take place among the White House and the two houses of Congress in an effort to get one budget acceptable to everyone. Failure to achieve a budget by the beginning of the fiscal year could mean shutting down the government and sending employees home. When this occurs, budget stop-gap bills are passed to temporarily appropriate money to keep the government operating.

The **1990 Budget Enforcement Act** was an effort to streamline the budget process and make it easier to arrive at a compromise budget. The law categorizes government expenditures as either mandatory or discretionary spending. **Mandatory spending** is required by law, to fund programs such as the **entitlement programs, Social Security, Medicare,** veterans' pensions, and payment on the national debt. **Discretionary spending** programs are not required by law and include defense, education, highways, research grants, and all government operations. Discretionary programs are the primary targets for making cuts to balance the budget.

TRADE POLICY

The United States is by far the richest nation in the world. The output of the economy of the state of California alone ranks among the top ten nations in the world. The economic outputs of each of the three cities of Los Angeles, Chicago, and New York rank among the output of the top 20 nations. For better or for worse, the United States is the largest producer and consumer of products.

Foreign nations depend on the United States as a market for their products, as we depend on them for ours. The **ratio of imported products to exported products** is called the **balance of trade. Trade deficits** occur when imports exceed exports. Trade deficits cause wealth to flow from a nation. When nations face trade deficits, they often place restrictions on imported goods. The nation facing the restrictions can take retaliation by imposing high import taxes or unfair regulations on products, effectively keeping out foreign goods. Trade wars can result, stopping trade between countries. Trade surpluses are the result of more money flowing into a country than out. The oil-producing nations have huge amounts of money flowing into their treasuries and therefore have large trade surpluses.

In an effort to promote trade, the United States signed the **General Agreement on Tariffs and Trade (GATT)**, which evolved into the World Trade Organization (WTO). The 125 members of the WTO account for 97 percent of the world's trade. The organization works to lower tariffs and quotas and reduce unfair trade practices.

In an effort to promote free trade between the United States, Canada, and Mexico, the three nations have signed the **North American Free Trade Agreement** (**NAFTA**), effectively removing import tariffs from one another's products. As an economic policy, NAFTA is controversial. It is opposed by U.S. industrial labor unions because of their fear that jobs will be lost to cheap Mexican labor. Others fear that the industrial capacity of the United States will be damaged because factories will move to Mexico where environmental laws are not strictly enforced. Those who support NAFTA claim it will improve the U.S. economy and will also create jobs in Mexico, resulting in less illegal immigration. Supporters also claim that a richer Mexico will purchase more American products. NAFTA has proven to be something of a mixed blessing. Its passage has led to cheaper labor (in Mexico) for many U.S. companies and an increase in trade between the two countries. Nevertheless, many American jobs have undeniably been sent south of the border, and many Mexican farmers are losing their land in a futile attempt to compete with American agribusinesses.

DOMESTIC POLICY

While economic policy is contentious (causes disputes), domestic policy is sometimes even more so because it gets to the very essence of the purposes of government. Liberals believe government has an obligation to provide for social welfare, to help the needy. Conservatives believe social-welfare programs are encroachments on individual liberties and responsibilities. They think these programs turn the government into an instrument used to create a permanent class of the underprivileged, dependent upon government handouts. Somewhere in between are the moderates who believe government should provide opportunities and limited help during difficult times.

The twentieth-century has seen a dramatic change in the way society perceives the role of government in providing for the basic needs of people. Before the Great Depression, there were no government programs to help people who suffered from the hardships of old age, disabilities, unemployment, and poverty. So many people needed help in the 1930s that the government had no choice but to enact programs to create jobs, provide housing, and feed the hungry. Later on, the **Great Society programs** of the Johnson administration expanded government welfare programs, but because of the expense and questions about their effectiveness, many of the Great Society programs were eliminated or scaled back during and after the Reagan administration.

Today there are two kinds of social-welfare programs.

- **Social insurance programs** are in reality **national insurance programs into which employers and employees pay taxes.** Because individuals pay into these programs, the benefits derived are considered by the public to have been earned. There seems to be little public debate over a citizen's "right" to Social Security.

- **Public assistance programs,** on the other hand, are not perceived as earned. These programs are a result of condition and a government responsibility to help the needy. Recipients are not required to pay into the system to get something out. Public assistance is considered by some to be a "handout" to the lazy. Because politicians understand this public perception, public-policy initiatives from both parties have concentrated on forcing people on public assistance to either seek work or enter work-training programs. The federal government has begun to provide states with block grants for initiating reform programs that put people on public assistance to work.

SOCIAL SECURITY

Social Security is an entitlement program mandated by law. The government must pay benefits to all people who meet the requirements of the program. Changing the law would require congressional action. Because the largest voting block of the electorate is those nearing or at retirement age, there is little chance of major changes to the system, even though the experts warn that the Social Security trust fund will go bankrupt in the near future. Currently, entitlement programs account for the largest expense in the federal budget.

In its original form Social Security only provided benefits to retired persons beginning at age 65. The program has now been expanded to include four categories of persons.

- Retired workers and their survivors who are presently age 65 and older receive monthly payments from the Social Security trust fund. To help maintain a recipient's standard of living, recipients are entitled to a **COLA** (cost of living adjustment) if the inflation rate exceeds 3 percent. COLAs put a strain on the ability of the trust fund to meet its obligations. Changes in the demographic composition of society are also putting a strain on the system. Society is aging, and the ratio of workers to retirees is declining. Because Social Security is a pay-as-you-go system, the money that is now paid into the system pays the present beneficiaries. As the ratio of workers to retirees continues to decline, workers will have to pay higher taxes to maintain the income of those who are retired.

- Insurance for the disabled provides monthly payments to those citizens who are permanently and totally disabled. The category of persons who fit the definition of disabled has been expanded to include the learning disabled and those dependent on drugs and alcohol.

- **Medicare** provides government assistance to people over 65 for health care. For those retirees who pay an additional tax on their social security benefit, Medicare part B will pay approximately 80 percent of their doctor's bills. The high cost of health care has nearly bankrupted Medicare.

- Temporary unemployment insurance for those out of work provides a weekly benefit, for a limited time. Each state government administers its own unemployment insurance program. Both the federal and state governments pay into a trust fund to provide the benefit. Each state determines the amount and duration of the benefit, with most around $200 a week for 26 weeks. The $200 must pay for all living expenses: rent, food, clothing, etc.

SOCIAL WELFARE

No matter how well intentioned the government has been, and no matter how much money has been spent, poverty has remained a perpetual problem for policy makers at both the state and federal levels. The first federal welfare programs were established by the Social Security Act in the 1930s. The largest and most controversial became known as Aid to Families with Dependent Children (AFDC).

All social welfare programs are designed to help targeted groups. Public assistance programs, known as welfare, target families whose total income falls below the federally determined minimum amount required to provide for the basic needs of a family. The present amount is approximately $17,000 for a family of four. The larger the family, the more income is required and the more money is paid out. Critics claimed that welfare was an incentive for families to have more children. Further complicating matters were complaints from recipients about a system that was degrading because investigators, looking for welfare cheaters, were invading their privacy.

In addition to AFDC, the federal government has established **supplemental public assistance programs** (known as SSI) to help the disabled and the aged who are living at or near the poverty level. To improve the diet and increase the buying power of the poor, the federal government also provides **food stamps**. Recipients use government-provided debit cards to help pay for food. Both SSI and the food-stamp program are federal programs administered through local and state agencies.

In an effort to reduce the number of people living on public assistance, the **Welfare Reform Act** was passed in 1996. Under the new law, social-welfare programs are funded by both the state and federal governments, with the federal government contributing the greatest share in the form of block grants. Block grants are important because they allow states to experiment with new types of programs designed to get people off welfare and into work programs. The administration of programs (the distribution of cash payments) and the incentives for finding work and providing job training are left to the states. The intent of the law is to reduce the welfare roles and force people to find work. This is accomplished by

- Abolishing Aid to Families with Dependent Children (AFDC), which has affected 22 percent of the families in the United States with children, replacing it with Temporary Assistance for Needy Families (TANF)

- Requiring adults to find work within two years or be cut off

- Placing a lifetime limit of five years for welfare eligibility, although it is possible to get a waiver if a recipient is actively seeking work

- Prohibiting aliens from receiving assistance

The political debate over public assistance centers around two issues: Who pays how much, and what is the fair standard to be used for the recipient? Both Democrats and Republicans have tried to reduce these programs. Cutting them, however, places more people at risk, reducing food stamp programs and school lunch programs, causing increased hunger. To make matters more complicated, the Welfare Reform Act moved millions off the welfare rolls of the states as it coincided with a boom in unemployment.

HEALTH CARE

One of the most vexing problems for policy makers is what to do about the high cost of health care. Americans spend more than 17 percent of the nation's **gross domestic product, or GDP** (the total of goods and services produced in a year), on health care. The United States has the most expensive health care system in the world and is the only fully industrialized nation without a national health care program. High costs have not guaranteed any longer life expectancy, nor better treatment than that found in other industrialized nations. Instead of a national program run by the government, most Americans rely on various types of insurance programs to pay for health care costs. The average cost for these insurance programs is at least $5,000 per year and is rising faster than the cost of living. The premiums for these health care programs are paid by workers and employers. For many reasons, but primarily because of cost, 30 percent of the population is without health insurance.

As with other government programs, the electorate is divided on how to solve the two issues of universal health care and the burden of health care costs. Voters seem to want increased coverage but there is little evidence to indicate they are willing to pay for it. The only tax increases the American electorate is willing to pay are the so-called "sin taxes" on alcohol and tobacco products, which will not generate enough revenues to provide increased coverage. Another basic issue for which there is no consensus is whether health benefits should be a government or privately administered program. With little public consensus, reform is difficult.

An ill-fated attempt at health care reform was made in the first Clinton administration. The proposed policy called for universal coverage and strict cost controls. The policy would have required increased taxes coupled with cost-cutting limits on the types of medical procedures allowable. The lack of public consensus killed the proposal within a year.

Some incremental changes to health care have been possible since the defeat of the Clinton program. Workers who change or lose their jobs can now maintain their health insurance for an extended time. Insurance companies are no longer permitted to deny coverage for pre-existing conditions. Mental health programs are now covered the same way as surgical procedures, and new mothers and their infants are guaranteed a 48-hour hospital stay.

The debate over health care continued during the 2000 presidential election. Both candidates agreed that something had to be done about both escalating costs and the increasing numbers of uninsured. The Democrats promoted a policy of a government-paid prescription drug program for senior citizens. The Republicans promoted a prescription-drug program run by insurance providers, but again there was no consensus.

Many taxpayers believe that taxes are too high, government is too big, and there is too much waste in federal programs. But, compared with the taxes paid in the 13 most industrialized nations, the United States' tax burden is almost the lightest—it ranks 12th. It appears that in the years ahead, as the population ages, either greater resources will be needed to pay for Social Security and health care benefits, or benefits will have to be cut.

SUMMARY

- Public policy is made when the government decides to take action to solve a societal problem, and consists of five steps:

  (1) defining the role of government,

  (2) agenda setting,

  (3) policy formulation,

  (4) policy implementation, and

  (5) policy evaluation.

- Economic policy has been one of the most important areas of public policy in American history. Policy makers have oscillated between supporting laissez-faire free market principles and redistributionist, interventionist policies.

- The United States has joined international trade organizations like the World Trade Organization (WTO) and the North American Free Trade Agreement (NAFTA) in order to boost our commerce with the rest of the world. Nevertheless, we still use tariffs and subsidies to protect large swathes of our industry and agriculture.

- Before FDR, the federal government did not engage in much domestic policy making, but since that era we have seen the rise of programs like Social Security, Welfare (through the Aid to Families With Dependant Children and new state-based systems) and Medicaid.

PRACTICE QUESTIONS

1. The Office of Management and Budget (OMB) is in charge of

    (A) assessing the nation's economic health
    (B) writing the national budget to reflect the interests of Congress
    (C) planning out the national budget for the president
    (D) providing long-term and highly theoretical economic advice
    (E) protecting the environment

2. Which of the following is NOT generally a step in the policy-making process?

    (A) Policy formulation
    (B) Abandoning governmental solutions for societal problems
    (C) Policy implementation
    (D) Policy evaluation
    (E) Agenda setting

3. Which of the following is an example of a policy that a believer in laissez-faire economics might support?

    (A) Giving the EPA greater power to fine factories that contribute to global warming
    (B) Increasing taxes across higher income groups to aid the poor
    (C) Creation of a law that protects unions and grants them collective bargaining rights
    (D) The implementation of a flat tax
    (E) Spending more money on farmers to support America's agricultural output

4. Which of the following people would NOT receive money from Social Security?

    (A) Retired workers
    (B) The widow of a retired worker
    (C) A quadriplegic
    (D) A worker who has just lost her job
    (E) A family that is chronically poor

5. When a nation's imports exceed its exports, the country is

    (A) running a trade deficit
    (B) running a trade surplus
    (C) in default
    (D) bankrupt
    (E) automatically expelled from the WTO

11

Civil Rights and Civil Liberties

CONCEPTS

- Why would Justice Thurgood Marshall blame the Supreme Court for the racial policies practiced in the United States before the *Brown* decision?

- Why did the Supreme Court allow the use of affirmative-action programs?

- Why is it said that the Warren Court took the handcuffs off the criminals and put them on the police?

- What mechanism did the Supreme Court use to ensure the rights of defendants in state criminal prosecutions?

- What impact has the interpretation of speech as a preferred right had on the government's power to censure?

- How does the Supreme Court interpret the right to privacy on matters dealing with human reproduction?

- How has the Supreme Court changed its reasoning in dealing with religious activities in schools financed by the public?

TERMS

- selective incorporation
- Fourteenth Amendment
- freedom of speech
- freedom of the press
- freedom of assembly
- freedom of religion
- slander
- libel
- obscenity
- preferred position doctrine
- prior restraint
- rights of the accused
- double jeopardy
- unreasonable search and seizure
- probable cause
- exclusionary rule
- objective good faith
- inevitable discovery rule
- cruel and unusual punishment
- implied right to privacy
- due process
- Jim Crow laws
- poll tax
- grandfather clause
- Civil Rights Act of 1964
- *de facto* segregation
- *de jure* segregation
- affirmative action
- Equal Rights Amendment
- abortion

How to Discuss a Court Case

First, an important tip: In responding to an essay question involving Supreme Court decisions, do not spend a lot of time giving narratives on the background of cases. Explain the essential questions and answers of cases, as well as the reasoning the Court used in the decision. The most important aspect of a case, for political science purposes, is its impact on government or society. When asked about a case, make sure the consequences of the decision are discussed. For example, the most important consequence of *Marbury v. Madison* is the establishment of judicial review, which is arguably the most important principle the Court ever enshrined. The consequence of *Heart of Atlanta Motel v. United States* is the affirmation of the power of Congress, through the use of the commerce clause, to end segregation by law in the United States.

The term **civil liberties** generally applies to those protections (enjoyed by all Americans) from the abuse of government power. The term **civil rights** is used specifically to describe protections from discrimination based on race, gender, or other minority status. Often, the term is used to refer specifically to the struggles of African Americans for equal status (e.g., the Civil Rights Movement).

The Extension of Civil Liberties Through American History

In *Barron v. Baltimore* (1833), the Supreme Court determined that the Bill of Rights restricted the national government but not the state governments. It was not until 1925 that the Court overturned this ruling, citing Fourteenth Amendment restrictions on the states ("no state shall... deprive any person of life, liberty, or property, without due process of law; nor deny to any person within its jurisdiction the equal protection of the laws"). That case, *Gitlow v. New York*, concerned freedom of speech and freedom of the press. The Court ruled that state limits on speech and the press could not exceed the limits allowed the national government.

Since then, the Court has applied the Bill of Rights to state law on a case-by-case basis. This process is called **selective incorporation.** Currently, the following rights have NOT been incorporated and may thus be restricted by the states:

- The Second Amendment right to bear arms
- The Third Amendment protection against forced quartering of troops in private homes
- The Fifth Amendment right to indictment by a grand jury
- The Seventh Amendment right to a jury trial in civil cases
- The Eighth Amendment protection against excessive bail and fines

All other provisions of the Bill of Rights, however, apply equally to the states and the national government. Thus, while the states may place restrictions on gun ownership (because the Second Amendment has not been incorporated), they may not deprive accused felons of their right to legal counsel (a right incorporated in *Gideon v. Wainwright*, 1963).

In defining individual rights, the Court has consistently weighed the rights of individuals against the needs of society at large. Therefore, none of the rights guaranteed in the Bill of Rights is absolute.

First Amendment Rights and Restrictions

The First Amendment guarantees **freedom of speech, freedom of the press, freedom of assembly,** and **freedom of religion.** None of these important rights, however, is absolute. Throughout the nation's history, the Supreme Court has ruled that these rights may be limited in the interest of the greater public good. It has also ruled, however, that such restrictions must be well justified, well defined, and limited only to those few instances in which the public welfare is genuinely threatened.

Freedom of Speech

The **most famous limit** on free speech is the **clear and present danger test.** In the case of *Schenck v. United States* (1919), Justice Oliver Wendell Holmes argued that a person may not falsely scream "fire!" in a crowded theater, because doing so would likely result in panic. The Court has also ruled that there is no constitutional protection for false defamatory speech (called *slander* when it is spoken and *libel* when it is in a more permanent form, such as print), obscenity, or speech intended to incite violence.

Since the 1940s, the Court has followed the **preferred position doctrine** in determining the limits of free speech. The doctrine reflects the Court's belief that freedom of speech is fundamental to liberty; therefore, any limits on free speech must address severe, imminent threats to the nation. They must also be limited to constraining those threats; any restriction that fails to meet this test would probably be overturned by the Supreme Court. The Court continues to protect offensive but nonthreatening speech such as flag burning (usually undertaken by protesters, who burn the flag as a symbolic indication that the country has failed to protect American values such as democracy and freedom for all).

Important Cases

Schenck v. U.S (1919). This case, decided by Chief Justice Oliver Wendell Holmes, established that speech which evokes "a clear and present danger" is not permissible. He famously used the example of someone falsely yelling "fire!" in a crowded theater as an example of prohibited speech.

Gitlow v. New York (1925). This case created the "Bad Tendency Doctrine," which held that speech could be restricted even if it only has a tendency to lead to illegal action. Though this element of the decision was quite restrictive, Gitlow also selectively incorporated freedom of speech to state governments.

Chaplinksy v. New Hampshire (1942). This case established that certain offensive types of speech—deemed "fighting words," could be prohibited.

Dennis v. U.S. (1951). In *Dennis*, the Court held that the federal government can limit speech even if it does not directly lead to action. In doing so, the Court was upholding the Smith Act—a law that made it a crime to support any communist organization.

Tinker v. Des Moines (1969). Students in an Iowa school were suspended for wearing black armbands to protest the Vietnam war. The Court ruled that this suspension was unconstitutional, and that public school students do not "shed their constitutional rights at the schoolhouse door."

Brandenburg v. Ohio (1969). Brandenburg, a leader in the Ku Klux Klan, made a speech at a Klan rally and was later convicted under an Ohio criminal syndicalism law. The law was found unconstitutional under the First and Fourteenth Amendments. The Court's main point was that states were not allowed to prevent or punish inflammatory speech unless it will lead to imminent lawless action.

Bethel School District v. Fraser (1986). This case gave public school officials the authority to suspend students for speech considered to be lewd or indecent.

Hustler Magazine v. Falwell (1988). In this much-publicized case, the Court held that intentional infliction of emotional distress was permissible First Amendment speech—so long as such speech was about a public official, and could not reasonably be construed to state actual facts about its subject.

Texas v. Johnson (1989). *Johnson* established that burning the American flag is an example of permissible free speech, and struck down numerous anti-flag burning laws.

U.S v. Eichman (1990). Following the *Johnson* case, *Eichman* invalidated the federal government's 1989 Flag Protection Act as an unconstitutional restriction of free speech.

Virginia v. Black (2002). This case stated that cross burning was the equivalent of "fighting words," and was thus unconstitutional.

Freedom of the Press

On occasion the government has tried to control the press, usually claiming national security interests. This occurred during the 1990 Persian Gulf War, when the Pentagon limited media access to the war zone and censored outgoing news reports. The media objected to these limitations. Such conflicts usually end up in the courts, where judges are forced to weigh conflicting national interests: the **need to be informed versus security concerns.** A previous similar case involved the Pentagon Papers (1971), a secret report on American involvement in Vietnam. The report was leaked to the *New York Times*, which published excerpts from the report. The government tried to halt further publication, claiming that national security was at stake. In that case, the Court rejected the government's efforts to prevent publication (called **prior restraint**), ruling that the public's need to be well informed outweighed the national security issues raised. The Pentagon Papers case demonstrates the preferred position doctrine.

An even more contentious issue involves the media's responsibility to reveal the sources of their information. The Supreme Court has ruled that reporters are not exempt from testifying in court cases and that they can be asked to name their sources. Reporters who refuse to do so, as many have, can be jailed. A number of states have enacted **shield laws** to protect reporters in state cases, but in other states and in federal cases reporters have no such protection.

As mentioned above, libel and obscenity are not protected by the First Amendment. In the case of *Miller v. California* (1973), the Court established a **three-part obscenity test:**

- Would the average person, applying community standards, judge the work as appealing primarily to people's baser sexual instincts?

- Does the work lack other value, or is it also of literary, artistic, political, or scientific interest?

- Does the work depict sexual behavior in an offensive manner?

Important Cases

Near v. Minnesota (1931). *Near* established that state injunctions to prevent publication violate the free press provision of the First Amendment and are unconstitutional. This case is important in that it selectively incorporates freedom of the press and prevents prior restraint.

New York Times v. Sullivan (1964). If a newspaper prints an article that turns out to be false but that the newspaper thought was true at the time of publication, has the newspaper committed libel? This case said no.

New York Times v. U.S. (1971). When Defense Department employee Daniel Ellsburg leaked some confidential files indicating that the war in Vietnam was going poorly, the government sought to prevent the publication of these "Pentagon Papers" by the New York Times. In this case, the Court held that executive efforts to prevent the publication violated the First Amendment were forbidden.

Hazelwood School v. Kuhlmeier (1988). In *Hazelwood*, the Court held that school officials have sweeping authority to regulate free speech in student run newspapers.

Freedom of Assembly and Association

The First Amendment protects the right of people to assemble peacefully. That right does not extend to violent groups or to demonstrations that would incite violence. Furthermore, the government may place reasonable restrictions on crowd gatherings, provided such restrictions are applied equally to all groups. Demonstrators have no constitutional right, for example, to march on and thereby close down a highway. They may not block the doorways of buildings. In short, crowd gatherings must not unnecessarily disrupt day-to-day life. That is why groups must apply for licenses to hold a parade or street fair.

The Court has also ruled that the combined rights of freedom of speech and freedom of assembly imply a **freedom of association**. This means that the government may not restrict the number or type of groups or organizations people belong to, provided those groups do not threaten national security.

Important Cases

DeJonge v. Oregon (1937). *DeJonge* is the landmark Supreme Court case that held that peaceable assembly for lawful discussion cannot be made a crime. It is also important in that it selectively incorporated the right to lawfully assemble on to all state governments.

Thornhill v. Alabama (1940). Labor unions have been controversial since the dawn of the industrial revolution—did their strikes constitute a form of unlawful assembly? In *Thornhill*, the Court held that strikes by unions were not unlawful.

Cox v. New Hampshire (1941). When a group of Jehovah's Witnesses were arrested for marching in New Hampshire without a permit, they claimed that permits themselves were an unconstitutional abridgment of their First Amendment freedoms. In *Cox*, the Court held that cities and towns could legitimately require parade permits in the interest of public order.

Grayned v. City of Rockford (1972). In *Grayned*, the Court held that demonstrations near schools that disrupted classes could legally be banned.

Lloyd Corporation v. Tanner (1972). This case allowed the owners of a shopping mall to throw out people protesting the Vietnam War. The key element here is that malls are private spaces, not public. As a result, protesters have substantially fewer assembly rights in malls and other private establishments.

Boy Scouts of America v. Dale (2000). Private organizations' First Amendment right of expressive association allows them to choose their own membership and expel members based on their sexual orientation even if such discrimination would otherwise be prohibited by anti-discrimination legislation designed to protect minorities in public accommodations. As a result of this case, the Boy Scouts of America were allowed to expel any member who was discovered to be homosexual.

Freedom of Religion

The Constitution guarantees the right to the free exercise of religion, meaning that the government may not prevent individuals from practicing their faiths. This right is not absolute, however. Human sacrifice, to give an extreme example, is not allowed. The courts have ruled that polygamy is not protected by the Constitution, nor is the denial of medical treatment to a child, regardless of individual religious beliefs. However, the Court has ruled that Jehovah's Witnesses cannot be required to salute the American flag and that Amish children may stop attending school after the eighth grade. In all cases, the **Court weighs individual rights to free religious exercise against society's needs.**

The Constitution also prevents the government from establishing a state religion (the establishment clause). The establishment clause has been used to prevent school prayer, government-sponsored displays of the Christmas nativity, and state bans on the teaching of evolution (because such bans were religiously motivated). However, the wall between church and state is not rock solid. The Court has allowed government subsidies to provide some aspects of parochial education (such as lunches, textbooks, and buses). It has also allowed for tax credits for non-public school costs. In deciding whether a law violates the establishment clause, the Court uses a three-part test, called the **Lemon test** after the case *Lemon v. Kurtzman* (1971):

- Does the law have a secular, rather than a religious, purpose?

- Does the law neither promote nor discourage religion?

- Does the law avoid "excessive entanglement" of the government and religious institutions?

Important Cases

Engel v. Vitale (1962). This landmark case prohibited state-sponsored recitation of prayer in public schools.

Abington School Dist. v. Schempp (1963). Given the Court's ruling in *Engel*, it's not surprising that in *Abington* they decided that the Establishment Clause of the First Amendment forbids state-mandated reading of the Bible, or recitation of the Lord's Prayer in public schools.

Epperson v. Arkansas (1968). In line with the Establishment Clause, *Epperson* prohibited states from banning the teaching of evolution in public schools.

Lemon v. Kurtzman (1971). This case dealt with state laws intending to give money to religious schools or causes. The Court held that in order to be consistent with the Establishment Clause, the money had to meet three qualifications: (1) it must have a legitimate secular purpose, (2) it must not have the primary effect of either advancing or inhibiting religion, and (3) it must not result in an excessive entanglement of government and religion. These qualifications are known as the "Lemon Test."

Wisconsin v. Yoder (1972). This case dealt with the Amish community's desire to pull their children from public school before the age of 16 so that they could help with farm and domestic work. The Court sided with the Amish and held that parents may remove children from public school for religious reasons.

THE RIGHTS OF THE ACCUSED

Rights granted to the accused are a fundamental protection against governmental abuse of power. Many of the these rights are found in the Fifth Amendment. Without them, the government could imprison its political opponents without trial or could guarantee conviction through numerous unfair prosecutorial tactics. However, these rights are also controversial. Anti-crime organizations and politicians frequently decry these protections when arguing that it is too difficult to capture, try, and imprison criminals. These accusations have grown louder and more frequent since the 1960s, when the Warren Court (the Supreme Court under Chief Justice Earl Warren) greatly expanded those protections that are granted to criminal defendants.

Important Cases

Weeks v. U.S. (1914). Though the Constitution is unequivocal when it forbids unlawful search and seizure, such ill-gotten evidence was still commonly used to prosecute defendants. Weeks established the Exclusionary Rule, which held that illegally obtained evidence could not be used in federal court.

Olmstead v. U.S. (1928). The Fourth Amendment clearly prohibits unlawful search and seizure. But do wiretaps of phone conversations fit this category? In *Olmstead*, the courts held that they did not, and allowed unlimited federal wiretapping of the nation's phones.

Powell v. Alabama (1932). The Constitution is clear in the Sixth Amendment when it guarantees all those accused of a federal crime the right to have a lawyer. But what about those accused of state crimes? Should they get a lawyer if they can't afford one? In *Powell*, the Court ruled that state governments must provide counsel in cases involving the death penalty to those who can't afford it.

Betts v. Brady (1942). The *Betts* case overruled *Powell* and established that state governments did not have to provide lawyers to indigent defendants in capital cases.

Mapp v. Ohio (1961). By 1961, the Exclusionary Rule meant that any unlawfully gathered evidence could not be introduced in federal court, but such evidence was introduced all the time in state courts. The Mapp case extended the Exclusionary Rule to the states, increasing the protections for defendents.

Gideon v. Wainwright (1963). This was a powerful repudiation of *Betts v. Brady*. Here, the Warren court strongly holds that all state governments must provide an attorney in all cases for those who can't afford one.

Escobedo v. Illinois (1964). *Escobedo* is another important Warren Court decision. Here, the Court held that any defendant who asked for a lawyer had to have one granted to him—or any confession garnered after that point would be inadmissible in court.

Miranda v. Arizona (1966). *Miranda* is the most dramatic and well-known of the Warren Court decisions. Here they find that all defendants must be informed of all their legal rights before they are arrested. It is thanks to *Miranda* that we all know the phrase "You have the right to remain silent…"

Katz v. United States (1967). Given the abuses of the FBI and J. Edgar Hoover, the court overturned *Olmstead* and held that warrants were, in fact, required to listen in on phone conversations.

Oregon v. Elstad (1985). What happens if someone immediately confesses before he or she is read their rights? Is the confession admissible? Here, the Court hold that such confessions are admissible.

NJ vs TLO

Protection from Self-Incrimination

The Constitution protects individuals from **self-incrimination.** A defendant cannot be forced to testify at trial, and the jury is not supposed to infer guilt when a defendant chooses to not testify. Furthermore, a defendant must be notified of his right to remain silent, his right to a lawyer, and his protection against self-incrimination at the time of his arrest. This precedent was established in the

1966 Supreme Court case *Miranda v. Arizona*. **Ernesto Miranda** had been arrested for kidnapping and rape, and, within two hours of his arrest, he had confessed to his crimes. His lawyer appealed the case on the grounds that Miranda had not been advised of his constitutional rights (e.g., the protection against self-incrimination and the right to legal counsel). In *Miranda*, the Supreme Court decided that the police had deprived Miranda of his **Fourteenth Amendment right to due process.** Those rights have since come to be known as Miranda rights.

For years, the courts rarely admitted into evidence confessions from arrestees who had not been properly "Mirandized." In recent years, however, the Supreme Court has defined some situations in which such confessions are admissible. In 1991, the Court ruled that a coerced confession does not automatically invalidate a conviction. Rather, an appeals court may consider all evidence entered at trial. If the court decides that a conviction was probable even without the confession, it may let the guilty verdict stand.

Protection from Unreasonable Search and Seizure

The **Fourth Amendment** limits the power of the government to search for evidence of criminal activity. When the police want to search private property, in most circumstances they must first go before a judge and justify the search. If the judge is convinced that the search is likely to uncover evidence of illegality—called **probable cause**—the judge issues a search warrant, which limits where the police may search and what they may take as evidence. Evidence found by police who disregard this procedure may not be admitted as evidence in trial. This is called the **exclusionary rule.** The Supreme Court applied the exclusionary rule to federal trials in 1911. In the 1961 case *Mapp v. Ohio*, the Court incorporated the exclusionary rule, thus making it applicable to state trials as well.

As with all constitutional rights, however, there are exceptions to this rule. In 1984, the Supreme Court established the **objective good faith** exception, which allows for convictions in cases in which a search was not technically legal (either because it violated the warrant or because the warrant itself was faulty) but was conducted under the assumption that it was legal. The Court has also determined that illegally seized evidence that would eventually have been found legally is also admissible in court. This principle is known as the **inevitable discovery rule.**

There are also circumstances under which the police may conduct a search without a warrant. Police may conduct an immediate search following a legal arrest, for example. Police may also conduct an immediate search of private property if the owner consents to that search. Evidence found in plain view may be seized immediately; if, for example, a person is growing marijuana on his front lawn, the police may seize that evidence without first acquiring a search warrant. Finally, police may conduct an immediate search if they have probable cause to believe they will find evidence of criminal activity, especially when they believe that evidence would disappear by the time they received a warrant and returned. The police would later have to demonstrate that they had probable cause in court.

Rights to an Attorney and a Speedy Trial

The **Sixth Amendment** guarantees criminal defendants the **right to an attorney in federal cases.** In 1932, the Supreme Court used the Fourteenth Amendment to incorporate this right in capital cases ("the Scottsboro boys" case). In the 1963 case *Gideon v. Wainwright*, the Court ruled that all criminal defendants in state courts were entitled to legal counsel. In both cases, the Court ruled that the state must provide a lawyer to defendants too poor to hire a lawyer. The Court has since extended this protection to misdemeanor cases, provided those cases could result in jail time for the defendant. However, the Court has held that states are not required to provide a lawyer to litigants in civil cases.

The Sixth Amendment also guarantees defendants **the right to a speedy trial.** The courts have become so overburdened with cases that the Supreme Court recently imposed a 100-day limit between the time of arrest and the start of a trial. The limit has had little practical effect, however, because both prosecutors and defense attorneys can request an extension to prepare their cases. Courts have generally granted such extensions. As a result, it is not unusual for a defendant to wait a year or more between his or her arrest date and a trial.

Protection from Excessive Bail and "Cruel and Unusual Punishment"

The **Eighth Amendment** states that "excessive bail shall not be required, nor excessive fines imposed, nor cruel and unusual punishments inflicted." The government is not required, however, to offer bail to all defendants. In 1984, Congress passed the Bail Reform Act to allow federal judges to deny bail to defendants considered either dangerous or likely to flee the country. The protection from excessive bail has *not* been incorporated, and states are therefore free to set bail as high as state law permits.

The **"cruel and unusual punishment"** clause of the Constitution lies at the heart of the debate over the **death penalty**. The Court has placed limits on when the death penalty can be applied; however, it has upheld the constitutionality of the death penalty when properly applied. Critics point to statistics that those convicted of killing blacks are far less likely to receive the death penalty than those convicted of killing whites. The Court has rejected this argument. In recent years, the Court has moved to make it easier for states to carry out the death penalty by limiting the number and nature of appeals allowed by convicted murderers on death row.

Important Cases

> *Furman v. Georgia* (1972). Here, the court looked at the patchwork quilt of nationwide capital punishment decisions and found that its imposition was often racist and arbitrary. In *Furman*, the Court ordered a halt to all death penalty punishments in the nation until a less arbitrary method of sentencing was found.

> *Woodson v. North Carolina* (1976). North Carolina tried to satisfy the Court's requirement that the imposition of the death penalty not be arbitrary—so they made it a mandatory punishment for certain crimes. The Court rejected this approach and ruled mandatory death penalty sentences as unconstitutional.

> *Gregg v. Georgia* (1976). Georgia was finally able to convince the Court that it had come up with a careful and fair system for trying capital offenses. As a result, the Court ruled that under adequate guidelines the death penalty did not, in fact, constitute cruel and unusual punishment. Thus *Gregg* allowed the resumption of the death penalty in America.

> *Atkins v. Virginia* (2002). Here, the United States lined up with most other nations in the world by forbidding the execution of defendants who are mentally retarded.

The Right of All Americans to Privacy

The right to privacy is not specifically mentioned in the Constitution. However, in the 1965 Supreme Court case of *Griswold v. Connecticut*, the Court ruled that the Bill of Rights contained an **implied right to privacy.** The Court ruled that the combination of the First, Third, Fourth, Fifth, Ninth, and Fourteenth Amendments added up to a guarantee of privacy. The *Griswold* case concerned a state law banning the use of contraception; the Supreme Court decision overturned that law. *Griswold* also laid the foundation for the landmark *Roe v. Wade* case of 1973, which legalized abortion.

Important Cases

Griswold v. Connecticut (1965). The Constitution never explicitly grants Americans a right to privacy, but the Court discovers one in this landmark and controversial case. Writing for the majority, Justice William O. Douglas noted that amendments like the Third, Fourth, and Ninth all cast "penumbras and emanations" which showed that the Founders really had intended for a right to privacy all along.

Roe v. Wade (1973). Though *Roe* is one of the most famous court cases in American history, legally it is really a subset of the *Griswold* decision. The court had already done the heavy lifting of discovering the right to privacy in the Constitution. As a result, in *Roe* they established national abortion guidelines by extending the inferred right of privacy from *Griswold*.

Webster v. Reproductive Health Services (1987). This case did not overturn *Roe v. Wade*, but it did give states more power to regulate abortion.

Planned Parenthood v. Casey (1992). A Pennsylvania law that would have required a woman to notify her husband before getting an abortion was thrown out, but laws calling for parental consent and the imposition of a 24 hour waiting period were upheld. All in all, the message was that states *can* regulate abortion but not with regulations that impose an "undue burden" upon women.

CIVIL RIGHTS

The AP U.S. Government and Politics Exam occasionally tests your knowledge of key civil rights legislation. Below is what you need to know about civil rights for the test.

Civil Rights and African Americans

Prior to the Civil War, most of the African American population in the U.S. consisted of slaves, who were denied virtually any legal rights whatsoever. Free blacks were also denied basic civil rights such as the right to vote and the right to equal protection under the law. Because the Supreme Court had ruled in 1833 that the Bill of Rights applied to the federal government only, states were free to enact discriminatory and segregationist laws. Many did so to ensure the oppression of African Americans.

The Civil War began the long, slow development toward equality of the races before the law. Here is a list of key events in that process.

- **The Civil War.** The Civil War was fought, at least in part, over the issue of slavery (the debate over the relative powers of the federal and state governments was also a major cause of the war). The war was more clearly defined as a war about slavery in 1863, when President Lincoln issued the **Emancipation Proclamation,** which declared the liberation of slaves in the rebel states. The Civil War also influenced the civil rights process in a less direct and less immediate way, as it resulted in an increase in the power of the federal government. One hundred years later, the increased power vested in the federal government would be the means of imposing and enforcing equal rights laws in the states.

- **Thirteenth Amendment.** The Thirteenth Amendment, ratified after the Civil War, made slavery illegal.

- **Fourteenth Amendment.** The Fourteenth Amendment, ratified during Reconstruction, was designed to prevent states in the South from depriving newly freed blacks of their rights. Its clauses guaranteeing **due process** and **equal protection** were later used by the Supreme Court to apply most of the Bill of Rights to state law. However, in the 1880s the Supreme Court interpreted the amendment narrowly, allowing the states to enact segregationist laws. The Fourteenth Amendment also made African Americans citizens of the nation and of their home states—the **Dred Scott case** (1857) had ruled that slaves and their descendants were not citizens.

- **Fifteenth Amendment.** The Fifteenth Amendment banned laws that would prevent African Americans from voting on the basis of their race or the fact that they previously were slaves.

- **Civil Rights Act of 1875.** The Civil Rights Act of 1875 banned discrimination in hotels, restaurants, and railroad cars, and also banned discrimination in selection for jury duty. The Supreme Court declared the Act unconstitutional in 1883.

- **Jim Crow laws and voting restrictions.** As the federal government exerted less influence over the South, states, towns, and cities passed numerous discriminatory and segregationist laws. The Supreme Court assisted the states by ruling that the Fourteenth Amendment did not protect blacks from discriminatory state laws, and that blacks would have to seek equal protection from the states, not from the federal government. In 1883, the Court also reversed the Civil Rights Act of 1875, thus opening the door to legal segregation. These segregationist laws are known collectively as **Jim Crow laws.** The states also moved to deprive blacks of their voting rights by imposing **poll taxes** (a tax that must be paid in order to vote) and literacy tests. To allow poor, illiterate whites to vote, some states passed **grandfather clauses** that exempted from these restrictions anyone whose grandfather had voted. Grandfather clauses effectively excluded blacks, whose grandparents had been slaves and therefore could not have voted.

- **Equal Pay Act of 1963.** This federal law made it illegal to base an employee's pay on race, gender, religion, or national origin. The Equal Pay Act was also important to the women's movement and to the civil rights struggles of other minorities.

- **Twenty-fourth Amendment (1964).** This outlawed poll taxes, which had been used to prevent blacks and poor whites from voting.

- **Civil Rights Act of 1964.** The Civil Rights Act of 1964 was a landmark piece of legislation. It not only increased the rights of blacks and other minorities, but also gave the federal government greater means of enforcing the law. The law banned discrimination in public accommodations (public transportation, offices, and so on) and in all federally funded programs. It also prohibited discrimination in hiring based on color and gender. Finally, it required the government to cut off funding from any program that did not comply with the law, and it gave the federal government the power to initiate lawsuits in cases of school segregation. States that had previously ignored federal civil rights mandates now faced serious consequences for doing so.

- **Voting Rights Act of 1965.** The Voting Rights Act was designed to counteract voting discrimination in the South. It allowed the federal government to step into any state or county in which less than 50 percent of the population was registered to vote, or in areas that used literacy tests to prevent voting. In those areas, the federal government could register voters (which is normally a function of the states).

- **Civil Rights Act, Title VIII (1968).** This banned racial discrimination in housing.

- **Civil Rights Act of 1991.** This law was designed to address a number of problems that had arisen in civil rights law during the previous decade. Several Supreme Court decisions had limited the abilities of job applicants and employees to bring suit against employers with discriminatory hiring practices; the 1991 act eased those restrictions.

Important Cases

Plessy v. Ferguson (1896). This case famously allowed southern states to twist the Equal Protection clause of the Fourteenth Amendment by allowing "separate but equal" facilities based on race.

Brown v. Board of Education of Topeka (1954). In this landmark case, a unanimous court led by newly appointed Chief Justice Earl Warren ruled the doctrine of "separate but equal" to be unconstitutional.

Brown v. Board 2ⁿᵈ (1955). One year later, the Warren Court saw that segregation was still ubiquitous. So in Brown II, they ordered schools to desegregate "with all due and deliberate speed."

Heart of Atlanta Motel, Inc. v. United States (1964). Did the Federal Civil Rights Act of 1964 mandate that places of public accommodation are prohibited from discrimination against blacks? Yes, said the Court.

Katzenbach v. McClung (1964). The Civil Rights Act of 1964 prohibited discrimination in public places, but what about in private businesses? The Katzenbach case established that the power of Congress to regulate interstate commerce extends to state discrimination statutes. This ruling made the Civil Rights Act of 1964 apply to virtually all businesses.

Regents of the University of California v. Bakke (1978). Alan Bakke was a white applicant who was rejected from medical school because of an affirmative action plan to boost the number of black students. The Court ruled that Bakke had been unfairly excluded and that quotas requiring a certain percentage of minorities violated the Fourteenth Amendment. But the Court also held that race-based affirmative action *was* permissible so long as it was in the service of creating greater diversity.

Grutter v. Bollinger (2003) and *Gratz v. Bollinger* (2003). These cases involved the University of Michigan Law School and the University of Michigan undergraduate school. Both used affirmative action, but the undergraduate school did so by giving minority applicants a large boost in the score used by officers deciding on admission. The Court threw out the undergraduate system of selection, but generally upheld *Bakke*.

Lawrence v. Texas (2003). The Court ruled that a Texas law that prohibited gays from engaging in consensual sodomy in private constituted an unreasonable invasion of privacy, as well as a violation of the Fourteenth Amendment due process clause.

Although the number of major new civil rights laws has decreased in the past decades, the fight for civil rights for African Americans and other minority groups is far from over. Although legally enforced segregation of public facilities no longer exists, racial segregation remains a national concern. Most public school systems remain essentially segregated because the neighborhoods that feed them are segregated. The impact of this *de facto* **segregation** (as opposed to *de jure* **segregation,** which is segregation by law) is increased by the disparity in average incomes among whites and blacks: Because many local school systems are supported by property taxes, lower-income neighborhoods end up with poorly funded, overcrowded schools. In the 1970s, the Supreme Court ruled that the government could bus children to different school districts to achieve the goal of integration, provided the affected districts had been intentionally segregated. Busing plans failed, however, due to public protest and the abandonment of cities by whites.

Furthermore, discrimination continues in employment, housing, and higher education. Because such discrimination is subtler—few employers tell job applicants, "I won't hire you because you're black"—it is more difficult to enforce antidiscrimination laws and punish offenders in these areas. **Affirmative action programs**, which seek to create special employment opportunities for blacks, women, and other victims of discrimination, address these questions but have become increasingly controversial and politically unpopular in recent years. In *Board of Regents of the University of California v. Bakke* (1978), the Supreme Court ruled that affirmative action programs could not use quotas to meet civil rights goals; however, it did say that gender and race could be considered among other factors by schools and businesses practicing affirmative action. Opponents of affirmative action programs argue that such programs penalize whites and thus constitute **reverse discrimination,** which is illegal under the Civil Rights Act of 1964.

Civil Rights and Women

The granting of equal rights for women in the United States is a relatively recent phenomenon. Women were not given the right to vote in all 50 states until 1920. Employment discrimination based on gender was not outlawed until 1964. As recently as the early 1990s, women were not guaranteed 12 weeks of unpaid leave from work after giving birth (this finally changed with the **Family and Medical Leave Act of 1993,** which gives this right to both mothers and fathers). Those who fought for the failed **Equal Rights Amendment** to the Constitution continue to argue that women do not yet have a full guarantee of equality under the law from the federal government.

Here is a list of events of the women's rights movement that the AP U.S. Government and Politics Exam sometimes tests.

- **Nineteenth Amendment (1920).** Granted women the right to vote.

- **Equal Pay Act of 1963.** This federal law made it illegal to base an employee's pay on race, gender, religion, or national origin. Prior to this bill, many businesses and organizations maintained different pay and raise schedules for their male and female employees. In fact, many continued to do so after the bill passed. Federal enforcement of the law, however, has helped narrow the gap between the salaries and wages of the genders.

- **Civil Rights Act of 1964.** The provision pertaining to gender discrimination was included in the Civil Rights Act of 1964 by an opponent of the bill. Representative Howard Smith of Virginia believed his proposal was ridiculous and would therefore weaken support for the bill. Much to his surprise, the bill passed with the gender provision included. The bill prohibits employment discrimination based on gender.

- **Title IX, Higher Education Act (1972).** This law prohibits gender discrimination by institutions of higher education that receive federal funds. Title IX has been used to force increased funding of women-only programs, such as women's sports. The **Civil Rights Restoration Act of 1988** increased its potency by allowing the government to cut off all funding to schools that violate the law (and not just to the specific program or office found in violation). As a result of these laws mandating equity in college athletics spending, colleges have eliminated many less popular men's sports, resulting in a backlash against Title IX and the Civil Rights Restoration Act.

As women have entered the workplace in greater numbers, the issue of sexual harassment at work has gained prominence. **Sexual harassment** is defined as any sexist or sexual behavior—physical or verbal—that creates a hostile work environment. It can range from suggestive remarks to attempts to coerce sex from a subordinate. Like other forms of discrimination, it is difficult to prove legally. Efforts to combat it range from public-awareness programs to sensitivity training to increased legal penalties for harassers.

Abortion has remained a controversial and prominent political issue since the Supreme Court affirmed a woman's right to an abortion in *Roe v. Wade* (1973). In that case, the court ruled that a woman's right to an abortion could not be limited during the first three months of pregnancy (increased limits are allowed as the development of the fetus progresses). Opponents of abortion, who call themselves *pro-life*, argue that the procedure is murder and should be criminalized. Those who support women's right to abortions (dubbed the *pro-choice* movement) argue that women should ultimately decide the ambiguous moral issues for themselves. Because of the very personal, life-and-death issues involved in the abortion debate, advocates on both sides of the issue feel very strongly, and as a result abortion is a major political issue. The decision in *Roe v. Wade* has influenced every election and Supreme Court nomination since; as a result of this case, candidates' opinions about the abortion issue are often the first thing the public learns about them. In most European countries, abortion rights were established legislatively (by laws). Many legal scholars believe that the judicial solution (left up to the courts) applied by the United States has opened the door to ideologues.

Other Major Civil Rights Advances

- **Age Discrimination Act of 1967.** As its name states, this law prohibits employment discrimination on the basis of age. The law makes an exception for jobs in which age is essential to job performance. An amendment to this law banned some mandatory retirement ages and increased others to 70.

- **Voting Rights Act of 1982.** This law requires states to create congressional districts with minority majorities in order to increase minority representation in the House of Representatives. The law has resulted in the creation of numerous strangely shaped districts, such as one in North Carolina that was 160 miles long and, at points, only several hundred yards wide. The Supreme Court nullified the district just described, leaving it unclear how the government may both achieve the goals of the Voting Rights Act and maintain the regional integrity of congressional districts.

- **Americans with Disabilities Act of 1990.** This law requires businesses with more than 24 employees to make their offices accessible to the disabled. It also requires public transportation, new offices, hotels, and restaurants to be wheelchair-accessible whenever feasible. Finally, it mandated the development of wider telephone services for the hearing-impaired.

- **Twenty-sixth Amendment (1971).** Extended the right to vote to 18-year-olds.

Other Important Cases

Federalism

Marbury v. Madison (1803). This most important of all decisions established **judicial review**—the Supreme Court's power to strike down acts of United States Congress which conflict with the Constitution.

McCulloch v. Maryland (1819). This case is important because it established a precedent of federal courts using judicial review to strike down Congressional legislation.

Gitlow v. New York (1925). *Gitlow* began the process of selective incorporation—the practice of transferring protections that Americans had from the federal government and applying them to state governments.

South Dakota v. Dole (1987). The federal government mandated the 21-year-old drinking age by threatening to withhold federal highway funds from all states that did not comply. In this case, such withholding was held to be constitutional.

United States v. Lopez (1995). Congress had used the Commerce clause to aggressively create legislation governing what seemed to be purely local matters. Here, the Court blocks them a bit by holding that the Commerce clause of the Constitution does not give Congress the power to regulate guns near state-operated schools.

Property Rights

Dartmouth College v. Woodward (1819). Here, the court rebuffed an attempt by the state of New Hampshire to take control of Dartmouth College by holding that Dartmouth's corporate charter qualified as a contract between private parties, with which the legislature could not interfere.

Barron v. Baltimore (1819). Here, the court held that the Fifth Amendment did not deny the states as well as the national government the right to take private property for public use without justly compensating the property's owner, and helped the states to engage in eminent domain.

Kelo v. New London (2005). Eminent Domain is usually used to seize private land and convert it to public use. In this case, the town of New London wanted to seize private land and turn it over to private developers. Was this legal? In a 5-4 decision, the court ruled that it was a legitimate use of eminent domain.

Executive Power

Korematsu v. United States (1944). This case was not the Supreme Court's finest hour, as it ruled that American citizens of Japanese descent could be interned and deprived of basic constitutional rights due to executive order.

U.S. v. Nixon (1974). In this case, Congress claimed that there was no such thing as executive privilege as it went after tapes that President Nixon had made of all his conversations in the Oval Office. The Court disagreed and allowed for executive privilege. But they forbid its usage in criminal cases, which meant that Nixon ultimately did have to turn over the tapes.

Clinton v. New York (1998). This case banned the presidential use of a line-item veto as a violation of legislative powers.

SUMMARY

- It is very important to remember that the Bill of Rights only protects Americans from the federal government. It wasn't until the passage of the Fourteenth Amendment and the advocacy of the twentieth-century Supreme Court that these freedoms were selectively incorporated to the states.

- Know about freedom of speech, clear and present danger and the preferred position doctrine.

- Freedom of the press is protected by the ban on prior restraint, but has limits (as in the case of slander or libel)

- The rights of the people to assemble generally can't be limited, though there are some exceptions to this rule.

- The Constitution forbids the creation of an official religion through the Establishment Clause, but also prevents the government from infringing on religious freedom through the Free Exercise Clause.

- We have seen a steady expansion of the rights of the accused, particularly since the decisions of the Warren Court.

- Rising from the disgrace of slavery and Jim Crow laws, the Court has acted in the latter half of the twentieth-century to protect racial minorities from discrimination. Today, most controversy swirls around the issue of Affirmative Action and whether it constitutes a form of reverse racism and thus constitutes a violation of the Fourteenth Amendment.

PRACTICE QUESTIONS:

1. The *Gratz* and *Grutter* cases served primarily to

   (A) reinforce primacy of "diversity" as established in *Bakke*
   (B) remove "diversity" as the focus of affirmative action
   (C) abolish affirmative action
   (D) justify affirmative action by noting that it "righted past wrongs"
   (E) establish a quota system

2. Prior Restraint (for non-student newspapers) was prohibited by

   (A) *Brown v. Board of Education*
   (B) *Betts v. Brady*
   (C) *Near v. Minnesota*
   (D) *Sheppard v. Maxwell*
   (E) President Johnson in 1967

3. The right to always have counsel present in court cases was established by

   (A) *Powell v. Alabama*
   (B) *Betts v. Brady*
   (C) *Gideon v. Wainwright*
   (D) *Escobedo v. Illinois*
   (E) *Miranda v. Arizona*

4. The Supreme Court case that allowed the resumption of the death penalty was

   (A) *Furman v. Georgia*
   (B) *Woodson v. North Carolina*
   (C) *Bunn v. North Carolina*
   (D) *Oregon v. Smith*
   (E) *Gregg v. Georgia*

5. The case that made it necessary to have a warrant to tap someone's phone was

   (A) *Hughes v. Superior Court*
   (B) *Adderly v. Florida*
   (C) *Olmstead v. U.S.*
   (D) *Katz v. U.S.*
   (E) *Reynolds v. U.S.*

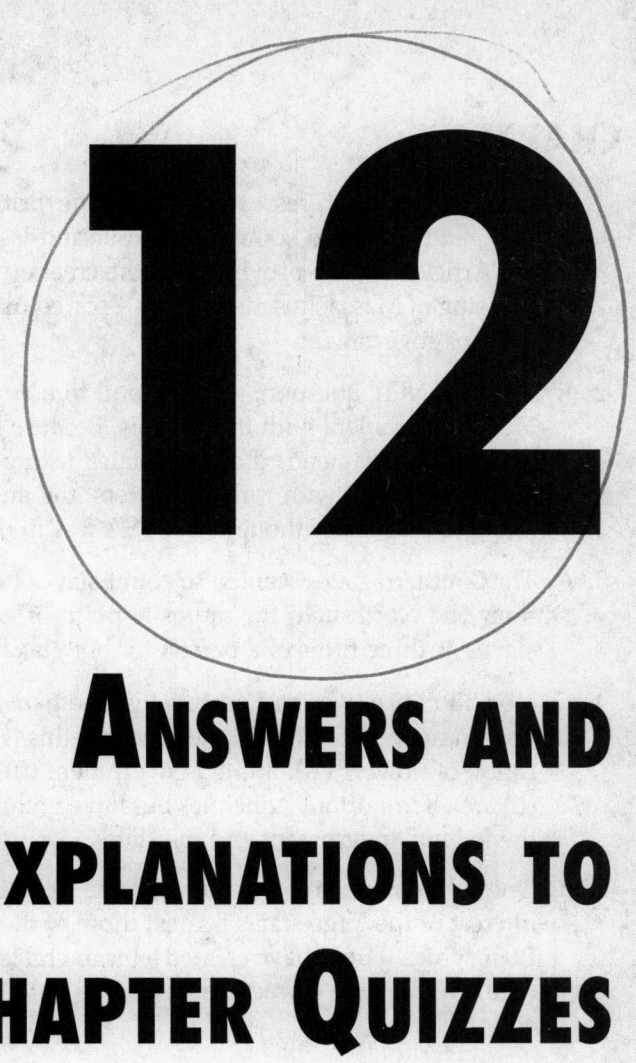

12

ANSWERS AND EXPLANATIONS TO CHAPTER QUIZZES

CHAPTER 5

1. **B** After feeling the pressure of the strong British central government, the founders of the new nation wanted something looser and less binding: the Articles of Confederation. But the Articles had no provision for the creation of a central army, and Shays's Rebellion—an uprising of Massachusetts farmers—scared many people and led to the desire for a stronger form of government.

2. **E** This is a NOT question, so be careful to note that it is asking which of the answer choices is NOT a problem with the Articles. Because the Articles had no strong army, were almost impossible to amend, did have states taxing trade with other states and did have states establishing ties with foreign powers, the answer is (E); after all, the states had so much freedom that many thought the USA was in danger of dissolution.

3. **A** The Southern states wanted to count slaves for the purpose of representation, but not taxation. The North held the opposite point of view. Ultimately they compromised, counting slaves as three-fifths of a person for both taxation and representation. Thus (A) is correct.

4. **C** No nation had ever had powers divided between a central government and strong regional governments before the United States—this was federalism, which makes (C) correct. Separation of powers (A), limited government (B), checks and balances (D) and judicial review (E) are all important principles but have nothing to do with the division of powers between the federal government and the states.

5. **B** One of the main sticking points at the Constitutional Convention was how to balance the interest of the large states against those of the small. The large states endorsed the Virginia Plan, which would have created a bicameral legislature in which the large states were dominant. So (B) is the correct response.

CHAPTER 6

1. **A** Small groups can often wield disproportionate power over public policy, and often this comes down to the strength, or intensity, of their feelings. So (A) is correct. Saliency (B) is the degree to which an issue is important to a particular group, while stability (C) is how much public opinion changes over time. (D) and (E) are not terms that are generally used to describe public opinion.

2. **D** This is a NOT question so we are looking for the one answer choice which is NOT a source of political socialization. Family (A), school (B), life experiences (C) and religion (E) are all major sources of political socialization due to the influence they have on people's world-views. Neither party really engages in large-scale indoctrination, making (D) the best choice.

3. **C** Liberals tend to want the government to use redistributionist policies to help the poor, making (C) correct. (A), (B), (D) and (E) are all examples of ideas that appeal more to conservatives.

4. **B** Conservatives are traditionally skeptical of any government attempts to control business and industry, and thus (B) is the answer here. (A), (C), (D) and (E) are all examples of ideas that appeal more to liberals.

5. **E** In this NOT question, we are asked to decide which factor does NOT determine ideological behavior. Race and ethnicity (A), religion (B), gender (C) and region (D) are all major factors in determining whether someone will be liberal or conservative. So (E) is the answer, as birth order has never been proven to have any relevance in this area.

CHAPTER 7

1. **D** Oftentimes, voters will become dissatisfied with the two parties in power and bolt to a new, third party. Ross Perot's Reform Party is a classic example of a "bolter" party, making (D) correct. (A), (B), (C) and (E) are all examples of ideological parties and are thus incorrect.

2. **B** In this NOT question, we are looking for the one example of a function that parties are NOT expected to do. Because the USA is a stable democracy, political parties are not expected to foment revolution, making (B) the answer. (A), (C), (D) and (E) are all examples of legitimate political party functions, making them the wrong choices.

3. **D** Cuban Americans (A), evangelicals (B), white southerners (C) and pro-lifers (E) all represent groups that are generally part of the Republican coalition. Mexicans and other non-Cuban Hispanics are far more likely to vote Democratic, making (D) correct.

4. **A** While many Americans may be skeptical of interest groups and the power that they wield, comparatively few resort to breaking the law and engaging in outright bribery, making (A) the answer here. (B), (C), (D) and (E) are all examples of tactics commonly used by interest groups to accomplish their goals.

5. **B** Unions and corporations have clear policy goals and want to elect candidates that will accomplish those goals. But federal law prohibits them from donating directly to candidates—thus the PAC was born. Because PACs are only allowed to accept and give out set amounts of money, (C) is incorrect and (B) is right. (A), (D) and (E) do not come close to defining the role and purpose of PACs.

CHAPTER 8

1. **E** States that use open primaries allow voters of any party to vote in one party primary of their choice, making (E) correct. (A), (B), (C) and (D) do not meet the definition of an open primary and are thus incorrect.

2. **D** Rules about campaign finance have changed since 2002, but one rule that has remained constant is that PACs can give candidates $5000 and no more than $5000 per election cycle. So (D) should be your choice.

3. **A** (B), (C), (D) and (E) are all examples of groups that assemble at nominating conventions, but the position of a party is known as its platform, and this is formed by (A) the platform committee.

4. **A** The president of the United States is the person who receives a majority of votes in the electoral college, making (A) correct. If a candidate only has a plurality of votes in the electoral college (C), then the House decides the president. Unanimity is nice, but not necessary for victory, making (E) wrong. The popular vote plays no role in who becomes president, making (B) and (D) wrong.

5. **B** Though there are exceptions, studies have overwhelmingly shown that the older and more educated a person is, the more likely they are to vote. The 65-year-old college professor is the oldest and best educated member of the group of choices, so (B) is correct.

CHAPTER 9

1. **B** Though he is mostly limited to ceremonial duties and to breaking the occasional tie, the vice president of the United States is officially the president of the Senate, making (B) correct. The majority leader (D) is the actual leader of the body, while the president *pro tempore* (C), also ceremonial, is outranked by the vice president. Neither the president (A) nor the chief whip (E) has leadership roles in the Senate.

2. **E** The power to choose a president (A), the power to propose amendments to the Constitution (B), treaty ratification (C) and confirmations (D) are all examples of non-legislative powers of Congress. To legislate means to make laws, and only (E) meets this definition.

3. **D** Controversial as it may be, the process of redistricting has always been controlled by state legislatures in the United States—making (D) correct. Though many experts have called for (E) nonpartisan commissions, currently only Iowa uses one to draw its district lines. The Senate (A) and the president (B) have no influence over districting. And while the Supreme Court (C) is empowered to rule on matters of redistricting, it rarely does so.

4. **A** The Constitution doesn't make any mention of the cabinet, but all presidents have had them, and as high ranking members of the executive branch, they must be chosen by the president and confirmed by the Senate, making (A) correct. The House does not confirm presidential appointments, so (B) is false. Neither the House (C) nor the Supreme Court (D) chooses cabinet officials. And as seen from (A), presidential choices for the cabinet do necessitate Senate approval, making (E) false.

5. **A** Because it is so informal and because its members need to give frank and unvarnished advice to the president, the EOP is exempt from Congressional oversight and is a favored tool of the presidency, making (A) correct. The fact that the EOP is unmentioned in the Constitution (B) does not detract from its power. It is not located in the Department of Defense (C), neither is it a dumping ground (D). And the vice president does not run it, making (E) false.

6. **C** The NSC is a key part of the EOP and Presidents have relied on it for many years, as NSC advisors like Henry Kissinger and Condoleezza Rice have used their positions to influence presidents. Its main function is to advise the president and to coordinate foreign policy (C), and to do so away from the prying eyes of Congress. None of the other answer choices correctly defines the NSC.

7. **D** Though the president gets to select all the judges who sit on the federal bench, district court judges all operate out of a specific state. By tradition, the senators from that state must approve of the president's selections to fill vacancies—this is known as senatorial courtesy, making (D) correct. Judicial appointments are not approved in the House (A), and Supreme Court Justices (B) are not subject to senatorial courtesy. Senators cannot appoint judges (C), nor are they immune to prosecution (E).

8. **C** Though Congress attempted to argue that executive privilege was not a real power of the presidency, the Supreme Court disagreed. However, they held that it could not be used to prevent criminal charges from being brought against the president, and thus (C) is correct. (A) is wrong because the legislative veto was ruled to be unconstitutional in the case of *INS v. Chadha*. (B) is false because impoundment was made illegal through the Budget Reform Act of 1974, and (D) is simply false. (E) is untrue because if Nixon had been tried, it would have been in the Senate, not the Court.

9. **E** From the presidency of Thomas Jefferson, but especially since that of Andrew Jackson, government jobs were given to political supporters—an arrangement known as the spoils system. The Pendleton Act, passed in 1883, ended this, so (E) is the answer. (A) refers to the Hatch Act, and (B), (C) and (D) are simply untrue.

10. **E** Also known as a sub-government, the alliance of Congressional committees, interest groups, and bureaucracies is so strong that it is often called an iron triangle, so (A) is correct. (A), (B), and (D) are all things that come in three, but none are known as iron triangles. (C) is false because iron triangles are fairly common in the United States.

CHAPTER 10

1. **C** The Office of Management and Budget (OMB) evolved out of the Bureau of the Budget—used by FDR to help guide the nation through the Great Depression. Its primary function is to plan the budget for the president, making (C) the correct response. The OMB exists to serve the president, not Congress, so (B) is incorrect. Assessing the nation's economic health (A) is more the job of the National Economic Council (NEC), and the NEC would also be in charge of (D). Protecting the environment (E) is the job of the EPA.

2. **B** Policy formulation (A), policy implementation (C), policy evaluation (D) and agenda setting (E) are all part of the policy-making process. But abandoning the government means abandoning policy-making, so (B) is the correct answer.

3. **D** A supporter of laissez-faire economic policy would be in favor of the free market, less regulation and fewer taxes. For these reasons, (E), (A), and (B) are wrong. Free marketers are traditionally skeptical of labor unions, making (C) wrong. A flat tax would mean an end to the progressive tax rate and less money paid in taxes overall, so (D) is the right choice.

4. **E** Retired workers (A), survivors of retirees (B), the handicapped (C), and the short-term unemployed (D) all receive benefits from Social Security. Though a family that is chronically poor may receive money from the government, they wouldn't get it from Social Security, so (E) is correct

5. **A** When a nation imports more than it exports, it is running a trade deficit, so (A) is right. A surplus (B) occurs when exports exceed imports. (C), (D) and (E) are all factually incorrect.

CHAPTER 11

1. **A** The cases of *Gratz* and *Grutter* in 2002 involved lawsuits against the University of Michigan by white students who did not get accepted as a result of affirmative action. Though many observers of the Court speculated that affirmative action might be overturned, ultimately the justices held upheld it and reinforced the *Bakke* case. So (A) is correct. Diversity remains the goal of affirmative action, so (B) is wrong. As seen above, (C) did not occur. Though many support affirmative action to right past wrongs, its legal foundation still rests on diversity, making (D) incorrect. Quotas have been illegal since *Bakke*, so (E) is incorrect as well.

2. **C** The state cannot engage in prior restraint, the prevention of publication of articles it might find offensive, and this was affirmed in the *Near* case, making (C) correct. (A) *Brown* ended segregation, (B) *Betts* provided lawyers for defendants who were mentally deficient, (D) *Sheppard* established rules about protecting defendants from being tried in the media and (E) President Johnson was never involved in prior restraint issues.

3. **C** Sometimes nicknamed "*Gideon's Trumpet*," the case of *Gideon v. Wainwright* established that all defendants have the right to counsel, so (C) is correct. *Gideon* overruled *Betts*, so (B) is wrong, and *Powell* (A) was overruled by *Brady* and is also wrong. *Escobedo* (D) said that the accused cannot be denied a lawyer after they ask for one, and *Miranda* (E) held that the arrested need to be informed of their rights.

4. **E** In the early 1970s, the Supreme Court ruled that the death penalty was being unfairly applied and banned it in the case of *Furman v. Georgia*, so (A) is incorrect. North Carolina tried to get capital punishment restored by making the death penalty mandatory in some cases, but in *Woodson v. North Carolina*, the Court struck down this approach, making (B) wrong. Finally, in *Gregg v. Georgia*, the Court allowed the death penalty to resume, making (E) correct. *Bunn* and *Smith* are both cases that deal with religious freedom and are incorrect.

5. **D** Originally, in *Olmstead v. U.S.*, the Court ruled that warrants were NOT necessary to tap phone lines, so (C) is wrong. *Katz* overruled *Olmstead* in 1967, and so (D) is correct. *Hughes* (A) is a case about labor picketing, *Adderly* (B) is about the legality of demonstrating near jails, and (E) *Reynolds* criminalized polygamy.

PART III

The Princeton Review AP U.S. Government and Politics Practice Tests and Explanations

13

PRACTICE TEST 1

UNITED STATES GOVERNMENT AND POLITICS

Two hours and 25 minutes are allocated for this examination: 45 minutes for Section I, which consists of multiple-choice questions; and 100 minutes for Section II, which consists of 4 mandatory essay questions. Section I is printed in this examination booklet. Section II is printed in a separate booklet.

SECTION I

Time—45 minutes

Number of questions—60

Percent of total grade—50

Section I of this examination contains 60 multiple-choice questions. Therefore, please be careful to fill in only the ovals that are preceded by numbers 1 to 60 on your answer sheet.

General Instructions

DO NOT OPEN THIS BOOKLET UNTIL YOU ARE INSTRUCTED TO DO SO.

INDICATE ALL YOUR ANSWERS TO QUESTIONS IN SECTION I ON THE SEPARATE ANSWER SHEET. No credit will be given for anything written in this examination booklet, but you may use the booklet for notes or scratchwork. After you have decided which of the suggested answers is best, COMPLETELY fill in the corresponding oval on the answer sheet. Give only one answer to each question. If you change an answer, be sure that the previous mark is erased completely.

Example: Sample Answer

Chicago is a

(A) state
(B) city
(C) country
(D) continent
(E) village

Many candidates wonder whether or not to guess the answers to questions about which they are not certain. In this section of the examination, as a correction for haphazard guessing, one-fourth of the number of questions you answer incorrectly will be subtracted from the number of questions you answer correctly. It is improbable, therefore, that mere guessing will improve your score significantly; it may even lower your score, and it does take time. If, however, you are not sure of the best answer but have some knowledge of the question and are able to eliminate one or more of the answer choices as wrong, your chance of getting the right answer is improved, and it may be to your advantage to answer such a question.

Use your time effectively, working as rapidly as you can without losing accuracy. Do not spend too much time on questions that are too difficult. Go on to other questions and come back to the difficult ones later if you have time. It is not expected that everyone will be able to answer all the multiple-choice questions.

Section I

Time—45 minutes

60 Questions

<u>Directions</u>: Each of the questions or incomplete statements below is followed by five suggested answers or completions. Select the one that is best in each case and then fill in the corresponding oval on the answer sheet.

1. The Constitution as ratified in 1788 most clearly reflects the framers' commitment to

   (A) the idea of direct democracy
   (B) the principle of limited government
   (C) the abolition of slavery
   (D) protecting the rights of the accused
   (E) maintaining the primacy of the states

2. Which of the following most accurately describes *The Federalist Papers*?

   (A) The Federalist party platform during the presidency of John Adams, the first Federalist president
   (B) A popular anti-British booklet of the pre-Revolutionary era
   (C) A collection of essays arguing the merits of the Constitution
   (D) A series of congressional acts defining the relationship between the federal and state governments
   (E) The laws under which the South was governed during Reconstruction

3. A Supreme Court that demonstrates a willingness to change public policy and alter judicial precedent is said to be engaging in

   (A) judicial activism
   (B) due process
   (C) judicial restraint
   (D) ex post facto lawmaking
   (E) judicial review

4. A writ of *certiorari* from the Supreme Court indicates that the Court

   (A) will review a lower court decision
   (B) has rendered a decision on a case
   (C) has decided not to hear an appeal
   (D) will recess until the end of the calendar year
   (E) plans to overturn one of its previous rulings

5. American foreign policy is directed primarily by the

   (A) House of Representatives
   (B) Senate
   (C) president
   (D) Supreme Court
   (E) federal bureaucracy

"We conclude that in the field of education the doctrine of 'separate but equal' has no place. Separate educational facilities are inherently unequal."

6. The Supreme Court issued this opinion in its ruling on which of the following cases?

   (A) *Gideon v. Wainwright*
   (B) *Marbury v. Madison*
   (C) *Engel v. Vitale*
   (D) *Regents of University of California v. Bakke*
   (E) *Brown v. Board of Education of Topeka*

7. Under which of the following circumstances is Congress LEAST likely to pass a bill the president has threatened to veto?

   (A) The president's public approval rating is extremely high.
   (B) A failed attempt has been made to develop a compromise bill with the White House.
   (C) The party controlling Congress is not the president's party.
   (D) The president has also expressed the possibility that he might not veto the bill.
   (E) Congressional leaders believe they have the votes necessary to override a veto.

GO ON TO THE NEXT PAGE

8. Which of the following best describes the practice of "ticket splitting"?

   (A) A presidential nominee selects a running mate who can appeal to voter groups whose support of the nominee is weak.
   (B) A voter chooses the presidential nominee of one major party, but chooses congressional nominees of the other major party.
   (C) A mayor orders the local police force to hand out fewer parking violations in the weeks leading up to the general election.
   (D) A delegate to a national party convention supports the front-runner but remains uncommitted on the party platform.
   (E) A member of Congress votes against legislation proposed by his or her party leader.

9. The Rules Committee is considered among the most powerful in the House of Representatives because it has great power over the

   (A) ethical conduct of House members
   (B) selection of federal judges
   (C) number of subcommittees that a standing committee may establish at any given time
   (D) scheduling of votes and the conditions under which bills are debated and amended
   (E) regulations governing federal elections

10. Compared with political parties in countries such as England and Israel, both of which have multiparty systems, American political parties are

    (A) less interested in influencing the outcome of elections
    (B) less clearly identified with consistent political ideologies
    (C) less effective at raising money from political supporters
    (D) better able to reflect the goals of their entire constituencies
    (E) more likely to organize around a single issue or goal

11. Which of the following people would most likely be accused of influence peddling?

    (A) A congressperson who retires to take a position teaching political science at a university
    (B) A former president who advises a current president on a particular foreign policy issue
    (C) A voter who researches the positions of all candidates in a race before choosing whom to support
    (D) A judge who consistently hands down the maximum sentence to convicted felons
    (E) An official who leaves the State Department to work as a paid consultant to foreign governments

12. The primary function of political action committees (PACs) is to

    (A) contribute money to candidates for election
    (B) coordinate local get-out-the-vote campaigns
    (C) promote the defeat of incumbents in the federal and state legislatures
    (D) organize protest demonstrations and other acts of civil disobedience
    (E) contact Congress to suggest legislation

13. Voters who rely exclusively on television network news coverage of national elections are most likely to be aware of

    (A) which special interest groups have endorsed which candidates
    (B) the relative strength of each candidate's support, as indicated by public opinion polls
    (C) candidates' positions on international issues
    (D) candidates' positions on domestic issues
    (E) candidates' congressional voting records

GO ON TO THE NEXT PAGE

14. Which of the following describe limitations that may constitutionally be placed on freedom of speech and freedom of the press?

   I. Under no circumstances may the government limit speech or censor the press.
   II. The government may censor the press in the interest of national and military security.
   III. The government may outlaw obscene publications.
   IV. The government may prevent individuals from engaging in "offensive" speech.

   (A) I only
   (B) II only
   (C) II and III only
   (D) III and IV only
   (E) II, III, and IV only

15. The Supreme Court holds original jurisdiction in all of the following types of cases EXCEPT

   (A) if the United States is a party in the case
   (B) in controversies in criminal law between a citizen and a state
   (C) in controversies under the Constitution, federal laws, or treaties
   (D) if a case is between citizens from different states
   (E) if cases arise under admiralty and maritime laws

16. Of the following, American federalism is most clearly exemplified by the

   (A) system of checks and balances among the three branches of the national government
   (B) process by which international treaties are completed
   (C) special constitutional status of Washington, DC
   (D) Tenth Amendment to the Constitution
   (E) president's power to grant reprieves and pardons

17. All of the following are specifically mentioned in the Constitution EXCEPT

   (A) judicial review
   (B) the national census
   (C) rules of impeachment
   (D) the State of the Union address
   (E) length of term of federal judgeships

18. Which of the following correctly states the relationship between the federal and state judiciaries?

   (A) Federal courts are higher courts than state courts and may overturn state decisions on any grounds.
   (B) The two are entirely autonomous, and neither ever hears cases that originate in the other.
   (C) The two are generally autonomous, although federal courts may rule on the constitutionality of state court decisions.
   (D) State courts are trial courts; federal courts are appeals courts.
   (E) State courts try all cases except those that involve conflicts between two states, which are tried in federal courts.

19. The line-item veto was found unconstitutional because

   (A) it gave executive powers to the legislature
   (B) it gave legislative powers to the bureaucracy
   (C) it gave legislative powers to the president
   (D) it delegated too many powers to the states
   (E) it permitted the Senate to use judicial review to reverse the House of Representatives

20. Among the executive branch's checks on the legislative branch is the president's power to

   (A) call special sessions of Congress
   (B) introduce bills to the floor of Congress
   (C) address Congress during its debate on bills
   (D) vote on acts of Congress
   (E) disband congressional committees

21. The amount of access cabinet secretaries have to the president is most likely to be controlled by the

   (A) vice president
   (B) president's chief of staff
   (C) national security advisor
   (D) chair of the Federal Reserve Board
   (E) president's press secretary

GO ON TO THE NEXT PAGE

22. Unlike a treaty, an executive agreement

(A) is not binding
(B) does not involve international relations
(C) does not require the Senate's approval
(D) can be enforced by the military
(E) automatically expires after one year

23. Successful candidates for the Republican presidential nomination tend to be more conservative than rank-and-file Republicans because

(A) moderate Republicans are less likely than conservative Republicans to gain widespread support in the general election
(B) most moderate Republicans have approved of the Democratic presidential candidate
(C) most rank-and-file Republicans do not care whether their party's nominee shares their political views
(D) party activists, whose political participation is disproportionate to their numbers, tend to be very conservative
(E) the Republican Party does not allow rank-and-file members to participate in the selection of the party's nominee

24. Those who argue that the House of Representatives is the government institution most responsive to the will of the public are most likely to cite as evidence the fact that

(A) congressional reelection campaigns are extremely costly
(B) term limits may soon restrict the number of years a congressperson may serve
(C) Congress has oversight power over many executive agencies
(D) average citizens may, on occasion, be called to testify before a congressional committee
(E) representatives must run for reelection every two years

25. Which of the following accounts for the fact that the power and prestige of the presidency have grown since 1932?

I. America's increased prominence in international affairs
II. continually improved public confidence in the federal government
III. the New Deal and other programs that have expanded federal responsibility
IV. the president's increased visibility, due to the development of mass media

(A) I only
(B) I and IV only
(C) I, III, and IV only
(D) II and IV only
(E) II, III, and IV only

26. Which of the following generally results when the Senate and House of Representatives pass different versions of the same bill?

(A) The president signs the version he prefers.
(B) The bill goes back to each house's committee and restarts the legislative process.
(C) All amendments to the bill are invalidated, and the original version of the bill is sent to the president to sign.
(D) The Senate's version of the bill is sent to the president because the Senate is the higher legislative body.
(E) The two legislative bodies form a conference committee.

GO ON TO THE NEXT PAGE

27. Which of the following is the most accurate statement about the voting behavior of Americans over the age of 65?

(A) They are as, or more, likely to vote than are members of other age groups because they have received the highest level of formal education of all age groups.

(B) They are as, or more, likely to vote than are members of other age groups because they believe that they have a personal stake in government policy.

(C) They are less likely to vote than are members of other age groups because it is difficult for them to get to the polls.

(D) They are less likely to vote than are members of other age groups because they are less likely to be aware of election schedules.

(E) They are less likely to vote than are members of other age groups because very few senior citizens run for political office.

28. A member of which of the following demographic groups is most likely to support a Republican presidential candidate?

(A) White male
(B) White female
(C) African American, male or female
(D) Youths under the age of 25, male or female
(E) Individuals earning below poverty-level wages, male or female

29. The Civil Rights Act of 1964 was passed to reinforce the

(A) presidential veto
(B) system of checks and balances
(C) states' power to challenge federal regulation
(D) Fourteenth Amendment
(E) Taft-Hartley Act of 1947

30. Which of the following best illustrates a use of the elastic clause?

(A) The Supreme Court allows a lower court ruling to stand by refusing to hear an appeal.
(B) A congressional committee prevents the full chamber from voting on legislation by delaying its report.
(C) Congress passes legislation establishing a national speed limit.
(D) A member of the House of Representatives introduces a bill to increase federal income tax rates.
(E) A governor issues an executive order requiring all state employees to submit to drug testing.

31. According to the *Federalist Papers*, federalism has which of the following effects on political factions?

(A) It provides a structured environment in which factions may flourish.
(B) It limits the dangers of factionalism by diluting political power.
(C) It allows factions to dominate on the national level while limiting their influence on state governments.
(D) It eliminates any opportunity for factions to form.
(E) It prevents factions by declaring them illegal.

32. The Constitution, as originally ratified, addressed all of the following weaknesses of the Articles of Confederation EXCEPT the

(A) lack of a chief executive office
(B) national government's inability to levy taxes effectively
(C) absence of a central authority to regulate interstate trade
(D) insufficiency of the government's power to raise an army
(E) omission of a universal suffrage clause

GO ON TO THE NEXT PAGE

33. Congress's power to determine national policy

    (A) usually increases as a president's popularity decreases, and vice versa
    (B) has declined steadily since the ratification of the Constitution
    (C) is severely limited by the "elastic clause" of the Constitution
    (D) increases during times of war
    (E) stems primarily from its control over the judicial branch

34. In recent years, presidents have come to rely most heavily on the advice of

    (A) the full cabinet
    (B) the vice president
    (C) congressional delegations
    (D) the White House staff
    (E) foreign ambassadors

35. Which of the following statements about the electoral college is correct?

    (A) Each state must split its electoral votes among all the candidates that receive votes.
    (B) Each state is equally represented in the electoral college.
    (C) The electoral college was created by an amendment to the Constitution.
    (D) The results of electoral college voting tend to distort the winner's margin of victory, when compared with the popular vote for president.
    (E) Each state's delegation to the electoral college consists of that state's U.S. senators and representatives.

36. Which of the following statements is true of congressional incumbents who run for reelection?

    (A) Incumbent senators are more likely to be reelected than are incumbent members of the House of Representatives.
    (B) Incumbents are prohibited by law from spending more on their reelection campaigns than their challengers spend.
    (C) Incumbents have a great advantage over challengers because they are better known and can raise campaign funds more easily.
    (D) Ever since the 1994 election, the majority of congressional incumbents have failed in their reelection attempts.
    (E) Most incumbents who run for reelection are unopposed in the general election.

37. Before serving in the House of Representatives or Senate, the greatest number of federal legislators

    (A) own and operate small businesses
    (B) are professional athletes
    (C) teach political science at the college level
    (D) work as journalists
    (E) earn law degrees

38. A member of the House of Representatives wishing to influence tax policy would most likely try to serve on which of the following committees?

    (A) Commerce
    (B) Ways and Means
    (C) Education and the Workforce
    (D) Resources
    (E) Judiciary

39. The spoils system of awarding civil service jobs was replaced by the merit system as a result of the

    (A) Truman Doctrine
    (B) Fair Labor Standards Act of 1961
    (C) National Industrial Recovery Act
    (D) Civil Rights Act of 1964
    (E) Pendleton Act of 1883

40. The boundary lines of congressional districts must be redrawn every 10 years to

    (A) reflect population shifts indicated by the national census
    (B) guarantee the turnover of the majority of congressional seats
    (C) make sure each state's congressional delegation exactly mirrors its residents' party affiliations
    (D) determine which party's leader will be named Speaker of the House
    (E) increase the number of female and minority members of Congress

GO ON TO THE NEXT PAGE

	Eligible voters	Registered voters	Votes cast	Turnout, registered voters	Turnout, all eligible voters
1986	178,566,000	118,399,984	64,991,128	54.89%	36.40%
1988	182,778,000	126,379,628	91,594,693	72.48%	50.11%
1990	185,812,000	121,105,630	67,859,189	56.03%	36.52%
1992	189,529,000	133,821,178	104,405,155	78.02%	55.09%
1994	193,650,000	130,292,822	75,105,860	57.64%	38.78%
1996	196,511,000	146,211,960	96,456,345	65.97%	49.08%
1998	200,929,000	141,850,558	73,117,022	70.6%	36.4%

Source: Federal Election Commission

41. The chart above best supports which of the following conclusions?

   (A) No more than half of all eligible voters ever participate in federal elections.
   (B) The number of registered voters always increases between elections.
   (C) Voters have been more dissatisfied with their electoral choices in the last decade than they were during the 1970s.
   (D) Voter turnout for midterm congressional elections is generally lower than it is for presidential elections.
   (E) Voter turnout for the 1996 presidential election was the lowest for any presidential election during the twentieth century.

42. Interest groups representing businesspeople and investors are often among the most successful lobbying groups in Washington, DC, for all of the following reasons EXCEPT

   (A) Such groups have the financial resources to mount sustained campaigns on their own behalf.
   (B) Many such groups have been in existence for several decades or more, allowing them to master the legislative system and to develop close ties with legislators.
   (C) In many districts, these groups' constituents make up the majority of voters.
   (D) These groups' constituents contribute heavily to many legislators' campaigns, and in doing so, gain greater access to legislators.
   (E) Economic lobbyists often campaign for obscure or minute changes to tax law about which the public knows little, and therefore frequently meet little opposition.

43. Of the following groups that have traditionally supported the Democratic Party, which would LEAST likely be cited by someone arguing that the Democrats represented only liberal constituencies?

   (A) White southerners
   (B) Labor union members
   (C) African Americans
   (D) Northern ethnic minorities
   (E) Environmentalists

44. The greatest number of American voters identify themselves as

   (A) liberal
   (B) conservative
   (C) progressive
   (D) reactionary
   (E) moderate

45. People who join a political party other than the one to which their parents belong most often do so because of

   (A) peer pressure
   (B) economic issues
   (C) religious beliefs
   (D) pressure from their employers
   (E) issues of international politics

46. Which of the following best describes the fate of most popular third-party movements?

   (A) They displace one of the two major parties and become major parties themselves.
   (B) They are ultimately abandoned by the public because their politics are perceived as too radical.
   (C) Their supporters become frustrated and withdraw from the political process.
   (D) They remain active participants in the American political system indefinitely.
   (E) They disintegrate when one or both of the major parties adopt the third party's goals.

GO ON TO THE NEXT PAGE

47. A constitutional amendment would be required to ban flag burning because that activity is currently protected by the right to

(A) due process
(B) assembly
(C) free exercise of religion
(D) protection against confiscation of private property
(E) free speech

48. The Supreme Court's decision in *Miranda v. Arizona* was based mainly on the

(A) Constitutional prohibition of ex post facto laws
(B) incorporation of the Fifth Amendment through the due process clause of the Fourteenth Amendment
(C) Eighth Amendment restriction against cruel and unusual punishment
(D) abolition of slavery by the Thirteenth Amendment
(E) full faith and credit clause of the Constitution

49. The Supreme Court has used the practice of selective incorporation to

(A) limit the number of appeals filed by defendants in state courts
(B) extend voting rights to racial minorities and women
(C) apply most Bill of Rights protections to state law
(D) hasten the integration of public schools
(E) prevent the states from calling a constitutional convention

50. The largest portion of the federal budget covers the costs of

(A) national defense
(B) social welfare programs
(C) interest on the national debt
(D) entitlement programs
(E) tax collection

51. Which of the following accurately describes congressional committees?

  I. The committee chairpersons always belong to the majority party.
  II. Seats on each committee are divided between the two major parties in exact proportion to the parties' representation in Congress.
  III. They recommend whether Congress should pass various pieces of legislation, and those recommendations are always approved by the full congressional body.
  IV. When a committee vote results in a tie, the vice president casts the tie-breaking vote.

(A) I only
(B) II only
(C) I and III only
(D) II and III only
(E) I, II, and IV only

52. The primary goal of the Gramm-Rudman Acts of 1985 and 1987 was to

(A) strengthen the military
(B) increase funding for social programs
(C) reduce the federal deficit
(D) limit the president's ability to conduct foreign policy
(E) allow citizens easier access to government records

53. The term "iron triangle" refers to the interrelationship of the

(A) president, Congress, and the Supreme Court
(B) electorate, Congress, and political action committees
(C) local, state, and federal governments
(D) State Department, the Pentagon, and the National Security Council
(E) federal bureaucracy, congressional committees, and lobbyists

GO ON TO THE NEXT PAGE

54. Media coverage of an issue is most likely to change public opinion when

(A) the issue directly affects few Americans and is one about which most Americans know very little

(B) coverage is extensive and is either overwhelmingly positive or overwhelmingly negative

(C) that issue is discussed in editorial columns and on broadcasts that emphasize news analysis, such as CNN's *Crossfire*

(D) a major newspaper runs a series of articles analyzing the issue in depth

(E) the media provide a diverse range of perspectives on the issue

55. Which of the following most accurately describes the right of American citizens to privacy?

(A) The right to privacy is determined entirely by the states on a case-by-case basis.

(B) The right to privacy is explicitly granted in the Preamble to the Constitution.

(C) The Supreme Court has ruled that the right to privacy is implied by the Bill of Rights.

(D) Common law requires the government to respect citizens' right to privacy.

(E) Americans have no right to privacy, but the government rarely violates individuals' privacy because to do so is not in the government's interest.

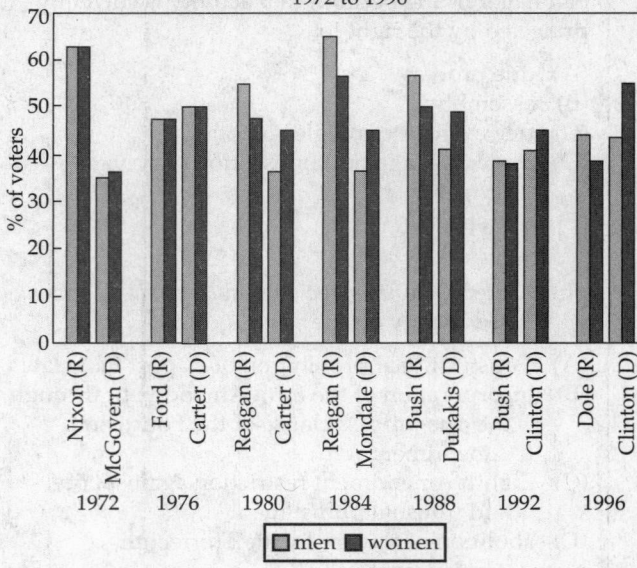

Presidential vote for majority party candidates, by gender, 1972 to 1996

Source: *New York Times*/CBS exit polls

56. The graph above supports which of the following conclusions about presidential elections?

(A) If only men had voted in the 1980 election, Jimmy Carter would have won.

(B) There is little difference in the level of support that the Republican Party receives from men and women.

(C) The gender gap was more prominent in the 1980s and 1990s than it was in the 1970s.

(D) In order for a Republican candidate to win, he or she must receive more votes from women than from men.

(E) The 1976 election was the closest in history.

GO ON TO THE NEXT PAGE

57. Which of the following factors would most likely explain why voter registration records underestimate the number of Independent voters in the United States?

(A) Independents are less likely than Republicans or Democrats to register to vote.
(B) Many Americans who consider themselves Independent do not participate in elections.
(C) Independents make up only a small portion of the electorate.
(D) Because Independents in many states are not allowed to participate in primary elections, many Independents register as either Republicans or Democrats.
(E) The majority of Independents are non-citizens who are not allowed to vote.

58. The difference between a pardon and a reprieve is

(A) a pardon lasts 10 years, a reprieve lasts one year
(B) a reprieve grants a release from legal punishment, while a pardon postpones it
(C) a pardon grants a release from legal punishment while a reprieve postpones it
(D) only state governors can issue pardons
(E) only state governors can issue reprieves

59. The government promotes preferential treatment for members of groups that have historically suffered from discrimination by means of

(A) the New Federalism
(B) affirmative action programs
(C) Social Security benefits
(D) bills of attainder
(E) gerrymandering

60. The exclusionary rule was established to

(A) create "separate but equal" facilities to facilitate racial segregation
(B) allow private organizations to restrict their memberships
(C) limit the government's ability to use illegally obtained evidence
(D) deny control of interstate commerce to the states
(E) provide the president with greater independence in negotiating foreign policy

STOP
END OF SECTION I

IF YOU FINISH BEFORE TIME IS CALLED, YOU MAY CHECK YOUR WORK ON THIS SECTION.
DO NOT GO ON TO SECTION II UNTIL YOU ARE TOLD TO DO SO.

UNITED STATES GOVERNMENT AND POLITICS

SECTION II

Time—100 minutes

<u>Directions:</u> You have 100 minutes to answer all four of the following questions. Unless the directions indicate otherwise, respond to all parts of all four questions. It is suggested that you take a few minutes to plan and outline each answer. <u>Spend approximately one-fourth of your time (25 minutes) on each question</u>. Illustrate your essay with substantive examples where appropriate. Make certain to number each of your answers as the question is numbered below.

1. Historians refer to five "party systems" in U.S. history.

    (a)   Define the term "party system."

    (b)   Evaluate the theory that the fifth party system, or "New Deal Coalition" that started in 1932 has come to an end.

    (c)   In support of your argument, cite the results of one election from the 1980s and one election from the 1990s.

GO ON TO THE NEXT PAGE

2. The debate over soft money has been a common and important feature of American politics.

   (a)   Define "soft money."

   (b)   Describe the opposing points of view expressed about soft money by the congressmen in this cartoon.

   (c)   Evaluate the arguments for and against soft money.

GO ON TO THE NEXT PAGE ⟶

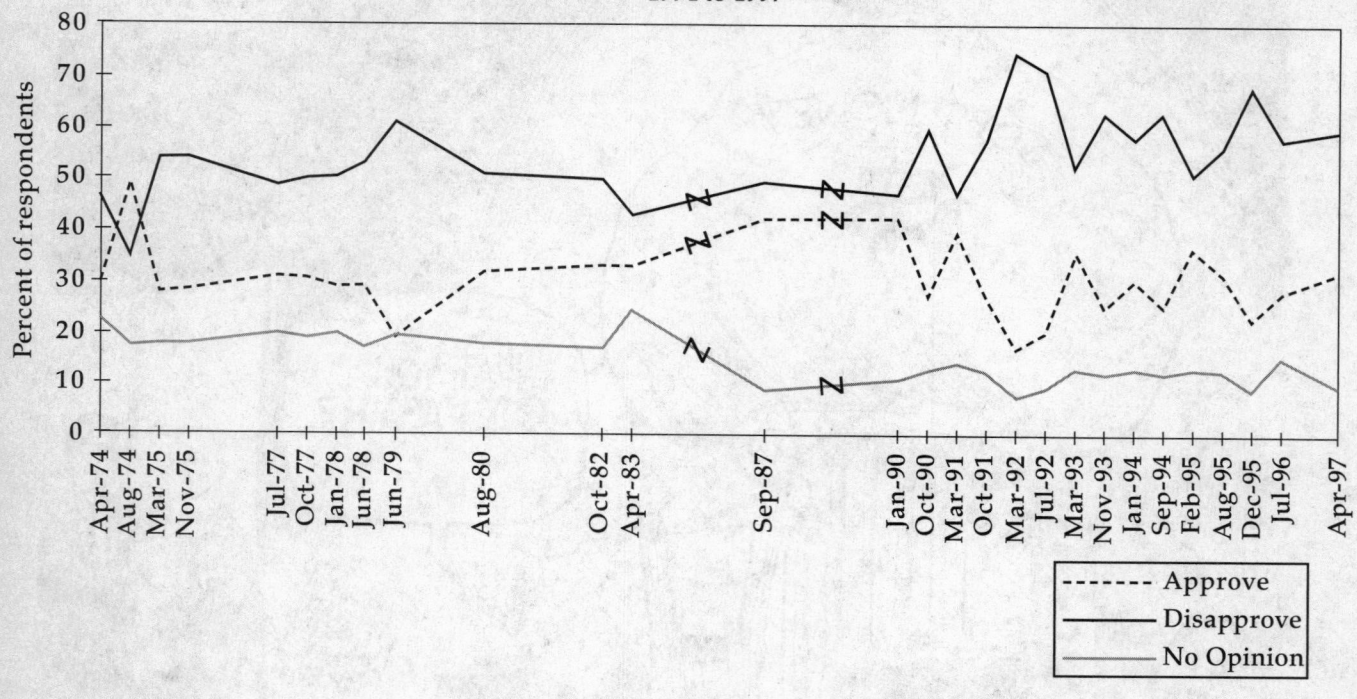

Answers to question: "Do you approve or disapprove of the way Congress is handling its job?"
1974 to 1997

Source: CBS poll

NOTE: Data for 1984–1986 and 1988–1989 not available.

3. Using the above graph and your knowledge of U.S. politics, perform the following tasks:

   (a)   Describe the overall trend in citizens' attitudes toward Congress. Assess the degree to which public opinion has changed since 1974.

   (b)   Explain the causes and results of ONE dramatic shift in public opinion indicated in the graph.

   (c)   Indicate to what extent the graph suggests that incumbent members of Congress will have difficulty winning reelection.

4. Political scandals involve investigations, prosecutions and possibly convictions of public officials.

   (a)   Describe two scandals that have occurred since 1960.

   (b)   Identify whether the allegations of impropriety surrounding these scandals were partisan or institutional in nature.

   (c)   Explain why scandals have been more prevalent in political life in recent years.

END OF EXAMINATION

14

PRACTICE TEST 1:
ANSWERS AND
EXPLANATIONS

ANSWER KEY

1.	B		31.	B
2.	C		32.	E
3.	A		33.	A
4.	A		34.	D
5.	C		35.	D
6.	E		36.	C
7.	A		37.	E
8.	B		38.	B
9.	D		39.	E
10.	B		40.	A
11.	E		41.	D
12.	A		42.	C
13.	B		43.	A
14.	C		44.	E
15.	B		45.	B
16.	D		46.	E
17.	A		47.	E
18.	C		48.	B
19.	C		49.	C
20.	A		50.	D
21.	B		51.	A
22.	C		52.	C
23.	D		53.	E
24.	E		54.	B
25.	C		55.	C
26.	E		56.	C
27.	B		57.	D
28.	A		58.	C
29.	D		59.	B
30.	C		60.	C

MULTIPLE-CHOICE SECTION: ANSWERS AND EXPLANATIONS

1. **B** The term *limited government* refers to the concept of defining government powers by means of a constitution. A constitution specifies what the government is allowed to do, and also what it may not do. In setting distinct limits on government power, the framers of the U.S. Constitution hoped to prevent the government from achieving the same level of power as had the British monarchy.

    Incorrect answers

    (A) *Direct democracy* refers to a form of democratic government in which all citizens vote on all issues. The Constitution established a representative democracy, in which citizens vote for representatives who, in turn, act on their behalf and assume the nation's legislative and executive duties.

    (C) The abolition of slavery did not occur until 1865 with the ratification of the Thirteenth Amendment. The framers of the Constitution did not seriously consider abolition.

    (D) As ratified in 1788, the Constitution did not yet have a Bill of Rights. The Bill of Rights was ratified in 1791; only then did the Constitution reflect a concern for protecting the rights of the accused.

    (E) Compared with the Articles of Confederation (which it replaced), the Constitution weakened the power of the states relative to the power of the federal government. Under the Articles, the states were mostly autonomous and exerted great control over the national government. The Constitution shifted the balance toward the federal government.

2. **C** *The Federalist Papers* is the collective name given to a group of essays written by Alexander Hamilton, James Madison, and John Jay in support of ratification of the Constitution. The essays were published anonymously in newspapers in New York and Virginia, two states in which ratification was both critical and uncertain.

    Incorrect answers

    (A) The Federalist Party did not have a platform. Party platforms are the product of political conventions, which did not become a part of American politics until after the demise of the Federalist Party.

    (B) This answer describes *Common Sense* by Thomas Paine and *The Rights of the British Colonies Asserted and Proved* by James Otis, among other documents.

    (D) The relationship described in this answer is defined by the U.S. Constitution.

    (E) The postwar South was governed under the Military Reconstruction Act of 1867.

3. **A** *Judicial activism* refers to the actions of a court that frequently strikes down or alters the acts of the executive and/or legislative branches. Activist judiciaries also are willing to overturn previous rulings. Judicial activism expands the court's impact on public policy.

Incorrect answers

(B) *Due process* refers to those rules that protect individuals from unfair treatment by the government. The due process clause of the Fourteenth Amendment prohibits the states from depriving citizens of life, liberty, or property without a fair and impartial hearing. The clause was intended to protect the rights of newly freed slaves in the post–Civil War South.

(C) *Judicial restraint* is the opposite of judicial activism. The term refers to judicial action that demonstrates an unwillingness to break with precedent or to overturn legislative and executive acts.

(D) An *ex post facto* law allows governments to prosecute citizens for acts that were legal at the time they occurred, but were later deemed illegal. Ex post facto laws are prohibited by the U.S. Constitution.

(E) *Judicial review* is the Supreme Court's power to overturn a law on the grounds that it is unconstitutional. Judicial review is not mentioned in the Constitution. The practice was established by Chief Justice John Marshall in the 1803 decision *Marbury v. Madison*.

4. **A** A writ of *certiorari* is a document issued by the Supreme Court that requests all the records pertaining to a case. When the Court issues a writ of *certiorari*, it indicates that the Court will consider the case. A writ of *certiorari* is issued when four of the nine justices agree to hear a case.

Incorrect answers

(B) The Supreme Court meets on Wednesdays and Fridays to vote on cases they have heard during the week. Afterward, one justice is chosen to write the majority opinion. Justices are given the chance to change their vote and to offer alternate concurring opinions (if they side with the majority but feel the majority opinion is either incomplete or incorrect) or dissenting opinions (if they disagree with the majority vote). Only when this process is complete does the Court hand down its final decision.

(C) When the Supreme Court decides not to hear a case, it simply rejects the appeal and the lower court decision stands. No writ is necessary.

(D) The Supreme Court meets 36 weeks a year, from the first week of October until June. It recesses occasionally to discuss cases and write decisions. No writ is necessary for a recess.

(E) The Supreme Court issues no official warning when it plans to overturn a previous ruling. When the Court agrees to hear a case concerning a subject on which it has already ruled, however, the possibility is great that the Court is considering altering at least part of its previous opinion.

5. **C** As chief of state, the president is the most powerful force in U.S. foreign policy. Because most congresspersons believe that the United States must present a strong, united front to the rest of the world, Congress allows the president a great deal of authority in setting foreign policy.

Incorrect answers

(A) The House is able to cut off funding for foreign policies it dislikes. As explained above, however, Congress is hesitant to take any action that would weaken the president's ability to conduct foreign policy.

(B) The Senate, like the House, can cut off funding for foreign policies. It also has the power to approve treaties and ambassadorial appointments. For the reasons given above, the Senate rarely challenges the president on foreign policy issues.

(D) The Supreme Court has very little direct influence over day-to-day foreign policy. Its one power in that regard is that it is the court of original jurisdiction for cases involving ambassadorial disputes.

(E) The federal bureaucracy is supposed to follow the instructions of Congress and the president. Although this is not always the case, the bureaucracy generally serves the president's policy goals. The president has the power to appoint many powerful officials within the bureaucracy, and these officials protect the president's interests.

6. **E** In 1954, the Supreme Court heard the anti-segregation case *Brown v. Board of Education of Topeka*, a lawsuit brought on behalf of Linda Brown (a black school-age child) by the NAACP. Then-future Supreme Court justice Thurgood Marshall argued the case for Brown. In its ruling, the Court overturned the "separate but equal" standard as it applied to education; "separate but equal" had been the law of the land since the Court had approved it in *Plessy v. Ferguson* (1896). In a 9 to 0 decision, the court ruled that "separate educational facilities are inherently unequal."

Incorrect answers

(A) *Gideon v. Wainwright* (1963) found that defendants in state criminal trials are entitled to legal representation even if they cannot afford it. *Gideon* thus resulted in the creation of state-sponsored public defenders.

(B) *Marbury v. Madison* (1803) established the principle of judicial review.

(C) *Engel v. Vitale* (1962) determined that forced prayer in public schools violated the "separation of church and state" clause of the Bill of Rights.

(D) *Regents of University of California v. Bakke* (1978) found that University of California's racial quota system of admissions violated the Civil Rights Act of 1964. This ruling complicated the implementation of many affirmative action programs by rejecting the use of simple quota systems. However, the Court also ruled that University of California could consider race as *one* of many factors in determining admission policy.

7. **A** Congress rarely passes a bill that it knows the president will veto because a presidential veto is extremely difficult to override (an override requires a two-thirds majority in both houses). When the president is very popular, the job of collecting that two-thirds majority becomes impossible. Veto overrides typically require members of the president's party to cross party lines and vote against the president. Such crossover votes only occur when a president is unpopular.

Incorrect answers

(B) When Congress has attempted and failed to draft a compromise bill with the president, it may pass the bill simply to force the president to reject it. This is particularly true of bills that are perceived as popular among a majority of a congressperson's constituents. For example, Congress may pass a tax reduction bill that it knows the president will veto to weaken the president politically. This is particularly likely to happen when Congress and the presidency are controlled by different parties.

(C) As explained above in answer choice (B), the opposing party to that of the president may pass a bill solely to force the president to veto it, and consequently lose political support.

(D) If the president has expressed some hesitancy about vetoing a bill, Congress may pass it simply to force a decision. Under such circumstances the possibility would remain that the president would sign the bill.

(E) If Congress has enough votes to override a veto, it will pass a bill. As explained in answer choice (B), such a situation would only occur when a president's public approval rating is low.

8. **B** *Ticket splitting* has become a common phenomenon in the past 30 years. In the distant past, the same party typically controlled the presidency and Congress. Since 1968, however, the Democrats have controlled both branches simultaneously for only six years, and the Republicans did not control both branches until 2002. All other years, control of Congress was split between the parties.

Incorrect answers

(A) This answer choice accurately describes an action typically taken by presidential candidates. However, it does not define *ticket splitting*.

(C) This answer choice describes an action that few politicians would attempt and fewer would admit to trying. Although it mentions *tickets*, it has nothing to do with *ticket splitting*.

(D) This answer captures the basic idea of *ticket splitting*, which occurs when a voter does not adhere to the party line. However, it does not define the term *ticket splitting* as it is conventionally used.

(E) Congresspersons vote along party lines between 60 and 80 percent of the time (the number varies from Congress to Congress and from issue to issue). The action described in this answer choice, then, is exceptional behavior. However, it does not define the term *ticket splitting* as it is conventionally used.

9. **D** Because the membership of the House of Representatives is so large, the process by which bills are debated and amended must be limited (in the Senate, which is smaller, fewer rules govern this process). The task of setting these limits falls to the House Rules Committee. Because the Rules Committee controls the terms of debate and the scheduling of floor votes, it is considered among the most powerful House committees. The majority party dominates the Rules Committee. During the 105th Congress, Republicans held nine seats on the committee, while Democrats held four (the number of Democrats and Republicans on any given committee is negotiated by the parties after each election. Generally, the majority party takes two-thirds of the seats on the most important committees to ensure the party's dominance of those committees).

Incorrect answers

(A) The House Ethics Committee investigates ethics charges against House members.

(B) The Senate has the power to provide "advise and consent" to the president on judicial nominees. The House has no power in this area.

(C) There is no single committee that sets a limit for the number of House subcommittees. The number of subcommittees is limited by budget and staffing considerations.

(E) The House Committee on Government Reform and Oversight considers changes to federal election procedures.

10. **B** Parties in multiparty systems tend to be smaller and more closely identified with particular ideologies and political goals. Parties in a two-party system, on the other hand, present more general platforms in order to win a simple majority of the electorate.

Incorrect answers

(A) Influencing the outcome of elections is a primary goal of all political parties. American political parties are no exception.

(C) American political parties are extremely effective at raising money. American elections are the costliest in the world.

(D) In a multiparty system, each party more closely mirrors the ideology and political goals of its members. The United States' two parties reflect only a narrow range of political perspectives, and many Americans' political views fall outside that range.

(E) American political parties rarely focus on a single goal or issue because doing so may alienate potential supporters. American political parties are organized around very general beliefs. The Democrats tend to believe that government intervention can be effective and so have a greater inclination toward regulation of businesses and social issues. Republicans tend to distrust government intervention and, in most instances, oppose government regulation.

11. **E** When government officials resign from office, many remain in Washington to work as consultants. Such individuals can use the contacts they made while in government to influence public policy. Often they work as or with lobbyists. The term *influence peddling* is used to describe their actions when they exploit their friendships with current government officials to achieve a political goal.

Incorrect answers

(A) *Influence peddling* refers specifically to actions that directly affect government policy.

(B) Although a former president may be trying to influence a current president, the action described does not define the term *influence peddling* as it is conventionally used.

(C) *Influence peddling* refers specifically to the actions of lobbyists. Therefore, this answer is incorrect.

(D) See the explanation for answer choice (C).

12. **A** Political action committees are organizations created for the purpose of raising political funds and distributing them to candidates.

Incorrect answers

(B) The primary purpose of PACs is to raise funds for electoral campaigns. The action described in this answer choice is performed both by political parties and by state and local governments.

(C) The vast majority of PAC contributions go to incumbents. The goal of PACs is to endorse the election of those who represent their points of view. They do not try to defeat all incumbents per se, but rather those who are their political opponents.

(D) The primary purpose of PACs is to raise funds for electoral campaigns. Although many PACs are affiliated with the types of public interest groups that organize protests, this is not something that PACs themselves generally do.

(E) See the explanation for answer choice (B).

13. **B** Network news programs tend to favor information that changes regularly and can be communicated quickly. Public opinion poll results fit both of these criteria. In contrast, candidates' positions on issues are often complex. Furthermore, they rarely change. Therefore, news programs may report such information once during an election, but they will not report it repeatedly as they do poll results. As a result, the network news audience is most likely to be aware of where candidates stand in the current polls. Choice (A), is the type of information that a news program may report once but will not report repeatedly, as they do poll results.

14. **C** The government may censor the press for security purposes, as it did during the Gulf War (I). The press is free to challenge such restrictions, however, and the courts do not always find in favor of the government. For example, when the Nixon administration attempted to suppress the Pentagon Papers, it argued that national security would be compromised by their publication. The courts disagreed, and the Pentagon Papers were published (II). The Supreme Court has also ruled that the government may ban obscene publications. Again, the courts ultimately determine what is and is not obscene.

Incorrect answers

(A) The explanation for answer (C) describes some of the circumstances under which the government may limit free speech.

(B) Statement II is correct; however, (B) is not the complete answer because statement III is also correct.

(D) Statement IV is incorrect. The government may not prevent speech merely because it is offensive. A prime example of such offensive speech is flag burning, which is protected by the First Amendment despite the fact that it offends many people. Furthermore, (D) does not include statement II, which accurately describes a circumstance under which the government may limit free speech.

(E) See the explanation for answer choice (D).

15. **B** The Supreme Court is denied jurisdiction in cases in which a state is a party in opposition to a citizen of that state.

Incorrect answers

(A) If the United States is a party, the federal courts have original jurisdiction.

(C) If the Constitution, federal laws, or treaties are in question, the Supreme Court holds original jurisdiction.

(D) If citizens from two different states are in conflict, the Supreme Court holds original jurisdiction.

(E) The Supreme Court holds original jurisdiction in "all cases of admirality and maritime jurisdiction."

16. **D** *Federalism* is a system under which the federal government shares power with the states. The Tenth Amendment to the Constitution reserves to the states all powers not granted the national government by the Constitution. Therefore, it is instrumental in defining the relationship between the two levels of government, which is the essence of federalism.

Incorrect answers

(A) The system of checks and balances among the three branches of the federal government concerns the national government only. Because Federalism involves the relationship between the states and the federal government, this cannot be the correct answer.

(B) International treaties are the sole responsibility of the federal government, and do not relate to the states in any way.

(C) Washington, DC, does have special constitutional status as the nation's capital. The federal government plays a role in governing the city, and the city is not represented in Congress. However, Washington's constitutional status has little influence on American Federalism.

(E) The president's power to grant reprieves and pardons is solely a function of the federal government. Because federalism involves the relationship between the states and the federal government, this cannot be the correct answer.

17. **A** *Judicial review* is the Supreme Court's power to overturn laws on the basis of their constitutionality. Judicial review is not mentioned in the Constitution. The practice was established by Chief Justice John Marshall in the 1803 decision *Marbury v. Madison*.

Incorrect answers

(B) The census must be taken every ten years, according to Article I, Section 2 of the Constitution, which states the following:
"The actual Enumeration shall be made within three years after the first meeting of the Congress of the United States, and within every subsequent term of ten years."

(C) The rules governing the impeachment of the president are contained in the body of the Constitution. To bring about an impeachment, the House of Representatives must vote to bring an impeachment trial (thus serving a role equivalent to that of a grand jury). The Senate serves as the trial jury, and the Supreme Court presides.

(D) Article II, Section 3 of the Constitution states that the president "shall from time to time give to the Congress information of the state of the union."

(E) The Constitution states that federal judges "both of the supreme and inferior courts shall hold their offices during good behavior." This means that judges are appointed for life and can only be removed for criminal or disgraceful behavior.

18. **C** Each state has its own set of laws, and violations of those laws are prosecuted in state courts. The federal government also has a set of laws, and violations of these are tried in federal courts. Occasionally the two legal systems overlap. For example, the defendants in the Oklahoma City bombing trial destroyed a federal building and killed federal employees, all federal crimes. Clearly the bombing also violated state laws prohibiting murder, destruction of property, and reckless endangerment. When this happens, the federal and state governments negotiate to decide who will try the case.

State cases, however, may be appealed to federal courts on constitutional grounds. Thus, although the two court systems are generally autonomous, they are not completely independent of each other.

Incorrect answers

(A) Federal courts may overturn state court decisions, but only on the grounds that a defendant's constitutional rights were violated. Federal courts may not rule on whether state courts have correctly applied state law (state Supreme Courts are the final arbiters of such cases).

(B) See the explanation for answer choice (C).

(D) This is an incorrect statement. Federal courts are not solely appeals courts.

(E) See the explanation for answer choice (C).

19. **C** The Constitution specifically delegates to the president the power to veto laws. It does not mention the power to veto parts of laws. The Supreme Court declared the line-item veto unconstitutional in *Clinton v. New York* on the grounds that the Constitution does not give the president the authority to cancel parts of taxing and spending bills because this would give the president too much legislative influence.

Incorrect answers

(A) The line-item veto gave legislative powers to the president, not executive powers to the legislature.

(B) The bureaucracy has no role in the line-item veto. The bureaucracy is responsible for carrying out the laws enacted by Congress and signed by the president. If the president's line-item veto power had been upheld, the bureaucracy would have had to implement the law as passed.

(D) The line-item veto did not involve the states.

(E) Judicial review is performed by the Supreme Court, not the Senate. If the Senate objects to a House bill, it merely votes against the bill.

20. **A** The president may, "on extraordinary occasions, convene both Houses, or either of them, and in case of disagreement between them, with respect to the time of adjournment, he may adjourn them to such time as he shall think proper." Otherwise, the president's powers to influence legislation are primarily political. As the most prominent political figure in the United States, the president can strongly influence public sentiment on legislation.

Incorrect answers

(B) The president may not introduce bills to the floor of Congress. He may recommend bills to Congress, but Congress is under no obligation to consider those bills.

(C) The president has no power to address Congress, except when he delivers his State of the Union address. Of course, the president does not need to speak on the floor of Congress to influence congressional votes, because his position on most bills is a matter of public record. As the leader of his party, the president also exerts some influence over the way congresspersons of his party vote.

(D) The president may not vote on congressional acts. He has a much greater power, however: the power to reject congressional legislation through a veto. The vice president votes in case of a tied vote in the Senate.

(E) The president has no power to disband congressional committees. Under extraordinary circumstances he may adjourn the entirety of Congress, but he has no special power to dissolve a committee. If he did, he could stop any congressional investigation of his administration by dissolving the committee in charge of the investigation. That, needless to say, would run counter to the system of checks and balances.

21. **B** Access to the president is handled primarily by the chief of staff, who screens requests from other executive officers to meet with the president. The chief of staff is often the president's closest confidant. He knows the president's agenda and can help coordinate executive actions to best accomplish those goals. The close relationship between the two allows the chief of staff to filter reports and any requests headed for the president's desk in an effort to keep the president from becoming overwhelmed. The chief of staff also mediates disputes among various cabinet offices.

Incorrect answers

(A) Vice presidents have as much or as little power as the president gives them. Al Gore was more active than most who preceded him. Other vice presidents have had very few official duties.

(C) The national security advisor is one of the president's top foreign policy advisors. However, he does not control the president's schedule. Answer (C), therefore, is incorrect.

(D) The chair of the Federal Reserve Board exerts tremendous influence over the American economy.

(E) The press secretary provides press releases and answers press queries on behalf of the president.

22. **C** An executive agreement is an agreement between the president and the leader of a foreign country. It is as binding as a treaty, but it does not require Senate approval. Because Congress controls government funding, it can exert influence over many executive agreements. However, Congress generally defers to the president in matters of foreign policy.

Incorrect answers

(A) Executive agreements are as binding as treaties. Otherwise, there would be little point in making an executive agreement.

(B) See the explanation for answer (C).

(D) Both executive agreements and treaties can be enforced by the military if necessary. Military force is always a last resort in matters of international dispute.

(E) There is no specified time limit for either executive orders or treaties.

23. **D** Those most active in both the Republican and Democratic parties tend to be further from the political center than are average or *rank-and-file* party members. Because party activists control much of the nomination process and because they are more likely than others to vote in primary elections, successful presidential nominees tend to reflect the political agendas of these activists. This has been particularly true of the Republican Party in recent years; most candidates for the Republican presidential nomination focus great effort on winning support from the party's small but powerful ultraconservative wing.

Incorrect answers

(A) The opposite is true. While conservative Republicans are generally more successful in the primaries, these same candidates have a more difficult time appealing to the moderate general electorate in November.

(B) Party members are expected to support their party's presidential candidate. If answer choice (B) were true, no Republican could ever win the presidency, because most Democrats and moderate Republicans would vote Democratic. Such a sizable coalition would win every election.

(C) People join the political party that most closely reflects their political views. Most Republicans do care whether their presidential nominee shares their views, at least on a few issues they consider important.

(E) Rank-and-file members participate in the Republican nominating process by voting in primary elections.

24. **E** The two-year term in the House of Representatives means that members no sooner win elections than they must start planning their reelection campaigns. As a result, House members are usually very responsive to the desires of their constituents. House members represent fewer constituents than do senators or the president, another reason that they more closely reflect the political will of their constituencies.

Incorrect answers

(A) Costly campaigns tend to make elected officials more responsive to the needs of potential donors but less responsive to other voters. Election campaigns for the House are less expensive than are senatorial and presidential campaigns.

(B) This answer simply does not address the question. Limits that may be placed on future representatives have no bearing on why someone today may characterize the House as the institution most responsive to the will of the public.

(C) The House and the Senate share oversight responsibilities. Therefore, congressional oversight would not explain why someone would consider the House more responsive than the Senate to the will of the public.

(D) Average citizens may be called to testify before either the House or the Senate. Therefore, this would not explain why someone would consider the House more responsive than the Senate to the will of the public. Also, those who are called to testify before Congress are usually called because of some specialized knowledge they possess and not because they represent the will of average citizens.

25. **C** America's increased prominence in foreign affairs (I) has increased the power of the president. As chief of state, the president receives and negotiates with foreign leaders. Congress generally allows the president great leeway in handling foreign relations. Therefore, as America's role in world affairs has increased, so too has the power of the presidency. Increased government responsibilities (III) are enforced and partly administered by the executive branch. As leader of the executive branch, the president has gained power as a result of this increased responsibility. Constant media exposure (IV) has given the American public greater awareness of each president since Franklin Roosevelt. The president is now better known and more widely heard than at any time in the past. This allows the president to influence voters in a way that no other elected official can.

Incorrect answers

(A) This answer is partly correct. However, statements III and IV are also true.

(B) This answer is partly correct. However, statement III is also true.

(D) Statement II is incorrect. Public confidence in the government has been in decline since the 1960s. The Vietnam War, the Watergate scandal, the Iran-Contra affair, and the government shutdown of 1993 are just a few of the events that have resulted in increased public cynicism toward the government.

(E) Statements III and IV are true, but so is statement I, which is not included in this answer choice. Also, statement II is incorrect (see explanation for answer (D)).

26. **E** The House and the Senate must pass the same version of a bill before the president may consider it. Often, the two houses pass different versions of the same bill. They then meet in conference committee to draft a compromise bill, which then returns to each house to be voted on again. Bills drafted by conference committees usually bypass the committee stage and are immediately scheduled for a floor vote in each house.

Incorrect answers

(A) The president may not sign a bill until an identical version of it has been passed by both the House and the Senate.

(B) Before a bill such as the one described returns to each house, the two houses meet to try to draft a compromise bill. Bills drafted by conference committees usually bypass the committee stage and are immediately scheduled for a floor vote in each house.

(C) See the explanation for answer choice (E).

(D) See the explanation for answer choice (E).

27. **B** Seventy percent of all Americans age 65 and over voted in the 1992 presidential election. That equaled the frequency with which Americans between ages 45 and 64 voted, and was higher than the voting frequency of younger Americans. Senior citizens depend on the government for Medicare and Social Security payments. They generally vote to protect these programs, and because they are a powerful voting bloc, politicians rarely even suggest cuts in spending for either program.

Incorrect answers

(A) Younger Americans hold proportionally more academic degrees than do senior citizens.

(C) Senior citizens are more likely to vote than are members of other age groups. See the explanation for answer (B).

(D) Senior citizens are more likely to vote than are members of other age groups. See the explanation for answer (B).

(E) Senior citizens are more likely to vote than are members of other age groups. See the explanation for answer (B).

28. **A** White males have preferred the Republican candidate for president in every election since 1972. White females, in contrast, favored Bill Clinton in 1992 and 1996, and have voted Democratic more frequently than have white males. The majority of youths voted for Democratic candidates Jimmy Carter (1976) and Bill Clinton (1996). African Americans have overwhelmingly identified themselves as Democrats since Franklin Roosevelt's presidency.

29. **D** The Fourteenth Amendment states that

"No state shall make or enforce any law which shall abridge the privileges or immunities of citizens of the United States; nor shall any state deprive any person of life, liberty, or property, without due process of law; nor deny to any person within its jurisdiction the equal protection of the laws."

The amendment proved ineffective, however, in preventing racial discrimination and segregation. Civil rights advocates had to struggle for almost 100 years more before the government banned all discrimination based on race, religion, gender, or national origin with the Civil Rights Act of 1964. The Civil Rights Act gave the government the power to enforce desegregation by cutting off federal funding to discriminatory programs. It also allowed the Justice Department to file desegregation suits. Choice (E) The Taft-Hartley Act of 1947 was designed to restrict some of the rights granted to unions by the Wagner Act of 1935. It prohibited closed shops (which required union membership as a prerequisite to hiring), restricted labor's right to strike, prohibited the use of union funds for political purposes, and gave the government broad power to intervene in strikes.

30. **C** Among the powers granted Congress by the Constitution is the right to pass laws "necessary and proper" to the performance of its duties. This section of the Constitution is called the *elastic clause* because it allows Congress to stretch its powers beyond those that are specifically granted it (called *enumerated powers*) by the Constitution. When Congress passed a national speed limit law in 1974, it invoked the elastic clause by citing its enumerated power to regulate interstate trade.

Incorrect answers

(A) The elastic clause pertains to Congress, not to the Supreme Court.

(B) This answer describes a common event, but it does not illustrate the elastic clause as described in the explanation for answer (C).

(D) Raising taxes is among Congress's enumerated powers. Therefore, the action described in answer (D) does not illustrate the elastic clause as described above in the explanation for answer (C).

(E) The elastic clause pertains to Congress, not to state executives such as governors.

31. **B** In "Federalist No. 10," James Madison warns of the dangers of political factions. He also acknowledges that political factions are inevitable. He concludes that American federalism, as embodied in the U.S. Constitution, checks the dangers of factions through the separation of powers, making it difficult for a faction to control the entire governing process. According to Madison, so many different regional and economic agendas are represented in federal and state government that it would be impossible for any single group to gain undue control.

Incorrect answers

(A) The *Federalist Papers* take a negative view of political factions and would not have approved of any political system that encouraged their growth.

(C) According to the *Federalist Papers*, Republican federalism limits the influence of political factions on all levels of the government.

(D) In "Federalist No. 10," Madison acknowledged that political factions form whenever people disagree and whenever individuals put their personal welfare above the best interests of the state. Political factions, he concluded, are inevitable in any system so long as humans remain human.

(E) The *Federalist Papers* were written in defense of the U.S. Constitution, which does not ban political factions.

32. **E** Each of the answer choices correctly identifies a weakness of the Articles of Confederation. However, neither the Articles nor the original Constitution had a universal suffrage clause. Under both, blacks and women were among those who had no right to vote, and states could add further restrictions on the right to vote. Many states allowed only property owners to vote, for example.

Incorrect answers

(A) Under the Articles of Confederation the national government was entirely dependent on the states to enforce national law, as it had no executive powers of its own. The Constitution rectified this problem by establishing the executive branch of government.

(B) Under the Articles of Confederation state governments held the power to impose trade tariffs. The Constitution grants this power to Congress.

(C) Under the Articles of Confederation the national government had no authority to regulate interstate trade. The Constitution grants this power to Congress.

(D) Under the Articles of Confederation the national government was dependent on the states to provide soldiers for national defense. This system proved unreliable at best. The Constitution grants Congress the power to raise an army.

33. **A** The Constitution is not precise in explaining how the president and Congress are to share power. As a result this relationship is dynamic, relying partially on the political popularity of the two institutions. When a president is popular—as Franklin Roosevelt was when he first took office—he can parlay that popularity into political clout and may dominate national policy decision-making. When a president is unpopular—as Truman was in the year preceding his reelection—then Congress gains the upper hand and can largely determine national policy on its own.

Incorrect answers

(B) Congress's power to determine national policy relies on the relative political strength of Congress and the president. Since the ratification of the Constitution, Congress has seen its powers grow and shrink in conjunction with its political fortunes.

(C) Congress's power is in fact expanded by the elastic clause, which grants Congress the right to pass laws "necessary and proper" to the performance of its duties. Congress regularly uses the elastic clause to broaden its scope of influence.

(D) During times of war, the president grows more powerful relative to Congress. Congress is hesitant to challenge the president in wartime, as most congresspersons believe that the country must remain unified during emergencies.

(E) Congress exerts little control over the judicial branch. It can pass laws, such as sentencing guidelines, that limit judicial action. The Senate confirms federal judicial appointments and so influences the judiciary in that way. By and large, however, the judiciary is independent of congressional influence.

34. **D** The White House staff consists of the president's closest advisors, often including those who have accompanied him throughout much of his political career. For example, during President Clinton's first term, he chose his longtime friend Thomas McLarty as chief of staff and his campaign chairman, Mickey Kantor, as U.S. trade representative. Cabinet officials, in contrast, are often chosen for political reasons. (Recent presidents are usually careful to select a cabinet that includes representatives of most minority constituencies.)

Incorrect answers

(A) Cabinet officials are often chosen for political reasons. Furthermore, they frequently place the goals of the agencies they represent above the president's priorities. As a result, the president does not rely primarily on the cabinet for advice.

(B) Vice presidents have as much or little influence on the president as the president allows them. Some, such as current Vice President Dick Cheney, have close relationships with the president.

(C) The president meets with congressional delegations on occasion to discuss pending legislation and negotiate compromises between the two branches, but he does not regularly seek congressional advice on policy matters.

(E) Foreign ambassadors are stationed overseas and confer with the president infrequently, if ever.

35. **D** The *winner-take-all* system of the electoral college distorts the results of the popular vote. In 1992, Ross Perot received 19 percent of the popular vote but 0 electoral votes. In 1996, President Clinton won 49 percent of the popular vote, Republican challenger Bob Dole received 41 percent, and Ross Perot received 8 percent. In the electoral college, however, Clinton won 70 percent, Dole 30 percent, and Perot 0 percent. The discrepancy was also apparent in 2000.

	% of Popular Vote	Electoral Vote	% of Electoral Vote
Gore	48.38	267	49.63
Bush	47.87	271	50.37
Nader	.42	0	0
Buchanan	2.74	0	0

The election of 2000 was one of the closest in American history. It was unusual because the winner of the popular vote lost the election in the electoral college. A difference of 400 to 500 popular votes in Florida would have given the election to Gore because he would have received all of Florida's electoral votes. As it turned out, Bush won the presidency by the minimum number of electoral votes possible, with Gore winning the national popular vote.

Incorrect answers

(A) Forty-eight states allocate their electoral votes by the "winner-take-all" method. The two exceptions are Maine and Nebraska, which give two electoral votes to the candidate who wins a plurality of the statewide vote, and one vote to the winner of each of the state's congressional districts. In 1996, Maine had four electoral votes, Nebraska had five.

(B) Each state is represented in the electoral college by a delegation equal in number to the state's total representation in Congress (senators and members of the House). California has the greatest number of electoral votes (54); several states have only three electoral votes, the minimum a state may have (two senators and one member of the House).

(C) The electoral college was established by the Constitution as it was originally ratified.

(E) Senators and representatives are prohibited from the electoral college by the Constitution. Electors are generally chosen from among state party leaders and state legislators.

36. **C** In 1996, 94 percent of incumbent representatives who ran for reelection won. In 1994, the year of supposed anti-incumbency, nearly 90 percent of all House incumbents won reelection campaigns. In short, incumbents have a huge advantage over challengers, primarily because voters are better acquainted with incumbents than with those who challenge them for office.

Incorrect answers

(A) Winning reelection to the Senate is considered slightly more difficult than winning reelection to the House. Because the Senate is a smaller legislative body than the House, each seat in the Senate is relatively more powerful than a seat in the House. As a result, Senate races are more hotly contested than House races.

(B) No such spending limits exist in House campaigns. Incumbents usually outspend their challengers by considerable sums during election campaigns.

(D) Even in 1994, the year of supposed anti-incumbency, nearly 90 percent of all House incumbents won reelection campaigns. In 1996, that number increased to 94 percent.

(E) Of 362 incumbents who ran for reelection in 1994, only 26 were unopposed. The great majority of incumbents face a challenger in the general election.

37. **E** 181 members (40 percent) of the 103rd Congress practiced law prior to serving office. Former businesspeople and bankers represented 30 percent of House membership. Educators made up 15 percent of the body; journalists held 24 seats (about 6 percent). In the Senate, lawyers make up an even greater portion: 58 percent of senators in 1993 had previously worked as lawyers. This fact should come as no surprise, given that the business of Congress is to pass laws. And as prominent members of the community, lawyers often have the standing to run for and win elected office.

38. **B** The House Ways and Means Committee controls tax and trade legislation. It is considered one of the most powerful committees in Congress.

Incorrect answers

(A) The Commerce Committee considers legislation on such topics as consumer affairs, medicine and medical research, energy, and national and international trade. It is a powerful committee and as such has some influence on tax policy, but not as much as the Ways and Means Committee, which considers all tax legislation before it reaches the floor of the House.

(C) The Education and the Workforce Committee considers legislation concerning national testing, public schools, and workplace issues.

(D) The Resources Committee considers legislation concerning the United States' natural resources.

(E) The Judiciary Committee considers legislation covering numerous topics such as patents, crime, immigration policy, telecommunications regulations, and Constitutional amendments.

39. **E** The Pendleton Act of 1883 was passed in response to charges of patronage in the awarding of government jobs (the "spoils system"). The Pendleton Act created the Civil Service Commission to oversee examinations for potential government employees.

Incorrect answers

(A) The Truman Doctrine was a foreign policy of the United States at the outset of the Cold War. Its goal was to contain Soviet expansion.

(B) The Fair Labor Standards Act of 1961 increased the minimum wage to $1.15 per hour.

(C) The National Industrial Recovery Act was a New Deal program that sought to revitalize U.S. industry during the Depression.

(D) The Civil Rights Act of 1964 banned discrimination in public places and gave the government the power to prosecute discriminatory institutions and businesses. It also allowed the government to cut off funding to segregationist and discriminatory programs.

40. **A** To maintain the "one person, one vote" principle of American government, Congress is required to redraw election districts every 10 years, in conjunction with the national census.

Incorrect answers

(B) Regardless of when congressional districts are redrawn, congressional incumbents are reelected at a rate of approximately 90 percent or more.

(C) Redistricting is a political battle in which the party in power attempts to draw districts in such a way as to increase their representation in Congress. Frequently, redistricting plans are challenged in court by the minority party.

(D) The Speaker of the House is chosen by the majority party in the House of Representatives.

(E) Redistricting can increase the number of female and minority congresspersons. In recent years, the courts have, on occasion, forced Congress to create minority districts and take other measures to increase minority representation. However, this has not historically been the purpose of redistricting. Congressional lines have been redrawn every ten years since the beginning of the republic, yet increased female and minority representation is a relatively recent phenomenon.

41. **D** The chart shows that between 66 percent and 78 percent of registered voters participate in presidential elections (1988, 1992, and 1996) but that only slightly more than half participate in midterm congressional elections (1986, 1990, and 1994).

Incorrect answers

(A) More than half of all eligible voters participated in the elections of 1988 and 1992. Furthermore, this chart only provides information for elections between the years 1986 and 1996. Therefore, any answer that draws a conclusion about elections in years before 1986, as answer (A) does, must be incorrect.

(B) The number of registered voters actually decreased between 1992 and 1994. Furthermore, this chart only provides information for elections between the years 1986 and 1996. Therefore, any answer that draws a conclusion about elections in years before 1986, as answer (B) does, must be incorrect.

(C) The chart provides no information about elections during the 1970s. Also, this answer assumes that voter satisfaction can be gauged by turnout rates, which is a disputable conclusion.

(E) Because this chart only provides information for elections between the years 1986 and 1996, answer (E), which requires you to draw a conclusion about all elections during the 20th century, must be incorrect.

42. **C** Businesspeople and investors constitute a small but powerful segment of U.S. society. They are the majority of voters in only a very few, very wealthy voting districts.

Incorrect answers

(A) Lobbyists representing businesses and investors are typically better funded than those representing the interests of people with lower incomes.

(B) Business lobbies, such as the U.S. Chamber of Commerce, are among the most enduring in Washington. Over their many decades in the capitol, these groups have made and maintained relationships with many important policy makers.

(D) Because election campaigns are so expensive, candidates must solicit funds. People who donate generously gain the candidate's friendship in return. Although legislators do not always follow their donors' suggestions—indeed they cannot because they have many different donors with diverse goals and interests—they must pay close attention if they expect to receive contributions to their next campaign.

(E) The most effective lobbies in Washington are those campaigning for obscure changes to regulations and tax codes. Because these issues are not widely followed by the public, lobbyists who pursue such changes encounter less opposition.

43. **A** Of the five groups mentioned, white southerners are easily the most conservative. In recent years this group's traditional support for the Democratic Party has dwindled to the point that many southern congressional seats that had been held by Democrats since the end of Reconstruction are now held by Republicans. Many southerners joined the Democratic coalition after the Civil War ended (the Republicans, remember, were the party of the abolition movement). This allegiance was strengthened during the New Deal, but has weakened since. A large segment of the white south adheres to conservative fundamentalist Christianity and is uncomfortable with the government activism and social programs associated with the Democratic Party.

Incorrect answers

(B) Labor unions are traditionally perceived as liberal, particularly concerning government regulation of the workplace.

(C) The majority of African Americans support some form of the liberal social programs that Democrats generally support and most Republicans oppose.

(D) Northern ethnic minorities are traditionally liberal on economic issues. Some, particularly those that are predominantly Catholic, can be conservative on social issues. However, they are generally more liberal in this regard than are white Southern fundamentalists.

(E) Environmentalism is strongly associated with liberalism, as many of its goals involve government regulation of America's natural resources.

44. **E** In a recurring poll taken by CBS News and the *New York Times*, the greatest number of Americans have identified themselves as political moderates every year since 1981. On average, slightly more than 40 percent of Americans call themselves moderates. About 33 percent consider themselves conservative, while approximately 20 percent call themselves liberals.

Incorrect answers

(A) See the explanation for answer (E).

(B) See the explanation for answer (E).

(C) Progressives consider themselves further to the political left than liberals. They make up an even smaller percentage of the American public than do liberals.

(D) *Reactionary* is a term used to describe extreme conservatives (the term originates from their adverse reaction to liberalism and to change in general).

45. **B** People usually join their parents' political party. When their political beliefs change, they do so as a result of economic issues. Of all political issues, economic issues have the greatest impact on personal politics.

Incorrect answers

(A) As people grow older, the views of their peers more greatly influence their political beliefs. Young people generally have little interest in politics, and as a result peer influence on their political beliefs is minimal. In any case, the economy has a greater influence on individual political outlooks.

(C) Because people generally have the same religious beliefs as their parents, religion is extremely unlikely to cause them to choose a party different from the one their parents have chosen.

(D) Employers rarely pressure employees to alter their party allegiance. They are somewhat more likely to seek their support for individual candidates or referenda. By and large, employers do not attempt to influence their employees' political beliefs.

(E) Most Americans do not follow issues in international politics closely, and these issues have little influence on the political beliefs of most.

46. **E** Of the many popular third parties in American history, only the Republican Party has progressed to the level of a major party. All others were absorbed by one or both of the major parties. The Populists, for example, campaigned for direct election of senators, a graduated income tax, and shorter workdays. Eventually both major parties took up these issues. As they did, the Populist coalition fell apart.

Incorrect answers

(A) There have been at least ten prominent third parties in American history. Of them, only the Republican Party went on to become a major party.

(B) A few third parties have had radical goals, but most radical parties never gain enough support to become "popular third-party movements." Some third parties grow around the popularity of a single individual: Ross Perot, George Wallace, and Theodore Roosevelt are some examples. Others champion progressive goals that are later adopted by one or both of the major parties. Examples of these include the Free Soil Party and the Populist Party. Even some of the Socialist Party's goals (especially those concerning workplace conditions) were later adopted by the Democratic Party.

(C) Some supporters of third parties become disenchanted when their candidates fail, but most rejoin the political mainstream.

(D) See the above explanation for question 45, answer (E).

47. **E** Because flag burning is usually done as an act of political protest, it is considered speech and is protected by the First Amendment.

48. **B** In *Miranda v. Arizona*, the main question was whether the Fifth Amendment protection against self-incrimination should be applied to state law. The court sided with Miranda and decided that the due process clause of the Fourteenth Amendment did apply to the Fifth Amendment, and that his confession was inadmissible in court. The Court then ruled that the police must advise a suspect of his rights before questioning begins. These rights have come to be known as *Miranda rights*.

Incorrect answers

(A) An *ex post facto* law allows governments to prosecute citizens for acts that were legal at the time they occurred but that later became illegal. Ex post facto laws are prohibited by the U.S. Constitution. For an explanation of the issues in the *Miranda* case, see the explanation for answer (B). (E): The states are required by the Constitution to accept the court judgments, licenses, contracts, and other civil acts of all the other states. This obligation is contained in the "full faith and credit" clause.

49. **C** In 1833, the Supreme Court ruled that the Bill of Rights applied to the federal government only and not to state governments. Since the early part of the twentieth-century, however, the Supreme Court has used the "due process" and "equal protection" clauses of the Fourteenth Amendment to extend *some* of the Bill of Rights protections, but has done so on a case-by-case basis. This process of incorporating *some* of the Bill of Rights protections to state law is called selective incorporation.

Incorrect answers

(A) See the explanation for answer (C).

(B) Voting rights have been extended to minorities and women by amendments to the Constitution and by various congressional civil rights acts.

(D) In the early 1970s, the Supreme Court upheld busing children to schools other than the ones closest to their homes to hasten integration. However, that is not what is meant by "selective incorporation." For a definition of this term, see the explanation for answer (C).

(E) See the explanation for answer (C).

50. **D** Entitlement programs include Social Security, veterans' pensions, civil-service pensions, and Medicare. Social Security alone accounts for 21 percent of the federal budget, making it the single largest government expenditure. National defense accounts for just under 20 percent of the budget, interest on the national debt accounts for 9 percent, and social welfare and tax collection costs account for even smaller shares.

51. **A** The majority party in each house controls all of that house's committees. The committee chair is always a member of the majority party.

Incorrect answers

(B) The number of Republicans and Democrats sitting on each committee is determined by negotiation, but the majority party always dominates the most important committees (usually by a two-to-one majority).

(C) Congress takes committee recommendations into consideration, but it does not follow all (or even most) of those recommendations.

(D) See the explanation for answer (B). Also, Congress takes committee recommendations into consideration, but it does not follow all (or even most) of those recommendations. Thus, statement III is also incorrect.

(E) Statement I is correct, but statements II and IV are incorrect. When a committee vote results in a tie, the result simply remains a tie vote.

52. **C** The Gramm-Rudman acts were intended to reduce budget deficits. Their best-known provision, in favor of automatic across-the-board budget cuts, was ruled unconstitutional by the Supreme Court. Although the laws failed to substantially reduce the federal deficit, they did heighten public awareness of the deficit issue.

53. **E** Iron triangles are sometimes referred to as *subgovernments*. They are formed by the close working relationship among various interest groups, congressional committees, and executive agencies that enforce federal regulations. Working together, these groups can exert a powerful collective influence over legislation and law enforcement.

54. **B** In general, media coverage affects which issues the public feels are important, but has little effect on the public's views on those issues. The exception is when media coverage is pervasive and overwhelmingly positive or negative, in which case it can alter public opinion. For example, in 1992 most Americans favored nationalized health care coverage. Polls also revealed that the public generally supported the major provisions of the Clinton health care proposal. Media coverage of the issue, however, was strongly negative. That, in conjunction with a well-coordinated campaign against the proposal led by health insurance companies and some medical associations, turned public opinion against the plan.

Incorrect answers

(A) When Americans don't care about an issue, they ignore media coverage of it. As a result, media coverage of these issues changes very few peoples' opinions.

(C) Relatively few Americans pay close attention to editorial pages and broadcasts. Of those who do, most are already strongly partisan and unlikely to be influenced by the opinions expressed in the forums.

(D) Even a major newspaper such as the *New York Times* reaches relatively few Americans directly. In-depth reports in major newspapers are read by even fewer Americans. Such a report may have a ripple effect, resulting in stories on broadcast news and television news magazines. However, as discussed in the explanation for answer (B) above, unless that coverage is pervasive and one-sided it will ultimately have little effect on public opinion.

(E) As discussed in the explanation for answer (B) above, media coverage is most likely to affect public opinion when it presents a single perspective on an issue. Diverse perspectives dilute the effect of media coverage on public opinion.

55. **C** In the 1965 Supreme Court case of *Griswold v. Connecticut*, the Court ruled that the Bill of Rights contained an implied right to privacy. The Court ruled that the combination of the First, Third, Fourth, Fifth, Ninth, and Fourteenth Amendments added up to a guarantee of privacy. The *Griswold* case concerned a state law banning the use of contraception. The Court decision overturned that law.

Incorrect answers

(A) The right to privacy is guaranteed by the federal government. States must comply with this protection under the Fourteenth Amendment.

(B) The right to privacy is implied by the Constitution; it is never directly stated. For more information, see the explanation for answer (C).

(D) Common law consists of the entire body of previous judicial decisions. It originated in medieval England and persists to this day, underlying much of American statute law (laws passed by legislatures). Common law does not guarantee the right to privacy.

(E) See the explanation for answer (C).

56. **C** The chart shows little difference between the presidential votes of men and women in both the 1972 and the 1976 elections. Starting with the 1980 election, however, a clear gender gap can be seen, with women consistently giving greater support to the Democratic candidate than men do.

Incorrect answers

(A) The chart shows that, had only men voted, Ronald Reagan would have won the 1980 election by a greater margin than he actually did.

(B) The chart shows that from 1980 forward a smaller percentage of women than men voted for the Republican presidential candidate.

(D) Because the chart illustrates only the percentage of votes from each gender, it is impossible to draw a conclusion about the number of votes that the candidates received from men and women.

(E) Because the chart only depicts election results from 1972 to 1996, it is impossible to draw a conclusion concerning every presidential election in history.

57. **D** Since the mid-1960s, Americans' loyalty to political parties has decreased. Many more Americans than ever before consider themselves Independents. Some of these voters continue to register as members of one of the major parties, however, because their home states allow primary voters to participate only in the election of their declared party. In some races, particularly in congressional contests where one party represents the vast majority of residents, elections are essentially decided during the primaries. To participate in these elections, some Independents register as Republicans or Democrats. As a result, voter registration records underestimate the number of Americans who consider themselves Independents.

Incorrect answers

(A) The question asks about voters. By law, people who do not register to vote cannot be voters.

(B) The question asks about voters. People who do not participate in elections are not voters.

(C) Independents make up 19 percent of the American electorate, according to a recent poll. Regardless, this answer would not explain why Independents are underrepresented by voter registration records.

(E) The question asks about voters. People who cannot participate in elections are not voters.

58. **C** The right to pardon is extended to both presidents and governors and is the full release from legal punishment. Presidents and governors can also issue reprieves, but a reprieve is merely a postponement of legal punishment.

59. **B** Programs designed to rectify social inequality based on past racial and gender discrimination are called affirmative action programs. Most such programs create special hiring and educational opportunities for women and racial minorities.

Incorrect answers

(A) The New Federalism was the name of Ronald Reagan's attempted reorganization of the federal government. Its goal was to shift governmental power from the national government to the states. The plan failed. States feared that the New Federalism would result in higher state budgets, resulting in unpopular tax increases.

(C) Social Security benefits are payments made to the elderly, disabled, and other entitled beneficiaries from a government trust fund. The source of the fund is a tax (called FICA) collected on payrolls and individual paychecks.

(D) A bill of attainder is a legislative act that applies to an individual or easily identified group in such a way as to constitute punishment. (For example, if the legislature passed a law that prevents Joe Bloggs from driving because Joe Bloggs is a political agitator.) Bills of attainder are unconstitutional.

(E) Gerrymandering refers to the process of dividing a geographical area into political divisions in such a way as to achieve an unlawful or ulterior goal. (For example, redrawing voting districts so that minority voters are split into different districts and their power consequently diluted.)

60. **C** The exclusionary rule holds that evidence obtained in unwarranted searches must be excluded from trial. It also requires the government to have just cause to search private property and to demonstrate that cause before a judge. The rule was established by the Supreme Court decision *Mapp v. Ohio*. The case involved Dollree Mapp, who had been convicted in Ohio for possession of obscene materials. Her original conviction was based on evidence found by police who were looking for evidence of illegal gambling. The police had not obtained a search warrant to search for either evidence of gambling or pornography, so the search was illegal.

Incorrect answers

(A) The Supreme Court decision *Plessy v. Ferguson* established the principle of "separate but equal," which was later overturned in *Brown v. Board of Education*.

(B) Because this involves excluding people, it is a tempting answer choice. However, this is not the meaning of the term *exclusionary rule*.

(D) Interstate commerce is controlled by the federal government under provisions of the Constitution. For an explanation of the exclusionary rule, see the explanation for answer (C).

(E) See the explanation for answer (C).

ESSAY SECTION: ANSWERS EXPLAINED

Remember that you need to answer all four essay questions in 1 hour and 40 minutes, so you do not have time to waste, nor can you skip any questions. Nevertheless, you should take time to brainstorm some ideas and to organize what you come up with before you start to write each response. Otherwise, your essays will probably be incomplete, disorganized, or both.

You must average 25 minutes or less per question, but that amount of time should be sufficient. Make sure you read each question carefully and respond directly to each of its components in your essay. The questions are about broad issues, but they ask for specific information. A general essay that fails to address specific concerns raised by the question will not earn a high score.

QUESTION 1

The five party systems this question refers to are in fact five historical periods. A fairly stable set of issues and fairly consistent party allegiances characterize a party system. The fifth party system, the subject of this question, began with the presidency of Franklin Roosevelt. The question is asking you whether this party system is still intact.

Even if you forgot or never saw the term "party system," you still could answer this question because it tells you that the fifth party system is the "New Deal coalition." If you know what that term means, you could probably assess the extent to which it is still intact, even if you don't know what a party system is.

Of course, formulating a successful answer requires more than simply recognizing the term "New Deal coalition." The question asks you to focus on the recent past and the present: Has the New Deal coalition persisted into the 1980s and 1990s? To what extent? Insofar as it has ended, what has taken its place? Is there a sixth party system, and, if so, what defines it?

A thorough answer to this question needs to accomplish the following four tasks:

- Explain the concept of a party system.

- Describe the characteristics of the fifth party system.

- Tell whether the fifth party system is still intact; if you say it is not, you need to tell what has replaced it.

- Use the outcomes of two elections, one from the 1980s, one from the 1990s, to defend your contention that the fifth party system is or is not intact.

Background Information—Party Systems in American History

A political party, of course, refers to an organization that represents certain ideas or individuals and runs candidates for office. A party system is a term for a set of political parties, issues, and voter alignments that endures over time. Most political scientists agree that the United States has had a series of five party systems, more or less along the following lines:

- **The First Party System (1790s to 1816).** The earliest government conflicts concerned the balance of power between the federal and state governments. Those who favored a strong central government included George Washington, Alexander Hamilton, and John Adams; they formed the leadership of the Federalist Party. Supporting the autonomy of the states were Thomas Jefferson and James Madison; their party was called the Democratic Republican Party. The Federalists were centered in New England. As the country expanded westward, they made up a proportionally smaller part of the electorate. Their pro-British sympathies during the War of 1812 finished them off, as they were widely perceived as traitors. For several years after the demise of the Federalists, the Democratic Republicans were the only major party. This period is known as the *Era of Good Feelings*.

- **The Second Party System (1830s to the 1850s).** During the 1820s, Andrew Jackson came to dominate the national political landscape. He was the most popular candidate in the 1824 election but lost in the electoral college; he returned to win the 1828 and 1832 elections. He led the Democratic Republican Party, which had now shortened its name to the Democratic Party. Eventually, a second party formed to represent those who opposed Jackson's policies. This group was called the Whigs, and they vehemently disagreed with Jackson's policies of Western expansion and destruction of the National Bank. During this period, the entire electoral system became more democratic. Laws requiring voters to own property were repealed, thus allowing all white men to vote. Parties held primary elections and conventions to choose their presidential candidates (previously presidential candidates had been selected by state legislatures and party leaders). The second party system fell apart due to the conflicts that caused the Civil War.

- **The Third Party System (Civil War to 1896).** In the 1840s and 1850s, the issue of slavery gave rise to a number of third parties. One, the Republican Party, grew strong enough to become a major party. It took the place of the Whig Party, which dissolved over internal disagreements about slavery. The Republicans dominated the national government during the war and Reconstruction at the expense of the Democrats, but afterward the two parties were evenly represented. The Democratic coalition was made up of white Southerners and the northern working class. The Republicans were supported by business, the middle class, and blacks (the Republican Party was, of course, the party of Abraham Lincoln). The Third Party System was undone by the rise of the Populist movement, which ultimately resulted in a major political realignment.

- **The Fourth Party System (1896 to 1932).** During the 1890s, a farmers' party called the People's Party (also called "the Populists") gained increased support for a number of government policies more favorable to the poor and working classes. In 1896 they joined the Democratic Party. As a result, some of the Democrats' more economically conservative constituencies abandoned them. As big-money interests threw their full support behind the Republicans, the Republican Party thrived. It dominated national politics until the Great Depression.

- **The Fifth Party System (1932 to present).** The Republicans' failure to prevent the Great Depression (probably an impossible task) and their unwillingness to alleviate its effects through government intervention resulted in another political realignment, this time greatly strengthening the Democratic Party. Franklin Roosevelt and the New Deal assembled a coalition made up of white ethnics (many of whom belonged to labor unions), Catholics, Jews, blacks, and southern whites (who benefited greatly from New Deal projects such as the WPA and the Tennessee Valley Authority). The New Deal coalition defined the Democratic Party as the party of the working class, the poor, and disenfranchised minorities. New Deal Democrats were those Democrats who believed that the government should play an active role in guaranteeing certain minimum living standards for all Americans. Those who disagreed aligned with the Republican Party.

Weakening of the New Deal Coalition

After World War II, the New Deal coalition showed some signs of weakening. The Truman administration, widely admired now, was not well liked by the public in its day. Although the majority of Americans considered themselves Democrats at the time, Republican Dwight Eisenhower won the presidency in 1952 and 1956. Still, throughout this period the Democrats continued to control both houses of Congress, and the party's fundamental support base did not change.

The continued strength of the New Deal coalition was apparent in the Democratic presidential victories of 1960 and especially 1964, when Lyndon Johnson won a landslide victory over Republican Barry Goldwater. Johnson's social agenda, called the Great Society, mirrored New Deal ideals and certainly appealed to much of the Democrats' core constituency.

However, Johnson's presidency also sowed seeds of dissension among the party faithful. The Great Society addressed the needs of poor Americans—particularly those of Southern blacks. These programs alienated many of the southern whites who formed a substantial portion of the Democrats' electoral base. Johnson also upset the liberal wing of the party with his Vietnam policy.

This set of circumstances brought an end to Democratic dominance of the White House. Over the next 24 years, Democrats held the presidency only during the four-year Carter administration. Still, throughout this 24-year period the Democrats continued to control the House of Representatives (and, for 18 of those years, the Senate as well). Furthermore, the political philosophy of the party and its supporters remained basically unchanged. The Democrats continued to believe in the effectiveness of government regulation and the need for government assistance. They also continued to support a liberal social agenda. The defection of southern whites had cost the Democrats the White House, but it had not otherwise fundamentally altered the American political landscape.

Has the Fifth Party System Come to an End?

There is not one correct response to this question. You have several ways to answer it, none of which is necessarily any better than the others; the strength of your answer depends on how clearly you articulate your position and, in particular, how effectively you identify and discuss appropriate elections from the 1980s and 1990s to support your view. Let's look at some possible answers.

- **No.** There are too many elements of continuity between the issues and partisan iden-tifications of voters across the past 60 years to say that a realignment has taken place.

  Some key groups in the New Deal coalition, notably African Americans and Jews, have continued to support Democratic candidates in the last several decades. Some of the members of the New Deal coalition who appeared to defect from the Demo-crats in 1968—such as the white southerners who instead supported Wallace's third-party bid or the Republican candidacy of Nixon that year—came back to the Democrats when they ran white southerners in 1976 (Carter) and 1992 (Clinton). In addition, many of the white, upper midwestern, Catholic union members who sup-ported Reagan in 1980 and 1984 over social issues such as busing and abortion did not vote to reelect Bush in 1992 when he was identified with an economic down-turn. In other words, evidence of clear partisan change is weak.

  The other component of a new party system is a new set of dominant issues. Here, too, there is reason to doubt that the fifth party system has ended.

  A true realignment would call for a major philosophical shift among the elec-torate, yet most Americans remain supportive of entitlements, some degree of government management of the economy, and government regulation of business. Fewer Americans support poverty-relief programs as they currently exist, but the jury is still out on whether they are willing to abandon the safety net entirely or have merely rejected the previous system for its many failings. Overall, almost half of all Americans consider themselves moderates, slightly up from the 1980s. Self-identified liberals make up 20 percent of the population, as they have for the past two decades, and the number of Americans who consider themselves conservative has also remained stable during that period, around 33 percent. Furthermore, Americans continued to elect Democrats to Congress throughout the 1980s, when the supposed shift to the political right was taking place. Election results of recent years demonstrate, more than anything, that Americans are fed up with "business as usual" in Washington, DC This was most evident in 1992, when almost 19 percent of voters supported Ross Perot, and in 1994, when voters gave the Democratic Congress a vote of no confidence by replacing them with Republicans. However, the "Republican revolution" of 1994 owed much to the resignation of many Democrats. Not many seats were actually won from incumbents. Had there been a true political realignment, moreover, the Republicans would have been able to easily implement their conservative agenda, and President Clinton would have had more difficulty winning reelection in 1996. Complicating matters further is the Democratic takeover of the House and Senate in 2004.

- **Yes.** If you choose to answer that the fifth party system is over, you still have a choice to make. You need to argue either that a sixth party system has replaced it, in which case you would have to describe it; or you would have to argue that nothing has re-placed it and we have entered an era of dealignment. Let's look at both possibilities.

You could argue that we are in a sixth party system. The presidential election of 1980 permanently altered the political landscape. Ronald Reagan's victory signaled a major shift to the political right of the entire electorate. This is further demonstrated by the fact that Bill Clinton had to reject much of the Democrats' traditional liberal agenda to win the elections of 1992 and 1996. Further proof that the New Deal coalition is dead is found in the 1994 midterm election, in which the Republicans gained control of both houses of Congress. The 1996 elections demonstrated that this was no fluke, as the Republicans maintained control of both houses despite the fact that Clinton won the presidential election handily. He could have been expected to provide coattails for Democratic legislative candidates. Republican control was also demonstrated by George W. Bush's election in 2000 and reelection in 2004.

Thus, the Republican party has shown over the last decade that it can win and hold the presidency, the House of Representatives, and the Senate as it was unable to do during the fifth party system. It has shown that it can attract support among majorities of groups that used to favor democrats, including white southerners, union members, and white northern ethnics. It has also shown strength among newly significant groups, such as suburbanites and westerners, who were relatively less important because there were fewer of them when Franklin Roosevelt put the New Deal coalition together.

Another way to argue that we have left the fifth party system is by asserting that, unlike earlier party systems, which ended with realignments, the fifth ended with *dealignment*, a period in which defining issues do not change completely, and certain voters' partisan identifications, rather than switching from one party to another, are weakened altogether.

Many political scientists believe that the current voting trend is best described as political dealignment. Prior to 1968, one party typically controlled both the executive and legislative branches of government. Since that year, however, there have been only six years of one-party control of these branches (1978 to 1980 and 1992 to 1994). Americans are more likely than ever to vote a split ticket. They are more likely to consider the merits and positions of a particular candidate than to merely consider his or her party affiliation. Overall, the parties that once wielded great power over the electoral process are less powerful than in previous years. In their place, media consultants have become the chief movers and shakers in political campaigns.

Thus, the New Deal coalition is dead, but no new coalition has come along to replace it.

- **It's too soon to tell.** At least one key constituency of the New Deal coalition has defected to the Republican Party: white southerners. The success of Democratic presidential candidates who are themselves white southerners—Carter and Clinton—does not mask the fact that Southern whites now vote Republican for Congress and governor with some consistency. Many of them still vote for Democratic state legislators, however, which suggests that the realignment is incomplete.

Democrats have also lost substantial support in the northern working class. Over the past 30 years, unions, many of which were core components of the New Deal coalition, have declined in proportion to the work force they enroll. White working-class Americans have also become disaffected from the Democratic Party, perceiving its social agenda on women and homosexuals to be too liberal. Increased support for Republicans has been especially pronounced among Catholics and the increasingly large conservative Christian component of the white working class. These groups have not become reliable Republicans, however, mistrusting the commitment of the party to real change on such issues as race, abortion, and gay rights.

It is therefore unclear what, if anything, has come along to replace the fifth party system. Given the tendency toward dealignment (discussed above), as well as the lack of a wholesale change in decisive issues and voter ideology, it is not yet evident that the fifth party system is really dead. Only further elections will tell.

Below is a detailed explanation of the issues pertaining to the essay questions. These reviews include much more information than you could possibly include in 25-minute essays. After the detailed explanation, we'll discuss writing strategies and provide a sample essay that would receive a grade of 5 (the highest grade possible).

Here's How to Crack It

1. Historians refer to five "party systems" in U.S. history.

    (a) Define the term "party system."
    (b) Evaluate the theory that the fifth party system, or "New Deal Coalition" that started in 1932 has come to an end.
    (c) In support of your argument, cite the results of one election from the 1980s and one election from the 1990s.

Always start by reading the question carefully. Reformulate it in your own words so you are sure what you are being asked. On the exam, the questions are in a green booklet; use some blank space in that green booklet to list everything that comes to mind about the party system and elections since 1980. Then, determine how you will answer the core question, whether the fifth party system has come to an end. Outline your essay, incorporating the best points from the list you brainstormed. Don't skip this step: The best essays are well planned. In order for your reader to follow you, you have to know where you are going before you start.

Avoid writing history. Even if you can provide a thoughtful discussion of each party system in U.S. history, the question does not ask for it and you won't have time to write an excellent answer as well as writing an uncalled-for history. Another pitfall to avoid: Even though you may recall hearing that the New Deal Coalition was not really consolidated until 1934 or later, ignore the matter. It is never a good idea to contradict a premise of a question.

Make it clear that you understand the issues involved in the question by defining key terms. It is hard to imagine an essay earning the highest score unless it defines "party system" and indicates key aspects of the fifth party system. Establish criteria that have to be met to convince you that this party system has ended. Make sure you discuss whether or not those criteria have been met.

Note that the question requires you to make reference to the outcomes of one election from the 1980s and one from the 1990s. Be sure to do this. Again, you will not get the maximum amount of credit for your answer if you do not. You will see that the discussion above suggests elections you could cite, regardless of the answer you give. Note that the specific requirement is to discuss the results of "one" election from each decade. An accurate treatment of one result from each decade is perfectly adequate. Citing another election can help your argument if it is relevant, but you do not need to do so. If a question asks for "at least one," you should probably cite two, but a request for some discussion of just one election in each decade really means just one election in each decade, not more.

Sample "Excellent" Essay

Political historians discuss five separate party systems in American history. The fifth began in 1932, at the beginning of the Roosevelt administration with the formation of the New Deal coalition. Through his New Deal, Roosevelt brought together backing from labor unions, poor farmers, minorities, and Southern whites. The New Deal made the Democrats the party of the poor and working classes, and the Republicans became the party of the wealthy. The New Deal also made the Democrats the party for those who believed in an active government; the Republicans opposed government intervention. The New Deal coalition held together through the late 1960s. Although it suffered some setbacks, such as the Eisenhower presidency, it remained strong enough that Lyndon Johnson could implement his New Deal–like Great Society program with this coalition's backing.

Ever since then, however, the New Deal coalition has been weakened by several factors. First, Johnson's Great Society and civil rights programs upset Southern white Democrats, particularly segregationists. Second, Johnson's support for the war in Vietnam angered liberals. These two factors permanently weakened the New Deal coalition. As a result, the Republicans gained control of the White House in 1968 and held it for most of the next 24 years. That does not mean, however, that the New Deal coalition and the fifth party system died. Democrats continued to control Congress throughout this period. Most Americans continued to believe in an activist government that maintained some control of the economy and industry, and provided a safety net to the poor.

Recent election results raise the question, however, of whether the New Deal coalition is now dead. The Democrats seem to have permanently lost two major constituencies: white Southerners and the working class, both of which have shifted to the Republican Party. Furthermore, another of its core constituencies, labor, has been weakened by decreasing union enrollments. These trends were evident in Ronald Reagan's 1980 victory and even clearer in his 1984 reelection and George Bush's 1988 victory. Still, during this period, the Democrats maintained control of Congress, evidence that the New Deal coalition was still alive. More compelling was the 1994 election, when the Democrats lost control of both houses of Congress for the first time since the 1920s. They did not regain control of Congress in 1996, despite the successful presidential campaign of their candidate, Bill Clinton.

However, to say that the fifth party system is dead, two things would have to be true: There would have to be a clear change in Americans' attitude toward the government, and there would have to be something concrete that had taken the fifth party system's place. It is difficult to say whether Americans have dramatically changed their attitudes about government. On the one hand, they are more cynical about politicians and the government. On the other hand, they still support most government programs and become angry when funding for them is cut.

More obviously, nothing has come along to take the place of the fifth party system. In 1994 and 1996, America saw the continuation of a trend that has been apparent since 1968: split-ticket voting. Americans are now more likely than ever to hand the executive branch to one party and the legislative branch to the other. Political scientists call this phenomenon "dealignment." The parties are weaker than in the past, and in their place are political media consultants and campaign strategists who work for individual candidates, not the parties.

Perhaps, then, the entire party system itself is dying, although at this point that is only speculation. Because the two major parties promote roughly the same ideology and represent most of the same constituencies as they have for many decades, I would say that the fifth party system is not dead yet. However, the coalitions that support it have certainly weakened considerably, leaving open the possibility of dramatic change in the near future.

QUESTION 2

What Is Soft Money?

"Soft money" is money donated by corporations and unions directly to political parties. Soft money contributions are supposed to be used for such general purposes as get-out-the-vote campaigns, voter registration drives, expenses involved in the day-to-day running of party headquarters, and campaign propaganda that relates to the party rather than to specific candidates: For example, T-shirts and balloons that say "Vote Democrat" as opposed to "Vote Clinton."

Corporations, unions, and trade groups are all prohibited by law from donating directly to candidates. Up until recently, they had been able to make unlimited soft-money contributions. According to the electoral watchdog organization Common Cause, the top 50 soft-money contributors in 1996 each donated an average of $800,000. Top donors such as Philip Morris, AT&T, and the Trial Lawyers Association each contributed more than $2 million. In 1996, the two parties raised a total of $260 million in soft money.

In 2002, Congress passed the Bipartisan Campaign Reform Act (BCRA), also known as the McCain-Feingold bill. This law made it illegal for the major political parties to raise and spend soft money, though other organizations still can and do. This law was upheld by the Supreme Court in *McConnell v. FEC* (2003).

Why Do the Congressmen in the Cartoon Want to Defend Soft Money, and Who Doesn't?

Soft money became an important source of campaign financing for several interrelated reasons.

- In the 1976 Supreme Court case *Buckley v. Valeo*, the Court ruled that election spending limits could not be imposed on candidates and parties. The Court ruled that, in politics, spending is equivalent to speech; spending limits, therefore, violate the First Amendment. The Court allowed for spending limits only when they are voluntary. For example, presidential candidates are eligible for federal matching funds, but only if they agree to comply with spending limits. The Court did, however, allow limits on the amount that an individual can contribute to a candidate or party, stating that "to the extent that large contributions are given to secure a political *quid pro quo* from current and potential office holders, the integrity of our system of representative democracy is undermined." As a result of the Court's partial rejection of spending limits, elections quickly grew more expensive. That trend escalated rapidly; in the 2000 election (the last presidential election before BCRA), candidates and parties spent more than $3.4 billion on campaigns.

- As noted above, federal law limits the amount of money an individual may contribute to general federal campaigns and individual candidates. In 1996, an individual could contribute no more than $20,000 to a political party, $2,000 to any single candidate, and no more than $25,000 total to any and all federal candidates during an election year. Finally, individuals could contribute no more than $5,000 to a PAC (political action committee). These limits, combined with the lack of limitation on campaign spending, lead the parties and candidates to pursue other funding options, such as soft money.

- Federal law also prohibits corporations, labor unions, and trade associations from contributing directly to candidates. Since 1978, however, the Federal Election Commission (FEC) has allowed corporations and unions to make unlimited donations to political parties for those general purposes described above. This money is what is known as "soft money." Every year since 1978, both parties expanded the purposes for which they used soft money. In 1996, for example, both parties used soft money for the first time to finance television ads. These ads did not specifically mention candidates and so may not have technically violated FEC regulations. However, in every other way they were virtually identical to individual campaign ads, and the intent of these ads was certainly the same as those of campaign advertisements.

- The FEC has very little enforcement power. Its rulings rarely come in time to affect election results. Most of its decisions, in fact, come long after elections are over. Furthermore, the commission's staff and funding have recently been cut drastically, leaving it even less capable of performing its function. In 1996, both parties pushed the limits of FEC regulations. Critics charge that the parties flagrantly broke the rules, knowing that punishment would come too late to change the election results.

- In 1996 the Supreme Court loosened restrictions covering party spending on behalf of candidates. While not removing all spending limits, the Court's decision indicated that any such limitations were subject to the Court's rejection on First Amendment grounds. Each party used the Court's decision to expand its use of soft money.

Before the passing of BCRA, soft money was a hot topic on Capitol Hill. Most congressmen wanted to defend soft money because it was in their interest to do so. Incumbents always receive the vast majority of all campaign contributions, and soft money contributions strengthened their reelection chances.

Congress was not unanimous on the subject, however. The Democratic Party wanted across-the-board limits on donations, while the Republicans did not. Donation limits would have hurt the Republicans, who receive more donations from wealthy Americans than the Democrats. Before the McCain-Feingold bill, the Republican Party raised 50 percent more in soft money than the Democratic Party.

The Republicans, conversely, wanted a ban on soft-money contributions from labor unions, and would have also accepted a ban on donations in congressional elections made from outside the candidate's district (House) or state (Senate). Democrats rejected the limit on contributions from labor unions for one obvious reason: Unions are strong supporters of the Democratic Party. They would have accepted such a ban if a similar one was placed on corporate donations. The Republicans, of course, rejected this idea; total corporate donations to the Republican Party far exceed union donations to the Democratic Party.

Democrats also rejected the Republican proposal for regional limitations on donations. This proposal would have particularly stung the Democrats in the House. Because many Republicans represent wealthy districts, a restriction on outside donations would not hurt them too badly; they would still be able to raise the necessary campaign funds from within their districts. Many Democrats, however, represent poor urban districts. A restriction on outside donations would deprive these Democratic candidates of much of their campaign funding. For these reasons, many Americans saw both sides of the debate as self-interested parties trying to gain electoral advantage, not as legitimate reformists trying to develop a fair system.

Despite the obstacles standing in the way of campaign finance reform, the collapse of Enron and other corporations created an atmosphere that allowed the McCain-Feingold/Shays-Meehan Campaign Finance Reform Act to make it through Congress. It is now known as the Bipartisan Campaign Reform Act, and the jury is still out as to whether it has truly curbed spending.

Should There Be Greater Restrictions on Soft Money? Why or Why Not?

Supporters of the ban on soft money argue that it is the only way to end the upward spiral of election costs. They also believe that such massive campaign contributions from corporations and unions make the average voter extremely cynical about the political process. Few voters believe that those who donate $1 million to a campaign expect nothing in return.

There are, however, legitimate arguments against limits on soft money. A recent *Time* magazine editorial pointed out that a limit on donations to political parties would merely increase the political power of issue advocacy groups, such as the Christian Coalition, the Sierra Club, and the National Rifle Association. These groups, like political parties, run televised advertisements and campaign for candidates. Unlike parties, issue advocacy groups are not required to disclose who donates to them or how much they donate. The net result, therefore, would be a system in which the public was less informed about corporate and union political donations.

Here's How to Crack It

2. The debate over soft money has been a common and important feature of American politics.

   (a) Define "soft money."

   (b) Describe the opposing points of view expressed about soft money by the congressmen in this cartoon.

   (c) Evaluate the arguments for and against soft money.

Any time an essay question comes with a cartoon, chart, graph, or quotation, graders will be looking to see whether you understand it. Always make sure to convey an understanding of such material, aside from answering whatever questions you are asked about it. In the case of this cartoon by Markstein, if, at some point, you explain his depiction of Congress at large and of Senators McCain and Feingold, it will be clear that you get the point of the cartoon.

As with any essay, you must define key terms in the question, whether or not you are explicitly asked to define them. Here you are specifically asked for the meaning of the term *soft money*, but you should have been prepared to define it even if you were not asked to do so.

Another component of the question has to do with the politics of soft money: Why do some in Congress favor it, while others seek to restrict it? You need reasonable explanations for holding each position.

Finally, you need to claim that soft money should or should not be further restricted. Whichever side you choose, you will have to justify your claim.

You should resist the tendency to answer each question separately, in a series of unconnected paragraphs. Try to craft an essay that addresses all the questions. A logical way to organize your essay would be to make each question the focus of one paragraph, with smooth transitions between them. The difference may not seem great, but the presentation is more impressive if you prove that you see the connections among the distinct questions by answering them all in one essay.

Sample "Excellent" Essay

"Soft money," the funds that flow from unions and corporations to political parties, has been the target of reformers and satirists in recent years. Unlike the hard money that goes directly from individuals to candidates, soft money is not restricted. As such, it is supposed to be used for only general party purposes, such as get-out-the-vote drives and advertisements for the party as a whole, rather than particular candidates. Parties have nevertheless found ways to avoid the regulations and gain individual electoral advantage from soft money. For that reason, among others, political cartoonists may criticize soft-money contributions. Because incumbents in general, and incumbent Republicans in particular, tend to benefit more than challengers, much support for soft money, like much opposition to it, is self-interest masquerading as public spirit. Partisan politics aside, there are reasons to worry about unlimited money being funneled into the political system.

Most members of Congress want to defend soft money because, as incumbents, they benefit from it more than those trying to unseat them. Because of limits on individual contributions, candidates depend on soft money, even if they misuse it. The Federal Election Commission is too understaffed to catch misuse of funds until after the election has been won. The cartoonist points out that the majority of Congress is dismayed to find that the opposition persists in trying to limit such an advantageous techniquefor reelection.

Some members of Congress, such as Senators McCain and Feingold (pictured in the cartoon), favor limits on soft money. Many of these members are Democrats who fear the greater fund-raising prowess of the Republican Party. A few good-government types on both sides of the aisle honestly worry about the corrupting influence of soft money, although some members win points with voters by speaking out against soft money while continuing to slyly accept such funds.

When the Supreme Court found, in *Buckley v. Valeo*, that most limitations on campaign contributions violate the right to free speech, it created a huge practical stumbling block to restrictions on soft money, and advanced a powerful argument against such limits. Certainly free speech is a value to cherish, but the authors of the First Amendment never imagined huge corporations and labor unions spending millions of dollars to elect candidates who would do their bidding. Those who give soft money expect something in return. Every person has one vote, but not every person has a huge checking account. To level the playing field between incumbents and challengers, Democrats and Republicans, and rich and poor, further restrictions on soft money are necessary, and the BCRA is a critical step in the right direction.

QUESTION 3

The first part of question 3 requires relatively little outside information. It is designed to test your ability to read a graph and draw conclusions based on your reading. You must then demonstrate a general understanding of the public's perception of Congress. The second part of the question does require outside information, as it asks for a historical cause for the shift in public opinion demonstrated in the graph. You have more than one good option to satisfy the second question; these options are discussed below in more detail than you would need to earn the highest score on this question. The last part of the question asks you to go well beyond the data in the graph and relate public perception of Congress as a whole with voters' perceptions of their own member of Congress. This part of the question demands information about the rate of reelection of incumbents and the recognition of an apparent paradox: People think little of Congress as an institution, but apparently like their own representatives well enough to reelect them quite often.

Describe the Overall Trend in Citizens' Attitudes Toward Congress. Assess the Degree to Which Public Opinion Has Changed Since 1974.

The trends reflected in this chart are ambiguous enough to allow you a couple of options. You could emphasize the upward trend in public disapproval of Congress. Conversely, you could focus on the fact that the public's approval rating of Congress, while fluctuating over the last 20 years, has generally hovered around the 30 percent mark, and so has not changed dramatically. Let's explore both options.

- Disapproval ratings have increased. In August of 1974, less than 50 percent of all Americans disapproved of the way Congress handled its job. That percentage dipped below 50 during the Reagan administration, but it rose above 50 percent during the Bush administration and has stayed there since. The upward trend in Americans' disapproval of Congress roughly corresponds to the drop in the number of Americans with no opinion of Congress. Even though Congress's approval rating has remained about the same over the last 20-plus years (approximately 30 percent), Americans overall are more dissatisfied with Congress than they were in the past.

- Approval ratings have remained relatively stable. In April of 1974, approximately 30 percent of all Americans approved of the job Congress was doing. In August 1997, Congress's approval rating was up slightly, to approximately 32 percent. The fluctuations in approval ratings of Congress throughout the period shown on the chart demonstrate that American opinion of Congress is volatile for the short term but relatively stable over the long term. The chart does show that disapproval ratings have increased during the period shown. However, it could be argued that this is a temporary aberration. Disapproval ratings were also high during the Ford administration (peaking at 55 percent) and reached 60 percent, slightly above their April 1997 level, during the Carter administration.

There is also a third option: acknowledge both trends. Any of these three options, if well executed, will get you on your way to a 5 on this essay.

Explain the Causes and Results of ONE Dramatic Shift in Public Opinion Indicated in the Graph.

The graph illustrates several dramatic changes in public opinion about Congress. Let's consider each.

- August 1974. Public approval of congressional performance reached its highest level for the period shown in the chart. In August of 1974, Richard Nixon was forced to resign from the presidency because Congress was initiating impeachment proceedings. The unusually high approval rating shows that the public agreed with this action. Public opinion of Congress often, although not always, fluctuates in inverse proportion to the president's popularity. In other words, when a president is popular, Congress tends to be less popular, particularly if its relationship with the president is adversarial. When a president is unpopular, however, Congress's approval ratings may increase, unless the public is generally dissatisfied with government, in which case everybody's approval ratings drop. In August of 1974, Richard Nixon's approval rating was abysmal (26 percent, the lowest recorded since 1936), and, not surprisingly, public approval of Congress soared.

- March 1975. Public disapproval of Congress jumps from 36 percent to 54 percent in just six months. The reason: economic woes. The United States entered a period of extended economic inflation during the mid-1970s. Conflicts in the Middle East led to increased oil prices and a gasoline shortage, doubling gas prices and forcing Americans to wait on line to buy gas for the first time since World War II. During this era, public approval of government was low: both Congress and President Ford were regarded by the public as incompetent.

- June 1979. Public disapproval of Congress reaches 60 percent. Again, economic problems resulted in a loss of confidence in the government, as the inflation rate exceeded 13 percent. Also, during this period American concern over nuclear weapons and energy peaked. The Three Mile Island nuclear disaster in March 1979 raised fears that the government was not properly regulating the nuclear energy industry. In June, Congress blocked passage of an arms reduction treaty with the Soviet Union.

- March 1992. Public approval ratings bottom out below 20 percent, and disapproval ratings soar above 70 percent. During this period, the Democratic Congress was continually at odds with Republican President George Bush Sr. The hot political issue during this period was the federal deficit, for which the public blamed both Congress and the president. Public opinion of the entire government was extremely low, as demonstrated by the fact that Ross Perot, a presidential candidate with no government experience, won 19 percent of the popular vote in the general election that year.

- December 1995. Public disapproval of Congress increases again in the aftermath of the federal government shutdown. In this case, the majority of Americans held Congress responsible for the shutdown. In particular, they blamed the Republican leadership and the many hard-line conservative representatives who had gained office during the "Republican revolution" in 1994.

To What Extent Does the Graph Suggest that Incumbent Members of Congress Will Have Difficulty Winning Reelection?

Regardless of the way you described public opinion in answering the first two parts of the question, it's clear that more people have disapproved of Congress than have approved of it almost without interruption for at least 25 years. From your study of congressional elections, however, you may recall that politicians that get elected to Congress, especially after they have gotten reelected once, tend to be quite successful at continuing to win reelection every two years after that, as long as they continue to run. This question asks you to consider whether disapproval of Congress as a whole translates into disapproval of individual representatives. The short answer is that it does not. Just as you may think little of professional athletes as a group yet still root for the home team, a negative assessment of the group does not translate into a negative assessment of every member in it. Members of Congress often run successfully for reelection by asking to be sent back to Washington to clean up the mess there, thus distancing themselves from Congress as an institution. Similarly, voters may see public spending elsewhere as a waste of their money while viewing spending in their own district as beneficial and a reason to reelect their representative who brought it home. You need to show in your essay that you are aware of and can account for the high rate of reelection of individual members of Congress in the face of the persistent disapproval of Congress as a whole.

Here's How to Crack It

3. Using the above graph and your knowledge of U.S. politics, perform the following tasks:

   (a) Describe the overall trend in citizens' attitudes toward Congress. Assess the degree to which public opinion has changed since 1974.

   (b) Explain the causes and results of ONE dramatic shift in public opinion indicated in the graph.

   (c) Indicate to what extent the graph suggests that incumbent members of Congress will have difficulty winning reelection.

Graders evaluating answers to this question want to see, first of all, that you can read a graph and draw conclusions based on the information it presents. They will be looking at your response to the second part of the question to see if you can recall a single historical event or set of circumstances that you can link to a shift in the public's opinion of Congress. You need to identify the event or circumstances as well as establish a probable connection to the poll data shown. In answering the third part, you need to demonstrate your familiarity with the high reelection rate of members of Congress and explain how it can coexist with the data in the graph. It is possible to address the three parts of the question in a straightforward manner. If you don't complicate your task with an elaborate introduction and conclusion, you could probably answer this question in less that 25 minutes, creating extra time for one of the other questions or for taking a short break between questions.

Sample "Excellent" Essay

Generally, negative public opinion of Congress over the last 25 years has fluctuated somewhat as a function of various events, and has failed to translate into electoral difficulties for individual members of Congress running for reelection.

Two major trends are noticeable in the chart. First, public disapproval of Congress has risen since 1974. In 1974, disapproval ratings were below 50 percent. They even dropped below 40 percent in April 1974. Since then, however, disapproval ratings have generally been above 50 percent and at times have been much higher. Approval ratings, on the other hand, have remained near 30 percent. Overall, it seems that public opinion of Congress has changed slightly for the worse since 1974. More people formerly had no opinion of Congress; most of those people seem to have shifted over to the disapproval category. This is probably because media coverage of Congress has grown more extensive and more negative over the past 20 years.

One dramatic shift in public opinion of Congress took place in December 1995, when the graph shows disapproval reaching the second highest peak recorded there, near 70 percent. The failure of both the president and Congress to agree on a budget caused a shutdown of all non-essential activities of the federal government. The Republican majority in Congress wanted to speed up deficit reduction and cut funding of social programs. When the Democratic president would not agree, Congress shut down the government rather than pass stop-gap appropriations bills. The public disapproved of the government shutdown and blamed Congress for it, resulting in much higher levels of disapproval.

Although disapproval of Congress has remained high, the public is not refusing to reelect incumbent representatives who seek to keep their seats. Members have expanded district office staffs, providing helpful, nonpartisan constituent services that keep their name recognition high and their individual popularity well above that of Congress as a whole. High levels of public spending allow representatives to claim credit for new buildings, roads, canals, and the like, and lead voters to appreciate the benefits their district is getting from their congressperson, even if they view Congress as a whole as spendthrift for repeating that spending in each of the other districts.

Thus Congress remains relatively unpopular, occasionally extremely so, but individual representatives are not tainted by that disapproval when they run for reelection.

QUESTION 4

Uh-oh. This question asks about an apparent increase in the frequency of political scandals. But your course didn't have a unit on corruption, did it? And the question is mandatory. How do you approach a question that is not obviously about one of the major topics you know about? First, read the question carefully to determine exactly what you are being asked, then go from there.

Your rereading of the question gives you the following information:

- You need to refer to two national political scandals since 1960.

- You need to identify partisan and institutional causes for them.

You can probably name at least two scandals in national politics since 1960. Remember Watergate, which toppled Richard Nixon for his role in covering up spying on his political opponents; Iran-Contra, when Reagan Administration officials sold arms to Iran and illegally diverted the proceeds to counter-revolutionaries in Nicaragua; and the series of investigations concerning Bill Clinton's role in the Whitewater land deal in Arkansas and the cover-up of an affair with a White House intern.

What can you say about the partisan and institutional factors involved in these scandals? Partisanship has to do with competition between the Republican and Democratic parties. Institutions include the major branches of the government—executive, legislative, judicial—and other permanent bodies that play a role in politics, such as the media. As you will see in the background discussion that follows, partisanship and institutional conflict figure prominently in these scandals.

Therefore, the question asks about competition between political parties and interaction between political institutions, two subjects you have studied and know something about.

Let's look at the cases of scandal we have identified and their institutional and partisan background. Then we can put it all together and crack this question.

Examples of Corruption

The cases of political scandals in national politics that come up most frequently in government courses are Watergate, Iran-Contra, and the contemporary Whitewater-Lewinsky example. There are others, of course, such as that involving former Speaker of the House Jim Wright and any number of others—in 1990, there were over 1,000 federal indictments and convictions of public officials—but let's stick to the cases that graders would expect you to know.

- Watergate. In June, 1972, five months before Richard Nixon was reelected president by a wide margin, five men who worked for Nixon's reelection effort were arrested while in possession of electronic bugging equipment at the headquarters of the Democratic Party in the Watergate building in Washington, DC. Over the next two years, indictments, prosecutions, and resignations of various officials linked to Nixon revealed the existence of attempts to cover up ties between the break-in and the president. The White House used the Federal Bureau of Investigation, the Central Intelligence Agency, even the Internal Revenue Service to investigate and attack Nixon's opponents. Televised Senate investigations drew popular attention. The revelation that Nixon had taped White House conversations led to a Supreme Court decision ordering Nixon to turn over the tapes to the House Judiciary Committee, which began developing articles of impeachment. In August, 1974, Nixon resigned.

- Iran-Contra. In 1985, a number of Americans who had been taken hostage in Lebanon were believed to be held by groups linked to the Iranian government. While publicly refusing to negotiate with terrorists, the Reagan administration secretly sold weapons to Iran in exchange for Iranian aid in winning the release of those captives. The proceeds from selling the arms were diverted to counter-revolutionaries, or "Contras," who were fighting the left-wing government of Nicaragua. At the time, Congress had banned U.S. aid to the Contras. The arms-for-hostages deal and illegal aid to the contras led to a Congressional investigation and indictments of various officials. Iran-Contra, along with the return of the Senate to a Democratic majority in the 1986 elections, weakened the Reagan administration in its final two years.

- Whitewater and Lewinsky. In 1994, Congress appointed former judge Kenneth Starr as a special prosecutor to investigate the Clintons' participation in the Whitewater land deal in Arkansas that occurred before Bill Clinton was elected president. The investigation went on to look at the suicide of administration official and Clinton friend Vince Foster; the circumstances surrounding the firing of the White House travel staff; the reasons that the Clinton White House came to have FBI files on Bush administration officials; President Clinton's perjury (lying under oath) and other attempts to cover up an affair with former White House intern Monica Lewinsky; and so on. The investigation culminated in the impeachment of President Clinton for perjury and obstruction of justice in the Paula Jones/Lewinsky grand jury investigation. The Senate did not convict the president because the charge did not rise to a high crime or misdemeanor against the government. Rather than face the probability of a post-presidential criminal trial for obstruction of justice, President Clinton negotiated an agreement with the special prosecutor to admit to perjury before a grand jury, in exchange for ending all criminal proceedings.

The Institutional Background of Scandals

In each of these scandals, the president and other administration officials come under allegations of impropriety. The investigations are carried out by Congress, with the aid of a special prosecutor. Thus, these scandals should be seen as instances of institutional conflict and competition. The executive and legislative branches have sought to dominate policy by any possible means, from skillful manipulation of the media, to clever policy initiatives, to prosecution of their foes. Furthermore, the judicial branch often figures in these cases, siding with Congress against the president by denying claims of executive privilege both in forcing Nixon to give Congress the tapes and in compelling testimony by Clinton officials and Secret Service agents guarding President Clinton. The media, too, increased their significance as a political institution after Watergate, when reporters Bob Woodward and Carl Bernstein became the heroic subject of books and movies and inspired a new generation of muckrakers by breaking the case wide open. Seen in this context, recent scandals are a chapter in the conflict for supremacy among political institutions that has been going on since the founding of the nation.

The Partisan Background of Scandals

The phenomenon of divided government—when one party controls Congress and the other controls the presidency—makes competition between institutions more likely and more virulent. In each of these three cases, split control contributed to scandal: Democrats controlling the House and Senate under Republican Nixon, Democrats controlling the House under Republican Reagan, and Republicans controlling the House and Senate under Democrat Clinton all used scandal as a way to weaken an administration with which they disagreed politically. Rarely do Democrats or Republicans go after members of their own party, even in a different branch of government.

Thus, the combination of institutional and partisan rivalries fed all three scandals.

Here's How to Crack It

4. Political scandals involve investigations, prosecutions and possibly convictions of public officials.

    (a)   Describe two scandals that have occurred since 1960.

    (b)   Identify whether the allegations of impropriety surrounding these scandals were partisan or institutional in nature.

    (c)   Explain why scandals have been more prevalent in political life in recent years.

The most important thing to remember when you see a question that is superficially unfamiliar is not to panic. Read the question carefully. Determine exactly what it asks. Brainstorm a list of considerations that seem relevant. Using this process will put you in the best possible position to come up with a coherent answer, even when you are not confident that you can write a convincing response.

In this case, start by listing two or three scandals with which you are familiar. Jot down a few facts about each. Identify the partisan and institutional components of the cases. See how they lead you back to political science issues with which you are familiar after all. Outline an essay that puts you on familiar footing while making sure to answer the question.

Don't forget that last part: Make sure you are answering the question! Even if you are not sure why a question is being asked, meeting some of the specific criteria it requests will give you a decent score. For this question, simply identifying two scandals and showing that you know what "partisan and institutional reasons" are will earn you points.

Finally, if you have put together the various factors involved here, you may be able to comment on the significance of the third part of the question, namely, "Political scandals seem to be on the rise." It is probably not the case that there is any more corruption today than a hundred or two hundred years ago, but there are stronger partisan and institutional reasons to attack one's enemies with charges of corruption. This explains the increase in allegations, investigations, prosecutions, and convictions, but the incidence of inappropriate behavior in American politics is as old as the republic itself, and probably no greater in recent years than at other times in its history.

Sample "Excellent" Essay

Political scandals seem to be on the rise. Investigations, prosecutions, and convictions of public officials have all increased. Looking at the scandals that engulfed Presidents Nixon and Clinton, we can see the partisan and institutional reasons that allegations of impropriety and attempts to punish public officials are a greater part of our political culture than they used to be.

Partisan conflict—when the parties disagree—has led to charges of misconduct. When the country is divided on questions of public policy and neither side can win a decisive victory for its views at the polls, charges of malfeasance serve as a way to weaken one's opponents and impose one's policy preferences in the absence of a clear electoral mandate.

Similarly, conflict among political institutions, especially the Presidency and Congress, has contributed to the apparent increase in scandals. Divided government, in which one party controls Congress and the other controls the White House, has been a near constant since 1968. As Congress has sought to restore the policy leadership it enjoyed for much of U.S. history but has lost in the 20th century, it has used allegations of misconduct to weaken the formidable powers of the executive branch. Courts and media have also been institutional players in the scandal game.

By the time Nixon won reelection in 1972, the country was split over the Vietnam War and the host of cultural issues raised in the late 1960s. Neither party could win control of both the White House and Congress in either 1968 or 1972. Thus, an atmosphere of intense partisan and institutional competition existed. The Watergate scandal, revolving around the cover-up of Nixon's role in spying on the Democrats, was an opportunity for Democrats who had been trounced in the 1972 presidential election to undermine the Republican president. As Nixon weakened and fell under the weight of Watergate, Congress imposed all kinds of limits on presidential power—the Budget Control Act, the War Powers Act, the Special Prosecutor Act—to restore the institutional balance. Democrats also forced a U.S. withdrawal from Vietnam. Thus, Watergate served partisan and institutional interests. The scandal was real enough, but without divided government, it probably never would have come to light.

Similarly, President Clinton came under fire because of partisan and institutional conflicts. Unable to retake the White House despite newfound control of Congress, Republicans used the tools left to them by congressional Democratic majorities of the past to continue to wield scandal in partisan and institutional combat. The special prosecutor, once a tool of Democrats in Congress, kept Clinton off balance and unable to dictate the public policy debate. He couldn't propose further health care reforms or take advantage of the newly balanced budget to expand government programs. As in Watergate, the President engaged in real misdeeds, but divided government made his actions into scandal for partisan and institutional reasons.

With the judiciary helping Congress limit the powers of the president by denying claims of executive privilege to both Nixon and Clinton, and the media fixating on every detail of the stories, the weaker institutions express their drive for more power by using allegations and prosecutions as a weapon against the executive branch. With neither party able to win clear policy mandates in elections, those institutions use investigations to weaken their partisan enemies.

15

PRACTICE TEST 2

UNITED STATES GOVERNMENT AND POLITICS

Two hours and 25 minutes are allocated for this examination: 45 minutes for Section I, which consists of multiple-choice questions; and 100 minutes for Section II, which consists of 4 mandatory essay questions. Section I is printed in this examination booklet. Section II is printed in a separate booklet.

SECTION I

Time—45 minutes

Number of questions—60

Percent of total grade—50

This examination contains 60 multiple-choice questions. Therefore, please be careful to fill in only the ovals that are preceded by numbers 1 to 60 on your answer sheet.

General Instructions

DO NOT OPEN THIS BOOKLET UNTIL YOU ARE INSTRUCTED TO DO SO.

INDICATE ALL YOUR ANSWERS TO QUESTIONS IN SECTION I ON A SEPARATE ANSWER SHEET. No credit will be given for anything written in this examination booklet, but you may use the booklet for notes or scratchwork. After you have decided which of the suggested answers is best, COMPLETELY fill in the corresponding oval on the answer sheet. Give only one answer to each question. If you change an answer, be sure that the previous mark is erased completely.

Example: Sample Answer

    Chicago is a   Ⓐ ● Ⓒ Ⓓ Ⓔ

    (A) state
    (B) city
    (C) country
    (D) continent
    (E) village

Many candidates wonder whether or not to guess the answers to questions about which they are not certain. In this section of the examination, as a correction for haphazard guessing, one-fourth of the number of questions you answer incorrectly will be subtracted from the number of questions you answer correctly. It is improbable, therefore, that mere guessing will improve your score significantly; it may even lower your score, and it does take time. If, however, you are not sure of the best answer but have some knowledge of the question and are able to eliminate one or more of the answer choices as wrong, your chance of getting the right answer is improved, and it may be to your advantage to answer such a question.

Use your time effectively, working as rapidly as you can without losing accuracy. Do not spend too much time on questions that are too difficult. Go on to other questions and come back to the difficult ones later if you have time. It is not expected that everyone will be able to answer all the multiple-choice questions.

Section I

Time—45 minutes

60 questions

Directions: Each of the questions or incomplete statements below is followed by five suggested answers or completions. Select the one that is best in each case and then fill in the corresponding oval on the answer sheet.

1. To which characteristic of American government does the term "federalism" refer?

   (A) The system of checks and balances within the national government
   (B) The power of the Supreme Court to review the constitutionality of laws
   (C) The Bill of Rights' protection of the rights of the accused
   (D) The process by which the size of each state's delegation to the House of Representatives is determined
   (E) The division and sharing of power between the national and state governments

2. The swift adoption of the Bill of Rights in the years following ratification of the Constitution demonstrates the

   (A) framers' unqualified commitment to individual rights
   (B) small states' determination to receive equal representation in the legislature
   (C) Northern states' support for abolitionism
   (D) states' fears of an overpowerful national government
   (E) Federalists' concerns that the system of checks and balances would weaken the national government

3. Which of the following is true of court cases in which one private party is suing another?

   (A) They are tried in civil court
   (B) The federal court system has exclusive jurisdiction over them
   (C) They are tried in criminal court
   (D) The state court system has exclusive jurisdiction over them
   (E) They are tried before a grand jury

4. The term "budget deficit" refers to the

   (A) annual increase in federal spending on the military
   (B) amount of interest on the national debt
   (C) difference between the initial budget proposals made by the president and Congress
   (D) period after the fiscal year ends during which the government operates without an official budget
   (E) amount the government spends in excess of its revenues

5. The legislative successes of the National Rifle Association, antiabortion activists, and other powerful interest groups demonstrate that

   (A) United States domestic policy has grown more conservative in the 1990s
   (B) the influence of political action committees has weakened in recent years
   (C) the power of interest groups depends on the degree of support for their positions in the White House
   (D) majority opinion on an issue can sometimes be overridden by the intensity of a minority's commitment to activism
   (E) the most powerful interest groups in the United States are generally those that support uncontroversial positions

GO ON TO THE NEXT PAGE

6. During the second half of the twentieth-century, the Supreme Court's position on free speech was that

   (A) free speech is essential to liberty and therefore may be abridged only under extreme circumstances
   (B) the government may never limit speech because free speech is protected by the First Amendment
   (C) state governments may place limits on free speech, but the national government may not because of the First Amendment
   (D) the government may limit speech that the majority of Americans finds offensive
   (E) the government may place limits on free speech in print and broadcast media but may not limit the spoken word

7. The national and state governments share all of the following powers EXCEPT the power to

   (A) administer elections
   (B) impose taxes
   (C) establish courts
   (D) borrow money
   (E) enact laws

8. Which group most frequently benefits from political action committee (PAC) donations?

   (A) Charitable organizations
   (B) Federal judges
   (C) Political interest groups
   (D) Research institutes
   (E) Incumbents running for reelection

9. The president executes a "pocket veto" by doing which of the following?

   (A) Publicly expressing rejection of a bill
   (B) Issuing an executive order invalidating a recently passed bill
   (C) Failing to sign a bill after Congress has adjourned
   (D) Recalling ambassadors from a peace negotiation
   (E) Refusing to seat a federal judge whom the Senate has confirmed

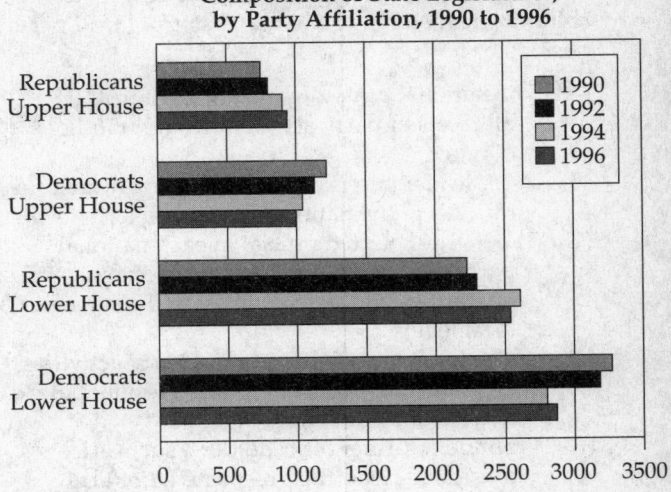

Composition of State Legislatures, by Party Affiliation, 1990 to 1996

10. The graph above supports which of the following conclusions?

   (A) If the trend shown on the chart continues, the Republican party will soon control most state legislatures.
   (B) In most states, registered Democrats outnumber registered Republicans.
   (C) Democrats had more seats than Republicans in state legislatures throughout the early 1990s.
   (D) The number of Republican governors increased between 1990 and 1996.
   (E) The Democrats and Republicans controlled an equal number of state legislatures in 1996.

GO ON TO THE NEXT PAGE

11. Which of the following is an accurate statement about the leadership of the two major political parties?

(A) The national party organization controls all facets of party activity throughout the country.
(B) Party leadership is dispersed among numerous officials at the national, state, and local levels.
(C) The highest elected official in each national party directs that party's activities and operations all the way down to the state and local levels.
(D) All major decisions concerning party activities are made during each party's presidential nomination conventions.
(E) Prominent former officeholders, such as ex-presidents, lead their respective political parties.

12. The media play a major role in establishing the public agenda by

(A) deciding how prominently to cover issue-related news stories
(B) refusing to publicize the opinions of any pundit deemed "too political"
(C) reviewing the accuracy of candidates' campaign advertisements
(D) reporting political news from foreign nations
(E) making available the complete text of presidential addresses and press releases

13. All of the following can be considered true about the impact of a higher level of education on voting habits EXCEPT

(A) voters are more likely to support government-enforced racial and sexual equality
(B) voters are more likely to support environmental protection efforts
(C) voters are more likely to support public prayer in schools
(D) voters are less likely to support restrictions on abortion rights
(E) voters are more likely to promote civil liberties

14. In *Gideon v. Wainwright*, the Supreme Court ruled that criminal defendants in state cases have the right

(A) to representation by an attorney
(B) not to incriminate themselves
(C) to a speedy trial
(D) not to be punished excessively
(E) to a jury trial

15. Under which of the following conditions are people most likely to vote?

(A) When they believe that none of the contested races is close
(B) When media coverage of the election is intense
(C) When the voter is unfamiliar with the candidates
(D) When the voter is unaffiliated with a political party
(E) During a midterm election

Questions 16–17 refer to the following amendment to the Constitution.

Amendment X

The powers not delegated to the United States by the Constitution, nor prohibited to the states, are reserved to the states respectively, or to the people.

16. The Tenth Amendment most often comes into conflict with which section of the Constitution?

(A) The "full faith and credit" clause
(B) The "necessary and proper" clause
(C) The provisions for the impeachment of a president
(D) The clause prohibiting states from coining money and entering into treaties
(E) The provisions for constitutional amendment

17. People who interpret the Tenth Amendment as greatly restricting the powers of the national government are often referred to as

(A) Federalists
(B) isolationists
(C) laissez-faire capitalists
(D) loose constructionists
(E) states' righters

18. Which committee in the House of Representatives determines the procedure by which bills are debated and amended?

(A) Ways and Means
(B) Judiciary
(C) Ethics
(D) Rules
(E) Government Reform

GO ON TO THE NEXT PAGE

19. The government often finds it difficult to make substantive changes to entitlement programs for which of the following reasons?

    (A) Most such programs were established by constitutional amendment.
    (B) These programs are extremely popular among their numerous beneficiaries.
    (C) Such programs are vital to national defense.
    (D) Most such programs primarily benefit the wealthy, a powerful political bloc.
    (E) These programs' budgets are determined by nonelected bureaucrats, not by Congress.

20. The relative stability of American public policy is achieved largely through

    (A) cooperation between the two major political parties
    (B) judicial activism
    (C) the Constitutional fragmentation of power
    (D) affirmative action programs
    (E) the delegation of unique reserved powers to each house of Congress

21. Uncertainty over the limits to presidential power is caused primarily by the fact that

    (A) the constitutional definition of those powers is broad and unspecific
    (B) most people agree that the Constitution places too many limits on presidential power
    (C) the Supreme Court consistently refuses to rule on cases concerning presidential powers
    (D) constitutional amendments have greatly increased presidential powers
    (E) some states cede more power to their governors than the national government cedes to the president

22. The responsibilities of the secretary of state are most likely to overlap with those of

    (A) the secretary of the interior
    (B) the secretary of the treasury
    (C) the speaker of the house
    (D) the president's chief of staff
    (E) the chief national security advisor to the president

23. In the past decade many states have moved forward the date of their presidential primary elections in an effort to

    (A) minimize the cost of running the election
    (B) convince the national government to move forward the date of the general election
    (C) restrict the number of entrants in the presidential race
    (D) focus greater national attention on their state primary races
    (E) increase the significance of their election results

24. Incumbent members of the House of Representatives win reelection more often than incumbent senators for all of the following reasons EXCEPT

    (A) representatives' constituents more often belong largely to the representative's party
    (B) senators have more political power than representatives, and Senate races are accordingly contested more aggressively
    (C) representatives may use federal funds to publicize their achievements via direct mail to constituents
    (D) representatives more often run uncontested
    (E) the fact that Senate races are held statewide generates more media coverage and thus more public awareness

25. A member of the president's cabinet is said to have "gone native" when that cabinet member

    (A) resigns to take a position as a consultant to lobbying groups
    (B) cedes control of his or her department to lifelong bureaucrats within the department
    (C) places his or her department's priorities above the president's
    (D) accepts bribes or expensive favors from businesses regulated by his or her department
    (E) suggests merging his or her department into another executive department

GO ON TO THE NEXT PAGE →

26. Congress would be required to use the "elastic clause" of the Constitution to

(A) change citizenship requirements
(B) impose workplace safety standards
(C) increase tax rates
(D) authorize the treasury to print money
(E) declare war

27. Which of the following is true of the Supreme Court?

(A) Every case appealed to the Supreme Court is ruled upon by the Court.
(B) The Court helps set the public agenda by deciding which appeals to hear.
(C) The Court hears all cases when two or more justices agree that the case has merit.
(D) In deciding cases, the chief justice's vote counts as two votes.
(E) The Court does not rule on cases in which five justices refuse to sign a single opinion.

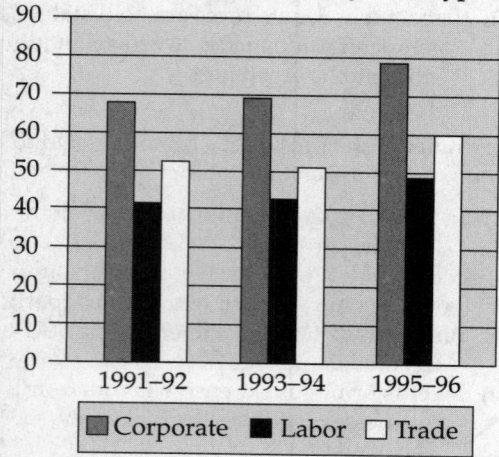

PAC Contributions to Candidates, in millions of dollars, by PAC Type

Corporate Labor Trade

28. Which of the following conclusions is supported by the graph?

(A) Corporations have more political influence than do labor unions.
(B) Trade PACs are the fastest growing sector of political activism in the United States.
(C) Corporate PACs are more likely to donate to Republican candidates than to Democratic candidates.
(D) In recent elections, PACs have contributed more than $150 million to different candidates.
(E) American workers had more disposable income in 1995–1996 than they had in 1993–1994.

29. Which of the following statements best describes the central constitutional issue concerning the death penalty?

(A) The death penalty violates the prohibition of double jeopardy.
(B) Different states use different means of executing convicts in capital cases.
(C) The death penalty arguably constitutes cruel and unusual punishment.
(D) Federal law and state law differ in their definitions of what constitutes a capital crime.
(E) Capital trials fail to meet the standard set by the "speedy and public trial" clause.

30. The Supreme Court has used the Fourteenth Amendment to apply portions of the Bill of Rights to state law by citing the amendment's

(A) prohibition on unreasonable search and seizures
(B) due process clause
(C) guarantee of privacy rights
(D) abolition of slavery
(E) "reserved powers" provision

31. The framers of the Constitution sought to insulate the Senate from public opinion by

(A) restricting Senate membership to those who previously served in the House of Representatives
(B) delegating the responsibility for electing senators to the state legislatures
(C) requiring all spending bills to originate in the House of Representatives
(D) empowering the Senate to provide advice and consent to the executive branch
(E) assigning exactly two senators to each state's congressional delegation

32. Under the Articles of Confederation, the national government had the power to

(A) negotiate treaties
(B) collect taxes
(C) establish a federal judiciary
(D) enforce its laws
(E) regulate interstate commerce

GO ON TO THE NEXT PAGE

33. Congress has attempted to protect independent regulatory agencies from political influence by requiring that each agency

(A) be led by a group of commissioners representing both major political parties
(B) plan policy cooperatively with the appropriate congressional committees
(C) reapply for funding at the end of each fiscal year
(D) submit all planned policy changes to the president for approval
(E) seek the advice and cooperation of the industries they regulate

34. Which of the following most accurately states the impact of the Civil Rights Act of 1964 on school desegregation in the south?

(A) Because it included no enforcement provisions, the Civil Rights Act of 1964 had no appreciable effect on school desegregation.
(B) By overturning the "separate but equal" principle, the Civil Rights Act of 1964 ended segregation in public schools.
(C) The Civil Rights Act of 1964 hastened school desegregation by cutting off federal funds to discriminatory school systems.
(D) The Civil Rights Act of 1964 sent federal troops to every segregated public school in the south to force school desegregation.
(E) The Civil Rights Act of 1964 required all southern public schools to mirror the racial demographics of their home states.

35. The rules governing the electoral college make it especially important for presidential candidates to

(A) win as many states as possible, regardless of the size of the states
(B) spend most of their time campaigning in the south
(C) campaign most aggressively among those who will be chosen as electors
(D) concentrate their campaign efforts on "battleground" states
(E) concentrate on the states in which they are farthest behind, to reduce the margin of their eventual losses in those states

36. The opinions of congressional committees often fail to accurately mirror public opinion because

(A) the membership of committees often overrepresents constituencies with the greatest stake in the committee's business
(B) most committees are too small to include representatives of all popular opinions
(C) the minority party controls nearly half of all committees
(D) committee members often lose track of their constituents' priorities because of their frequent contact with special-interest lobbyists
(E) committee members rely primarily on their legislative aides to develop their positions on committee business

37. The absence of a political party solely dedicated to labor and working class issues in the United States

(A) proves U.S. politicians are not concerned about serving working-class constituencies
(B) is the result of government restrictions placed on the political activities of labor unions
(C) reflects the difficulty of unifying a party around a single issue in a "winner-take-all" format
(D) demonstrates that, in the United States, most political issues regarding workers have been decided in the workers' favor
(E) illustrates that race, not class, is the primary political division in the United States

38. In the majority of cases, federal programs are implemented by

(A) private businesses working as subcontractors to the government
(B) state and local governments, by means of federal funding
(C) Congress, through the local offices of its elected representatives
(D) the federal courts, by means of criminal prosecutions
(E) federal agencies, through their many local offices in cities and towns

GO ON TO THE NEXT PAGE

39. Which of the following is an accurate statement about the federal court system?

   (A) The creation of new federal courts requires a constitutional amendment.
   (B) The creation of new federal courts requires the unanimous consent of all 50 states.
   (C) The Supreme Court has the sole power to create new federal courts.
   (D) Congress has the power to create new federal courts.
   (E) The number of federal courts is fixed by the Constitution and cannot be changed.

40. Both the War Powers Act of 1974 and the Budget and Impoundment Control Act of 1974 represent efforts by Congress to limit the powers of the

   (A) Joint Chiefs of Staff
   (B) House Ways and Means Committee
   (C) Central Intelligence Agency
   (D) secretary of defense
   (E) president

41. An open primary is a primary election in which

   (A) voters registered as "independents" may not vote
   (B) candidates do not specify the office for which they are running
   (C) voters may register at their polling place on election day
   (D) candidates need not announce their candidacy until the day of the primary
   (E) voters may vote in the election of a party other than the one to which they are registered

42. Which of the following describes an unintended result of the Federal Election Campaign Act of 1974?

   (A) Limits were placed on the amount of money individuals could donate to a federal election campaign.
   (B) Federal funding became available to presidential candidates who agree to abide by spending limits.
   (C) Candidates drastically decreased the amount of money spent on television advertising.
   (D) Thousands of political action committees were created to raise funds for candidates.
   (E) The number of third-party campaigns for the presidency decreased dramatically.

43. Politicians and political reporters are natural adversaries; the adversarial nature of their relationship, however, is tempered by the fact that

   (A) younger politicians who are more comfortable with the media are gradually displacing older politicians
   (B) government regulations on interaction between the two groups are very strict
   (C) each group is dependent on the other to perform its job effectively
   (D) very few media outlets will cover a story that is embarrassing to a political leader
   (E) most government activity is classified and therefore inaccessible to the media

44. All of the following contribute to lower voting rates among Americans in the 18-to-25 age bracket EXCEPT

   (A) college attendance in a state other than one's home state
   (B) frequent relocation of one's primary residence
   (C) the remoteness of most political issues to the daily lives of young people
   (D) the fact that the minimum voting age in some states is 21
   (E) military service

45. Which of the following defines the salience of a political issue?

   (A) The amount of coverage the issue receives in the major news media
   (B) The degree to which public opinion on the issue is likely to shift quickly
   (C) The number of people affected by the issue
   (D) The degree to which the issue can be addressed through government action
   (E) The importance of the issue to a particular individual or group

46. When the Democratic Party pursues liberal social policies, it is most likely to alienate which of its traditional bases?

   (A) People holding advanced academic degrees
   (B) Northeastern city dwellers
   (C) Southerners
   (D) Jewish Americans
   (E) Urban African Americans

GO ON TO THE NEXT PAGE

47. Under Chief Justice Earl Warren, the Supreme Court

(A) greatly expanded the rights of criminal defendants
(B) greatly limited the power of the federal government over the states
(C) established the principle of judicial review
(D) refused to enforce the Sherman Antitrust Act
(E) weakened the constitutional division between church and state

48. The Supreme Court case *Regents of University of California v. Bakke* concerned which of the following issues?

(A) The rights of students to protest on a publicly funded campus
(B) In-class prayer at a publicly funded school
(C) The rights of students to carry concealed weapons on campus
(D) Accommodations for disabled students at publicly funded schools
(E) The use of racial quotas in public university admissions

49. The principles of freedom—"we hold these truths to be self-evident, that all men are created equal"— stated in the Declaration of Independence were influenced by the beliefs of political philosopher

(A) Thomas Hobbes
(B) Niccolo Macchiavelli
(C) Jonathan Edwards
(D) John Locke
(E) John Calvin

50. In "Federalist No. 10," James Madison argues that a federal system of government reduces the danger of political factions by

(A) creating insurmountable obstacles to the founding of factions
(B) making it difficult for one faction to gain the power necessary to govern
(C) requiring equal representation of all factions within the government
(D) restricting factional political activity to the state level only
(E) allowing federal agencies to strictly regulate the activities of factions

51. Under which of the following circumstances does a president usually experience a reduction in political power?

I. The president is in the final two years of his or her second term
II. The number and severity of international crises is increasing
III. Different parties control Congress and the White House
IV. The economy is strong and the president's approval ratings are high

(A) I only
(B) I and II only
(C) I and III only
(D) II and III only
(E) II, III, and IV only

52. House members are more concerned about their committee assignments than are senators because

(A) House members may serve on only one committee at a time
(B) Senate committees have relatively little power to alter legislation
(C) bills in the Senate must pass through all committees before reaching the floor
(D) senators may change their committee assignments whenever they wish
(E) the rules make it extremely difficult for representatives to influence legislation on the House floor

53. Which of the following is true of most third parties in U.S. history?

(A) They arose and succeeded during times of prosperity
(B) They were created to protest wars
(C) At some point they won a majority of seats in Congress
(D) They flourished during periods of widespread dissatisfaction
(E) They arose in response to increased government regulation

GO ON TO THE NEXT PAGE

54. Failed felony prosecutions at the state level are sometimes retried at the federal level

(A) on appeal by state prosecutors
(B) under the "double jeopardy" provision of the Constitution
(C) because new evidence has voided the state-level verdict
(D) as a result of a gubernatorial veto
(E) as civil liberties violations

55. Which of the following is true of Congress's power of oversight?

(A) Congressional oversight activities most often take place at the committee and subcommittee levels.
(B) State challenges to congressional oversight have severely weakened Congress's oversight powers.
(C) Congressional oversight is primarily directed at the judicial branch.
(D) Constituent input does not influence congressional oversight.
(E) Congressional oversight primarily concerns Congress's power to discipline its own members.

56. Which of the following statements about voting patterns is NOT true?

(A) Non-whites are more likely to vote Democratic than are whites.
(B) Women are more likely to vote Democratic than are men.
(C) Low-income Americans are more likely to vote Democratic than are upper-income Americans.
(D) Fundamentalists are more likely to vote Democratic than are non-religious Americans.
(E) Homosexuals are more likely to vote Democratic than are heterosexuals.

57. Considered as a single group, the Small Business Administration, the Small Business committees in the House and Senate, and small business advocacy groups are an example of

(A) an iron triangle
(B) a conference committee
(C) a regulatory agency
(D) dual Federalism
(E) a third party

58. Which of the following is true of federal judges?

(A) They serve four-year terms that coincide with the presidential term.
(B) They are appointed for life and can only be removed by impeachment.
(C) They are elected by Congress and serve ten-year terms.
(D) They are appointed for life and cannot be removed from office.
(E) They are appointed by the Supreme Court to life terms.

59. Filibusters are less likely to occur in the House of Representatives than in the Senate because

(A) Senate decorum forbids one senator from attempting to stop another's speech
(B) the House meets for substantially fewer hours per day than does the Senate
(C) Senate sessions, unlike House sessions, are open to the public
(D) debate in the House is in most instances strictly regulated by the rules
(E) all speeches in the House are delivered by the House Speaker

60. Which of the following is true of congressional redistricting?

(A) The responsibility for redrawing congressional districts belongs to congressional committees.
(B) It is a noncontroversial process because it has few political ramifications.
(C) It occurs every 10 years to reflect changes in population according to the census.
(D) The Supreme Court has ruled that legislators may not consider racial demographics when redrawing districts.
(E) When redrawing districts, the chief concern of legislators is to maintain the integrity of neighborhoods.

STOP
END OF SECTION I

IF YOU FINISH BEFORE TIME IS CALLED, YOU MAY CHECK YOUR WORK ON THIS SECTION.
DO NOT GO ON TO SECTION II UNTIL YOU ARE TOLD TO DO SO.

UNITED STATES GOVERNMENT AND POLITICS

SECTION II

Time—100 minutes

Directions: You have 100 minutes to answer all four of the following questions. Unless the directions indicate otherwise, respond to all parts of all four questions. It is suggested that you take a few minutes to outline each answer. Spend approximately one-fourth of your time (25 minutes) on each question. Illustrate your essay with substantive examples where appropriate. Make certain to number each of your answers as the question is numbered below.

1. Since the 1960s, Congress has addressed the problem of gender bias on numerous occasions.

   (a) Select one of the following laws and describe how it has attempted to address the problem of gender bias in American society.
   - the Equal Pay Act of 1963
   - the Civil Rights Act of 1964

   (b) Assess the effectiveness of that law.

   (c) Select one of the following legislative actions and describe how it has attempted to address the problem of gender bias in American society.
   - Title IX of the Higher Education Act of 1973
   - the Equal Rights Amendment to the Constitution

   (d) Assess the effectiveness of that action.

2. Traditionally, presidential candidates have relied on strong support from their national party organization.

   (a) Describe how national party organizations have historically aided their candidates.

   (b) Describe how this dynamic has changed in recent presidential elections.

   (c) Discuss THREE factors that have helped bring about this change.

GO ON TO THE NEXT PAGE

3. The media have a large influence on American politics.

   (a) Describe why the media are so important and why they have such influence.

   (b) Identify and describe THREE examples of media coverage that have influenced American politics in the past twenty years.

   (c) Evaluate the argument that in politics, the media tend to overemphasize stories that are easy to tell at the expense of those that are more complicated.

"The prosecution of [impeachments] will seldom fail to agitate the passions of the whole community, and to divide it into parties more or less friendly or inimical to the accused. In many cases it will connect itself with pre-existing factions, and will enlist all their animosities, partialities, influence, and interest on one side or the other, and in such cases there will always be the greatest danger that the decision will be regulated more by the comparative strength of parties, than by the real demonstrations of innocence or guilt."

—Alexander Hamilton, *Federalist 65*

4. The House of Representatives has twice impeached sitting presidents, both of whom avoided removal from office by the Senate.

   (a) Define impeachment and removal, and describe the process of impeachment and removal as listed in the Constitution.

   (b) Assess the accuracy of Hamilton's observations as applied to both cases of presidential impeachment.

   (c) Identify the strengths and weaknesses of checks and balances in dealing with Hamilton's concerns.

END OF EXAMINATION

16

Practice Test 2: Answers and Explanations

ANSWER KEY

1.	E		31.	B
2.	D		32.	A
3.	A		33.	A
4.	E		34.	C
5.	D		35.	D
6.	A		36.	A
7.	A		37.	C
8.	E		38.	B
9.	C		39.	D
10.	C		40.	E
11.	B		41.	E
12.	A		42.	D
13.	C		43.	C
14.	A		44.	D
15.	B		45.	E
16.	B		46.	C
17.	E		47.	A
18.	D		48.	E
19.	B		49.	D
20.	C		50.	B
21.	A		51.	C
22.	E		52.	E
23.	E		53.	D
24.	C		54.	E
25.	C		55.	A
26.	B		56.	D
27.	B		57.	A
28.	D		58.	B
29.	C		59.	D
30.	B		60.	C

MULTIPLE-CHOICE SECTION: ANSWERS EXPLAINED

1. **E** *Federalism* is a government system under which the national government shares power with subnational governments. Under federalism, both the national and state governments are granted *exclusive* powers. They share many other *concurrent* powers, such as the powers to tax and write laws.

   Incorrect answers

   (A) The term *system of checks and balances* refers to the manner in which government power at the national level is divided to prevent any single office or faction from gaining control of the government. It applies specifically to the national government; *federalism* refers to the relationship between the national and state governments.

   (B) The power of the Supreme Court to review the constitutionality of laws is called *judicial review*.

   (C) The Bill of Rights' protection of the rights of the accused occasionally has an impact on Federalism, as when the Supreme Court requires the state laws to conform to provisions in the Bill of Rights. However, this answer does not provide the definition of the term *federalism*.

   (D) The size of state delegations to the House of Representatives is determined by the national census, which is taken every 10 years.

2. **D** During the ratification debate, the Constitution received its strongest opposition from those objecting to its lack of a Bill of Rights, which raised fears that the new government may grow too powerful and suppress individual rights. Had supporters of the Constitution not conceded the speedy addition of a Bill of Rights after ratification, the Constitution may never have received the necessary support.

   Incorrect answers

   (A) Had the Framers been wholeheartedly committed to individual rights, the Constitution would originally have included a Bill of Rights. Its later addition reveals that the framers did not consider a Bill of Rights necessary.

   (B) The Bill of Rights enumerates the rights of individuals and thus provides protection against an overpowerful national government. Answer (B) refers to a concession the small states received during the framing of the body of the Constitution. That concession resulted in the creation of the Senate, where all states receive equal representation.

   (C) The Bill of Rights is silent on the issue of slavery, so it cannot be cited as evidence of abolitionism in the North.

   (E) The system of checks and balances is laid out in the body of the Constitution, not in the Bill of Rights.

3. **A** *Civil court* is the venue for lawsuits. It is where disputes between two private parties, such as individuals or corporations, are settled (as opposed to *criminal court*, where the state tries accused criminals).

Incorrect answers

(B) Suits may be filed in either state or federal court, depending on the nature of the case.

(C) *Criminal court* is where the state tries accused criminals.

(D) Suits may be filed in either state or federal court, depending on the nature of the case.

(E) A *grand jury* hears preliminary evidence in a criminal case. Its job is to decide whether prosecutors have enough evidence to bring an indictment against the accused. When a grand jury indicts, the case moves on to the criminal courts.

4. **E** A *budget deficit* is the difference between government income and government spending, when spending is greater than income. When income is greater, this difference is called a *budget surplus*.

Incorrect answers

(A) See the explanation for answer (E).

(B) Interest on the national debt may contribute to the deficit, but it is not synonymous with the term *budget deficit*.

(C) See the explanation for answer (E).

(D) Occasionally the federal fiscal year ends before Congress and the president can agree on a new budget. When this happens, Congress usually passes emergency spending bills to cover government expenses. This can contribute to *budget deficits*, because it is more expensive to run the government on this *ad hoc* basis, but the situation described is not synonymous with the term *budget deficit*.

5. **D** Many successful interest groups—such as those cited in the question—represent minority positions. Their power derives from the fact that the minorities they represent base their votes almost exclusively on a candidate's position on that issue. The intensity of their commitment overrides their numerical disadvantage, because their opposition more often considers other issues when voting. Accordingly, they form a less powerful voting bloc on any single issue.

Incorrect answers

(A) In fact, domestic policy has grown more liberal during the period described. Such a policy shift is common under Democratic administrations.

(B) Political action committees have remained powerful in recent years and will continue to do so as long as current campaign-finance laws and practices remain in place.

(C) No, both the NRA and antiabortion rights activists were opposed by the Clinton White House, yet both remained influential in Washington, DC.

(E) The groups described are powerful AND they support extremely controversial positions.

6. **A** This answer choice encapsulates the *preferred position doctrine*, framed by the Supreme Court in the 1940s.

    Incorrect answers

    (B) The Supreme Court has accepted limits on free speech, most notably in *Schenck v. United States*, in which the Court established the "clear and present danger" limit on speech.

    (C) This was, in fact, true between 1830 and 1925. In 1830, the Court ruled in *Barron v. Baltimore* that the Bill of Rights applied only to the national government, not to state governments. In 1925, however, the Court ruled in *Gitlow v. New York* that free speech was protected from state infringement by the "due process" clause of the Fourteenth Amendment. Since the 1940s, the Court's position on free speech has been the *preferred position doctrine* (see above).

    (D) The First Amendment protects offensive speech. A classic example of protected offensive speech is graphic pornography; most Americans find it offensive, yet it proliferates nonetheless.

    (E) The exact same First Amendment rights that protect print and broadcast media protect individuals as well.

7. **A** The power to administer elections is reserved to the states. All powers described in the other answer choices are concurrent powers, granted to both the national and the state governments.

8. **E** PACs contribute primarily to incumbents because 1) incumbents usually win their elections, and 2) the PACs hope to gain influence with the candidate by donating to his or her campaign.

9. **C** A *pocket veto* can only be used on bills passed in the final days of a congressional session. The Constitution requires the president to sign a bill within 10 days of its reaching his desk. If the president fails to sign a bill while Congress is in session, the bill is returned to Congress, whereupon it becomes law. (Presidents who wish to express disapproval of a law, but not veto it, occasionally use this constitutional process.) However, if Congress is not in session, the bill cannot be returned to Congress, so it simply dies. This process is called a pocket veto.

    Incorrect answers

    (A) While using the pocket veto, the president may or may not express disapproval of the bill. A public rejection of the bill, however, is not a necessary element of a pocket veto.

    (B) See the explanation for answer choice (C).

    (D) See the explanation for answer choice (C).

    (E) The situation described in this answer choice does not describe a pocket veto. Furthermore, it describes an extremely unlikely scenario because the president must first nominate federal judges before the Senate can confirm them.

10. **C** Compare each of the four "Democratic Upper House" bars with the corresponding "Republican Upper House" bars on the bar graph. In each case, the Democratic bar is larger. The same holds true for the lower houses. If you did *not* choose this answer, perhaps the wording of the answer choice confused you. The answer choice does *not* say that Democrats held majorities in the majority of legislative chambers, an assertion that the bar graph does not support. Rather, it simply says that Democrats had more seats in all the legislatures. That is precisely what this graph shows.

Remember that graph questions on the AP Government and Politics Exam ask only that you identify indisputable conclusions. Do not try to "read between the lines" and interpret the data—you will only get into trouble that way.

Incorrect answers

(A) While the chart does demonstrate an increase in Republican representation in state legislatures, this answer choice goes too far in drawing its conclusion. The trend shown is simply not dramatic enough to support this assertion.

(B) This chart does not include information about registered voters and therefore cannot support the conclusion drawn in this answer choice.

(D) This chart does not include information about governors and therefore cannot support the conclusion drawn in this answer choice.

(E) This chart does not include information about party representation in individual state legislatures and therefore cannot support the conclusion drawn in this answer choice.

11. **B** As in U.S. government, power in political parties is spread out among various national, state, and local officials. National party organizations exert little influence over local party officials and elected officers. In contrast, the national party organizations in parliamentary democracies (such as Britain) tightly control the activities and votes of party members in government.

Incorrect answers

(A) This statement is true of national parties within parliamentary governments, but not of those within the United States federal government.

(C) The president and his counterpart in the opposition party are too busy running the government to direct party activities. Both serve as important fundraisers and ideological leaders of their parties, but neither typically spends much time on day-to-day party operations.

(D) If the parties waited for their nominating conventions (which occur once every four years) to make important decisions, they would never get anything done. In fact, important decisions of any kind are rarely made at conventions, which are instead carefully choreographed pageants designed to sell the party's candidates to voters.

(E) Gerald Ford, Jimmy Carter, and George H. W. Bush all played minimal roles in their political parties.

12. **A** By covering some events heavily and down playing others, the media help set the public agenda. The amount of exposure given to an issue by the media directly affects whether the public perceives that issue as important. Furthermore, because the public relies on the media for information, the way in which the media present news (and the frequency with which they report certain stories) naturally influences the public's viewpoint.

Incorrect answers

(B) Pundits who are "overly political" are in high demand during elections.

(C) News media play an important role in elections by dissecting campaign advertisements. However, this highly specified task does not "play a major role in establishing the public agenda."

(D) Except in times of crisis, most Americans pay little attention to news from overseas. Consequently, political reporting from overseas usually has little impact on the public agenda.

(E) Again, this answer describes a media service of interest to only a small portion of the voting public.

13. **C** Support for prayer in schools is weakest among those with higher levels of education. The less education a person has, the more likely that person is to support school prayer (Gallup poll, 1992).

Incorrect answers

(A) Government-enforced racial and sexual equality is more likely to be supported as the level of education rises due to the impact of understanding historical and social causes and effects of segregation and discrimination.

(B) The more educated, the more likely voters are to hold progressive or liberal views about the environment.

(D) The more educated, the more likely voters are to hold progressive or liberal views about abortion.

(E) The more educated, the more likely voters are to hold progressive or liberal views about civil liberties.

14. **A** In 1963, Clarence Earl Gideon won an appeal of his criminal conviction. His appeal argued that the state of Florida had denied him a fair trial because its court had refused to provide him with a defense attorney. The Supreme Court agreed, ruling that Florida had violated Gideon's right to due process under the Fourteenth Amendment. Because of *Gideon v. Wainwright*, poor defendants are now entitled to court-appointed attorneys in felony cases. (B), Self-incrimination was the central issue in *Miranda v. Arizona*. Each of the incorrect answers describes a right guaranteed by the Bill of Rights, but not the one tested in *Gideon*.

15. **B** The better informed voters are of an election and its central issues, the more likely they are to vote. Media coverage provides the primary source of election information for most Americans. Accordingly, voter turnout usually increases as media coverage increases. Turnout is lowest in local elections, which are poorly publicized, and highest during national elections, which are highly publicized. This is especially true of presidential elections, which receive the most publicity of all U.S. elections.

Incorrect answers

(A) Voters are less likely to vote when they believe their vote cannot influence the outcome of the election, as in the situation described by this answer choice.

(C) Voters are more likely to vote when they perceive stark differences between the candidates. When they are unfamiliar with the candidates, they are less likely to vote.

(D) Independents vote less frequently than do voters registered as Democrats or Republicans.

(E) Voters turn out in greater numbers for a presidential election. Without the drawing power of a presidential election, midterm elections attract fewer voters to the polls.

16. **B** The "necessary and proper" clause, often referred to as the *elastic* clause, allows Congress to pass laws "necessary and proper" to the performance of its duties. Congress can use this clause to expand its authority, often by citing its power to regulate interstate commerce. The "necessary and proper" clause comes into conflict with the Tenth Amendment because Congress uses this clause to gain control in areas previously under state supervision. Avid states' rights advocates argue that these Congressional actions usurp the states' reserved powers.

Incorrect answers

(A) The "full faith and credit" clause requires states to honor one another's laws, licenses, and so on. Because it does not involve infringements on state governments by the national government, it does not pertain to the Tenth Amendment.

(C) The provisions for the impeachment of a president pertain only to the national government and so cannot come into conflict with the Tenth Amendment.

(D) The clause prohibiting states from coining money and entering into treaties appears in the body of the Constitution. These powers are "delegated to the United States by the Constitution," as acknowledged in the Tenth Amendment, and so do not conflict with the amendment.

(E) The provisions for constitutional amendment lay out a process for amending the Constitution that does not infringe on states' rights and therefore do not conflict with the Tenth Amendment.

17. **E** *States' righters* believe that the Constitution limits the national government to its specifically enumerated powers. They also believe that the vast majority of governance should be left entirely to the states.

Incorrect answers

(A) The term *Federalist* refers either to those who support the federal system or to members of the Federalist Party, which existed from the late 1700s until the late 1810s. Either way, it describes a person who supports a strong central government.

(B) The term *isolationist* refers to a person who believes that the government should avoid involvement with foreign governments and nations.

(C) The term *laissez-faire capitalist* refers to a person who believes the government should regulate the economy as little as possible.

(D) The term *loose constructionist* refers to a person who believes the national government should use the elastic clause to expand its powers. Loose constructionists argue that the national government may do anything not expressly forbidden by the Constitution. They do not see the Tenth Amendment as a significant limitation of federal power.

18. **D** Because the membership of the House is so large, the process by which the House debates and amends bills must be regulated. The task of setting these limits falls to the House Rules Committee. Because the Rules Committee controls crucial aspects of the legislative process, it is the most powerful committee in the House. The Speaker of the House nearly always chairs this committee.

Incorrect answers

(A) The Ways and Means Committee has jurisdiction over tax and trade legislation. It is an extremely powerful committee.

(B) The Judiciary Committee is a powerful committee with a wide range of responsibilities. It has jurisdiction over matters concerning the judiciary, immigration, and constitutional amendments. This committee heard the evidence in the impeachment proceedings against Bill Clinton and reported to the full membership of the House, recommending impeachment.

(C) The Ethics Committee determines the rules of proper behavior for representatives. It punishes those who violate the rules.

(E) The Committee on Government Reform performs oversight on executive agencies.

19. **B** Entitlement programs include Social Security and Medicare. Many people, especially among the elderly, rely on these programs to cover living and medical expenses. Recipients of entitlements form a large and powerful voting bloc. Consequently, it is considered political suicide even to suggest substantial reductions in entitlement benefits.

Incorrect answers

(A) Entitlement programs are created by acts of Congress. Social Security was established during the New Deal; Medicare was created as part of Lyndon Johnson's Great Society program.

(C) Entitlement programs are not defense-related. See the explanation for answer choice (B).

(D) Entitlement recipients do indeed constitute a powerful political bloc, but the vast majority of entitlement recipients are not wealthy. In fact, most are extremely protective of their entitlements precisely because they have very little money.

(E) Congress can alter entitlement budgets, although in theory these budgets are supposed to be separately funded (through payroll withholding taxes) and thus "untouchable." If Congress and the president were unable to alter entitlement budgets, these budgets would not be the hot political issue that they are.

20. **C** The fact that power is divided among so many different government branches and agencies guarantees slow, conservative government action. Only during times of extreme crisis—such as during the Great Depression—can the government move quickly AND effect substantial change. Otherwise, the conflicting interests of the many parties involved slow both the process and the rate of change, resulting in relatively stable policy.

Incorrect answers

(A) The two major parties rarely cooperate. The lack of cooperation between them, in fact, slows the political process, increasing political stability.

(B) Judicial activism—the process by which courts change policy by reinterpreting the law—decreases stability by effecting rapid change to the legal system. The Warren Court's alterations of criminal rights, for example, quickly changed policing and trial procedures in the United States.

(D) Affirmative action programs, which attempt to redress previous racial and gender inequality, are a recent phenomenon. Because American public policy has always been relatively stable, this cannot be the correct answer.

(E) The delegation of specific powers to the House and Senate plays an important role in the functioning of the legislature, but it does not have a major influence on the stability of public policy.

21. **A** The Constitution provides a broad outline of the president's duties but does not define them specifically. Nor does the Constitution enumerate the limits on those powers, except in the broadest of terms. Consequently, presidents are often left to define for themselves the limits of their powers under such mandates as "Commander in Chief" and "Head of State." Presidential power is accordingly fluid, dependent on the popularity and skills of the office holder. Franklin D. Roosevelt was able to establish an extremely strong presidency; Presidents Ford and Carter, conversely, found their presidencies limited by post-Watergate mistrust of the executive branch.

Incorrect answers

(B) Whether the Constitution places too many or too few limits on presidential power is a subject of endless debate. "Most people" do not agree that the presidency is too weak.

(C) The Supreme Court is not unwilling to rule on such cases. In the 1930s, the Court frequently struck down Roosevelt's New Deal programs on constitutional grounds. In the 1970s, the Court decided against the Nixon administration several times, in each instance ruling that Nixon had overstepped his authority as president.

(D) No constitutional amendments have increased presidential power. One amendment limits the number of terms a president may serve. This amendment arguably decreases presidential power by creating a "lame duck" period for second-term presidents, during which presidents' ability to influence Congress invariably declines.

(E) This is simply not an issue in the debate over presidential power.

22. **E** The secretary of state is responsible for international relations. The chief national security advisor consults with the president on foreign policy matters. Consequently, the responsibilities of the two officials overlap. This was most evident in the late 1960s and early 1970s, when President Nixon clearly favored the advice of national security advisor Henry Kissinger over that of Secretary of State William Rogers.

Incorrect answers

(A) The secretary of the interior is responsible for administering public lands, such as national parks and wildlife refuges, within the United States.

(B) The secretary of the treasury oversees the Treasury Department.

(C) The Speaker of the House leads the House of Representatives. The Speaker is always a member of the majority party in the House.

(D) The president's chief of staff manages the president's schedule and controls access to the president.

23. **E** In primary elections, momentum translates into donations, the lifeblood of the campaign. Accordingly, early victories are extremely important. Because of this emphasis placed on early primaries, many states have pushed their primary dates forward. By enhancing the prominence of their primaries, states hope to influence the direction of the campaign, perhaps even gaining promises of increased federal support from candidates hopeful of winning in their states.

Incorrect answers

(A) State expenses in elections are not a major concern to the states. While candidates spend many millions, the states' expenses are confined to maintaining voting machines, hiring poll workers, and so on. Changing the primary date would do little to alter these costs, which are nominal at any rate.

(B) General elections are always held on the first Tuesday of November. There is no public interest in changing that date.

(C) Other factors—primarily the ability to raise money—restrict the number of entrants in the presidential race. While moving primary dates forward may have exacerbated this situation, this was not the states' intent in changing their primary dates.

(D) State-level primary races rarely generate national attention. The exception to this rule is the rare controversial primary, such as when David Duke, an ex-member of the Ku Klux Klan, ran in—and won—Louisiana's Republican primary for governor in 1990.

24. **C** Neither senators nor representatives are allowed to use federal funding to finance their campaigns.

Incorrect answers

(A) Senators represent entire states, in which party identification is rarely lopsided. A representative from an inner-city district, however, may have a constituency that is 95 percent Democratic.

(B) In terms of political currency, a Senate seat is simply more valuable than a seat in the House. The length of term in office, the limited number of seats in the chamber, and the special powers of the body all confer extra status on senators. Accordingly, Senate races are usually hotly contested. House incumbents, conversely, frequently run uncontested.

(D) See the explanation for answer choice (B).

(E) House races rarely generate much media attention. Senate races always do, at least within the state (and often nationally as well). This increased public interest makes it more difficult for Senate incumbents to win reelection.

25. **C** Cabinet members head executive departments. As they work with the bureaucrats within their departments, many come to see themselves as their department's chief advocate within the administration. As such, they grow more concerned with their department's priorities and less concerned with the president's, a process referred to as "going native." This is why presidents more often turn to their personal advisors than to cabinet members for advice.

26. **B** The Constitution does not specifically grant Congress the authority to impose workplace safety standards. Congress does so by citing its power to regulate interstate commerce and exercising the elastic clause, which allows Congress to pass laws "necessary and proper" to the execution of its enumerated powers.

Incorrect answers

NOTE: All of the incorrect answers appear in Article I, Section 8 of the Constitution.

(A) The Constitution specifically empowers Congress to "establish a uniform rule of naturalization."

(C) The Constitution specifically empowers Congress to "collect taxes, duties, imposts, and excises."

(D) The Constitution specifically empowers Congress to "coin money [and] regulate the value thereof."

(E) The Constitution specifically empowers Congress to declare war.

27. **B** The Supreme Court hears less than 5 percent of all appeals. It chooses its cases carefully, fully aware that each Court decision could have a major impact on society. In choosing its cases, the Court helps set the public agenda. Whenever the Court agrees to hear an abortion case, for example, abortion immediately leaps to the top of the public agenda, with activists on all sides of the issue stepping up activities.

Incorrect answers

(A) The Court hears less than 5 percent of all appeals.

(C) Four or more justices must agree to hear a case. When four justices reach this agreement, the court issues a writ of *certiorari* requesting all transcripts for the case.

(D) The vote of the chief justice counts as one vote, as do the votes of all nine members of the Court.

(E) The Court will rule in favor of one side or another even if the justices cannot reach a majority agreement on a single opinion. For example, five justices may vote in favor of one party. They may not agree, however, on why the party has won the case. All five justices may then write separate opinions, or (more often) several will sign on to one justice's opinion, while another justice will offer a separate *concurring opinion* on the case.

28. **D** Add the totals of all PAC contributions in each of the recent elections. In each election, the sum is greater than $150 million. Remember that this is only the tip of the iceberg: Candidates raise money from private donors and many other sources as well.

Remember that graph questions on the AP Government and Politics Exam ask only that you identify indisputable conclusions. Do not try to "read between the lines" and interpret the data—you will only get into trouble that way.

29. **C** Former Supreme Court justices William Brennan and Thurgood Marshall were among the numerous legal experts who have argued that the death penalty constitutes "cruel and unusual punishment." While theirs is the minority opinion, it is one that is widely held among opponents of the death penalty.

Incorrect answers

(A) The double jeopardy clause protects individuals from a second prosecution once a court has found them "not guilty."

(B) The Constitution addresses this issue only in its "cruel and unusual punishment" clause, and then only if the states impose the death penalty in a cruel manner. While hanging and the electric chair were arguably "cruel and unusual," the most common form of execution today—lethal injection—is less so.

(D) Federal and state laws vary on most issues. This is a fundamental feature of federalism and is not particularly controversial.

(E) This may be an issue in some death penalty cases, but it is not the central constitutional issue concerning the death penalty.

30. **B** The process described in this question is called *selective incorporation*. You should have been able to use process of elimination to answer this question, because none of the incorrect answers appears in the Fourteenth Amendment.

Incorrect answers

(A) The Fourth Amendment guarantees this right.

(C) The Constitution does not explicitly guarantee this right. The Supreme Court has found an implied right to privacy, however, in the combined effect of the Bill of Rights and the Fourteenth Amendment.

(D) The Thirteenth Amendment abolished slavery.

(E) The "reserved powers" provision appears in the Tenth Amendment.

31. **B** Under the provisions of the Constitution as ratified in 1789, state legislatures selected senators. The framers considered the House of Representatives to be the "people's house," as evidenced by the provision for direct election of representatives. The Seventeenth Amendment (1913) provided for the direct election of senators.

Incorrect answers

(A) No such restriction appears in the Constitution.

(C) While the Constitution does in fact require all spending bills to originate in the House, the purpose of this provision was not to insulate the Senate from public opinion. Rather, the purpose was to increase the accountability of those who spent the people's money.

(D) While the Constitution does in fact give this power to the Senate, the purpose of this provision was not to insulate the Senate from public opinion. Rather, the purpose was to reinforce the system of checks and balances.

(E) The purpose of this provision was to create one legislative body in which each state received equal representation, not to insulate the Senate from public opinion.

32. **A** Under the Articles of Confederation, the states remained nearly autonomous, united in a loose confederation empowered to perform only those few tasks necessary to the maintenance of a single nation. The framers of the Articles left the national government dependent on the states to collect taxes and enforce its laws, tasks that the states could not be compelled to perform and which therefore were performed erratically, if at all. The Articles did not empower the national government to create a judiciary or regulate interstate commerce. Of the powers listed in the answer choices, only the power to negotiate treaties belonged to the national government.

33. **A** Federal law requires that a panel of commissioners drawn from both parties lead independent regulatory agencies. Commissioners serve long terms that do not usually coincide with the changes of presidential administrations. All of these provisions are intended to protect regulatory agencies from the political pressures of electoral politics. In reality, of course, political pressures cannot be avoided, given the weighty impact of regulatory agencies' decisions. Politicians, businesses, and public-interest groups all work hard to influence regulatory policy.

    Incorrect answers

    (B) Regulatory agencies must often defend their decisions before congressional committees, but they are not required to plan policy cooperatively with them. Furthermore, interactions with Congress increase the political pressure on regulators.

    (C) This process increases political pressure on regulatory agencies by leaving them dependent on Congress.

    (D) Interactions between the president and regulatory agencies increase the political pressure on those agencies.

    (E) Regulatory agencies are not required to seek the advice of the industries they regulate, although almost all do as a matter of course. Such interactions, however, increase political pressure on regulatory agencies.

34. **C** The government could not immediately enforce the 1954 Supreme Court decision *Brown v. Board of Education* because it had little enforcement power. Short of sending troops to force integration, the government had few powers over uncooperative states. The Civil Rights Act of 1964 changed that by allowing the government to cut off funding to discriminatory school systems. The loss of federal funding would have crippled many school systems and so persuaded many to comply with *Brown*.

    Incorrect answers

    (A) See the explanation for answer choice (C).

    (B) *Brown v. Board of Education* overturned the "separate but equal" principle. See the explanation for answer choice (C).

    (D) See the explanation for answer choice (C).

    (E) The process described in this answer choice would have been impossible, given residential segregation. To make each public school population mirror state residential demographics would require transporting some students many, many miles. The impracticality of this answer choice should have helped you eliminate it.

35. **D** The winner-take-all arrangement in the electoral college places a high premium on victory in battleground states, which are determined by used polling data. Presidential candidates spend relatively little time in strongly ideological states such as New York (Democratic) or Texas (Republican), preferring states like Florida and Pennsylvania where the vote is up for grabs.

Incorrect answers

(A) It is possible for a candidate to win more than half the states in the electoral college and still lose the election. California alone has as many electoral votes as the 15 least populous states combined!

(B) Though the south has swung from being solidly Democratic to being solidly Republican, its importance is not absolute and can vary from election to election.

(C) Because the votes of electors always reflect their home state's election results, candidates need not campaign among electors at all.

(E) The winner-take-all arrangement of the electoral college encourages candidates to give up on states in which they are farthest behind and to concentrate instead on those in which they have a chance of winning.

36. **A** A good example is the Agriculture Committee, which is invariably populated almost entirely by congresspersons from agricultural states. Accordingly, agricultural consumers and other constituencies with an interest in agriculture are underrepresented on this committee. This pattern holds true throughout the many special-interest committees in Congress.

Incorrect answers

(B) Membership in congressional committees is reasonably large, certainly large enough to include representation of all popular opinions. Congress simply chooses not to populate its committees in that manner.

(C) The majority party controls every committee. The chairperson is a member of the majority party, and more than half the seats on every committee go to majority party members. The fact that the minority party controls some committee seats tends to make committee members more broadly representative of public opinion, not less.

(D) This is a pretty good distracter answer. However, most members of Congress keep constant tabs on their constituents' priorities through regular polling.

(E) Even if this were so, it would not explain why the opinions of committee members do not accurately reflect public opinion.

37. **C** Winning an election in a two-party system requires coalition building, which is not possible when one of the parties clings to one issue or ideological position. But it is possible in electoral systems (based on proportional representation) that allow for single-cause parties, such as the German Green party, to win a share of the seats in parliaments.

Incorrect answers

(A) U.S. politicians must serve all classes in their constituency to win in a two-party system.

(B) During the early and middle parts of the last century there was an expansion of the power of labor and unions in the economy, society, and politics.

(D) The struggle between different interests within the two-party system has not led to the domination of labor, or any other interest in the political representation of party.

(E) Race, although represented as a political cleavage within the parties, does not rank as high as class standing and political affiliation.

38. **B** The majority of federal programs are administered through *grants-in-aid* to the states. The federal government provides the states with a set of guidelines and the money to carry them out, but leaves administration of the programs to the states.

39. **D** The Constitution empowers Congress to create new federal courts (see Article III, Section 1).

40. **E** The War Powers Act requires the president to seek periodic approval from Congress for any substantial troop commitment. The bill was passed in response to the Vietnam War. The Budget and Impoundment Control Act requires congressional approval of presidential impoundments of federal funds. The bill was passed in response to impoundments made by President Nixon, who tried to cut federal spending by impounding, or refusing to allocate, funds Congress had appropriated. Both bills sought to limit the president's powers by requiring the president to seek congressional approval for specific actions.

41. **E** In an *open primary*, voters enter the voting booth and then decide in which party's primary they wish to vote. They may vote in only one party's primary, however; they may not hopscotch across the ballot, for example, by voting in the Democratic primary for president and then the Republican primary for governor. Voting in such a manner is only permitted in a *blanket primary*.

    Incorrect answers

    (A) Independents may vote in open and blanket primaries. They may not vote in closed primaries, which are limited only to members of the respective parties (i.e., Democrats may vote only in the Democratic primary and Republicans may vote only in the Republican primary).

    (B) There is no such primary election as the one described in this answer choice. See the explanation for answer choice (E).

    (C) See the explanation for answer choice (E).

    (D) There is no such primary election as the one described in this answer choice. See the explanation for answer choice (E).

42. **D** The FECA was intended to reduce the influence of money on election campaigns by limiting donations from individuals, corporations, and interest groups. To achieve this goal, the FECA allowed interest groups to form political action committees to advance their political goals. These PACs are subject to donation limits. As a result, thousands of new PACs arose to solicit funds for various causes. Consequently, money became an even more important factor in elections.

    Incorrect answers

    (A) This answer describes an intended result of the FECA.

    (B) This answer describes an intended result of the FECA.

    (C) The amount of money spent on televised campaign advertising continues to increase from election to election.

    (E) Since the passage of the FECA, there have been several credible third-party candidates, for example, John Anderson in 1980 and Ross Perot in 1992. The FECA does not appear to have dampened third-party presidential efforts.

43. **C** Politicians need to reach the public for a number of reasons: to rally support and to publicize their reelection efforts, to name two. Political reporters need politicians as well: Without quotes to put in their news stories and confidential information from political insiders, the media would not be able to report the news. Each group needs the other, a fact that softens the antagonistic nature of their relationship.

Incorrect answers

(A) There is no real distinction between younger and older politicians' comfort level with the media. Some of the most savvy handlers of the press are older politicians, whose experiences have taught them how to manipulate the press.

(B) The First Amendment prevents the government from regulating press activity in nearly all situations.

(D) Most media outlets will gladly cover a story embarrassing to a politician if they believe their audiences are interested. For one obvious example, consider the coverage of Bill Clinton's affair with Monica Lewinsky.

(E) Most government activity is accessible to the public. When information is classified, it tends to exacerbate the antagonistic relationship between the media and politicians. The media try to uncover the classified information (to find out whether it is newsworthy), much to the annoyance of the government.

44. **D** The Twenty-sixth Amendment to the Constitution established a uniform voting age of 18 for the entire nation. This answer states the facts incorrectly.

Incorrect answers

(A) Many people in this age bracket attend college out of state. This requires them to either register in the new state (some states will not allow such students to register, requiring them to vote in their old home states instead) or vote in their former state of residence by absentee ballot. Both of these procedures are complicated enough to discourage some from voting.

(B) Many people in this age bracket move frequently, requiring them to register at their new place of residence. Some do not, preferring instead not to vote.

(C) Many people in this age bracket simply do not see the pertinence of most political issues to their daily lives. This results in a lower voting rate.

(E) People in this age bracket serving in the military must vote by absentee ballot. This discourages some from voting.

45. **E** For a discussion of the different aspects of public opinion on issues, see Chapter 6.

46. **C** Among its traditional constituencies, the Democratic Party has the weakest hold on the south, where the party's progressive social policies are often at odds with the general conservatism of the region. For decades, the Democratic Party could count on solid support from the south merely because the Republican Party was "the party of Lincoln" and was thus "responsible" for the Civil War. In recent years, however, the Republican Party has made major inroads in the region.

Incorrect answers

(A) People holding advanced academic degrees generally support the liberal social policies advanced by traditional Democrats.

(B) Northeastern city dwellers generally support the liberal social policies advanced by traditional Democrats.

(D) Jewish Americans generally support the liberal social policies advanced by traditional Democrats.

(E) Urban African Americans generally support the liberal social policies advanced by traditional Democrats.

47. **A** The Warren Court issued a number of landmark decisions expanding the rights of the accused. Among these decisions, *Miranda v. Arizona* protected defendants against self-incrimination, *Gideon v. Wainwright* guaranteed accused felons the right to legal counsel, and *Mapp v. Ohio* established the *exclusionary rule*, which disallows the use in trial of improperly obtained evidence.

Incorrect answers

(B) Warren Court decisions increased the power of the national government over the states by forcing the states to comply with the Bill of Rights.

(C) The principle of judicial review was established in 1803 by Chief Justice John Marshall in *Marbury v. Madison*.

(D) The Supreme Court of the late 1800s employed unusual definitions of the Sherman Anti-Trust Act to subvert its intent. The Warren Court covers a later period (the 1950s and 1960s).

(E) The Warren Court strengthened the division between church and state in several rulings. In its most noteworthy decision on the subject, the Court prohibited school prayer.

48. **E** This 1978 case concerned a white male who had been denied admission to the University of California at Davis medical school. The student, Alan Bakke, discovered that Davis had reserved 16 of the 100 slots in the class specifically for minority students. Bakke discovered further that some of the students admitted in those slots had lower MCAT scores and college GPAs than him. Bakke argued reverse discrimination, pointing out that minority students could compete for all 100 slots in the class but that he could compete for only 84, resulting in an unfair reduction of his chances of admission. The Court agreed with Bakke, but its decision was a complicated one that still allowed colleges to use affirmative action, so long as they did so in the name of diversity and avoided setting quotas.

49. **D** Thomas Jefferson's Declaration of Independence reflects John Locke's philosophy regarding natural rights and the participation of the individual in politics.

Incorrect answers

(A) Thomas Hobbes held a pessimistic view of humanity and favored a strong monarchy with limitations on individual liberty.

(B) Niccolo Macchiavelli wrote *The Prince*, which advocates a strong, centralized leader, and an "ends justify the means" school of political thought.

(C) Jonathan Edwards, an early colonial theologian, felt that rights were granted to people by God, not by government.

(E) John Calvin, a protestant reformer, advocated a theocracratic type of government.

50. **B** In the most famous of the *Federalist Papers*, James Madison bemoaned the evils of political factions and explained how a federal republic, by dividing power among many parties, minimizes the damage that factions can cause. AP U.S. Government and Politics questions referring to the *Federalist Papers* almost invariably center on this essay and, more particularly, on this point. Make sure you know it.

51. **C** As a president enters the final two years of his second term, his political influence diminishes. Through the second midterm election of his tenure, the president carries considerable influence with the electorate and therefore can persuade Congress to cooperate through threats (e.g., "I will campaign against you, and you will lose"). Once that threat has passed, the president, no longer able to run for reelection, loses political capital. Congress accordingly defers to him less frequently. A president saddled with a Congress led by the opposing party will also experience a diminution in power because his ability to implement his programs will meet a challenge from the legislature. Bill Clinton proved adept at accomplishing some goals despite opposition from a Republican Congress; nonetheless, divided control of the legislative and executive branches unquestionably weakens a president.

International crises strengthen a president. Congress is reluctant to challenge a president when the United States is challenged abroad, preferring instead to present a united front to the world. Presidents always thrive when the economy is strong and approval ratings are high. Because the United States is a republican democracy, popularity confers substantial political power because popularity translates into votes.

52. **E** Senators have much greater leeway to alter legislation on the Senate floor than representatives have on the House floor. The size of the House prohibits lengthy debate and a prolonged amendment process. To complete its work on legislation, the House imposes strict rules on floor debates and amendments. All such work in the House is done in committee, making a representative's committee assignments a critical aspect of his or her ability to accomplish political goals.

Incorrect answers

(A) Like senators, House members may serve on several committees simultaneously.

(B) Senate committee members enjoy all the same powers as House committee members.

(C) The committee system works in roughly the same manner in both legislative chambers. A Senate bill does not have to pass through every committee. Were this procedure in place, it would certainly grind the legislative process to a halt.

(D) A special committee assigns committee membership in the Senate. The House uses the same procedure.

53. **D** Third parties arise primarily out of discontent with the two major parties. The Republicans, for example, arose to represent Northern abolitionists, who could not find a voice in either of the two major parties of the 1840s and 1850s. The Populists gave farmers a political outlet in the 1890s; the Socialists represented disaffected workers in the early 1900s.

Incorrect answers

(A) During times of prosperity, most Americans pay little attention to politics. The interest level of most Americans is too low during such periods to support a third party.

(B) While some third parties fit this description, most do not.

(C) Unless you count the Republicans as a third party, no third party has ever won a majority of seats in Congress. By the time a party accomplishes this feat, it has become one of the two major parties.

(E) While some third parties fit this description, most do not.

54. **E** The dual judicial system of the United States encompasses state and federal courts. Usually the two domains remain distinct, but some crimes are prosecutable in both systems. Recently, the federal government has sought to correct perceived injustices in state courts—primarily in high-profile acquittals—by prosecuting the accused in federal court. Some such defendants include the police officers who were captured on videotape beating Rodney King in Los Angeles, and a young African American who stabbed a rabbinical student in Brooklyn during a racially charged riot. In these and other similar cases, the government charges the accused with violating the civil rights of their victims, thereby bringing the case within the jurisdiction of the federal courts.

Incorrect answers

(A) The constitutional prohibition of double jeopardy prevents state prosecutors from appealing a case in which the defendant is found not guilty.

(B) The double jeopardy clause would seem to prevent such double prosecutions but does not for the reasons given in the explanation for answer choice (E).

(C) New evidence alone cannot provide grounds for a new trial unless it can be proven that the accused in some way participated in hiding the evidence. If this were not the case, the government could theoretically withhold evidence from a trial. If the government did not get the "guilty" verdict it desired, it could then introduce the new evidence and try the defendant again.

(D) Governors may pardon convicts, but they may not veto "not guilty" verdicts.

55. **A** Both houses of Congress have standing committees that handle government oversight. Other committees provide oversight in the course of their business as they review the actions of regulatory agencies and other executive departments whose work coincides with the committee's area of concern. Oversight by the full body of either house would simply be too time-consuming, which is why oversight is performed in committee.

Incorrect answers

(B) Congress oversees the workings of the federal government, particularly the executive branch. The states have not challenged this power of oversight.

(C) Congressional oversight focuses primarily on the executive branch.

(D) Constituent input influences nearly everything that Congress does, including performing its oversight duties.

(E) Congressional oversight focuses primarily on the executive branch. Both houses maintain committees on ethics to regulate and discipline errant legislators.

56. **D** The fundamentalist vote is largely Republican, in large part because of Ronald Reagan and George W. Bush's efforts to win these voters with his conservative social agenda.

Incorrect answers

(A) The Democratic commitment to poverty relief programs attracts minority voters, many of whom are disproportionately represented in lower-income groups.

(B) Women support Democratic candidates more frequently than do men. The Democratic Party's commitment to gender issues such as equal pay and maternity leave has helped the party in this area.

(C) The Democratic commitment to poverty relief programs, along with Republican antagonism toward such programs, persuades many poor Americans to vote Democratic.

(E) The conservative social agenda of the Republican Party, combined with the Democratic commitment to government-enforced equal rights, persuades many homosexuals to vote Democratic.

57. **A** Iron triangles—also called *subgovernments*—result from the workings of particular federal agencies, congressional committees that provide oversight for those agencies, and related public interest groups. Members of these groups forge relationships through constant interaction and form a strong bond because they are often pursuing the same goals. Consider the example cited by the question. Advocacy groups for small businesses pursue legislation beneficial to their constituents. The Small Business Administration champions these goals, both for the benefit of small businesses and because new small business initiatives strengthen the agency (by providing it with new tasks to perform). Congressional committees dealing with small business issues support the goals as a means of serving an important constituency: those who own or work at small businesses. This type of alliance can grow extremely powerful, dominating a particular area of policy.

Incorrect answers

(B) A *conference committee* is a committee composed of members of the House and Senate. Conference committees meet when the House and Senate have passed differing versions of the same bill. Their goal is to work out a compromise bill that both houses can pass.

(C) A *regulatory agency* regulates a particular area of policy. The Environmental Protection Agency, the Nuclear Regulatory Commission, and the Federal Communications Commission are some examples of regulatory agencies. Regulatory agencies are part of the executive branch of government.

(D) The term *dual federalism* refers to a federal system in which the national and local governments have separate and distinct responsibilities.

(E) A third party is a political party other than the Democratic or Republican parties.

58. **B** To protect federal judges from political influence, the framers of the Constitution gave judges tenure for life. Judges serve "during good behavior" and can be removed from office only by impeachment.

59. **D** Guidelines issued by the Rules Committee strictly limit debate in the House; in most cases, representatives may speak on a bill for no more than five minutes. A *filibuster* is a speech of indefinite length, given by a senator in an effort to derail a particular Senate action, or to force a concession on that action. A three-fifths majority vote is required to end debate (such a vote is called a vote of *cloture*). A cloture vote is one of only two means to end a filibuster. The other is a unanimous consent agreement.

Incorrect answers

(A) The Senate prides itself on having greater civility than the House, but this decorousness does not extend to suffering interminable speeches without protest.

(B) House sessions are roughly the same length as Senate sessions.

(C) Sessions of both chambers are open to the public.

(E) All members of the House, not just the Speaker, may speak on the floor of the chamber.

60. **C** The Constitution requires that a census be taken every 10 years for the express purpose of apportioning seats in the House of Representatives. See Article I, Section 2, paragraph 3 of the Constitution.

Incorrect answers

(A) State legislatures are responsible for redrawing congressional districts.

(B) Redistricting has huge political ramifications. Seats in Congress are won and lost depending on where the lines are drawn, and whichever party is in power attempts to redraw the districts to its political advantage. This occasionally results in oddly shaped districts whose constituents have little in common other than their political party.

(D) The Supreme Court has interpreted the Voting Rights Act to mean that states must consider racial demographics when redrawing districts, to remedy previous practices used to artificially reduce minority representation in the House. The result of this ruling has been to dramatically increase minority representation in the House.

(E) Legislators' chief concern in redistricting is political outcomes, not allowing neighbors to be in the same district. Opposite sides of a street may fall into different districts.

ESSAY SECTION: ANSWERS EXPLAINED

QUESTION 1

You receive full credit for this essay if you correctly identify two of the four congressional actions mentioned in the question and accurately assess the effectiveness of each of those legislative actions.

The Equal Pay Act of 1963

The Equal Pay Act outlaws wage discrimination based on gender. The law also outlaws wage discrimination based on skin color, religion, or nationality (you need not mention the latter fact in your essay to receive full credit, but it is useful information).

Here are several assessments of the effectiveness of the Equal Pay Act of 1963. Your essay only needs to include one accurate assessment to receive full credit.

- The law increased awareness of the problem of unequal pay for equal work. It persuaded some employers to end wage discrimination in their businesses.

- The law was initially difficult to enforce. It requires women to file a complaint against their employer, an action many workers hesitate to take for fear of reprisal (firing, workplace harassment, and so on).

- Because the law did not prohibit employment discrimination, it allowed employers to favor men in hiring for prestigious, higher-paying jobs. Thus, the law did little to remedy the fundamental problem of workplace discrimination. Even after the Equal Pay Act became law, women remained "ghettoized" in low-paying clerical, teaching, and nursing jobs.

- As the government passed more civil liberties laws and as the public grew more aware and supportive of gender rights issues, the Equal Pay Act became a useful tool for those fighting for women's rights.

- Women and men still do not earn the same money for the same work; therefore, the effectiveness of the Equal Pay Act has been limited at best.

The Civil Rights Act of 1964

The Civil Rights Act prohibits employment discrimination based on gender. The difference between the Equal Pay Act and the Civil Rights Act is that the Equal Pay Act did not prevent employers from awarding better jobs to men based on gender. Instead, it merely required them to pay the same wages to men and women performing the same jobs. The Civil Rights Act corrected this problem. The law also outlaws employment discrimination based on skin color, religion, or nationality (again, you need not mention this in your essay to receive credit, but it is good to know). The following are several assessments of the Civil Rights Act.

- The law increased awareness of the problem of gender discrimination in hiring. It persuaded some employers to end gender discrimination in their businesses.

- The law did not immediately end gender discrimination. Enforcement required legal action, which in turn required women to complain when they believed they had been victims of gender discrimination. Because of the time, effort, expense, and risk involved in lodging such a complaint, many women were unwilling to do so.

- Although the Civil Rights Act changed the law, it did not change the deeply in-grained attitudes of employers, judges, government officials, and so on. This proved another obstacle to enforcement. At least in its early years, enforcement of the gender discrimination provisions of the Civil Rights Act of 1964 met with considerable institutional resistance.

- Eventually, as societal attitudes toward gender issues changed, the Civil Rights Act of 1964 became a powerful tool in forcing businesses to change their hiring practices. The law, in combination with the Equal Pay Act, proved a powerful tool for those willing to sue businesses over discrimination.

- The United States has not achieved gender equality in the workplace; therefore, the Civil Rights Act of 1964 has not been entirely effective.

Title IX of the Higher Education Act of 1972

Title IX prohibits gender discrimination at colleges and universities which receive federal aid. Here are some assessments of Title IX.

- Title IX employed the federal government's most powerful enforcement tool: the cessation of federal aid. Because noncompliant schools risk losing essential funding, Title IX has been easier to enforce than either the Equal Pay Act or the Civil Rights Act. The threat of lost funding is a powerful one.

- Title IX ended public funding for all-male schools, increased financial aid to female students, and encouraged the development of women's studies and other gender-related academic disciplines. It has had a tremendous impact on college athletics. On some campuses it has dramatically increased funding to women's sports programs. On others, it has resulted in a reduction of men's programs (to erase the difference between spending on men's and women's programs).

- Congress strengthened Title IX in 1988 by passing a law stating that all programs at a school are subject to Title IX even if only one or two programs at the school receive federal funding. This action, taken in response to a Supreme Court ruling, increased the effectiveness of Title IX in eliminating gender bias on publicly funded campuses.

The Equal Rights Amendment to the Constitution

The ERA would have inserted into the Constitution a prohibition against all gender discrimination. Although it received the necessary support in Congress, it did not receive the required approval from three-fourths of the states. Here are some assessments of the ERA.

- The Equal Rights Amendment generated a tremendous amount of public interest in the gender rights issue. By placing the issue at the forefront of the public agenda, the ERA made it easier for women's rights activists to publicize their message.

- The Equal Rights Amendment also generated considerable opposition to the women's rights movement. This may have reinforced gender bias in some quarters.

- The Equal Rights Amendment failed to gain the necessary support of three-quarters of the states. In this regard, the ERA was a failure.

- The struggle for the ERA (and the public outcry in the aftermath of its failure) resulted in the passage of numerous state-level anti gender-bias laws. Sixteen states now have equal rights amendments in their constitutions. Considered in this light, the ERA was effective in advancing the cause of gender equality.

Here's How to Crack It

1. Since the 1960s, Congress has addressed the problem of gender bias on numerous occasions.

    (a) Select one of the following laws and describe how it has attempted to address the problem of gender bias in American society.
    - the Equal Pay Act of 1963
    - the Civil Rights Act of 1964

    (b) Assess the effectiveness of that law.

    (c) Select one of the following legislative actions and describe how it has attempted to address the problem of gender bias in American society.
    - Title IX of the Higher Education Act of 1973
    - the Equal Rights Amendment to the Constitution

    (d) Assess the effectiveness of that action.

Describe two of the four congressional actions accurately, then state one reason why they were or were not effective in addressing the problem of gender bias.

SAMPLE "EXCELLENT" ESSAY

While most of the major civil rights advancements of the 20th century were spearheaded by the Supreme Court, Congress also played a prominent role. More specifically, it has addressed the issue of gender rights on many occasions. Among the most prominent examples of its efforts are the Equal Pay Act of 1963 and Title IX of the Higher Education Act.

The Equal Pay Act of 1963 outlaws wage discrimination based on sex. Before the Equal Pay Act, it was legal to pay women and men different amounts for doing the same jobs. The feminist movement in the United States did not become very strong until the 1970s, but there was still support in Congress for the act—even if most justified its passage due to economic considerations. Interestingly enough, one of the major reasons for the bill's passage was to prevent employers from using women as a source of cheap labor that would depress the prevailing wage.

How effective was the Equal Pay Act? At first, it was not very good at preventing the payment disparities it was designed to eliminate. It was difficult to enforce and forced injured parties to engage in time-consuming litigation against their employers. It also failed to get at the deeper problem of sex discrimination, because employers were still allowed to discriminate when it came to hiring. So rather than pay a man more than a woman for doing the same job, the employer could just promote the man and then pay him the appropriate (male) wage for the new job. Still, as the women's movement became more powerful with passage of the Civil Rights Act of 1964, the Equal Pay Act became increasingly effective.

Title IX of the Higher Education Act is one of the most controversial laws passed in recent time. The law itself called for an end to sex discrimination in schools and threatened to cut off federal funding to any school, college or university that engaged in discriminatory practices. Because many schools, public and private, are very reliant on federal funds, they complied quite readily.

The question of effectiveness needs to be broadened to the issue of athletics. In 1979, the Department of Health defined Title IX as requiring schools to spend equal amounts of money on male and female athletics. Because far fewer women have joined sports teams, this has forced many schools to kill male sports that are less popular (like wrestling or track) in order to keep the proportion of spending the same. Critics claim that this quota system is devastating male sports for no good reason, while defenders say that Title IX has led to increased spending that resulted in a generation of empowered athletic American women.

QUESTION 2

You receive full credit if you identify three factors that have decreased the reliance of presidential candidates on their political parties and explain how they have done so. Identifying more than three factors will not earn you extra credit. If you identify three factors that have decreased the reliance of presidential candidates on their political parties but do not explain how they have done so, you will receive half credit.

Factors and Explanations

- Voters no longer identify with political parties as strongly as they once did. America has more voters that consider themselves Independents than at any other point in her history. Those who identify with one of the major parties are more likely than ever before to vote a split ticket. All of this has weakened the parties' hold on the electorate. Consequently, the "prestige by association" that presidential candidates once gained from their parties has been greatly diminished, and they have thus begun to campaign more independently than ever before.

- Campaign finance legislation limits the amount of money parties can contribute to their candidates. Accordingly, candidates have been forced to look elsewhere for the financial support their parties once provided. This has shifted candidate allegiance from the parties to the PACs, interest groups, and individuals whose donations sustain their increasingly expensive campaigns.

- In various regions and among various voting blocs, dislike for one party or the other has handicapped some presidential candidates. Candidates have learned that by maintaining the ability to distance themselves from their parties, they can overcome a region's or bloc's dislike of their party. In both 1992 and 1996, for example, Bill Clinton successfully disassociated himself from the traditional Democratic image to gain support from some southern conservatives. In 1980 and 1984, Ronald Reagan was able to create enough distance between the public image of himself and his party to draw a majority of working-class votes.

- Once, candidates needed their parties to publicize their names and messages. Now they can use television and the internet to bypass their parties. Television exposure has supplanted party rallies, leaflets, and door-to-door canvassing as the preferred method of gaining visibility.

- Recent developments in polling and market research have made it much easier for individual candidates to track public opinion and respond accordingly. Where candidates once relied on their parties to give them the "lay of the land" in various regions, today they rely on pollsters (who work exclusively for their campaigns) to provide such information.

Here's How to Crack It

2. Traditionally, presidential candidates have relied on strong support from their national party organization.

   (a) Describe how national party organizations have historically aided their candidates.

   (b) Describe how this dynamic has changed in recent presidential elections.

   (c) Discuss THREE factors that have helped bring about this change.

Brainstorm before you write. Make a list of all possible factors you may discuss in part (c). Consider the list carefully. Which factors most clearly contributed to the weakening of parties' hold on their presidential candidates? Which ones can you explain quickly and clearly? Choose the three best factors for you.

Do not write about four, five, or six factors. Graders can only give you credit for three, no matter how many more you come up with.

Sample "Excellent" Essay

Once, there was a time when candidates were selected behind closed doors by party bosses in smoke-filled rooms. Up until the mid-20th century, parties dictated positions to candidates, and candidates relied on the organizational efforts of their parties to achieve elected office. Recently, however, the dynamic has shifted. Whereas candidates once ran as representatives of their parties, in recent times candidates have run more and more independently, emphasizing their party ties when advantageous, and distancing themselves from their parties in other situations.

The new "candidate-centered" campaign has come about as a result of numerous factors. First and foremost is the prominent role television plays in modern political campaigns. In the past, candidates have depended on their national party organizations to rally the party faithful and acquaint themselves with voters. Television allows candidates to bypass the party organization and speak directly to the voting public en masse. Without television and other mass media, the age of candidate-centered campaigns could never have arisen.

Another factor is the recently accelerated primary schedule, which has forced candidates to develop powerful campaign machines early in the election cycle. The new schedule places a high premium on early electoral success, meaning that candidates must arrive in New Hampshire with much of their primary campaign machine intact. Long before they can expect any help from the national party, candidates must raise large amounts of campaign money, publicize their messages, and begin all-important polling and voter tracking. The development of such independent full-service campaign organizations has altered the political landscape, leading candidates to rely more on their campaign organizations and less on their parties.

Changes in American voting patterns have helped to accelerate this process. Voters no longer identify with political parties as strongly as they once did. Many more now consider themselves independents. Others who identify with one of the major parties are more likely than ever before to vote a split ticket. All of this has weakened the parties' hold on the electorate. Consequently, presidential candidates have less to gain from the parties and so campaign more independently than they once could.

Question 3

You receive full credit if you clearly state your position on the subject, identify three examples, and explain how each of the three examples supports your position. Note that whereas there are basically only two positions to take—agreeing or disagreeing—there are literally hundreds of possible examples you could provide to support either argument. Here are the two positions, support for both, and examples that support the positions. You could, of course, provide different support and examples while still receiving full credit.

Positions and Examples

Agree: The media focus on stories that can be told easily and quickly while ignoring or downplaying stories that are complicated or ambiguous.

How you may argue this position:

- Most Americans receive their news from television. The average news story on television runs between one and three minutes. Nearly one-quarter of the news stories on network news are less than one minute in length. This is rarely enough time to cover a complicated or nuanced story.

- News reporting on television plays to the medium's strength: the ability to present dramatic pictures. Television news stories are often immediate and dramatic, but they rarely present historical background or in-depth analysis of the issues surrounding a story. Consequently, coverage is superficial. Complexity and ambiguity are ignored, in favor of easily-digestible video and sound bites.

- Most modern newspapers follow the lead of *USA Today* in providing summary coverage of national and international news. They also devote more space to features, sports, and celebrity news, all of which fall under the category of stories that can be told quickly and easily. Only a few U.S. newspapers consistently provide in-depth news coverage and analysis.

Examples you may use to support this argument:

- The 2000 presidential campaign: The media spent a great deal of time covering inconsequential aspects of the race (Al Gore kissing his wife at the Democratic National Convention, George W. Bush's religious devotion, and chad counting) and as a result did not show the dramatic ideological divide between the two men.

- Afghanistan: The media did very little to cover the October, 2001, United States invasion of Afghanistan. News outlets focused almost exclusively on the hunt for Osama bin Laden and neglected to report on the potential long-term results of this military action (especially once the invasion of Iraq began).

- O. J. Simpson trial: The sheer magnitude of coverage the trial received was well beyond its significance to society. Simpson trial coverage demonstrated that the media prefer sensationalistic, personality-driven stories to complex, "hard news" stories.

- Presidential impeachment: The news media focused on the lurid details of Clinton's affair with Monica Lewinsky. Still, most Americans were unclear about the mechanics of the impeachment process even after seeing numerous stories about impeachment. Again, the media focused on the sensational, easily understandable aspects of the story but failed to inform Americans on the more complicated aspects.

Disagree: The media do not focus on stories that can be easily and quickly told while ignoring or downplaying stories that are complicated or ambiguous.

How you may argue this position:

- While it is true that some media focus on easy stories and avoid complex stories, it is not universally true of the media. PBS, all-news cable stations, National Public Radio, *The New York Times*, *The Wall Street Journal*, *The Washington Post*, and literally dozens of magazines and journals often provide complex, in-depth coverage of the news. Media serve their audiences, so it is a mistake to blame mainstream media for the apparent lack of depth and breadth of its coverage. They cover stories in this manner because this is what the mass media audience wants. Those who want more complexity in their news coverage have ample access to such sources.

Examples you may use to support this argument:

- Yugoslavia: The tragic ethnic battles in the former Yugoslavia have torn the region apart for nearly a decade. Despite the complexity of the story and the remoteness of it to the daily lives of most Americans, the press has covered this story since the outset. Although one may argue that the coverage was not prominent enough—given the severity of the situation—it is also important to note that the fully-detailed story was available to anyone with an interest in pursuing it. In these and many other foreign news matters, the media does its job of providing the news, even though only a small number of Americans demonstrate interest in these stories.

- Y2K crisis: Again, the media reported extensively on a story that was difficult for many Americans to understand. Coverage of the Y2K issue disproves the often-made accusation that the media drop complicated stories, especially those that cannot be easily adapted to television reporting.

- In 1997, three reporters for *The Seattle Times* won the Pulitzer Prize for their investigation into abuses in a federally sponsored housing program for Native Americans. This is just one of many examples of investigative pieces that are neither easily told nor digested. Yet this story, and dozens of other investigative reports like it every year, result in a better-informed public and call for much-needed societal reform.

- Finally, you may cite any or all of the examples provided for the opposite point of view. You could conceivably argue that media coverage of any or all of those stories (e.g., the 2000 presidential campaign or the invasion of Afghanistan) was both thorough and appropriate. The fact that Americans were uninformed on the central issues of those stories, you may conclude, pertains to the salience of those issues to their lives. Because Americans did not feel the need to remain fully informed on these stories, they ignored or forgot detailed reporting on the issues.

Here's How to Crack It

3. The media has a large influence on American politics.
   (a) Describe why the media are so important and why they have such influence.
   (b) Identify and describe THREE examples of media coverage that have influenced American politics in the past twenty years.
   (c) Evaluate the argument that in politics, the media tend to overemphasize stories that are easy to tell at the expense of those that are more complicated.

Choose your position. Brainstorm a list of examples that support your position. Choose three that you would like to write about. Make sure to clearly identify your examples. Remember that the question specifies that your examples must be drawn from the previous two decades. Do not provide examples that are more than ten years old. Do not write about more than three examples. Graders can only give you credit for three, no matter how many more you come up with.

Write an introductory paragraph explaining your position. Follow with one paragraph for each of your three examples. Write a conclusion if you have time.

SAMPLE "EXCELLENT" ESSAY

A common criticism of the news media is that it focuses on stories that do not demand thought or attention from the audience. Stories that can be easily told—those with a clear beginning, middle, and end, or those with just enough drama to "hook" an audience—are favored over more substantial stories that, because of their complexity, may lack a clear resolution or require background information. This bias is particularly evident in television news, where stories must be short and must have "good visuals." Sadly, however, the trend has even found its way into print media. Newspaper articles are shorter, and the number of stories that newspapers cover is smaller than ever before.

Several recent examples confirm the validity of this criticism. The biggest—or at least, most widely covered—story of the past decade was not a war, the fall of a government, or a natural disaster. It was the murder of a celebrity's wife and her friend. Because the celebrity—former football star O. J. Simpson—was the chief suspect in the case, the trial that followed received enormous publicity. The amount of coverage this story received—many news shows led with O. J. stories nightly, and the story dominated the front pages of newspapers for months—was grossly disproportionate to its importance. While the Simpson story was not an "important story," it was a "good story," in that it had interesting characters, a clear narrative thread, and a "whodunit" aspect. Unsurprisingly, the media favored this easy-to-tell story over more complex ones.

Even when the media cover important issues, they often overlook the complexity of those issues. Consider the coverage of presidential elections. The media focus on those aspects that can be told and digested quickly, such as the "horse race" aspects of campaigns and polling. They play candidate "sound bites" but do not excerpt long passages from candidates' speeches. They focus on the "inside politics" of each candidate's campaign organizations. What they do not do is report in-depth on the candidates' positions. Consequently, in 1992 , most every American knew who was ahead in the polls. They knew the name of Bill Clinton's alleged mistress, and where she bought her dresses. However, they did not know the candidates' positions on the federal budget or international affairs.

Media coverage of "hard news" is especially lacking when the news occurs overseas. Such stories invariably require the audience to have some understanding of the cultures and histories of the foreign nation that is the subject of the report. The media ignore these stories as much as possible, both because the media believe that American audiences do not care about these stories and because the stories are difficult to report quickly. Only when a story is accompanied by compelling visual images does it have a chance to crack the media blockade. Thus, millions of Americans watched when the corpse of an American soldier was dragged through the streets of Somalia, but very few knew why the United States was in Somalia in the first place, or why there may be animosity toward the American soldiers stationed there.

American news reporting is not entirely bad. The First Amendment allows a diversity of news sources to flourish, and some do an excellent job of covering the news. However, the mainstream media—those that provide news to the vast majority of Americans—consider the importance of a story as only one of many factors in deciding whether to report it. How quickly and interestingly the story can be told, it seems, is more important to those who decide what constitutes "news."

QUESTION 4

You receive full credit if you correctly identify Andrew Johnson and Bill Clinton, state clearly whether Hamilton's quotation applies to each case, and correctly describe and analyze the various roles of the House, Senate, and Supreme Court as effective checks in the impeachment process.

Identification

Clearly identify Andrew Johnson and Bill Clinton as the two impeached presidents in question. Even though the question does not specifically ask you to do so, you will not receive full credit if you fail to cite them both by name.

In Each Case, Is Hamilton's Quotation Accurate?

- Congress impeached Andrew Johnson for violation of the Tenure of Office Act, a law that forbade Johnson to fire certain federal appointees to the executive branch. Johnson fired Secretary of War Stanton, a radical Republican who opposed Johnson's plans for Reconstruction. Hamilton's assessment of the impeachment process accurately describes Johnson's situation. Johnson's impeachment certainly "agitated the passions of the whole community" and "divided it into parties more or less friendly or inimical to the accused." These "pre-existing factions," divided over the nature of Reconstruction, were similarly divided over Johnson's impeachment. Republicans, who held the majority in Congress, lined up against Johnson. Democrats, arguing that the Tenure of Office Act violated the system of checks and balances (by giving Congress undue power over the executive branch) lined up behind Johnson. The outcome was regulated by "the comparative strength of the parties," as the vast Republican majority in the post–Civil War Congress assured Johnson's impeachment and very nearly his conviction by the Senate. Seven senators crossed party lines to vote for Johnson's acquittal, allowing Johnson to escape removal from office by a single vote. The Supreme Court later found the Tenure of Office Act unconstitutional, a fact that further underscores the political nature of Johnson's impeachment.

- Congress impeached Bill Clinton for crimes arising from the cover-up of an extra-marital affair. Clinton was accused of having lied about the affair in a deposition in a civil suit and then again before a federal grand jury. He was also accused of encouraging others to lie, thereby obstructing justice, and of using the powers of his office to impede investigations into his wrongdoings. Do Hamilton's statements apply to Clinton's impeachment? Regardless of your personal feelings about Clinton's culpability, you should be ready to acknowledge the accuracy of Hamilton's warnings as they apply to the Clinton impeachment. The congressional vote for Clinton's impeachment fell almost exclusively along party lines, fulfilling Hamilton's warning of "pre-existing factions... [enlisting] all their animosities, partialities, influence, and interest in on one side or the other." You may also point out that Congress rushed its impeachment vote to maintain the Republican party-line advantage. Midterm elections had reduced the Republican majority in the upcoming session, and Republican leaders feared that defections in the next Congress could deny them a majority for impeachment. You may also make the argument that the charges against Clinton, while embarrassing, did not rise to the level of "high crimes and misdemeanors" and were only so defined because of "the comparative strength of parties."

The Effectiveness of the System of Checks and Balances

Simply put, Hamilton's primary concern was that factions, or parties, would taint the impeachment process by infusing it with partisan agenda. The Constitution addresses the problem of factions through the system of checks and balances, which divides power to make it difficult for a faction to gain control of the government.

The Constitution allows for impeachment as a check on the power of the president. But it also places a series of checks in the impeachment process as a protection against hasty or imprudent congressional action. Chief among these checks is the division of trial responsibilities between the two houses of Congress. The House of Representatives is empowered to bring impeachment charges (not only against the president, but also against the vice president and other civilian government officials, including federal judges). Impeachment by the House requires only a majority vote. Impeachment trials occur in the Senate, where a two-thirds majority vote is required for conviction. Thus the system works to make impeachment possible (requiring merely a simple majority vote) but conviction difficult. It also places the ultimate responsibility for determining the fate of the accused in the hands of the Senate, which the framers regarded as the more cautious and deliberative of the legislative bodies. The chief justice of the Supreme Court presides over impeachment trials. This stipulation serves several purposes. First, it prevents an obvious conflict of interest; if not for this provision, the vice president would preside over the trial as president of the Senate. Additionally, it involves a second branch of government—the judicial branch—in this important process. As a representative of a separate, ostensibly less political branch of government, the chief justice provides a check on Senate power and injects an element of impartiality into a very partisan process.

The system of checks and balances works to prevent the excesses of political factions in the impeachment process. History provides the evidence: Congress has impeached only two presidents, neither of whom was removed from office. In one other instance—that of Richard Nixon—the House would surely have impeached and the Senate may well have convicted the president, had Nixon not resigned first. The charges against Nixon, however, more clearly fit the definition of "high crimes and misdemeanors" than did the charges in either of the two presidential impeachments to reach the Senate.

Here's How to Crack It

"The prosecution of [impeachments] will seldom fail to agitate the passions of the whole community, and to divide it into parties more or less friendly or inimical to the accused. In many cases it will connect itself with pre-existing factions, and will enlist all their animosities, partialities, influence, and interest on one side or the other, and in such cases there will always be the greatest danger that the decision will be regulated more by the comparative strength of parties, than by the real demonstrations of innocence or guilt."

—Alexander Hamilton, *Federalist 65*

4. The House of Representatives has twice impeached sitting presidents, both of whom avoided removal from office by the Senate.

    (a) Define impeachment and removal, and describe the process of impeachment and removal as listed in the Constitution.

    (b) Assess the accuracy of Hamilton's observations as applied to both cases of presidential impeachment.

    (c) Identify the strengths and weaknesses of checks and balances in dealing with Hamilton's concerns.

Correctly identify the two presidents who have been impeached. Do not write about Richard Nixon, as he resigned before the House could impeach him. Recall the basic details of both impeachment trials, being careful to apply Hamilton's quotation to your recollection. Was Hamilton correct or not? Your narratives must address this question. Then discuss the roles of the House of Representatives, Senate, and Supreme Court in the impeachment process. Answer the question: Do they provide sufficient checks and balances against the abuse of power?

SAMPLE "EXCELLENT" ESSAY

In *Federalist 65*, Alexander Hamilton warned that presidential impeachments could be politically motivated. Pointing out that impeachments "will seldom fail to agitate the passions of the whole community," Hamilton observed that pre-existing factions, such as political parties, could use impeachment to advance their political goals, regardless of the validity of their charges. Hamilton's words proved prophetic, accurately foretelling the impeachments of Andrew Johnson and Bill Clinton.

Andrew Johnson was impeached for violating the Tenure of Office Act, which forbade the president to fire certain federal appointees, among them the secretary of war. Johnson ignored the law and fired the secretary of war, who was a holdover from the Lincoln Administration and a political enemy of the president. As Hamilton predicted, Johnson's impeachment "agitated the passions of the whole community" and "divided it into parties more or less friendly or inimical to the accused." Republicans, especially the radical faction of the party, lined up against Johnson, while Democrats supported him. Again, as Hamilton predicted, the outcome of the impeachment was regulated by "the comparative strength of the parties." The vast Republican majority in the post–Civil War Congress assured Johnson's impeachment and very nearly brought about his conviction by the Senate. Johnson won acquittal by a single vote.

Bill Clinton was impeached for crimes arising from the cover-up of an extramarital affair. As did Johnson, Clinton faced accusation by a Congress controlled by his political opposition. The House vote on Clinton's impeachment fell almost entirely along party lines, showing how the process could be influenced by "pre-existing factions...[enlisting] all their animosities, partialities, influence, and interest on one side or the other." Did President Clinton's actions rise to the level of "high crimes and misdemeanors"? Almost every House Republican voted "yes," and almost every House Democrat voted "no." This mirrors Hamilton's observation that such matters could be decided by "the comparative strength of parties [rather] than by real demonstrations of innocence or guilt."

Fortunately, the framers of the Constitution installed a system of checks and balances to make politically-motivated impeachment extremely difficult. In impeachment, the most important check is the division of trial responsibilities between the two houses of Congress. The House of Representatives brings impeachment charges through a majority vote. Impeachment trials occur in the Senate, where a two-thirds majority vote is required for conviction. This system makes impeachment feasible but removal difficult. The framers intentionally gave the Senate the power to remove the president from office, regarding that legislative body as the more cautious of the two. Another check on the system requires the chief justice of the Supreme Court to preside over impeachment trials. The chief justice lends an air of impartiality to the proceedings. As a non-elected official, the chief justice is uniquely situated to defend the Constitution. Unlike House and Senate members, the chief justice can do his job unaffected by the latest poll results.

Glossary

adversary system   A system of law where the court is seen as a neutral area where disputants can argue the merits of their cases.

affirmative action   Government-mandated programs that seek to create special employment opportunities for African Americans, women, and other victims of past discrimination.

amendment   Addition to the Constitution. Amendments require approval by two-thirds of both houses of Congress and three-quarters of the states. The first ten amendments make up the Bill of Rights.

amicus curiae **briefs**   "Friend of the court" briefs that qualified individuals or organizations file in lawsuits to which they are not a party, so the judge may consider their advice in respect to matters of law that directly affect the cases in question.

appellate jurisdiction   Term used to describe courts whose role is to hear appeals from lower courts.

Articles of Confederation   The United States' first constitution. The government formed by the Articles of Confederation lasted from 1781 (the year before the end of the Revolutionary War) to 1789. The government under the Articles proved inadequate because it did not have the power to collect taxes from the states, nor could it regulate foreign trade to generate revenue from import and export tariffs.

bicameral   Consisting of two legislative houses. The United States has a bicameral legislature; its two houses are the House of Representatives and the Senate.

Bill of Rights   First ten amendments to the U.S. Constitution. The Bill of Rights guarantees personal liberties and limits the powers of the government.

blanket primary   Primary election in which voters may select a candidate from any party for each office. Blanket primaries use the same procedure as general elections.

block grants   Federal money given to states with only general guidelines for its use. The states have the authority to decide how the money will be spent.

bread-and-butter issues   Those political issues are specifically directed at the daily concerns of most working-class Americans, such as job security, tax rates, wages, and employee benefits.

broad constructionism   Belief that the Constitution should be interpreted loosely when concerning the restrictions it places on federal power. Broad constructionists emphasize the importance of the elastic clause, which allows Congress to pass laws "necessary and proper" to the performance of its duties.

Brown v. Board of Education   The 1954 case in which the Supreme Court overturned the "separate but equal" standard as it applied to education. In a 9-to-0 decision, the court ruled that "separate educational facilities are inherently unequal." "Separate but equal" had been the law of the land since the Court had approved it in *Plessy v. Ferguson* (1896).

budget deficit   Condition that arises when federal expenditures exceed revenues; in other words, when the government spends more money than it takes in.

budget resolution   Set of budget guidelines that must pass both houses of Congress in identical form by April 15. The budget resolution guides government spending for the following fiscal year.

categorical grants   Federal aid given to states with strings attached. To receive the money, the states must agree to adhere to federally mandated guidelines for spending it.

caucus   Meeting of local party members for the purpose of choosing delegates to a national party convention. The term also refers to a meeting of the Democratic members of the House of Representatives.

census   The process, mandated by the Constitution, by which the population of the United States is officially counted every 10 years. Census data is then used to help distribute federal money and to **reapportion** congressional districts.

checks and balances   The system that prevents any branch of government from becoming too powerful by requiring the approval of more than one branch for all important acts.

civil court   Court in which lawsuits are heard. In contrast, criminal cases are heard in **criminal court**.

civil disobedience   Nonviolent civil disobedience requires activists to protest peacefully against laws they believe unjust and to be willing to accept arrest as a means of demonstrating the justice of their cause. The notion was popularized by nineteenth-century American writer Henry David Thoreau and was practiced by Martin Luther King Jr.

civil liberties   Those protections against government power embodied in the Bill of Rights and similar legislation. Civil liberties include the right to free speech, free exercise of religion, and right to a fair trial.

civil rights   Those protections against discrimination by the government and individuals. Civil rights are intended to prevent discrimination based on race, religion, gender, ethnicity, physical handicap, or sexual orientation.

Civil Rights Act of 1964   Federal law that made segregation illegal in most public places, increased penalties and sentences for those convicted of discrimination in employment, and withheld federal aid from schools that discriminated on the basis of race or gender.

civil service system   Method of hiring federal employees based on merit rather than on political beliefs or allegiances. This system replaced the **spoils system** in the United States.

class action suit   A lawsuit filed on behalf of a group of people, and whose result affects that group of people as a whole. Interest groups such as the NAACP often use these as a means of asserting their influence over policy decisions.

clear and present danger test   Interpretation by Justice Oliver Wendell Holmes regarding limits on free speech if it presents clear and present danger to the public or leads to illegal actions; for example, one cannot shout "Fire!" in a crowded theater.

closed primary   Primary election in which voting is restricted to registered members of a political party.

cloture   A motion in the Senate to end debate, often used in the event of a filibuster. A cloture vote requires a three-fifths majority of the Senate.

coalition   A combination of groups of people who work together to achieve a political goal. The coalition on which the Democratic Party rests, for example, is made up of Northern urban dwellers, Jews, African Americans, and labor unions. Coalitions also form among legislators who work together to advance or defeat a particular bill.

commander-in-chief   The president's role as leader of all United States military forces. This is one of the executive powers authorized in the Constitution.

concurrent powers   Constitutional powers shared by the federal and state governments.

conference committee   Congressional committee that includes representatives of both houses of Congress. Their purpose is to settle differences between the House and Senate versions of bills that have been passed by their respective legislatures.

Congressional Budget Office   Congressional agency of budget experts who assess the feasibility of the president's plan and who help create Congress's version of the federal budget.

congressional district   The geographically defined group of people on whose behalf a representative acts in the House of Representatives. Each state is divided into congressional districts of equal population, with larger states having more districts and representatives than small states. Congressional districts are reapportioned every ten years according to new census data.

conservative   A political ideology that tends to favor defense spending and school prayer and to disapprove of social programs, abortion, affirmative action, and a large, active government. Conservatives are generally affiliated with the Republican party.

constitutional convention   An as-of-yet untried method by which the Constitution may be amended. To call a constitutional convention, two-thirds of all state legislatures must petition the federal government; not to be confused with the Constitutional Convention when the Constitution was written.

cooperative federalism   Preeminent form of U.S. federalism since the passage of the Fourteenth Amendment. The Fourteenth Amendment initiated the long demise of **dual federalism** by providing the national government the means to enforce the rights of citizens against state infringement. The Progressive Era, the New Deal, and the Great Society all increased federal involvement in state government. The result is a system called cooperative federalism in which the national and state governments share many powers.

criminal court   Court in which criminal trials are heard. In contrast, lawsuits are heard in **civil court**.

dealignment   A recent trend in which voters act increasingly independent of a party affiliation. This is partially the result of television because candidates can appeal directly to the electorate without relying on their party. One consequence is **split-ticket voting,** which leads to a **divided government** in which neither party controls both the executive and the legislative branch.

delegated powers   Constitutional powers granted solely to the federal government.

direct democracy   Form of government in which all enfranchised citizens vote on all matters of government. In contrast, in a representative democracy, voters choose representatives to vote for them on most government issues.

divided government   A government in which the presidency is controlled by one party and Congress is controlled by the other. This has become a common occurrence in recent decades as voters have begun to act more independent of parties and increasingly vote **split tickets.**

double jeopardy   The act of trying an individual a second time after he has been acquitted on the same charges. Double jeopardy is prohibited by the Constitution.

dual federalism   Form of U.S. federalism during the nation's early history. During this period, the federal and state governments remained separate and independent. What little contact most Americans had with government occurred on the state level, as the national government concerned itself primarily with international trade, construction of roads, harbors, and railways, and the distribution of public land in the West.

due process   Established legal procedures for the arrest and trial of an accused criminal.

elastic clause   The section of the Constitution that allows Congress to pass laws "necessary and proper" to the performance of its duties. It is called the elastic clause because it allows Congress to stretch its powers beyond those that are specifically granted to it (enumerated) by the Constitution.

electoral college   Constitutionally established body created for the sole purpose of choosing the president and vice president. During general elections, voters choose a presidential ticket. The winner in each state usually receives all of that state's electoral votes in the electoral college. A majority of electoral votes is required for victory in the electoral college; if such a majority cannot be reached, the election result is determined by the House of Representatives.

eminent domain   The power of the government to take away property for public use as long as there is just compensation for property taken.

entitlement programs   Social insurance programs that allocate federal funds to all people who meet the conditions of the program. Social Security is the largest and most expensive entitlement program. Because they are a form of **mandatory spending**, it is incredibly difficult to cut funds to entitlement programs during the budgetary process.

Equal Rights Amendment   Failed Constitutional amendment that would have guaranteed equal protection under the law for women (1970s).

establishment clause   Section of the Constitution that prohibits the government from designating one faith as the official religion of the United States.

exclusionary rule   Rule that prohibits the use of illegally obtained evidence at trial. The Supreme Court has created several exceptions to the exclusionary rule, notably the **objective good faith** rule and the **inevitable discovery** rule.

executive agreement   Presidential agreements made with foreign nations. Executive agreements have the same legal force as treaties but do not require the approval of the Senate.

executive privilege   The right of the president to withhold information when doing so would compromise national security (e.g., in the case of diplomatic files and military secrets). Executive privilege is not mentioned in the Constitution. It is, rather, part of the **unwritten Constitution**.

ex post facto **laws**   If allowed, these laws would punish people for actions that occurred before such actions were made criminal.

extradition   Process by which governments return fugitives to the jurisdiction from which they have fled.

Federal Reserve Board   Executive agency that is largely responsible for the formulation and implementation of monetary policy. By controlling the monetary supply, the Fed helps maintain a stable economy.

federalism   Term describing a system under which the national government and local governments (state governments, in the case of the United States) share powers. Other federal governments include Canada, Switzerland, and Australia.

Federalist Papers A series of essays written by James Madison, Alexander Hamilton, and John Jay to defend the Constitution and persuade Americans that it should be ratified. These documents presented the concerns and issues the framers faced as they created a blueprint for the new government.

Fifteenth Amendment (1870) Prohibited states from denying voting rights to African Americans. Southern states circumvented the Fifteenth Amendment through literacy tests and poll taxes.

filibuster A lengthy speech that halts all legislative action in the Senate. Filibusters are not possible in the House of Representatives because strict time limits govern all debates there.

First Amendment Protects the rights of individuals against the government by guaranteeing the freedom of speech, the press, religion, and assembly.

fiscal year Twelve-month period starting on October 1. Government budgets go into effect at the beginning of the fiscal year. Congress and the president agree on a **budget resolution** in April to guide government spending for the coming fiscal year.

Freedom of Information Act (1974) Act which declassified government documents for public use.

Fourteenth Amendment (1868) Prevented the states from denying "due process of law" and "equal protection under the law" to citizens. The amendment was specifically aimed at protecting the rights of newly freed slaves. In the twentieth century, the Supreme Court used the amendment to strike down state laws that violate the Bill of Rights.

front-loading Because early primaries have grown increasingly important in recent years, many states have pushed forward the date of their primary elections. Political analysts refer to this strategy as front-loading.

full faith and credit clause Section of the Constitution that requires states to honor one another's licenses, marriages, and other acts of state courts.

general election Election held on the first Tuesday of November, during which voters elect officials.

gerrymandering The practice of drawing congressional district lines to benefit one party over the other.

***Gideon v. Wainwright* (1963)** Supreme Court case in which the Court ruled that a defendant in a felony trial must be provided a lawyer free of charge if the defendant cannot afford one.

Gramm-Rudman-Holings Bill (1985) Set budget reduction targets to balance budget but failed to eliminate loopholes.

Great Compromise Settlement reached at the Constitutional convention between large states and small states. The Great Compromise called for two legislative houses: One in which states were represented by their populations (favoring the large states) and one in which states received equal representation (favoring the small states).

Great Society President Lyndon B. Johnson's social/economic program, aimed at raising the standard of living for America's poorest residents. Among the Great Society programs are Medicare, Medicaid, Project Head Start, Job Corps, and Volunteers in Service to America (VISTA).

***Griswold v. Connecticut* (1965)** Supreme Court decision in which the Court ruled that the Constitution implicitly guarantees citizens' right to privacy.

Hatch Act (1939) A congressional law that forbade government officials from participating in partisan politics and protected government employees from being fired on partisan grounds; it was revised in 1993 to be less restrictive.

House of Representatives Lower house of U.S. Congress, in which representation is allocated to states in direct proportion to their population. The House of Representatives has sole power to initiate appropriations legislation.

House Rules Committee Determines the rules for debate of each bill, including whether the bill may be amended. This is the most powerful committee in the House. The Senate, which is smaller, has no rules for debate.

impeachment Process by which a president, judge, or other government official can be tried for high crimes and misdemeanors. Andrew Johnson was impeached but was found not guilty and was not removed from office.

indictment A written statement of criminal charges brought against a defendant. Indictments guarantee that defendants know the charges against them so they can plan a defense.

inevitable discovery Exception to the exclusionary rule that allows the use of illegally obtained evidence at trial if the court determines that the evidence would eventually have been found by legal means.

initiative Process through which voters may propose new laws. One of several Progressive Era reforms that increased voters' power over government.

interest group Political group organized around a particular political goal or philosophy. Interest groups attempt to influence public policy through political action and donations to sympathetic candidates.

iron triangle Also called *subgovernment*. Iron triangles are formed by the close working relationship among various interest groups, congressional committees, and executive agencies that enforce federal regulations. Working together, these groups can collectively exert a powerful influence over legislation and law enforcement.

Jim Crow laws State and local laws passed in the post–Reconstruction Era South to enforce racial segregation and otherwise restrict the rights of African Americans.

joint committee Congressional committee composed of members of both houses of Congress, usually to investigate and research specific subjects.

judicial activism Term referring to the actions of a court that frequently strikes down or alters the acts of the executive and/or legislative branches.

judicial restraint Term referring to the actions of a court that demonstrates an unwillingness to break with precedent or to overturn legislative and executive acts.

judicial review The power of the Supreme Court to declare laws and executive actions unconstitutional.

killer amendment Amendment to a bill proposed by its opponents for the specific purpose of decreasing the bill's chance of passage.

Ku Klux Klan Nativist hate group founded during the Reconstruction Era. The Klan terrorized African Americans throughout the south, especially those who attempted to assert their civil rights. The Klan also preaches hatred of Catholics and Jews.

legislative oversight One of Congress's most important tasks. In order to check the power of the executive branch, congressional committees investigate and evaluate the performance of corresponding executive agencies and departments.

liberal   Descriptive of an ideology that tends to favor government spending on social programs, affirmative action, a woman's right to an abortion, and an active government, and to disfavor defense spending and school prayer. Liberals are generally affiliated with the Democratic Party.

limited government   Principle of government that states that government powers must be confined to those allowed it by the nation's Constitution.

line-item veto   Power held by some chief executives (e.g., governors) to excise some portions of a spending bill without rejecting the entire bill. The purpose of this power is to allow executives to eliminate frivolous appropriations. The president's claim to the line-item veto was denied by the Supreme Court.

mandate   Level of support for an elected official as perceived through election results.

Marbury v. Madison **(1803)**   Supreme Court decision that established the principle of **judicial review**.

Marshall, John   Third Chief Justice of the Supreme Court (he served from 1800 to 1835). A Federalist who worked to increase the powers of the federal government over the states. Marshall established the principle of **judicial review**.

Miranda v. Arizona **(1966)**   Supreme Court case in which the Court ruled that, upon arrest, a suspect must be advised of the right to remain silent and the right to consult with a lawyer.

national convention   Occasion at which a political party officially announces its presidential nominee and reveals its party platform for the next four years. Today's national conventions are merely media events; nominees have already been determined by primary election results.

National Organization of Women (**NOW**)   Feminist political group formed in 1967 to promote legislative change. NOW lobbied for the failed **Equal Rights Amendment** to the Constitution.

National Security Council   Presidential advisory board established in 1947. The NSC consults with the president on matters of defense and foreign policy.

Nineteenth Amendment (1920)   Granted voting rights to women.

nomination   Endorsement to run for office by a political party.

objective good faith   Exception to the exclusionary rule that allows the use of illegally obtained evidence at trial if the court determines that police believed they were acting within the limits of their search warrant when they seized the evidence.

Office of Budget and Management   Executive branch office responsible for drawing up the president's proposals for the federal budget.

open primary   Primary election in which voters may vote in whichever party primary they choose, though they must select that party before entering the voting booth.

original jurisdiction   Term used to describe a court's power to initially try a case. Courts in which cases are first heard are those with original jurisdiction in the case. By contrast, appellate courts hear challenges to earlier court decisions.

override   The Constitutional power of Congress to supersede a president's veto by a two-thirds majority in both houses. Such a vote is difficult to achieve, however, so overrides are fairly rare.

PAC   see **political action committee**.

pardon   Cancellation of criminal punishment. Presidents and governors have the power to grant pardons to those awaiting trial and to those convicted of crimes.

platform   Statement of purpose and policy objectives drafted and approved by political parties at their national conventions. Party platforms rarely exert much influence on day-to-day politics.

Plessy v. Ferguson (1896)   Supreme Court ruling that "separate but equal" facilities for different races are not unconstitutional. This ruling opened the door to 75 years of state-sanctioned segregation in the south.

pocket veto   If the president fails to approve a bill passed during the last ten days of a congressional session, the bill does not become law. This process is called a pocket veto.

political action committee (PAC)   The fundraising apparatus of interest groups. Donations to and contributions from PACs are regulated by federal law. PACs contribute heavily to the reelection campaigns of representatives and senators sympathetic to the PAC's political agenda.

political party   Group of people with common political goals which hopes to influence policy through the election process. Parties run candidates for office who represent the political agenda of party members. They therefore serve as an institutional link between the electorate and politicians.

policy implementation   The process by which executive departments and agencies put legislation into practice. Agencies are often allowed a degree of freedom to interpret legislation as they write guidelines to enact and enforce the law.

Populists   Political party of the late 1800s. The Populists primarily represented farmers and working-class Americans. They sought inflationary economic policies to increase farm income. They also lobbied for a number of Democratic reforms that would later be adopted by the Progressives, such as direct election of senators.

pork barrel   Budget items proposed by legislators to benefit constituents in their home state or district. Such expenditures are sometimes unnecessary but are passed anyway because they are politically beneficial.

president *pro tempore*   Individual chosen to preside over the Senate whenever the vice president is unavailable to do so. The president *pro tempore* is chosen by the Senate from among its members.

primary elections   Form of election held by the majority of states, during which voters select the nominees for political parties. Winners of primary elections appear on the ballot during the **general election**.

prior restraint   Censorship of news material before it is made public.

privileges and immunities clause   Section of the Constitution stating that a state may not refuse police protection or access to its courts to U.S. citizens because they live in a different state.

progressive income tax   A progressive tax increases tax rates for people with higher incomes. Those citizens at the poverty level, for example, may pay few or no taxes. Middle-class citizens may be taxed at a 15 percent rate, while the wealthy are taxed at two or three times that rate. The goal of a progressive tax is to allow those with greater need to keep more of what they earn while taking more from those who can best afford it.

quorum   The minimum number of people required for the legislature to act.

realignment   Occurs when a party undergoes a major shift in its electoral base and political agenda. The groups of people composing the party coalition may split up, resulting in a vastly different party. Realignments are rare and tend to be signaled by a critical election. The last realignment occurred during the New Deal, when many working-class and ethnic groups joined together under the Democratic party.

reapportionment   The process by which congressional districts are redrawn and seats are redistributed among states in the House. Reapportionment occurs every ten years, when census data reports shifts in the population of districts. Each district must have an equal number of residents. States may lose or gain seats during reapportionment, but the total House membership remains 435.

recall election   Process through which voters can shorten an office holder's term. One of several Progressive Era reforms that increased voters' power over government.

referendum   Process through which voters may vote on new laws. One of several Progressive Era reforms that increased voters' power over government.

regulatory agency   Executive agency responsible for enforcing laws pertaining to a certain industry. The agency writes guidelines for the industry, such as safety codes, and enforces them through methods such as inspection.

representative democracy   Form of government under which citizens vote for delegates who in turn represent citizens' interests within the government. In contrast, a **direct democracy** requires all citizens to vote on all government issues. The United States is a representative democracy.

reserved powers   Constitutional powers that belong solely to the states. According to the Tenth Amendment, these powers include any that the Constitution does not either specifically grant the national government or deny the state governments.

Roe v. Wade **(1973)**   Supreme Court case that decriminalized abortion.

runoff primary   Election held between top two vote-getters in a primary election, when neither received a legally required minimum percentage of the vote. Many states require a runoff when no candidate receives at least 40 percent of the primary vote for his or her party.

sampling error   Margin of error in public opinion poll. Most polls are accurate within a margin of ± 4 percent.

saving amendment   Amendment to a bill proposed in hopes of softening opposition by weakening objectionable elements of the bill.

Schenck v. United States   Supreme Court case involving limits on free speech rights. The Schenck case established the "clear and present danger" principle in determining what type of speech could be restricted.

search warrant   Document issued by the courts to allow the police to search private property. To obtain a warrant, the police must go before a judge and explain 1) where they want to search, and 2) what they are looking for. A search warrant also limits where the police may search and what they may take as evidence (Fourth Amendment).

select committee   Temporary committee of Congress, usually created to investigate specific issues.

selective incorporation   Process by which the Supreme Court has selectively applied the Fourteenth Amendment to state law.

Senate   Upper house of Congress, in which each state has two representatives. The Senate has the sole power to approve cabinet, ambassadorial, and federal judicial appointments. International treaties must receive two-thirds approval from the Senate.

senatorial courtesy   A check placed on the president by which candidates for the federal bureaucracy must first be approved by a vote within the Senate.

separation of powers   The system that prevents any branch of government from becoming too powerful by dividing important tasks among the three branches. Also called the system of **checks and balances**.

shield law   Law guaranteeing news reporters the right to protect the anonymity of their sources. Many states have passed shield laws, but there is no federal shield law.

Sixteenth Amendment (1913)   Authorized Congress to impose and collect federal income taxes.

soft money   Political donations made to parties for the purpose of general party maintenance and support, such as get-out-the-vote campaigns, issue advocacy, and advertisements that promote the party (but not individual candidates). Soft money contributions to political parties were banned in 2002 by the Bipartisan Campaign Reform Act (BCRA).

Speaker of the House   Individual chosen by members of the House of Representatives to preside over its sessions.

split-ticket rating   Choosing candidates from different parties for offices listed on the same ballot. Voters have been more inclined to vote a split ticket in recent decades. This trend has led to **divided government**.

spoils system   The political practice of trading government jobs and preferences for political and financial support. President Andrew Jackson was the first to be widely accused of using the spoils system to reward political friends and supporters.

standing committee   A permanent congressional committee.

strict constructionism   Belief that the Constitution should be read in such a way as to limit the powers of the federal government as much as possible. Strict constructionists emphasize the importance of the Tenth Amendment, which reserves to the states all powers not explicitly granted to the federal government.

supremacy clause   Section of the Constitution that requires conflicts between federal and state law to be resolved in favor of federal law. State constitutions and laws that violate the U.S. Constitution, federal laws, or international treaties can be invalidated through the supremacy clause.

Supreme Court   Highest court in the United States. The only federal court specifically mentioned in the U.S. Constitution.

The Patriot Act (2001)   Act passed in response to the terrorist attacks of September 11, 2001, granting broad police authority to the federal, state, and local governments to interdict, prosecute, and convict suspected terrorists.

Thirteenth Amendment (1865)   Abolished slavery.

Three-fifths Compromise   Agreement reached at the Constitutional Convention between Southern and Northern states. The South wanted slaves counted among the population for voting purposes but not for tax purposes; the North wanted the exact opposite. Both sides agreed that three-fifths of a state's slave population would be counted toward both congressional apportionment and taxation.

Twenty-fourth Amendment (1964)   Outlawed poll taxes, which had been used to prevent the poor from voting.

Twenty-second Amendment (1951)   Limited the number of years an individual may serve as president. According to the Twenty-second Amendment, a president may be elected no more than twice.

Twenty-sixth Amendment (1971)   Lowered the voting age from 21 to 18.

United Nations   International organization established following World War II. The United Nations aims to preserve international peace and foster international cooperation.

unanimous consent decree   Agreement passed by the Senate that establishes the rules under which a bill will be debated, amended, and voted upon.

unwritten Constitution Certain deeply ingrained aspects of our government that are not mentioned in the Constitution, such as political parties, political conventions, and cabinet meetings.

veto The power held by chief executives (e.g., the president or governors) to reject acts of the legislature. A presidential veto can be overridden by a two-thirds majority vote of both houses of Congress.

Voting Rights Act of 1965 Federal law that increased government supervision of local election practices, suspended the use of literacy tests to prevent people (usually African Americans) from voting, and expanded government efforts to register voters. The Voting Rights Act of 1970 permanently banned literacy tests.

War on Poverty Those programs of President Lyndon Johnson's **Great Society** that were specifically aimed at assisting the poor. Among these programs was Volunteers in Service to America (VISTA), Medicaid, and the creation of the Office of Economic Opportunity.

War Powers Act Law requiring the president to seek periodic approval from Congress for any substantial troop commitment. Passed in 1973 in response to national dissatisfaction over the Vietnam War.

Warren Court (1953–1969) The Supreme Court during the era in which Earl Warren served as Chief Justice. The Warren Court is best remembered for expanding the rights of minorities and the rights of the accused.

Watergate The name of the hotel in which spies working for President Richard Nixon's 1972 reelection campaign were caught breaking into Democratic National Headquarters. The name Watergate soon became synonymous with a number of illegal activities undertaken by the Nixon White House. The resulting scandal forced Nixon to resign the presidency in 1974.

writ of *habeas corpus* A court order requiring an explanation as to why a prisoner is being held in custody.

writ of *certiorari* A legal document issued by the Supreme Court to request the court transcripts of a case. A writ of *certiorari* indicates that the Court will review a lower court's decision.

THE CONSTITUTION OF THE UNITED STATES OF AMERICA

[Note: text in *italics* indicates that a section of the Constitution is no longer in effect.]

PREAMBLE

We the people of the United States, in order to form a more perfect union, establish justice, insure domestic tranquillity, provide for the common defense, promote the general welfare, and secure the blessings of liberty to ourselves and our posterity, do ordain and establish this Constitution for the United States of America.

Article I

Section 1. All legislative powers herein granted shall be vested in a Congress of the United States, which shall consist of a Senate and House of Representatives.

Section 2. The House of Representatives shall be composed of members chosen every second year by the people of the several states, and the electors in each state shall have the qualifications requisite for electors of the most numerous branch of the state legislature.

No person shall be a Representative who shall not have attained to the age of twenty-five years, and been seven years a citizen of the United States, and who shall not, when elected, be an inhabitant of that state in which he shall be chosen.

Representatives *and direct taxes*[1] shall be apportioned among the several states which may be included within this union, according to their respective numbers, *which shall be determined by adding to the whole number of free persons, including those bound to service for a term of years, and excluding Indians not taxed, three-fifths of all other Persons.*[2] The actual Enumeration shall be made within three years after the first meeting of the Congress of the United States, and within every subsequent term of ten years[3], in such manner as they shall by law direct. The number of Representatives shall not exceed one for every thirty thousand, but each state shall have at least one Representative; and until such enumeration shall be made, the state of New Hampshire shall be entitled to choose three, Massachusetts eight, Rhode Island and Providence Plantations one, Connecticut five, New York six, New Jersey four, Pennsylvania eight, Delaware one, Maryland six, Virginia ten, North Carolina five, South Carolina five, and Georgia three.

When vacancies happen in the Representation from any state, the executive authority[4] thereof shall issue writs of election to fill such vacancies. The House of Representatives shall choose their speaker and other officers; and shall have the sole power of impeachment.

Section 3. The Senate of the United States shall be composed of two Senators from each state, *chosen by the legislature thereof* [5], for six years; and each Senator shall have one vote.

Immediately after they shall be assembled in consequence of the first election, they shall be divided as equally as may be into three classes. The seats of the Senators of the first class shall be vacated at the expiration of the second year, of the second class at the expiration of the fourth year, and the third class at the expiration of the sixth year,[6] so that one third may be chosen every second year; *and if vacancies happen by resignation, or otherwise, during the recess of the legislature of any state, the executive thereof may make temporary appointments until the next meeting of the legislature, which shall then fill such vacancies.*[7]

No person shall be a Senator who shall not have attained to the age of thirty years, and been nine years a citizen of the United States and who shall not, when elected, be an inhabitant of that state for which he shall be chosen. The vice president of the United States shall be President of the Senate, but shall have no vote, unless they be equally divided. The Senate shall choose their other officers, and also a President *pro tempore*[8], in the absence of the vice president, or when he shall exercise the office of President of the United States. The Senate shall have the sole power to try all impeachments. When sitting for that purpose, they shall be on oath or affirmation. When the President of the United States is tried, the Chief Justice shall preside: And no person shall be convicted without the concurrence of two thirds of the members present.

Judgment in cases of impeachment shall not extend further than to removal from office, and disqualification to hold and enjoy any office of honor, trust or profit under the United States: but the party convicted shall nevertheless be liable and subject to indictment, trial, judgment and punishment, according to law.

Section 4. The times, places and manner of holding elections for Senators and Representatives, shall be prescribed in each state by the legislature thereof; but the Congress may at any time by law make or alter such regulations, except as to the places of choosing Senators.

The Congress shall assemble at least once in every year, *and such meeting shall be on the first Monday in December*[9], unless they shall by law appoint a different day.

Section 5. Each House shall be the judge of the elections, returns and qualifications of its own members, and a majority of each shall constitute a quorum[10] to do business; but a smaller number may adjourn from day to day, and may be authorized to compel the attendance of absent members, in such manner, and under such penalties as each House may provide.

Each House may determine the rules of its proceedings, punish its members for disorderly behavior, and, with the concurrence of two thirds, expel a member.

Each House shall keep a journal of its proceedings, and from time to time publish the same, excepting such parts as may in their judgment require secrecy; and the yeas and nays of the members of either House on any question shall, at the desire of one fifth of those present, be entered on the journal.

Neither House, during the session of Congress, shall, without the consent of the other, adjourn for more than three days, nor to any other place than that in which the two Houses shall be sitting.

Section 6. The Senators and Representatives shall receive a compensation for their services, to be ascertained by law, and paid out of the treasury of the United States. They shall in all cases, except treason, felony and breach of the peace, be privileged from arrest during their attendance at the session of their respective Houses, and in going to and returning from the same; and for any speech or debate in either House, they shall not be questioned in any other place.

No Senator or Representative shall, during the time for which he was elected, be appointed to any civil office under the authority of the United States, which shall have been created, or the emoluments[11] whereof shall have been increased during such time: and no person holding any office under the United States, shall be a member of either House during his continuance in office.[12]

Section 7. All bills for raising revenue shall originate in the House of Representatives; but the Senate may propose or concur with amendments as on other Bills.

Every bill which shall have passed the House of Representatives and the Senate, shall, before it become a law, be presented to the President of the United States; if he approve he shall sign it, but if not he shall return it[13], with his objections to that House in which it shall have originated, who shall enter the objections at large on their journal, and proceed to reconsider it. If after such reconsideration two thirds of that House shall agree to pass the bill, it shall be sent, together with the objections, to the other House, by which it shall likewise be reconsidered, and if approved by two thirds of that House, it shall become a law[14]. But in all such cases the votes of both Houses shall be determined by yeas and nays, and the names of the persons voting for and against the bill shall be entered on the journal of each House respectively. If any bill shall not be returned by the President within ten days (Sundays excepted) after it shall have been presented to him, the same shall be a law, in like manner as if he had signed it, unless the Congress by their adjournment prevent its return[15], in which case it shall not be a law.

Every order, resolution, or vote to which the concurrence of the Senate and House of Representatives may be necessary (except on a question of adjournment) shall be presented to the President of the United States; and before the same shall take effect, shall be approved by him, or being disapproved by him, shall be repassed by two thirds of the Senate and House of Representatives, according to the rules and limitations prescribed in the case of a bill.

Section 8. The Congress shall have power to lay and collect taxes, duties, imposts and excises, to pay the debts and provide for the common defense and general welfare of the United States; but all duties, imposts and excises shall be uniform throughout the United States;

- To borrow money on the credit of the United States;

- To regulate commerce with foreign nations, and among the several states, and with the Indian tribes;

- To establish a uniform rule of naturalization, and uniform laws on the subject of bankruptcies throughout the United States;

- To coin money, regulate the value thereof, and of foreign coin, and fix the standard of weights and measures;

- To provide for the punishment of counterfeiting the securities and current coin of the United States;

- To establish post offices and post roads;

- To promote the progress of science and useful arts, by securing for limited times to authors and inventors the exclusive right to their respective writings and discoveries;

- To constitute tribunals inferior to the Supreme Court;

- To define and punish piracies and felonies committed on the high seas, and offenses against the law of nations;

- To declare war, grant letters of marque and reprisal[16], and make rules concerning captures on land and water;

- To raise and support armies, but no appropriation of money to that use shall be for a longer term than two years;

- To provide and maintain a navy;

- To make rules for the government and regulation of the land and naval forces;

- To provide for calling forth the militia to execute the laws of the union, suppress insurrections and repel invasions;

- To provide for organizing, arming, and disciplining the militia, and for governing such part of them as may be employed in the service of the United States, reserving to the states respectively, the appointment of the officers, and the authority of training the militia according to the discipline prescribed by Congress;

- To exercise exclusive legislation in all cases whatsoever, over such District (not exceeding ten miles square) as may, by cession of particular states, and the acceptance of Congress, become the seat of the government of the United States[17], and to exercise like authority over all places purchased by the consent of the legislature of the state in which the same shall be, for the erection of forts, magazines, arsenals, dockyards, and other needful buildings; and

- To make all laws which shall be necessary and proper for carrying into execution the foregoing powers, and all other powers vested by this Constitution in the government of the United States, or in any department or officer thereof.[18]

Section 9. *The migration or importation of such persons as any of the states now existing shall think proper to admit, shall not be prohibited by the Congress prior to the year one thousand eight hundred and eight, but a tax or duty may be imposed on such importation, not exceeding ten dollars for each person.*[19]
The privilege of the writ of habeas corpus[20] *shall not be suspended, unless when in cases of rebellion or invasion the public safety may require it.*

- No bill of attainder[21] or ex post facto law[22] shall be passed.

- *No capitation, or other direct, tax shall be laid, unless in proportion to the census or enumeration herein before directed to be taken.*[23]

- No tax or duty shall be laid on articles exported from any state.

- No preference shall be given by any regulation of commerce or revenue to the ports of one state over those of another: nor shall vessels bound to, or from, one state, be obliged to enter, clear or pay duties in another.

- No money shall be drawn from the treasury, but in consequence of appropriations made by law; and a regular statement and account of receipts and expenditures of all public money shall be published from time to time.

- No title of nobility shall be granted by the United States: and no person holding any office of profit or trust under them, shall, without the consent of the Congress, accept of any present, emolument, office, or title, of any kind whatever, from any king, prince, or foreign state.

Section 10. No state shall enter into any treaty, alliance, or confederation; grant letters of marque and reprisal; coin money; emit bills of credit; make anything but gold and silver coin a tender in payment of debts; pass any bill of attainder, ex post facto law, or law impairing the obligation of contracts, or grant any title of nobility.

No state shall, without the consent of the Congress, lay any imposts or duties on imports or exports, except what may be absolutely necessary for executing its inspection laws; and the net produce of all duties and imposts, laid by any state on imports or exports, shall be for the use of the treasury of the United States; and all such laws shall be subject to the revision and control of the Congress.

No state shall, without the consent of Congress, lay any duty of tonnage, keep troops, or ships of war in time of peace, enter into any agreement or compact with another state, or with a foreign power, or engage in war, unless actually invaded, or in such imminent danger as will not admit of delay.

Article II

Section 1. The executive power shall be vested in a President of the United States of America. He shall hold his office during the term of four years, and, together with the vice president, chosen for the same term, be elected, as follows:

Each state shall appoint, in such manner as the Legislature thereof may direct, a number of electors, equal to the whole number of Senators and Representatives to which the State may be entitled in the Congress: but no Senator or Representative, or person holding an office of trust or profit under the United States, shall be appointed an elector.

The electors shall meet in their respective states, and vote by ballot for two persons, of whom one at least shall not be an inhabitant of the same state with themselves. And they shall make a list of all the persons voted for, and of the number of votes for each; which list they shall sign and certify, and transmit sealed to the seat of the government of the United States, directed to the President of the Senate. The President of the Senate shall, in the presence of the Senate and House of Representatives, open all the certificates, and the votes shall then be counted. The person having the greatest number of votes shall be the President, if such number be a majority of the whole number of electors appointed; and if there be more than one who have such majority, and have an equal number of votes, then the House of Representatives shall immediately choose by ballot one of them for President; and if no person have a majority, then from the five highest on the list the said House shall in like manner choose the President. But in choosing the President, the votes shall be taken by States, the representation from each state having one vote; a quorum for this purpose shall consist of a member or members from two thirds of the states, and a majority of all the states shall be necessary to a choice. In every case, after the choice of the President, the person having the greatest number of votes of the electors shall be the vice president. But if there should remain two or more who have equal votes, the Senate shall choose from them by ballot the vice president.[24]

The Congress may determine the time of choosing the electors, and the day on which they shall give their votes; which day shall be the same throughout the United States.

No person except a natural born citizen, or a citizen of the United States at the time of the adoption of this Constitution[25], shall be eligible to the office of President; neither shall any person be eligible to that office who shall not have attained to the age of thirty five years, and been fourteen years a resident within the United States.

In case of the removal of the President from office, or of his death, resignation, or inability to discharge the powers and duties of the said office, the same shall devolve on the vice president, and the Congress may by law provide for the case of removal, death, resignation or inability, both of the President and vice president, declaring what officer shall then act as President, and such officer shall act accordingly, until the disability be removed, or a President shall be elected.[26]

The President shall, at stated times, receive for his services, a compensation, which shall neither be increased nor diminished during the period for which he shall have been elected, and he shall not receive within that period any other emolument[27] from the United States, or any of them.

Before he enter on the execution of his office, he shall take the following oath or affirmation: "I do solemnly swear (or affirm) that I will faithfully execute the office of President of the United States, and will to the best of my ability, preserve, protect and defend the Constitution of the United States."

Section 2. The President shall be commander in chief of the Army and Navy of the United States, and of the militia of the several states, when called into the actual service of the United States; he may require the opinion, in writing, of the principal officer in each of the executive departments, upon any subject relating to the duties of their respective offices, and he shall have power to grant reprieves and pardons for offenses against the United States, except in cases of impeachment.

He shall have power, by and with the advice and consent of the Senate[28], to make treaties, provided two thirds of the Senators present concur; and he shall nominate, and by and with the advice and consent of the Senate, shall appoint ambassadors, other public ministers and consuls, judges of the Supreme Court, and all other officers of the United States, whose appointments are not herein otherwise provided for, and which shall be established by law: but the Congress may by law vest the appointment of such inferior officers, as they think proper, in the President alone, in the courts of law, or in the heads of departments.

The President shall have power to fill up all vacancies that may happen during the recess of the Senate, by granting commissions which shall expire at the end of their next session.

Section 3. He shall from time to time give to the Congress information of the state of the union, and recommend to their consideration such measures as he shall judge necessary and expedient; he may, on extraordinary occasions, convene both Houses, or either of them, and in case of disagreement between them, with respect to the time of adjournment, he may adjourn them to such time as he shall think proper; he shall receive ambassadors and other public ministers; he shall take care that the laws be faithfully executed, and shall commission all the officers of the United States.

Section 4. The President, vice president and all civil officers of the United States, shall be removed from office on impeachment for, and conviction of, treason, bribery, or other high crimes and misdemeanors.

Article III

Section 1. The judicial power of the United States, shall be vested in one Supreme Court, and in such inferior courts as the Congress may from time to time ordain and establish. The judges, both of the supreme and inferior courts, shall hold their offices during good behavior, and shall, at stated times, receive for their services, a compensation, which shall not be diminished during their continuance in office.

Section 2. The judicial power shall extend to all cases, in law and equity, arising under this Constitution, the laws of the United States, and treaties made, or which shall be made, under their authority; to all cases affecting ambassadors, other public ministers and consuls; to all cases of admiralty and maritime jurisdiction; to controversies to which the United States shall be a party; to controversies between two or more states; between a state and citizens of another state[29]; between citizens of different states; between citizens of the same state claiming lands under grants of different states, and between a state, or the citizens thereof, and foreign states, citizens or subjects.

In all cases affecting ambassadors, other public ministers and consuls, and those in which a state shall be party, the Supreme Court shall have original jurisdiction. In all the other cases before mentioned, the Supreme Court shall have appellate jurisdiction, both as to law and fact, with such exceptions, and under such regulations as the Congress shall make.

The trial of all crimes, except in cases of impeachment, shall be by jury; and such trial shall be held in the state where the said crimes shall have been committed; but when not committed within any state, the trial shall be at such place or places as the Congress may by law have directed.

Section 3. Treason against the United States, shall consist only in levying war against them, or in adhering to their enemies, giving them aid and comfort. No person shall be convicted of treason unless on the testimony of two witnesses to the same overt act, or on confession in open court.

The Congress shall have power to declare the punishment of treason, but no attainder of treason shall work corruption of blood, or forfeiture except during the life of the person attainted.[30]

Article IV

Section 1. Full faith and credit shall be given in each state to the public acts, records, and judicial proceedings of every other state.[31] And the Congress may by general laws prescribe the manner in which such acts, records, and proceedings shall be proved, and the effect thereof.

Section 2. The citizens of each state shall be entitled to all privileges and immunities of citizens in the several states.

A person charged in any state with treason, felony, or other crime, who shall flee from justice, and be found in another state, shall on demand of the executive authority of the state from which he fled, be delivered up, to be removed to the state having jurisdiction of the crime.[32]

No person held to service or labor in one state, under the laws thereof, escaping into another, shall, in consequence of any law or regulation therein, be discharged from such service or labor, but shall be delivered up on claim of the party to whom such service or labor may be due.[33]

Section 3. New states may be admitted by the Congress into this union; but no new states shall be formed or erected within the jurisdiction of any other state; nor any state be formed by the junction of two or more states, or parts of states, without the consent of the legislatures of the states concerned as well as of the Congress.

The Congress shall have power to dispose of and make all needful rules and regulations respecting the territory or other property belonging to the United States; and nothing in this Constitution shall be so construed as to prejudice any claims of the United States, or of any particular state.

Section 4. The United States shall guarantee to every state in this union a Republican form of government, and shall protect each of them against invasion; and on application of the legislature, or of the executive (when the legislature cannot be convened) against domestic violence.

Article V

The Congress, whenever two thirds of both houses shall deem it necessary, shall propose amendments to this Constitution, or, on the application of the legislatures of two thirds of the several states, shall call a convention for proposing amendments, which, in either case, shall be valid to all intents and purposes, as part of this Constitution, when ratified by the legislatures of three fourths of the several states, or by conventions in three fourths thereof, as the one or the other mode of ratification may be proposed by the Congress; provided that no amendment which may be made prior to the year one thousand eight hundred and eight shall in any manner affect the first and fourth clauses in the ninth section of the first article; and that no state, without its consent, shall be deprived of its equal suffrage in the Senate.

Article VI

All debts contracted and engagements entered into, before the adoption of this Constitution, shall be as valid against the United States under this Constitution, as under the Confederation.

This Constitution, and the laws of the United States which shall be made in pursuance thereof; and all treaties made, or which shall be made, under the authority of the United States, shall be the supreme law of the land[34]; and the judges in every state shall be bound thereby, anything in the Constitution or laws of any State to the contrary notwithstanding.

The Senators and Representatives before mentioned, and the members of the several state legislatures, and all executive and judicial officers, both of the United States and of the several states, shall be bound by oath or affirmation, to support this Constitution; but no religious test shall ever be required as a qualification to any office or public trust under the United States.

Article VII

The ratification of the conventions of nine states, shall be sufficient for the establishment of this Constitution between the states so ratifying the same.

Done in convention by the unanimous consent of the states present the seventeenth day of September in the year of our Lord one thousand seven hundred and eighty seven and of the independence of the United States of America the twelfth. In witness whereof We have hereunto subscribed our Names,

Signed:
    G. Washington—President, and 38 representatives of the states

AMENDMENTS TO THE CONSTITUTION

[Note: Amendments I through X are collectively known as the "Bill of Rights."]

Amendment I (1791)

Congress shall make no law respecting an establishment of religion, or prohibiting the free exercise thereof [35]; or abridging the freedom of speech, or of the press; or the right of the people peaceably to assemble, and to petition the government for a redress of grievances.

Amendment II (1791)

A well regulated militia, being necessary to the security of a free state, the right of the people to keep and bear arms, shall not be infringed.

Amendment III (1791)

No soldier shall, in time of peace be quartered in any house, without the consent of the owner, nor in time of war, but in a manner to be prescribed by law.

Amendment IV (1791)

The right of the people to be secure in their persons, houses, papers, and effects, against unreasonable searches and seizures, shall not be violated, and no warrants shall issue, but upon probable cause, supported by oath or affirmation, and particularly describing the place to be searched, and the persons or things to be seized.

Amendment V (1791)

No person shall be held to answer for a capital[36], or otherwise infamous crime[37], unless on a presentment or indictment of a grand jury, except in cases arising in the land or naval forces, or in the militia, when in actual service in time of war or public danger; nor shall any person be subject for the same offense to be twice put in jeopardy of life or limb[38]; nor shall be compelled in any criminal case to be a witness against himself, nor be deprived of life, liberty, or property, without due process of law; nor shall private property be taken for public use, without just compensation.

Amendment VI (1791)

In all criminal prosecutions, the accused shall enjoy the right to a speedy and public trial, by an impartial jury of the state and district wherein the crime shall have been committed, which district shall have been previously ascertained by law, and to be informed of the nature and cause of the accusation; to be confronted with the witnesses against him; to have compulsory process for obtaining witnesses in his favor, and to have the assistance of counsel for his defense.

Amendment VII (1791)

In suits at common law, where the value in controversy shall exceed twenty dollars, the right of trial by jury shall be preserved, and no fact tried by a jury, shall be otherwise reexamined in any court of the United States, than according to the rules of the common law.

Amendment VIII (1791)

Excessive bail shall not be required, nor excessive fines imposed, nor cruel and unusual punishments inflicted.

Amendment IX (1791)

The enumeration in the Constitution, of certain rights, shall not be construed to deny or disparage others retained by the people.

Amendment X (1791)

The powers not delegated to the United States by the Constitution, nor prohibited by it to the states, are reserved to the states respectively, or to the people.

Amendment XI (1795)

The judicial power of the United States shall not be construed to extend to any suit in law or equity, commenced or prosecuted against one of the United States by citizens of another state, or by citizens or subjects of any foreign state.

Amendment XII (1804)

The electors shall meet in their respective states and vote by ballot for President and vice president, one of whom, at least, shall not be an inhabitant of the same state with themselves; they shall name in their ballots the person voted for as President, and in distinct ballots the person voted for as vice president, and they shall make distinct lists of all persons voted for as President, and of all persons voted for as vice president, and of the number of votes for each, which lists they shall sign and certify, and transmit sealed to the seat of the government of the United States, directed to the President of the Senate.

The President of the Senate shall, in the presence of the Senate and House of Representatives, open all the certificates and the votes shall then be counted; the person having the greatest number of votes for President, shall be the President, if such number be a majority of the whole number of electors appointed; and if no person have such majority, then from the persons having the highest numbers not exceeding three on the list of those voted for as President, the House of Representatives shall choose immediately, by ballot, the President. But in choosing the President, the votes shall be taken by states, the representation from each state having one vote; a quorum for this purpose shall consist of a member or members from two-thirds of the states, and a majority of all the states shall be necessary to a choice. And if the House of Representatives shall not choose a President whenever the right of choice shall devolve upon them, *before the fourth day of March next following*[39], then the vice president shall act as President, as in the case of the death or other constitutional disability of the President.

The person having the greatest number of votes as vice president, shall be the vice president, if such number be a majority of the whole number of electors appointed, and if no person have a majority, then from the two highest numbers on the list, the Senate shall choose the vice president; a quorum for the purpose shall consist of two-thirds of the whole number of Senators, and a majority of the whole number shall be necessary to a choice. But no person constitutionally ineligible to the office of President shall be eligible to that of vice president of the United States.

Amendment XIII (1865)

Section 1. Neither slavery nor involuntary servitude, except as a punishment for crime whereof the party shall have been duly convicted, shall exist within the United States, or any place subject to their jurisdiction.

Section 2. Congress shall have power to enforce this article by appropriate legislation.

Amendment XIV (1868)

Section 1. All persons born or naturalized in the United States, and subject to the jurisdiction thereof, are citizens of the United States and of the state wherein they reside.[40] No state shall make or enforce any law which shall abridge the privileges or immunities of citizens of the United States; nor shall any state deprive any person of life, liberty, or property, without due process of law; nor deny to any person within its jurisdiction the equal protection of the laws.

Section 2. Representatives shall be apportioned among the several states according to their respective numbers, counting the whole number of persons in each state[41], excluding Indians not taxed. But when the right to vote at any election for the choice of electors for President and vice president of the United States, Representatives in Congress, the executive and judicial officers of a state, or the members of the legislature thereof, is denied to any of the *male* inhabitants of such state, being *twenty-one* years of age, and citizens of the United States, or in any way abridged, except for participation in rebellion, or other crime, the basis of representation therein shall be reduced in the proportion which the number of such *male* citizens shall bear to the whole number of male citizens *twenty-one* years of age in such state.[42]

Section 3. No person shall be a Senator or Representative in Congress, or elector of President and vice president, or hold any office, civil or military, under the United States, or under any state, who, having previously taken an oath, as a member of Congress, or as an officer of the United States, or as a member of any state legislature, or as an executive or judicial officer of any state, to support the

Constitution of the United States, shall have engaged in insurrection or rebellion against the same, or given aid or comfort to the enemies thereof. But Congress may by a vote of two-thirds of each House, remove such disability.

Section 4. The validity of the public debt of the United States, authorized by law, including debts incurred for payment of pensions and bounties for services in suppressing insurrection or rebellion, shall not be questioned. But neither the United States nor any state shall assume or pay any debt or obligation incurred in aid of insurrection or rebellion against the United States, or any claim for the loss or emancipation of any slave; but all such debts, obligations and claims shall be held illegal and void.

Section 5. The Congress shall have power to enforce, by appropriate legislation, the provisions of this article.

Amendment XV (1870)

Section 1. The right of citizens of the United States to vote shall not be denied or abridged by the United States or by any state on account of race, color, or previous condition of servitude.

Section 2. The Congress shall have power to enforce this article by appropriate legislation.

Amendment XVI (1913)

The Congress shall have power to lay and collect taxes on incomes, from whatever source derived, without apportionment among the several states, and without regard to any census of enumeration.

Amendment XVII (1913)

The Senate of the United States shall be composed of two Senators from each state, elected by the people thereof, for six years; and each Senator shall have one vote. The electors in each state shall have the qualifications requisite for electors of the most numerous branch of the state legislatures.

When vacancies happen in the representation of any state in the Senate, the executive authority of such state shall issue writs of election to fill such vacancies: Provided, that the legislature of any state may empower the executive thereof to make temporary appointments until the people fill the vacancies by election as the legislature may direct.

This amendment shall not be so construed as to affect the election or term of any Senator chosen before it becomes valid as part of the Constitution.

Amendment XVIII (1919)

Section 1. After one year from the ratification of this article the manufacture, sale, or transportation of intoxicating liquors within, the importation thereof into, or the exportation thereof from the United States and all territory subject to the jurisdiction thereof for beverage purposes is hereby prohibited.

Section 2. The Congress and the several states shall have concurrent power to enforce this article by appropriate legislation.

Section 3. This article shall be inoperative unless it shall have been ratified as an amendment to the Constitution by the legislatures of the several states, as provided in the Constitution, within seven years from the date of the submission hereof to the states by the Congress.[43]

Amendment XIX (1920)

Section 1. The right of citizens of the United States to vote shall not be denied or abridged by the United States or by any state on account of sex.

Section 2. The Congress shall have power to enforce this article by appropriate legislation.

Amendment XX (1933)

Section 1. The terms of the President and vice president shall end at noon on the twentieth day of January, and the terms of Senators and Representatives at noon on the third day of January, of the years in which such terms would have ended if this article had not been ratified; and the terms of their successors shall then begin.[44]

Section 2. The Congress shall assemble at least once in every year, and such meeting shall begin at noon on the third day of January, unless they shall by law appoint a different day.

Section 3. If, at the time fixed for the beginning of the term of the President, the President elect shall have died, the vice president elect[45] shall become President. If a President shall not have been chosen before the time fixed for the beginning of his term, or if the President elect shall have failed to qualify, then the vice president elect shall act as President until a President shall have qualified; and the Congress may by law provide for the case wherein neither a President elect nor a vice president elect shall have qualified, declaring who shall then act as President, or the manner in which one who is to act shall be selected, and such person shall act accordingly until a President or vice president shall have qualified.

Section 4. The Congress may by law provide for the case of the death of any of the persons from whom the House of Representatives may choose a President whenever the right of choice shall have devolved upon them, and for the case of the death of any of the persons from whom the Senate may choose a vice president whenever the right of choice shall have devolved upon them.

Section 5. Sections 1 and 2 shall take effect on the fifteenth day of October following the ratification of this article.

Section 6. This article shall be inoperative unless it shall have been ratified as an amendment to the Constitution by the legislatures of three-fourths of the several states within seven years from the date of its submission.

Amendment XXI (1933)

Section 1. The eighteenth article of amendment to the Constitution of the United States is hereby repealed.

Section 2. The transportation or importation into any state, territory, or possession of the United States for delivery or use therein of intoxicating liquors, in violation of the laws thereof, is hereby prohibited.[46]

Section 3. This article shall be inoperative unless it shall have been ratified as an amendment to the Constitution by conventions in the several states, as provided in the Constitution, within seven years from the date of the submission hereof to the states by the Congress.

Amendment XXII (1951)

Section 1. No person shall be elected to the office of the President more than twice, and no person who has held the office of President, or acted as President, for more than two years of a term to which some other person was elected President shall be elected to the office of the President more than once. But this article shall not apply to any person holding the office of President when this article was proposed by the Congress, and shall not prevent any person who may be holding the office of President, or acting as President, during the term within which this article becomes operative from holding the office of President or acting as President during the remainder of such term.

Section 2. This article shall be inoperative unless it shall have been ratified as an amendment to the Constitution by the legislatures of three-fourths of the several states within seven years from the date of its submission to the states by the Congress.

Amendment XXIII (1961)[47]

Section 1. The District constituting the seat of government of the United States shall appoint in such manner as the Congress may direct:

A number of electors of President and vice president equal to the whole number of Senators and Representatives in Congress to which the District would be entitled if it were a state, but in no event more than the least populous state; they shall be in addition to those appointed by the states, but they shall be considered, for the purposes of the election of President and vice president, to be electors appointed by a state; and they shall meet in the District and perform such duties as provided by the twelfth article of amendment.

Section 2. The Congress shall have power to enforce this article by appropriate legislation.

Amendment XXIV (1964)

Section 1. The right of citizens of the United States to vote in any primary or other election for President or vice president, for electors for President or vice president, or for Senator or Representative in Congress, shall not be denied or abridged by the United States or any state by reason of failure to pay any poll tax or other tax.

Section 2. The Congress shall have power to enforce this article by appropriate legislation.

Amendment XXV (1967)

Section 1. In case of the removal of the President from office or of his death or resignation, the vice president shall become President.

Section 2. Whenever there is a vacancy in the office of the vice president, the President shall nominate a vice president who shall take office upon confirmation by a majority vote of both Houses of Congress.

Section 3. Whenever the President transmits to the President pro tempore of the Senate and the Speaker of the House of Representatives his written declaration that he is unable to discharge the powers and duties of his office, and until he transmits to them a written declaration to the contrary, such powers and duties shall be discharged by the vice president as Acting President.

Section 4. Whenever the vice president and a majority of either the principal officers of the executive departments or of such other body as Congress may by law provide, transmit to the President pro tempore of the Senate and the Speaker of the House of Representatives their written declaration that the President is unable to discharge the powers and duties of his office, the vice president shall immediately assume the powers and duties of the office as Acting President.

Thereafter, when the President transmits to the President pro tempore of the Senate and the Speaker of the House of Representatives his written declaration that no inability exists, he shall resume the powers and duties of his office unless the vice president and a majority of either the principal officers of the executive department or of such other body as Congress may by law provide, transmit within four days to the President pro tempore of the Senate and the Speaker of the House of Representatives their written declaration that the President is unable to discharge the powers and duties of his office. Thereupon Congress shall decide the issue, assembling within forty-eight hours for that purpose if not in session. If the Congress, within twenty-one days after receipt of the latter written declaration, or, if Congress is not in session, within twenty-one days after Congress is required to assemble, determines by two-thirds vote of both Houses that the President is unable to discharge the powers and duties of his office, the vice president shall continue to discharge the same as Acting President; otherwise, the President shall resume the powers and duties of his office.

Amendment XXVI (1971)

Section 1. The right of citizens of the United States, who are 18 years of age or older, to vote, shall not be denied or abridged by the United States or any state on account of age.

Section 2. The Congress shall have the power to enforce this article by appropriate legislation.

Amendment XXVII (1992)

No law, varying the compensation for the services of the Senators and Representatives, shall take effect, until an election of Representatives shall have intervened.

NOTES

[1] This clause says that the government may only assess taxes on the states on the basis of population. Amendment XVI changed this by allowing the government to tax individuals' incomes.

[2] *Other persons* meant slaves. Amendment XIII abolished slavery, and Amendment XIV nullified the *three-fifths* clause.

[3] This is the clause that requires a national census every 10 years. The census is taken to apportion Congressional representation; it is also used by Congress to decide how to distribute federal funding.

[4] The *executive authority* of a state is the governor.

[5] Amendment XVII changed this; senators are now elected by state voters, not by the state legislature.

[6] This section applied only to the first two Senates to guarantee senatorial elections every two years from the beginning of the Republic.

[7] Amendment XVII changed this by allowing the governor to make such temporary appointments.

[8] The president *pro tempore* presides over Senate when the vice president is not present.

[9] Amendment XX changed this date to January 3.

[10] *Quorum* means the minimum number of people required for the legislature to act. In other words, the Senate cannot begin a session unless at least 51 members are in attendance. Once a session has begun, however, the senators may leave the floor.

[11] *Emoluments* means payments.

[12] A Congressperson cannot hold a second government job. This is a central component of the *separation of powers* within the U.S. government.

[13] The President's veto power.

[14] Congress can override a presidential veto with a two-thirds vote in both houses.

[15] This is called a *pocket veto* by the president. He does not return the bill to Congress, but because Congress has adjourned, the bill does not become law. Congress must then re-pass the law in its next session to force the president to consider it again.

[16] *Letters of marque and reprisal* allow private citizens to arm their boats so that they can attack enemy ships. In other words, Congress has the power to license private navies (called *privateers*). Given the circumstances of modern warfare, the chances that Congress will ever again exercise this power are pretty small.

[17] This section refers to the District of Columbia (Washington, DC)

[18] This is the elastic clause.

[19] This section prohibited Congress from outlawing the importation of slaves until the year 1808. In 1808, Congress did in fact outlaw the import of slaves.

20 A *writ of habeas corpus* is used by a defendant to appear before a judge, who determines whether the government has the right to hold the defendant as a prisoner. A defendant's right to a writ of habeas corpus is what prevents the government from arresting and imprisoning people without just cause.

21 A *bill of attainder* is a law that finds an individual guilty of a capital offense (usually treason). Because it denies an individual's right to a fair trial, it is prohibited by the Constitution.

22 An *ex post facto* law is one that declares an action a crime retroactively.

23 Amendment XVI negated this section by altering Congress' power to impose taxes.

24 Amendment XII overrides this section of the Constitution.

25 This clause was inserted to provide for the first presidents, who as colonists had been born British subjects.

26 This entire paragraph was modified by Amendments XX and XXV.

27 *Emolument* means payment.

28 This paragraph enumerates several key features of the system of *checks and balances*.

29 Amendment XI prohibits an individual from using the federal courts to sue a state other than her state of residence.

30 This paragraph says that if Congress finds a person guilty of treason, it may punish that person but not his heirs.

31 States must accept the actions of each others' governments. Every state must accept every other state's driver's licenses, marriage licenses, legal decisions, and so on.

32 The process described in this section is called *extradition*.

33 This section refers to escaped slaves. It was nullified by Amendment XIII.

34 This means that federal law takes priority when federal law and state law conflict. In *McCulloch v. Maryland*, Chief Justice Marshall interpreted this to mean that the federal government could nullify laws that contradicted federal law.

35 *Free exercise* means the freedom to practice whatever religion you choose.

36 A *capital* crime is one punishable by death.

37 An *otherwise infamous crime* is one that is considered serious enough to be punishable by imprisonment.

38 This is the *double jeopardy* clause. A person cannot be tried again if a court finds him not guilty in a prior trial.

39 Amendment XX changed this date to January 20th.

40 This sentence grants citizenship to the former slaves.

41 This sentence overrides the *three-fifths* clause in the body of the Constitution.

42 This section grants voting rights only to males over the age of 21. Amendment XIX extended voting rights to women; Amendment XXVI lowered the voting age to 18.

43 Amendment XVIII was repealed by Amendment XXI.

44 This amendment shortened the amount of time that a president serves after he has been voted out of office.

45 *President elect* refers to someone who has been elected president but has not yet taken the oath of office. Whenever the presidency changes hands by election, there is a president elect between Election Day and Inaugural Day.

46 Amendment XXI repealed prohibition but it did not prohibit state and local governments from imposing prohibition. This section makes it a federal crime to transport liquor to a dry county (area in which alcoholic beverages are prohibited).

47 This amendment gave residents of the District of Columbia the right to vote for president.

Index

Third Amendment, 50, 137, 145
third parties, 69–70
Third Party System, 208
Thirteenth Amendment, 52, 146
Thomas, Clarence, 108
Thornhill v. Alabama, 140
Three-Fifths Compromise, 44
Three Mile Island, 219
three-part obscenity test, 139
three-strike rule, 124
Time, 63
Tinker v. Des Moines, 138
Title IX Higher Education Act, 101, 149, 266
titles of nobility, 47
trade policy, 128
treaties, 47, 48
trial, 144
Truman, Harry, 105, 209
Twelfth Amendment, 52
Twentieth Amendment, 53
Twenty-Fifth Amendment, 53
Twenty-First Amendment (Prohibition), 49
Twenty-Fourth Amendment, 52, 146
Twenty-Second Amendment, 53
Twenty-Sixth Amendment, 53, 150
Twenty-Third Amendment, 53
20/20, 63
two-party system, 69

unemployment insurance, 130
unifying the party, 86
United Auto Workers, 75
United States v. Lopez, 150
University of Michigan, 147
unreasonable search and seizure, 142, 143
U.S. Citizenship and Immigration Services
        (USCIS), 105
U.S. Term Limits v. Thornton, 93
U.S. Trade Representative, 105
U.S. v. Eichman, 139
U.S. v. Nixon, 151

veto, 48, 54, 96–97
Vietnam War, 53, 63, 70, 103, 138, 139, 140
Virginia Plan, 44
Virginia v. Black, 139
voter exit polls, 59, 88–89

voter turnout, 70, 71, 73, 82, 88
voting
    electoral college and, 32, 33, 70, 87
    literacy tests, 146
    poll taxes, 146
    voting age, 53
    voting rights, 52, 93–94, 145–146, 150
Voting Rights Act of 1965, 52, 100, 147, 150

Wagner Act, 100
Wallace, George, 70
war
    Civil War, 145, 146
    declaration of war, 46, 47, 103
    drug war, 124
    Gulf War, 59, 63, 103, 104, 139
    Vietnam War, 53, 63, 70, 103, 138, 139, 140
War Powers Act, 100, 103
Warren, Earl, 142
Washington, George, 54, 208
Webster v. Reproductive Health Services, 145
Weeks v. U.S., 142
welfare, 47, 62, 73, 126, 128–131
Welfare Reform Act, 101, 130
Wesberry v. Sanders, 93
Whigs, 208
winner-take-all system, 87
Wisconsin v. Yoder, 141
women and civil rights, 148–149, 265
Woodson v. North Carolina, 144
WPA, 209
writ of *certiorari,* 108
writ of habeas corpus, 47

Zamarripa, Sam, 94

ABOUT THE AUTHOR

Tom Meltzer, a Columbia University graduate, is the author or coauthor of six Princeton Review books, including *The Best 366 Colleges*, *Cracking the CLEP*, and *Illustrated Word Smart*. He has taught and developed materials for The Princeton Review since 1998. He currently resides in North Carolina.

The Princeton Review

Completely darken bubbles with a No. 2 pencil. If you make a mistake, be sure to erase mark completely. Erase all stray marks.

1. YOUR NAME: _____
(Print) Last First M.I.

SIGNATURE: _____ **DATE:** ___/___/___

HOME ADDRESS: _____
(Print) Number and Street

_____ **E-MAIL:** _____
City State Zip

PHONE NO.: _____ **SCHOOL:** _____ **CLASS OF:** _____
(Print)

IMPORTANT: Please fill in these boxes exactly as shown on the back cover of your test book.

OpScan iNSIGHT™ forms by Pearson NCS EM-255325-1:654321
Printed in U.S.A.

© The Princeton Review, Inc.

5. YOUR NAME

First 4 letters of last name				FIRST INIT	MID INIT

(Bubble grid A–Z, 6 columns)

2. TEST FORM

_____

6. DATE OF BIRTH

MONTH	DAY	YEAR
○ JAN		
○ FEB		
○ MAR	0 0	0 0
○ APR	1 1	1 1
○ MAY	2 2	2 2
○ JUN	3 3	3 3
○ JUL	4 4	4
○ AUG	5 5	5
○ SEP	6 6	6
○ OCT	7 7	7
○ NOV	8 8	8
○ DEC	9 9	9

3. TEST CODE   4. PHONE NUMBER

(Bubble grid 0–9, multiple columns)

7. SEX
○ MALE
○ FEMALE

8. OTHER
1 Ⓐ Ⓑ Ⓒ Ⓓ Ⓔ
2 Ⓐ Ⓑ Ⓒ Ⓓ Ⓔ
3 Ⓐ Ⓑ Ⓒ Ⓓ Ⓔ

Begin with number 1 for each new section of the test. Leave blank any extra answer spaces.

SECTION 1

(Answer bubbles 1–100, each with options A B C D E)

1 Ⓐ Ⓑ Ⓒ Ⓓ Ⓔ   26 Ⓐ Ⓑ Ⓒ Ⓓ Ⓔ   51 Ⓐ Ⓑ Ⓒ Ⓓ Ⓔ   76 Ⓐ Ⓑ Ⓒ Ⓓ Ⓔ
2 Ⓐ Ⓑ Ⓒ Ⓓ Ⓔ   27 ...   52 ...   77 ...
... through 100

Completely darken bubbles with a No. 2 pencil. If you make a mistake, be sure to erase mark completely. Erase all stray marks.

1. YOUR NAME: _____
(Print)   Last   First   M.I.

SIGNATURE: _____ **DATE:** ___ / ___ / ___

HOME ADDRESS: _____
(Print)   Number and Street

E-MAIL: _____

City   State   Zip

PHONE NO.: _____ **SCHOOL:** _____ **CLASS OF:** _____
(Print)

IMPORTANT: Please fill in these boxes exactly as shown on the back cover of your test book.

OpScan *i*NSIGHT™ forms by Pearson NCS EM-255325-1:654321
Printed in U.S.A.

© The Princeton Review, Inc.

5. YOUR NAME

First 4 letters of last name				FIRST INIT	MID INIT
Ⓐ	Ⓐ	Ⓐ	Ⓐ	Ⓐ	Ⓐ
Ⓑ	Ⓑ	Ⓑ	Ⓑ	Ⓑ	Ⓑ
Ⓒ	Ⓒ	Ⓒ	Ⓒ	Ⓒ	Ⓒ
Ⓓ	Ⓓ	Ⓓ	Ⓓ	Ⓓ	Ⓓ
Ⓔ	Ⓔ	Ⓔ	Ⓔ	Ⓔ	Ⓔ
Ⓕ	Ⓕ	Ⓕ	Ⓕ	Ⓕ	Ⓕ
Ⓖ	Ⓖ	Ⓖ	Ⓖ	Ⓖ	Ⓖ
Ⓗ	Ⓗ	Ⓗ	Ⓗ	Ⓗ	Ⓗ
Ⓘ	Ⓘ	Ⓘ	Ⓘ	Ⓘ	Ⓘ
Ⓙ	Ⓙ	Ⓙ	Ⓙ	Ⓙ	Ⓙ
Ⓚ	Ⓚ	Ⓚ	Ⓚ	Ⓚ	Ⓚ
Ⓛ	Ⓛ	Ⓛ	Ⓛ	Ⓛ	Ⓛ
Ⓜ	Ⓜ	Ⓜ	Ⓜ	Ⓜ	Ⓜ
Ⓝ	Ⓝ	Ⓝ	Ⓝ	Ⓝ	Ⓝ
Ⓞ	Ⓞ	Ⓞ	Ⓞ	Ⓞ	Ⓞ
Ⓟ	Ⓟ	Ⓟ	Ⓟ	Ⓟ	Ⓟ
Ⓠ	Ⓠ	Ⓠ	Ⓠ	Ⓠ	Ⓠ
Ⓡ	Ⓡ	Ⓡ	Ⓡ	Ⓡ	Ⓡ
Ⓢ	Ⓢ	Ⓢ	Ⓢ	Ⓢ	Ⓢ
Ⓣ	Ⓣ	Ⓣ	Ⓣ	Ⓣ	Ⓣ
Ⓤ	Ⓤ	Ⓤ	Ⓤ	Ⓤ	Ⓤ
Ⓥ	Ⓥ	Ⓥ	Ⓥ	Ⓥ	Ⓥ
Ⓦ	Ⓦ	Ⓦ	Ⓦ	Ⓦ	Ⓦ
Ⓧ	Ⓧ	Ⓧ	Ⓧ	Ⓧ	Ⓧ
Ⓨ	Ⓨ	Ⓨ	Ⓨ	Ⓨ	Ⓨ
Ⓩ	Ⓩ	Ⓩ	Ⓩ	Ⓩ	Ⓩ

2. TEST FORM

_____

3. TEST CODE   4. PHONE NUMBER

⓪	⓪	⓪	⓪	⓪	⓪	⓪	⓪	⓪	⓪	⓪
①	①	①	①	①	①	①	①	①	①	①
②	②	②	②	②	②	②	②	②	②	②
③	③	③	③	③	③	③	③	③	③	③
④	④	④	④	④	④	④	④	④	④	④
⑤	⑤	⑤	⑤	⑤	⑤	⑤	⑤	⑤	⑤	⑤
⑥	⑥	⑥	⑥	⑥	⑥	⑥	⑥	⑥	⑥	⑥
⑦	⑦	⑦	⑦	⑦	⑦	⑦	⑦	⑦	⑦	⑦
⑧	⑧	⑧	⑧	⑧	⑧	⑧	⑧	⑧	⑧	⑧
⑨	⑨	⑨	⑨	⑨	⑨	⑨	⑨	⑨	⑨	⑨

6. DATE OF BIRTH

MONTH		DAY		YEAR	
◯ JAN					
◯ FEB					
◯ MAR	⓪	⓪	⓪	⓪	
◯ APR	①	①	①	①	
◯ MAY	②	②	②	②	
◯ JUN	③	③	③	③	
◯ JUL		④	④	④	
◯ AUG		⑤	⑤	⑤	
◯ SEP		⑥	⑥	⑥	
◯ OCT		⑦	⑦	⑦	
◯ NOV		⑧	⑧	⑧	
◯ DEC		⑨	⑨	⑨	

7. SEX
◯ MALE
◯ FEMALE

8. OTHER
1 Ⓐ Ⓑ Ⓒ Ⓓ Ⓔ
2 Ⓐ Ⓑ Ⓒ Ⓓ Ⓔ
3 Ⓐ Ⓑ Ⓒ Ⓓ Ⓔ

Begin with number 1 for each new section of the test. Leave blank any extra answer spaces.

SECTION 1

1 Ⓐ Ⓑ Ⓒ Ⓓ Ⓔ	26 Ⓐ Ⓑ Ⓒ Ⓓ Ⓔ	51 Ⓐ Ⓑ Ⓒ Ⓓ Ⓔ	76 Ⓐ Ⓑ Ⓒ Ⓓ Ⓔ
2 Ⓐ Ⓑ Ⓒ Ⓓ Ⓔ	27 Ⓐ Ⓑ Ⓒ Ⓓ Ⓔ	52 Ⓐ Ⓑ Ⓒ Ⓓ Ⓔ	77 Ⓐ Ⓑ Ⓒ Ⓓ Ⓔ
3 Ⓐ Ⓑ Ⓒ Ⓓ Ⓔ	28 Ⓐ Ⓑ Ⓒ Ⓓ Ⓔ	53 Ⓐ Ⓑ Ⓒ Ⓓ Ⓔ	78 Ⓐ Ⓑ Ⓒ Ⓓ Ⓔ
4 Ⓐ Ⓑ Ⓒ Ⓓ Ⓔ	29 Ⓐ Ⓑ Ⓒ Ⓓ Ⓔ	54 Ⓐ Ⓑ Ⓒ Ⓓ Ⓔ	79 Ⓐ Ⓑ Ⓒ Ⓓ Ⓔ
5 Ⓐ Ⓑ Ⓒ Ⓓ Ⓔ	30 Ⓐ Ⓑ Ⓒ Ⓓ Ⓔ	55 Ⓐ Ⓑ Ⓒ Ⓓ Ⓔ	80 Ⓐ Ⓑ Ⓒ Ⓓ Ⓔ
6 Ⓐ Ⓑ Ⓒ Ⓓ Ⓔ	31 Ⓐ Ⓑ Ⓒ Ⓓ Ⓔ	56 Ⓐ Ⓑ Ⓒ Ⓓ Ⓔ	81 Ⓐ Ⓑ Ⓒ Ⓓ Ⓔ
7 Ⓐ Ⓑ Ⓒ Ⓓ Ⓔ	32 Ⓐ Ⓑ Ⓒ Ⓓ Ⓔ	57 Ⓐ Ⓑ Ⓒ Ⓓ Ⓔ	82 Ⓐ Ⓑ Ⓒ Ⓓ Ⓔ
8 Ⓐ Ⓑ Ⓒ Ⓓ Ⓔ	33 Ⓐ Ⓑ Ⓒ Ⓓ Ⓔ	58 Ⓐ Ⓑ Ⓒ Ⓓ Ⓔ	83 Ⓐ Ⓑ Ⓒ Ⓓ Ⓔ
9 Ⓐ Ⓑ Ⓒ Ⓓ Ⓔ	34 Ⓐ Ⓑ Ⓒ Ⓓ Ⓔ	59 Ⓐ Ⓑ Ⓒ Ⓓ Ⓔ	84 Ⓐ Ⓑ Ⓒ Ⓓ Ⓔ
10 Ⓐ Ⓑ Ⓒ Ⓓ Ⓔ	35 Ⓐ Ⓑ Ⓒ Ⓓ Ⓔ	60 Ⓐ Ⓑ Ⓒ Ⓓ Ⓔ	85 Ⓐ Ⓑ Ⓒ Ⓓ Ⓔ
11 Ⓐ Ⓑ Ⓒ Ⓓ Ⓔ	36 Ⓐ Ⓑ Ⓒ Ⓓ Ⓔ	61 Ⓐ Ⓑ Ⓒ Ⓓ Ⓔ	86 Ⓐ Ⓑ Ⓒ Ⓓ Ⓔ
12 Ⓐ Ⓑ Ⓒ Ⓓ Ⓔ	37 Ⓐ Ⓑ Ⓒ Ⓓ Ⓔ	62 Ⓐ Ⓑ Ⓒ Ⓓ Ⓔ	87 Ⓐ Ⓑ Ⓒ Ⓓ Ⓔ
13 Ⓐ Ⓑ Ⓒ Ⓓ Ⓔ	38 Ⓐ Ⓑ Ⓒ Ⓓ Ⓔ	63 Ⓐ Ⓑ Ⓒ Ⓓ Ⓔ	88 Ⓐ Ⓑ Ⓒ Ⓓ Ⓔ
14 Ⓐ Ⓑ Ⓒ Ⓓ Ⓔ	39 Ⓐ Ⓑ Ⓒ Ⓓ Ⓔ	64 Ⓐ Ⓑ Ⓒ Ⓓ Ⓔ	89 Ⓐ Ⓑ Ⓒ Ⓓ Ⓔ
15 Ⓐ Ⓑ Ⓒ Ⓓ Ⓔ	40 Ⓐ Ⓑ Ⓒ Ⓓ Ⓔ	65 Ⓐ Ⓑ Ⓒ Ⓓ Ⓔ	90 Ⓐ Ⓑ Ⓒ Ⓓ Ⓔ
16 Ⓐ Ⓑ Ⓒ Ⓓ Ⓔ	41 Ⓐ Ⓑ Ⓒ Ⓓ Ⓔ	66 Ⓐ Ⓑ Ⓒ Ⓓ Ⓔ	91 Ⓐ Ⓑ Ⓒ Ⓓ Ⓔ
17 Ⓐ Ⓑ Ⓒ Ⓓ Ⓔ	42 Ⓐ Ⓑ Ⓒ Ⓓ Ⓔ	67 Ⓐ Ⓑ Ⓒ Ⓓ Ⓔ	92 Ⓐ Ⓑ Ⓒ Ⓓ Ⓔ
18 Ⓐ Ⓑ Ⓒ Ⓓ Ⓔ	43 Ⓐ Ⓑ Ⓒ Ⓓ Ⓔ	68 Ⓐ Ⓑ Ⓒ Ⓓ Ⓔ	93 Ⓐ Ⓑ Ⓒ Ⓓ Ⓔ
19 Ⓐ Ⓑ Ⓒ Ⓓ Ⓔ	44 Ⓐ Ⓑ Ⓒ Ⓓ Ⓔ	69 Ⓐ Ⓑ Ⓒ Ⓓ Ⓔ	94 Ⓐ Ⓑ Ⓒ Ⓓ Ⓔ
20 Ⓐ Ⓑ Ⓒ Ⓓ Ⓔ	45 Ⓐ Ⓑ Ⓒ Ⓓ Ⓔ	70 Ⓐ Ⓑ Ⓒ Ⓓ Ⓔ	95 Ⓐ Ⓑ Ⓒ Ⓓ Ⓔ
21 Ⓐ Ⓑ Ⓒ Ⓓ Ⓔ	46 Ⓐ Ⓑ Ⓒ Ⓓ Ⓔ	71 Ⓐ Ⓑ Ⓒ Ⓓ Ⓔ	96 Ⓐ Ⓑ Ⓒ Ⓓ Ⓔ
22 Ⓐ Ⓑ Ⓒ Ⓓ Ⓔ	47 Ⓐ Ⓑ Ⓒ Ⓓ Ⓔ	72 Ⓐ Ⓑ Ⓒ Ⓓ Ⓔ	97 Ⓐ Ⓑ Ⓒ Ⓓ Ⓔ
23 Ⓐ Ⓑ Ⓒ Ⓓ Ⓔ	48 Ⓐ Ⓑ Ⓒ Ⓓ Ⓔ	73 Ⓐ Ⓑ Ⓒ Ⓓ Ⓔ	98 Ⓐ Ⓑ Ⓒ Ⓓ Ⓔ
24 Ⓐ Ⓑ Ⓒ Ⓓ Ⓔ	49 Ⓐ Ⓑ Ⓒ Ⓓ Ⓔ	74 Ⓐ Ⓑ Ⓒ Ⓓ Ⓔ	99 Ⓐ Ⓑ Ⓒ Ⓓ Ⓔ
25 Ⓐ Ⓑ Ⓒ Ⓓ Ⓔ	50 Ⓐ Ⓑ Ⓒ Ⓓ Ⓔ	75 Ⓐ Ⓑ Ⓒ Ⓓ Ⓔ	100 Ⓐ Ⓑ Ⓒ Ⓓ Ⓔ

NOTES

NOTES

NOTES

NOTES

NOTES

NOTES

NOTES

NOTES